An Open Map

RECENCIES SERIES: RESEARCH AND RECOVERY IN TWENTIETH-CENTURY AMERICAN POETICS

MATTHEW HOFER, SERIES EDITOR

RECENCIES

This series stands at the intersection of critical investigation, historical documentation, and the preservation of cultural heritage. The series exists to illuminate the innovative poetics achievements of the recent past that remain relevant to the present. In addition to publishing monographs and edited volumes, it is also a venue for previously unpublished manuscripts, expanded reprints, and collections of major essays, letters, and interviews.

Also available in the Recencies Series:

Imagining Persons: Robert Duncan's Lectures on Charles Olson edited by Robert J. Bertholf and Dale M. Smith
The Collected Letters of Charles Olson and J. H. Prynne edited by Ryan Dobran
The Olson Codex: Projective Verse and the Problem of Mayan Glyphs by Dennis Tedlock
The Birth of the Imagination: William Carlos Williams on Form by Bruce Holsapple
The Maltese Falcon to Body of Lies: Spies, Noirs, and Trust by Robert von Hallberg
The Oppens Remembered: Poetry, Politics, and Friendship edited by Rachel Blau DuPlessis
How Long Is the Present: Selected Talk Poems of David Antin edited by Stephen Fredman
Loose Cannons: Selected Prose by Christopher Middleton
Amiri Baraka and Edward Dorn: The Collected Letters edited by Claudia Moreno Pisano
The Shoshoneans: The People of the Basin-Plateau, Expanded Edition by Edward Dorn and Leroy Lucas

For additional titles in the Recencies Series, please visit unmpress.com.

An Open Map

The Correspondence of Robert Duncan and Charles Olson

EDITED BY **ROBERT J. BERTHOLF** AND **DALE M. SMITH**

University of New Mexico Press • Albuquerque

© 2017 by the University of New Mexico Press
All rights reserved. Published 2017
Printed in the United States of America
22 21 20 19 18 17   1 2 3 4 5 6

First paperback edition, 2020
Paperback ISBN: 978-0-8263-5428-0

Library of Congress Cataloging-in-Publication Data
Names: Duncan, Robert, 1919–1988 author. | Olson, Charles, 1910–1970 author.|
Bertholf, Robert J. editor. | Smith, Dale, 1967– editor.
Title: An Open Map: The Correspondence of Robert Duncan and Charles Olson /
edited by Robert J. Bertholf and Dale M. Smith.
Description: Albuquerque: University of New Mexico Press, 2017. |
Includes bibliographical references and index. |
Identifiers: LCCN 2017029441 (print) | LCCN 2017039140 (ebook) |
ISBN 9780826358974 (E-book) | ISBN 9780826358967 (cloth: alk. paper)
Subjects: LCSH: Duncan, Robert, 1919–1988—Correspondence. | Olson, Charles, 1910-1970—
Correspondence. | Poets, American—20th century—Correspondence.
Classification: LCC PS3507.U629 (ebook) | LCC PS3507.U629 Z48 2017 (print) |
DDC 811/.54 [B]—dc23
LC record available at https://lccn.loc.gov/2017029441

Designed by Felicia Cedillos
Composed in Minion Pro 10.5/14.25

Charles Olson, "Bud pink enclosing," no date [ca. April 1956], Robert Duncan Collection, The Poetry Collection of the University Libraries, University at Buffalo, The State University of New York.

Contents

Appendix

*Guggenheim Letters: Charles Olson on Robert Duncan, Robert Duncan on
Charles Olson*   221

Preface

DALE M. SMITH

Robert J. Bertholf (1940–2016) began work on the Robert Duncan–Charles Olson correspondence in 1978, when he visited the Archives and Special Collections at the Thomas J. Dodd Research Center at the University of Connecticut. Four years later, in a letter to Robert Duncan, Bertholf related his progress on the material:

> This morning I finished the second run through the Duncan/Olson letters [all have been transcribed and are now in typed versions]. There are words, and even phrases in Olson's hand that escape me, at times because of the Xerox copy and at times because of Olson's hand. Jack Clarke will help there. And then I am going to Storrs at the end of May to go over all of them again with the originals. There are notes to be finished, and a lot of small matters: the big matters have been done at this point.

Work on the letters continued intermittently during Bertholf's curatorship of the Poetry Collection of the University Libraries at the University at Buffalo, where he guided textual scholars for nearly thirty years and collaborated with the Poetics program. Many of the textual problems, especially the deciphering of difficult words and phrases in the letters, were clarified in conversations with Jack Clarke, a beloved Blake scholar in the English Department, and with the support of Robert Creeley of the Poetics program.

Beyond his duties as a scholar and mentor, however, Robert Bertholf was devoted to the creative particulars of place and the people around him, a dynamic space that Robert Duncan and Charles Olson would have called a temenos. I first met Robert in Buffalo just as he was retiring from the Poetry Collection in 2007. We met again the following year when he moved to Austin, where I was finishing doctoral research at the University of Texas. Robert came from a generation of men and women whose understanding of poetry included a humane and sympathetic connection to the world and to the conditions that give shape to creative precincts of study. As seen in the frank admissions and enthusiasm for art announced in the correspondence of Duncan and Olson, Robert mixed friendly and playful banter with a sense of urgency and a serious understanding of the poetry he encountered. His prodding humor was instructive and gave me permission to be at ease in myself as a scholar. Robert, like many other poets I have known, showed me that the lines between scholarship and art, between critical inquiry and everyday acts of attention, remain fluid and interactive; no rigid method ever intervened to supplant the primary attunements and affections he brought to diverse areas of study. Indeed, he was a man committed to his enthusiasms. I say all of this to honor his memory, to acknowledge my ongoing delight in our friendship, and to give some testament to the joy I took in working with him.

In 2011, as I was moving with my family to Toronto, Ontario, Robert added a large cardboard box to my moving load. It wasn't until a few months later that I examined the contents and was surprised to discover the manuscripts of *An Open Map: The Correspondence of Robert Duncan and Charles Olson* (which became the current volume) and *Imagining Persons: Robert Duncan's Lectures on Charles Olson* (which is a separate volume also published by the University of New Mexico Press). I immediately suggested that we finish both projects, and so began our formal obligation to these important documents of mid-century poetics. When Robert died suddenly in February 2016, he knew that the texts would be published, and he was thrilled that his many years of work would find a home at the University of New Mexico Press.

Robert Bertholf never approached small tasks: his scholarly publications reflect his devotion to American open-form poetry, with special emphasis on the writing of Robert Duncan and his life partner, the visual artist and collagist Jess. Bertholf's many publications include *Robert Duncan: Scales of the Marvelous* (with Ian Reid) (1979), *William Blake and the Moderns* (1982), *Robert Duncan: A Descriptive Bibliography* (1986), *A Great Admiration: H.D./Robert Duncan Correspondence, 1950–1961* (1991), *Jess: A Grand Collage, 1951–1993* (with Michael Auping and Michael Palmer) (1993), Robert Duncan's *Selected Poems* (1993) and *A Selected Prose* (1995), and *The Letters of Robert Duncan and Denise Levertov* (with Albert Gelpi, 2004). While these books took priority over the Duncan-Olson correspondence, the letters nonetheless informed Robert's understanding of the material. In a 1982 letter to Duncan, he observed:

Most interesting to me was the emerging continuity between the comments

in the letters to Olson late 1950s and into the 1960s about poetics, the syllable and the comments from that recent visit. The attention has remained the
same. I thought I had so misdirected my attention to the larger message that
I'd lost sight of the smaller events of the syllables, the line, the poetics of the
poems. As it happens, there was another request for an article, and the poetics of the poem will play a large part in the discussion. I feel like I've found
the poems, again, in a new direction of understanding.

Robert's willingness to revise his position and renew his understanding of
open-form poetry has been crucial for the subsequent publications of Duncan's
work. The notes and glossary in the current volume likewise benefit from Robert's devotion to the history and contexts of mid-century publication and literary institutions. The primary individuals and the little magazines that sustained
poetry in the 1950s and '60s form the significant background to the correspondence, and Robert's knowledge of the publications and the key cultural events
behind them support the overall trajectory of this volume.

In my work on this project, I hope to increase knowledge and to display some
of Robert's commitment to poetry and its possibilities as public documentation
derived from the private sources of experience and thought. I am grateful to
have had the opportunity to contribute to the work here. And while I am pleased
to see this volume in print, I cannot help but feel the loss of a terrific friend
whose enjoyment of life, including the life animating these letters, deepened the
joy of others.

Acknowledgments

The editors express their gratitude to Christopher Wagstaff and Mary Margaret Sloan, the co-trustees of the Jess Collins Trust, for their support of this project and for permission to publish Robert Duncan's letters to Charles Olson. We especially thank Christopher Wagstaff for his attention to the manuscript during the final editing stage. Thanks also go to Dodd Research Center archivist Melissa Watterworth Batt for her support in the preparation of this volume. The work here could not have happened without the insights and contributions of a large community of scholars and writers committed to the writings of Duncan and Olson and to the traditions of poetics they formed. We are grateful for early involvement in this project by John Clarke, Robert Creeley, and Marta Werner, who helped in the transcription of the original letters and offered many insights. We also thank James Maynard and the staff of the Poetry Collection for their assistance, especially Roumiana Velikova for helping us prepare the final typescript.

Generous comments and insightful critiques of the manuscript from University of New Mexico Press reviewers Ammiel Alcalay and Peter O'Leary helped clarify the scope and final shape of the current book; we are grateful for their support and correspondence. Christopher Beach's book *ABC of Influence: Ezra Pound and the Remaking of American Poetic Tradition* and Michael André Bernstein's essay "Bringing It All Back Home: Derivations and Quotations in Robert Duncan and the Poundian Tradition" both helped improve our understanding of Duncan's relationship to Pound and his ideas about literary traditions.

Elise McHugh, University of New Mexico Press editor, offered enthusiasm and insight throughout the publication process. We are indebted especially to Merryl A. Sloane for her careful editing of the final manuscript and to the production team at the University of New Mexico Press for their care in the final typographic preparation of this volume.

We could not have accomplished this work without the conversation and financial support of a network of friends, correspondents, and institutions at different phases of production. The Faculty of Arts, Ryerson University, generously bestowed a grant in support of this project, for which we are grateful. Our thanks go also to David Abel, Steven Carter, Michael Cavuto, Dennis Denisoff, Benjamin Friedlander, Morgan Holmes, Adam Katz, Kevin Killian, Duncan McNaughton, Hoa Nguyen, Simon Pettet, Don Share, Kyle Schlesinger, Roger Snell, Jeffrey Walker, and Kyle Waugh. The work could not have appeared without Anne Bertholf's faith and generosity, and to her we owe our deepest thanks.

Works by Charles Olson published during his lifetime are held in copyright by the Estate of Charles Olson. Previously unpublished works by Charles Olson are the copyright of the University of Connecticut Libraries. Used with permission.

Letters by Charles Olson and Robert Duncan are held at the University of Connecticut in the Charles Olson Research Collection in Archives and Special Collections at the Thomas J. Dodd Research Center.

The letters from Jonathan Williams, Cid Corman, and Robert Creeley to Duncan and the unmailed letters to Charles Olson are housed in the Robert Duncan Collection in the Poetry Collection of the University Libraries, University at Buffalo, the State University of New York. We are grateful to these institutions for their support and permission to reproduce the archived material.

Letters dated circa December 15, 1953; June 17, 1954; August 8, 1954; August 14, 1955; August 28, 1955; June 4, 1957; February 7, 1959; February 6, 1960; March 9, 1963; June 29, 1964; and December 18, 1969, were published in *Sulfur* 35 (1994): 87–118. The letter dated circa December 15, 1953, was also published previously as "near-far Mister Olson," *Origin*, 1st ser., 12 (1954): 210–11. More recently, the letters dated June 19 and 21, 1955; August 21, 1955; and August 24, 1955, appeared in *Poetry* (September 2017).

Note on the Text

In transcribing these letters, we have attempted to be as faithful to the original correspondence as possible. The configuration of the material on the page has been retained, though slight discrepancies have entered in the translation from handwriting and typescript to print. The use of contractions such as "shld" and "wld" have been retained as have the special spellings of words when a pun of sound or usage was intended. Casual spelling and typing errors have been corrected silently. Both Duncan and Olson used square brackets (and they did not always close them or parentheses). Editorial insertions, therefore, are indicated with curly brackets. Ellipses in the text are from the original letters and should not be read as editorial omissions.

Both poets often mentioned authors and historical figures, works, and occurrences without explanation. The notes and glossary identify some of the specific people, publications, and other references mentioned in the letters.

Introduction

Love and the Idea of Form

DALE M. SMITH AND ROBERT J. BERTHOLF

> Go today to San Francisco, & shall look up the Cali4nians,
> starting with Robert Duncan.
>
> —CHARLES OLSON TO EZRA POUND, August 24, 1947

The correspondence of Robert Duncan and Charles Olson is one of the foundational literary exchanges in American poetry in the second half of the twentieth century. The letters provide the facts and circumstances of what lies under the published literary history, and they illuminate the pathway from imaginative conception to the published texts by recounting the poetics of formation. So much of these poets' published work was based on intense discussions that took place off the printed page, often in letters that debated the value of form and wisdom in poetry. They never lived close to one another and spoke on the telephone rarely, so the primary medium of exchange between them was the letter, as it was between Robert Creeley and Olson and between Duncan and Denise Levertov. Olson's *Maximus Poems* also are written as "letters," indicating the rhetorical importance of addressing specific individuals and communities in the conception of his poetics. The intersection of the letters and the poetry show the active commitments behind a body of work that emphasized a close readership: the authorial perspective required testing in the form of an ongoing flow of correspondence.

Both men initiated a novel stance toward poetry in the mid-twentieth century, and they met each other with huge accomplishments, an inquiring declarative intelligence, wide-ranging interests in history and occult literature, and the urgent demand to be a poet. The rich context of Duncan's creative practice nourished an approach to writing that, with Olson, struggled to articulate a new basis for poetics; their shared goal was to reestablish the uses of poetry beyond the domain of literature to confront a larger cultural and historical field of action. Literary and coterie contexts mattered, but the terms of their individual encounters with poetry drew on a variety of disciplines and areas of study that applied to a larger cultural context. The stakes of Duncan's and Olson's poetic activities, as shown in their writings and announced in their letters, focused on the individual in specific precincts of study and perception: the articulated goal of writing was to enter the complex energies they perceived and participated in as a process of discovery at the thresholds of subjective and linguistic encounters. Poetry as it was then presented by the New Critical literary tradition was a vehicle for topics formalized through individual talent and virtuosic invention. But Duncan and Olson approached the art's open field, as they called it, to document the act of creative pursuit with the material intervention of language, which they used to scrutinize an array of interests and concerns relevant to the poet's particular motives.

Duncan's *The Opening of the Field* (1960) and Olson's *The Distances* (1960) combine with Creeley's *For Love* (1962) to complete the tripartite foundation for the group of poets who activated the propositions of an open-form poetry through the dynamic correspondence they all shared. The accomplishments of this new group of poets were consolidated in Donald Allen's anthology *The New American Poetry* (1960). The publication of that volume designated the various groups of authors that had begun to participate in open forms of writing practiced in resistance to New Criticism and to the models of closed-form verse then promoted in academia and the literary public sphere. The expansion of writing about the American geographic experience inevitably led also to new social and political encounters in poetry, which confronted the homogenization of postwar culture through the confessed plights of societal dropouts and other outcasts. Jack Kerouac, Allen Ginsberg, LeRoi Jones (later, Amiri Baraka), and Diane di Prima exemplified a new energy in writing presented at the counterculture's margins, where Duncan and Olson established their close bonds. Behind the public events of book publications and readings, their ongoing formulations of poetry were enriched in the privacy of their letters.

The letters also were concerned with the beginning and growth of little magazines, where literary revolutions typically first appear. *Origin* (first issue in the spring of 1951), edited by Cid Corman, was a pivotal magazine in the formation of the new poetics, and Olson was key to its scope and development. He wrote at times stinging criticism directed at Corman about how to run the magazine, and Corman responded with favor to Olson's vision of the journal as a statement of mid-century American poetics. Corman also wrote extensively to Duncan and Creeley, who, with Olson, cultivated the context for the "company" of poets (as Creeley often called them),[1] establishing the momentum of agreement in the poetics of open forms that was at the heart of the bond between Duncan and Olson. William Carlos Williams, Levertov, Paul Blackburn, William Bronk, Corman, and many others helped make *Origin* the place where the new writers established a substantive body of work.

Corman's efforts at *Origin* were matched by Robert Creeley's editing of the *Black Mountain Review* (first issue in the spring of 1954). The Black Mountain school of poets cohered through a dynamic approach to writing inspired by the central figures of Olson, Duncan, Creeley, and Levertov (who called herself a second-generation Black Mountain poet), and grew to encompass diverse approaches to writing as seen in the works of poets published in the *Black Mountain Review*, such as Joel Oppenheimer, Ed Dorn, Blackburn, Michael Rumaker, Larry Eigner, and Jonathan Williams. Both Duncan and Olson published poems and essays in this journal. Additionally, two other magazines come into the letters: John Wieners's *Measure* and Gerrit Lansing's *Set*. Again, the obligation of these editors was to prepare a context for the company of poets whose works attempted to fully articulate a stance toward poetry that was outside the institutionalizing culture of commercial and university press publishing.

The poets who published in these magazines invented forms that reflected their positions at the margins of the Cold War era; it was a moment hostile to nonstandard speech, typography, and phrasing—all of which were used in open forms of poetry. It was also a historical period that was especially resistant to modes of feeling and perspectives on reality that were outside the institutional forms of categorization. The decades just after the Second World War anticipated our own cultural moment in distressing ways insofar as conditions of language use, then as now, were so often shaped by the common linguistic and rhetorical bonds of a largely commercial and socially regimented society. A long-lasting epistolary connection, however, granted Duncan and Olson the room to improvise arguments and conjectures in an atmosphere of their own making in words. There were few opportunities for face-to-face meetings. Travel was expensive and time consuming; long-distance phone conversations were costly and potentially open to wiretaps in an era of political conformism; and the fast-paced modes of digital communication we take for granted had yet to produce expectations of instant responses to occasional queries or more frequent rounds of shared information. Indeed, the pace of the letters is not rushed; they tend to breathe, with periods of intense weekly conversations separated by longer stretches of silence. (There is no record of letters between Duncan and Olson during all of 1962, for instance, though they pick up with a passion the following year.)[2] The correspondence provided room to expand ideas, encounter new terms, and discover individual trust in the creative adventure of writing.

Duncan and Olson's relationship in poetry and letters, then, provided a space for social identification outside the normative Cold War public sphere. Intellectual challenges and dedications of feeling between the men reinforced their individual perceptions and shaped their poetics. When notice of the publication of poems in the little magazines or the lists of trade publishers reached them, they praised each other as makers in a long transmission of cultural labor. Each read out a poetics in the works of the other and, by so doing, generated the principles that redefined American avant-garde poetry after 1950.

Robert Duncan: 1919–1947

Self-identity emergent in the context of poetry was crucial to Duncan. He was named Edward Howard Duncan at birth, but his adoptive parents changed his name to Robert Edward Symmes; in 1941, he began calling himself Robert Duncan.[3]

Duncan's mother died a few hours after giving birth to him on January 7, 1919, in Oakland, California; Duncan's father, a laborer, put him up for adoption; and in August he was taken into the home of Edwin Joseph Symmes and Minnehaha Harris Symmes, both followers of a branch of theosophical hermeticism established in the nineteenth century by Helena Petrovna Blavatsky. Duncan's upbringing was steeped in the rituals and conversations of the Oakland Hermetic Brotherhood, and his family encouraged self-reflection, the study of spiritual and occult traditions, and the adventure of self-discovery in Greek, Roman, and German mythologies. The seminal works that informed his childhood imagination, to which he referred frequently as a mature poet, included G. R. S. Mead's translations and studies of the trismegistic literature in the three-volume *Thrice-Greatest Hermes*; L. Frank Baum's many books of Oz, published in the first two decades of the century; and the work of Scottish novelist George MacDonald, whose stories *The Light Princess*, *The Princess and the Goblin*, *The Princess and Curdie*, and others project a complex and unorthodox Christian theology through the pleasures of fantasy. These books informed Duncan's personal mythology while the modernist writings of H.D., Ezra Pound, D. H. Lawrence, and Virginia Woolf— introduced to him by his senior high school teacher Edna Keogh—connected the depth of his spiritualist and mythological training to an applied poetics.[4] As a student at Berkeley he first read Gertrude Stein and T. S. Eliot before following his lover Ned Fahs to Philadelphia in 1938; he remained on the East Coast for nearly a decade, working odd jobs and exploring relationships in creative communities and sexual partnerships.

During the decade prior to the commencement of the letters collected here,

Duncan established a literary relationship with Anaïs Nin, who helped see his first work into print in *Poetry*; she also introduced him to Henry Miller, Kenneth Patchen, and others at the Phoenix Community, an artists commune in Woodstock, New York. Duncan founded his own journal *Ritual* (later renamed the *Experimental Review*); and he came out publicly and politically in Dwight Macdonald's *Politics* magazine with "The Homosexual in Society" (1944), an essay that provoked John Crowe Ransom to withdraw Duncan's previously accepted poem "Toward an African Elegy" from publication in the *Kenyon Review*. Duncan had been dishonorably discharged as a "sexual psychopath" from the army after only three months, and he had an equally unsuccessful and brief marriage to Marjorie McKee in 1943.

Duncan worked as a dishwasher and typist, attended anarchist meetings on both coasts, and cultivated friendships in diverse literary communities. He returned in 1946 to California, where he completed poems that would appear in his first book, *Heavenly City, Earthly City* (1947). When he met Olson, Duncan had fully established literary friendships with Pauline Kael, Kenneth Rexroth, James Broughton, Jack Spicer, Robin Blaser, William Everson, and Madeline Gleason. He re-enrolled the following year at the University of California with Spicer and Blaser in the Civilization of the Middle Ages program, studying with Ernst Kantorowicz, a medievalist whose influence would remain with Duncan as he later developed his own style of pedagogy and public performance.

When he met Olson, the twenty-eight-year-old Duncan had recently returned from a pilgrimage to visit Ezra Pound in Washington, DC, having spent two afternoon sessions at St. Elizabeths psychiatric hospital with the modernist figure. Duncan identified closely with Pound's poetics, and the California native had recently published "The Years as Catches" in George Leite's *Circle*, a small Bay Area journal inspired by Poundian poetics. Pound invigorated writers like Duncan and Olson who wanted to confront the social, creative, and political homogenization of society rather than seek posts in the increasingly managed industries of publication and pedagogy. Pound's adaptation of Ernest Fenollosa's description of Chinese ideography encouraged a broad apprehension of cultural and historical material through the vividness of concretely written expression, an approach favored by both Duncan and Olson.

Charles Olson: 1910–1947

Olson was born on December 27, 1910, in Worcester, Massachusetts, to Karl Joseph Olson, a US postal worker and Swedish immigrant, and Mary Theresa Hines, the Catholic daughter of Irish immigrants. In 1915, the Olsons began summering in the Cape Ann resort town of Gloucester, a maritime location that would occupy the poet's imagination throughout his life and form the primary domain of his epic, *The Maximus Poems* (1960). It was an area that appealed to the creative impulses of visual artists like Marsden Hartley (whom Olson would meet in New York in 1940–1941) and poets like T. S. Eliot, another itinerant visitor to Gloucester as a boy with his family, whose "The Dry Salvages" (in *Four Quartets*, 1943) in part describes significant features of Cape Ann.

Olson graduated in 1928 from Worcester Classical High School, where he excelled in Latin and public speaking. As captain of the debate team, he took third place at the 1928 national oratory championship in Washington, DC, winning a trip that summer to Europe; in Ireland, he met the poet W. B. Yeats. Olson attended Wesleyan University, worked during the summers in the post office in Gloucester, and in 1932 graduated with a BA, which was followed by an MA in English the next year. His thesis was on Herman Melville, and he was then awarded the Olin Fellowship by Wesleyan University to do research on Melville's library, a project that put Olson in touch with Melville's granddaughter Eleanor Metcalf and others who provided the young scholar access to the Melville family papers. Olson was admitted to Harvard's American Civilization program as a doctoral candidate in 1936, the same year he met the novelist Edward Dahlberg, whose work and mentorship would influence Olson forcefully in the years ahead, particularly as Olson directed efforts toward a definitive book on Melville. In 1939, Olson was awarded a Guggenheim Fellowship to complete his research on Melville and abruptly left the Harvard graduate program, having finished his coursework but not his dissertation.

By 1941, Olson was living in New York City, eventually finding employment as a part-time publicist with the American Civil Liberties Union and then as an editorial assistant at the Common Council for American Unity, an organization dedicated to serving the interests of immigrant citizens. In 1942, as the United States entered the war in Europe, Olson moved with his young common-law wife, Constance "Connie" Wilcock, to Washington, DC, where he took a position with the Foreign Language Division of the Office of War Information. He thrived in the competitive and political atmosphere of a public relations office, persuading immigrant citizens through press releases and radio speeches to support America's efforts in the war.[5] His deepening engagement with the Democratic Party resulted in an offer of the position of director of the Foreign Nationalities Division of the Democratic National Committee by 1944. Although he successfully contributed to Franklin D. Roosevelt's final election that same year, Olson soon quit politics, resolving to turn his attention back to writing. He resumed work on his Melville book, eventually publishing it as *Call*

Me Ishmael (1947); he had published his first poem, "Pacific Lament," in the *Atlantic Monthly* the year before.

Late in 1945, Olson had defended Ezra Pound, who had been arrested for treason in Italy and had only recently returned to the United States to stand trial. While Olson found the elder poet's fascist politics despicable, he was in awe of the literary achievement of *The Cantos* (the first complete edition was published in 1954) and other works. He attended Pound's trial as a legal reporter and was present for Pound's November 27 arraignment. Olson maintained contact and was an early visitor of the poet when Pound was moved to St. Elizabeths psychiatric hospital after federal courts declared him insane; Olson made careful notes of their meetings. Pound took an interest in *Call Me Ishmael*, which was accepted for publication by Reynal and Hitchcock, a New York trade publisher. Pound's advocacy on behalf of Olson also resulted in the publication of the chapbook *Y & X* (1948) with Black Sun Press.

When Olson finally met Duncan in September 1947, both men had the influence of Ezra Pound to thank for the development of their understanding of poetry and for the intersection of their lives that month in California.

Publications and Meetings: 1947–1970

The letters presented in this volume begin soon after Duncan and Olson met in 1947 on the campus of the University of California at Berkeley, where Olson had traveled to study archival documents at the Bancroft Library related to the California gold rush. The correspondence continues until the end of December 1969, just a short time before Olson's death. For a period in the 1950s, each wrote back quickly, excited by the questions of poetry under discussion. During the 1960s, the letters between the poets are less frequent, but no less intense. Both Duncan and Olson arrived at a mature poetics, which they tested and explored in the private world of letters, while in the public world of poetry they published their major books.

Duncan, under the influence of the collage art of his life partner Jess Collins, moved away from the romanticist structures of his early writing and toward a poetry that claimed direct statement as its motive and a collection of sources—"derivations," as Duncan called them—as its fabric. Olson, on the other hand, published two volumes of *Maximus* poems in 1953 and 1956. He answered Duncan's publication of *The Opening of the Field* (1960) with his own *The Distances* (1960) and a collected edition of *The Maximus Poems* (1960) brought out by a combined effort of the Jargon Society (which had published the two previous editions of the poems) and Corinth Books. A collection of Olson's essays appeared as *Human Universe and Other Essays* (1965); Creeley edited and introduced Olson's *Selected Writings* (1966), which brought together the poetry, essays, and letters in a fulsome display of Olson's achievements. (Creeley had published Olson's *Mayan Letters* from his Divers Press in 1953.) Another *Maximus* volume appeared in 1968 as *Maximus Poems IV, V, VI*.

In the second decade of their correspondence, Duncan published two big books of poems, *Roots and Branches* (1964) and *Bending the Bow* (1968), in which he demonstrated a poetics of derivation, and he continued moving further into open forms with two series of poems: "Structure of Rime" and "Passages." In 1966, he published two books written early in his career, *The Years as Catches* and *A Book of Resemblances*. Also in the 1960s, Duncan wrote *The H.D. Book*, portions of which appeared in literary journals over the next two decades. This unusual work lays out a personal encounter with poetry in myths and Gnostic narratives, and the cultural histories and contexts in which D. H. Lawrence, Ezra Pound, William Carlos Williams, and H.D. approached writing. Similarly, Duncan's *The Truth and Life of Myth* (1968) explored the myths, lore, and mysteries of poetic transmission between generations of authors in an establishment of literary affinities across time.

The Berkeley conversations were among the few face-to-face meetings Duncan and Olson ever had. Other than these 1947 encounters in California, Duncan, Jess, and Harry Jacobus stayed one night in February 1955 at Black Mountain College, where Olson served as the school's rector from 1951 to 1956. Black Mountain College was a liberal arts institution of higher learning that had opened in 1933 near Asheville, North Carolina. The school's emphasis on applied learning and art was based on principles of education laid out by John Dewey, and its pedagogical model was connected to the progressive education movement. Its reputation as an art school was enhanced under the stewardship of Josef and Anni Albers, two influential Bauhaus designers who directed Black Mountain's art program from 1933 to 1949. The school saw its final days under Olson's guidance, finally closing permanently in 1957. In addition to the many writers who spent time at Black Mountain—Creeley, Dorn, Fielding Dawson, Arthur Penn, Buckminster Fuller, among others—an impressive number of visual artists and performers, such as Basil King, John Cage, Merce Cunningham, Robert Rauschenberg, and Cy Twombly, also taught or attended courses there. Olson invited Duncan to teach at the college between March and September 1956, and some of their interactions are described below.

Besides their brief residency together at Black Mountain, they saw each other when Olson gave lectures and readings in San Francisco in February and March 1957 and again during Duncan's northeastern reading tour in April 1960, which included performances at Dartmouth and Yale. Duncan also met Olson for the Spring Poetry Festival that year at Wesleyan University, where they both performed. They met again in Buffalo in April 1964, after the sudden death of Olson's second wife, Betty Kaiser. The friends conversed briefly in San Francisco in April 1967, and Duncan visited Olson in New York City in early 1970, shortly before Olson's death on January 10.

Of note are two major poetry conferences in which both men participated: in Vancouver during the summer of 1963 and at Berkeley in the summer of 1965. The Vancouver Poetry Conference, hosted by the University of British Columbia, was a landmark event in North American open-form poetry. The eighteen-day schedule was organized by UBC English professor Warren Tallman and his wife, Ellen Tallman, whose connections to Berkeley profoundly shaped the event; Robert Creeley, who at the time was a visiting professor in the Department of English, also was a key organizer. The conference included workshops, lectures, and readings with leading Canadian and American poets, including George Bowering, Fred Wah, Michael Palmer, Clark Coolidge, and Allen Ginsberg. The 1965 Berkeley Poetry Conference was a two-week event beginning on July 12, which featured many of the poets included in Donald Allen's *The New American Poetry* (1960). Duncan was a key organizer of the event, and on July 23 he introduced what was supposed to be a poetry reading by Olson who, instead, used the occasion to speak extemporaneously for three hours (this momentous event is discussed further below).

Wisdom and the Idea of Form

The correspondence collected here is divided into five chronological sections that highlight important movements and developments in the conversation between Duncan and Olson. In part I, "'near-far Mister Olson' (1947–1955)," the letters follow up on their initial 1947 Berkeley meeting. Duncan, for instance, sends Olson a copy of the first issue of the *Berkeley Miscellany*, a small journal he published in 1948–1949. In response, Olson puts Duncan in touch with Cid Corman, the editor of *Origin*, initiating an important publishing contact for the West Coast poet. In 1951, Olson joins the faculty of Black Mountain College, and he shares information with Duncan about life and events at the college, with an emphasis on small press publishing. (Duncan's *Song of the Border-guard* is typeset in 1952 as a Black Mountain broadside designed by Cy Twombly, who was then a student at the college.) Olson also introduces Duncan to the poet and publisher of the Jargon Society, Jonathan Williams. Behind their collective push to secure publications and shape the direction of small magazines to suit their growing understanding of open-form writing, Pound and William Carlos Williams remain constant points of conversation as the younger poets attempt to extend the sense of their own poetics.

The arrival to Duncan of Olson's *In Cold Hell, in Thicket* (1953) begins a new momentum in the conception of poetic practice, and Duncan makes explicit the importance to him of Olson's presence in his ongoing poetic thinking. Indeed, "'near' means everything," he writes to Olson around December 15, 1953, articulating a feeling of close connection in the poetry despite the obvious geographic fact of their physical separation. "These pieces in scatterd magazines and these books now," Duncan continues, "are those 'friends coming from far quarters' that Confucius finds one of three civilized pleasures." Duncan discovers in Olson his own capacities as a writer who seeks "a revelation of language not personality." For Duncan, poetry leads to a kind of wisdom in the "counsels of the language." One goal of poetry, then, for Duncan, is its formalization of wisdom.

Responding on December 21, 1953, Olson acknowledges Duncan's "technical achievement compared to [his] often very damned often inadequacy." For Olson, Duncan's praise is a testament of affection first of all: "to have you say these things gives me *the* sense of having done the job, the sense of that comradeship, that central love." He then asks Duncan to publish the letter as an enthusiastic statement on Olson's poetics in the first issue of the *Black Mountain Review*. Olson, however, also challenges his friend's position regarding the value of wisdom in poetry. For Olson, "that's the trouble with wisdom. It isn't a measure. And thus has to go, from language (not knowing abt art)." Olson's dispute over wisdom brings to light a central element of his poetic stance: individuals are secondary in the permitted documentations of the energy sustained by an acknowledged flow or movement of perception. The goal is to see out into a world glimpsed only fleetingly. To hold closely to one's wisdom is to separate from that outer force of the world, to be entrapped by confidence and identification rather than to be in submission to outside forces or observable facts. "Doesn't it honestly," Olson argues,

> come to, to love? that all springs up, there? And that what springs up is
> *energy*, with which to do anything, think (which is to be wise), cut wood
> (& i mean for no other reason than to keep warm), push something, ahead,
> make it different, etc., anything, all that all the vocabulary—the words you
> seek to make gnomic by doublet—are valid enuf as reductive (that is, that
> they do analyze validly the worlds love opens one's eyes to.

Olson goes on to explain that "thinking is analytical" and is a "single statement" whereas "writing is not thinking. . . . Writing is what love is." For Olson, the act of writing participates in the active moment of perception open to any possibility: writing should not impose one's stamp of preconceived ideas or values; value is associated instead with a willingness to give oneself completely to the creative demands of a given situation. Measures of durations of time and space are facts that guide Olson's position. "And that a poem / is not wise, even if it is," he continues,

> —that any wisdom also is solely
> a quality of the moment of time of that poem in which there are
> wisdoms. There are obviously seizures which have nothing to do with
>   wisdom
> at all.
> And they are very beautiful.

The particular force of Olson's objection to wisdom is then elaborated publicly in his essay "Against Wisdom as Such" (1954), which appears in the first issue of the *Black Mountain Review* and is a response to Duncan's essay "Pages from a Notebook," published a year earlier in the *Artist's View*. So the private correspondence enters public debate, and Olson risks Duncan's good will in a forceful public statement that opposes his friend's own strong view.[6]

Duncan, however, generously replies to Olson in an August 8, 1954, letter, announcing right away, "I ain't going to rise in defense of my bewilderings—this matter of clarification is too important and, if there were no other measure of it, I shld. say that it is the keener excitement in writing backs up your point." Duncan acknowledges Olson's claim to measure and love in poetry as a primary directing force of the poet's attention. He also clarifies what he means by "knowledge and control," observing: "For motion to be free and energies just here: the real must be distinguishd from the unreal. Things must be discriminated and acknowledged." For Duncan, a problem exists regarding the ability of poetry to exact truth in the world. Volition and validity can be at odds, particularly when engaged with the vagaries of imagination. He writes, "But in made-up things, in the imagination the will has range of a different kind. Words like genuine and false, truth and lie, up and down (where there is nor up nor down as it's named), great and small are anything and everything we design."

For Duncan, wisdom is not a presence or a position to claim subjectively in the composition of a poem, but is instead, as Olson argues, a measure that determines the truth in possibilities that "senses discover." The worry over language's bewitching sensual properties set against the demand for certainty would have been a keen concern for Duncan, whose reading of Plato at the time kept him attuned to the philosophical conundrum in ancient Greece between knowledge and its expression, the tense philosophical distinctions of dialectic and rhetoric. The individual poet in the process of composition must come to participate in the larger generative possibilities that allow a poem into existence. Such process-based concerns include an awareness of language, conditions, and facts propelled by speech or authorial stance, all compelled by the energetic endowment of the moment, the place from which imagination enters new conditions of form.

In the spring of 1955, Duncan traveled with Jess to Banyalbufar, Majorca, where they remained off and on until February 1956. Although the twelve letters in part II, "Duncan in Majorca (1955–1956)," cover a period of less than a year, they require emphasis largely due to Duncan's and Olson's mutual expansion of poetic form beyond literary strategies to include cultural and historical particularities. The medieval iconography and architecture of Southern Europe, moreover, provoked extended reflection on cultural energy and its transmission in formal structures. Duncan's interest in the medieval period began at Berkeley as a student under Ernst Kantorowicz in the Civilization of the Middle Ages program from the spring of 1948 to the fall of 1951.[7] His journey with Jess to Spain, therefore, brought Duncan close to the architecture and iconography that ultimately led him toward an expanded theorization of his own poetic practice as it confronted Olson's. The discussion of form in this part begins when Olson responds point by point to Duncan's essay "Notes on Poetics Regarding Olson's 'Maximus.'" For Olson, the German naturalist Ernst Haeckel's distinction between ontogeny and phylogeny is crucial for understanding the individual transformation of energy into form as it meets a larger historical and cultural framework. This scientific basis for understanding form underlies the ensuing months-long conversation. The interest of both poets focuses on existing figures of art in relation to historical periods when the motivating influences of culture shifted the terms of production and value. Writing on August 14, 1955, on the difference between medieval art and the new humanist emphasis of the Renaissance, Duncan observes the following:

> Wherever the spatial knowledge does not exist, the iconography does not exist. The images are not signs and with the "renaissance" everything is lost of the order; the icons are humanize{d} and became idols; the terror and majesty of the romanesque is superceded by piety and luxury.

Basing these insights on his viewing of the apse of Santa Maria de Taüll in

Barcelona, Duncan seeks to map historical emergences of creative energy onto his own poetic affinities with Olson and Creeley:

> The created thing then, as now, emerges from the thing seen (the painter's necessary book), the thing embodied as a sign in the thing seen/heard (the book, the word, and the letters—the world emerges from vowels and consonants), and the thing as heard (the musician's necessary book—and hence here the trumpet, the harps and lutes).

Olson, however, moves the question of form back to the location of individuals, away from things "seen/heard" to insist on "those energies (fuerza) which you at that moment are" (letter 32). For Olson, a "question persists: when is a transformation possible to the reductive materials????" The understanding of form as it is worked out in the Majorca letters combines a respect for artifacts and an acknowledgment not only of cultural or historical shifts but of the many interacting and conflictive energies that shape the motives of individuals to use the given cultural material. Christ Pantokrator, whose image is depicted at Santa Maria de Taüll, then, reaches out to the present as a sign, not a symbol, of the measure Olson evokes. "A word is a speed," he writes on August 21, 1955, "which fuerza hath, / happen the great bodied spirit is // The book / is what we make."

In March 1956, after part II of these letters, Duncan travels from Majorca to North Carolina to accept a temporary position offered by Olson in the final months of Black Mountain College. Taking over for Creeley, Duncan offers a course called Ideas and the Meaning of Form; the class convened at eight each morning, introducing students to an intense scrutiny of vowels, consonants, syllables, prosody, sentences, and paragraphs.[8] By contrast, Olson taught late into the evening, often requiring students to remain in class beyond midnight. A competition developed between the two instructors over the students' affections, with Duncan eventually satirizing Olson's Black Mountain presence in his play *Origins of Old Son*, in which Old Son is an oversized baby in diapers. The parody of Olson reveals Duncan at the beginning of his most potent poetic period when he had started composing poems that ultimately would make up *The Opening of the Field*. There are many ways to consider the lampooning of his friend, and certainly the friendship of Duncan and Olson in the letters does not abate. Beyond the obvious satiric play involved in its form, *Origins of Old Son* brings out mythic insight and friendly provocation in an intense, isolated community with two strongly shamanic figures at the height of their creative powers. As Peter O'Leary suggests, the play may have been an opportunity for Duncan to establish creative balance and to settle his own energies as he learned to teach in the context of higher education for the first time.[9]

Despite any competitive frays remaining from the men's time at Black Mountain, the twenty-five letters in part III, "'Haven't you, from of 'Wisdom as Such' on, given me myself' (1956–1957)," resume in September 1956, shortly after Duncan returns to San Francisco to take a position as the assistant director of the Poetry Center at San Francisco State University. While Olson remains at Black Mountain to deal with the closing of the college, Duncan relays the news and gossip of the San Francisco poetry scene and arranges for Olson to perform at the Poetry Center and to lecture at other West Coast locations early the following year.[10] After the February 21, 1957, reading by Olson at the Poetry Center, Duncan hosts a series of talks by the New England poet based on his Black Mountain course lectures, which focus on the process philosophy of Alfred North Whitehead. Additionally, on May 13, 1957, Duncan shares news that he has secured an agreement for publication with Grove Press of *The Opening of the Field* and advocates on Olson's behalf for a book that will eventually appear as *The Distances* (both published in 1960).

The support of Grove enlivens their spirits and validates the decade of work they have done together in poetry—work that had until then appeared mainly in small presses (Duncan's *Letters* [1958], published with Jargon, is one important example). "Well, and it's this Event of a possible book of yours that is the flower that I keep watching this green plant for," Duncan writes to Olson on June 4, 1957. But the sense of their roles as outsiders still preoccupies Duncan in that same letter: "Reading Joyce's *Letters*, I notice him searching, in the form of reading and coercing reviewers, for where was any reaction to his work. Just beyond that feeling, is there any response? is another feeling of a nonindividual significance to the act." While Olson is concerned with the legalities and economics of closing Black Mountain, Duncan's energies continue to focus on publishing possibilities, and his advocacy of Olson reveals a deep attachment to his friend along with a faith in their individual achievements. On August 24, 1957, Duncan writes:

> RE: Your book, Grove, etc. It's begun to seep into their comprehension that your work gives us all measure, that you move to excel what you have accomplished, and I've dinnd it into Mr. {Donald} Allen's skull that every published work from you is a necessity for anybody seriously at the work. What comes out of his skull is that this Olson thing is a loaded literary event. O.K. if that gets more in circulation.
>
> I take it that he wants to "launch" you—and try not to shudder visibly.

What I urge is that you get into print a solid collection (including *Cold Hell* poems) (and *Y&X*) of the work extra-Maximus=this for the book. For *Evergreen Review* a group of Maximus cantos, with a prose piece will illustrate the scene. Allen wants an essay on your work—and I am preparing (most of the text is already in notebooks) the second section of my essay on *Maximus*.

Duncan's ambition in this part of the correspondence comes through on behalf of Olson and himself as he strives to secure a living as well as a reputation in poetry. With the closing of Black Mountain College, Olson would soon be without a position to support himself and his family, and Duncan's meager wages ($150 a month) at the Poetry Center did not go far. To that end, Duncan asks Olson for a reference on September 29 for a Guggenheim Fellowship (both men wrote letters of support for Guggenheim applications, which are included in the appendix to this volume). Olson, with his second wife, Betty, and their young son, returns to Gloucester after the closing of the school, continuing their economic precariousness.

But the material circumstances of their lives are secondary to their personal affinities. "You are," Duncan writes on October 5, "dear Charles, first of my sense of the kin." The honor he bestows on Olson, and the advocacy he extends on his behalf, acknowledges depths that go beyond merely careerist ambition. The bonds of their friendship have found root in a psychic domain for Duncan, who in the same letter acknowledges Olson's influence on him: "Haven't you, from of 'Wisdom as Such' on, given me myself; and certainly as I came to find that the dance had been, was, is there: 'came to' in the midst of, your hand was there in the round." Duncan articulates a vitalist understanding of their joint endeavors to bring the energy and speed of their words to bear in a larger cultural commons. As both men shape their lives on the edges of various educational and publishing institutions, Duncan verifies their motives in the shared obligations of their friendship. "I have this certainty," he writes, "that you, like me, thrive upon, spring up from a community not of imitation but of volition. It's into life we'll have will or no our initiations; not into the kind."

"Kaos or Kosmos"

The last decade of Olson's life departs in fortune from Duncan's during the same period, roughly 1958 to 1970. While Olson struggles to maintain his domestic life and creative pursuits after the closing of Black Mountain College, Duncan travels widely across North America in support of his publications. With financial help from Barbara Joseph, a close Berkeley friend, Duncan and Jess purchase a home in San Francisco by 1967, and they are able to meet their domestic needs with the fees earned by Duncan's extensive poetry readings and Jess's art sales. By contrast, Olson faces an often-dire economic situation after his return to Gloucester from Black Mountain, and he makes only intermittent attempts at employment: he is a visiting professor of poetry in 1963–1965 at the University at Buffalo, for instance, and he takes a brief position at the University of Connecticut just before he is diagnosed with cancer. Duncan's busy reading schedule may have contributed to a reduction in their correspondence, though they cross paths when Duncan is on the East Coast and at the 1963 Vancouver Poetry Conference and the 1965 Berkeley Poetry Conference. During this time, Duncan also grows increasingly preoccupied with the Vietnam War, directing energy to his correspondence with Levertov as their relationship began to suffer under vehement disagreements about the role of poetry in resistance to the war.[11]

The letters between Duncan and Olson continue to reinforce a close bond, though their relationship in the correspondence becomes more and more focused on mutually sustaining the values and beliefs established in earlier conversations. As they complete work independently for Grove Press (Duncan's *Opening of the Field* and Olson's *The Distances*), both continue to support the other's ambitions. Duncan, for instance, provides a letter of recommendation for Olson's Guggenheim application; Olson, in his management of the liquidation of Black Mountain College, ensures that Duncan receives compensation for his teaching and keeps him informed on details related to the school's closing.

But Duncan also is thinking closely about their position in his derived lineage of modernist writers. The letters in part IV, "Projecting Verse, Opening the Field (1958–1961)," are concerned about the editing of comprehensive anthologies of new writing being undertaken by Donald Allen, Barney Rosset, and Jonathan Williams. As these editors begin to shape representative publications of the new poetry inspired by Duncan, Olson, and Creeley, Duncan on March 10, 1958, argues for the importance of a collection of writing that exposes "PROCESS" rather than focusing on individual groupings of writers. "Let interaction of texts (form/content) be the design," he writes. "Present a constellation" that features himself, Olson, and Creeley at the center. He is interested in an "insistent design of determinants / and derivations, & relations," establishing Louis Zukofsky, Pound, Lawrence, and Williams as essential figures behind them. Olson agrees with Duncan in letter 69, suggesting a representative sample from the Black Mountain group along with Pound, Williams, and the Bay Area poet Philip Whalen. The constellation of poets that eventually makes it to print in Donald Allen's influential *New American Poetry* (1960) does in fact feature Creeley, Duncan, and Olson, the latter appearing as the central, unifying figure. The focus on process also is foregrounded in essays published with Allen's anthology to show how these poets approached open-form writing.

While Duncan's social presence in the world of poetry is increasing, Olson's retreat into his Gloucester home at 28 Fort Square begins a shift in the dynamics of the correspondence, which now has a greater focus on poetics and the intersection of the studies pursued by both men along with a special emphasis on cosmology. In November–December 1959, Olson writes:

> events
> in the cosmos
> are as the crystals
> in the gene
> the tree
> which emerges
> is the multifoliate
> rose
> Love
> is
> God

For Olson, the cosmos establishes relation; it moves attention away from individual concerns to include an acknowledgment of the interaction of dynamic energies. The pursuit of his studies increasingly occupies Olson's attention, particularly as the winter solstice approaches, a dark period each year as his birthday grows near and as the earth reaches its greatest distance from the sun—a period often of anxiety and reflection for him. In 1959, he is particularly concerned with the idea of measure in poetry as it relates to him individually and in terms of the cosmos, and it is particularly relevant that these two cosmological poets should increase each other's awareness in letters whenever possible. For instance, on December 23, Olson writes:

> the 'ANCIENTS' (including Alchemie, both
> European and Tibetan (? or China?)
>
> knew the NECESSITIES
> of the soul IN
> And OF the   And FOR the
> KOSMOS

Olson goes on to confide in his friend about his own inability to understand the relation of his modern sense of soul to the ancient rites of encounter he so wants to retrieve; poetry is increasingly a place of a potential discovery "in ancient circular life." An orientation to cosmological significance, moreover, has opened a range of study and understanding that directs attention away from the Cold War emphasis on rigidly secular and social attitudes of cultural bearing. Olson instead wants to make

> the admission
> that one is living
> in the presence
> of a larger
> life: BUT FACT [PRAXIS]—what I take it has been
>   MISSING.

Duncan responds in early January 1960, a few days before his own birthday (he and Olson held it to be significant that they both were Capricorns in the zodiac wheel), arguing for the importance of "driv{ing} the word straight as he can into peril" (letter 81). Where Olson's letters are impassioned, if convoluted, and lunge forward into the chaos of person and his surroundings, cosmological and actualized in environmental energies, Duncan's "middle-class household" grasp of their shared actualities in poetry tends, in the letters, toward diagram and illustrations of areas for poetic understanding. "Facts," "concepts," "surroundings," and "meanings" all compose the interactive grounds on which poetry enacts "co-ordinations of sensory and visceral being."

The February 1960 correspondence continues to push matters of cosmos to the fore of their articulated stances toward poetry. Duncan stresses "atomic reality" and "elemental life" as fundaments to any understanding of creative energy. Importantly, the terms of their encounters with the cosmos remove human measure from any centralized position, opening pathways to understanding an "adventure into the Kosmos," as Duncan stresses: "the atomic reality make{s} man *not the center*." He sees individuals in relation to a larger whole as "events," Whitehead's term, which is used by both men to describe an individual projection of form accessed in imagination, "that 'we' may be extend{ed} as a sum of a progression of imagined *events*." For Duncan, the terms of soul, spirit, sensual experience, cosmos, and universe are interchangeable points of entry in the imaginative encounter of events made possible through poetry. Although the adventure of their relationship in letters had begun over a dispute regarding the place of wisdom in poetry, they both now approach a sense of form in the elemental terms of a private correspondence; their exchange articulates and exemplifies the creative bounty available through an open-field poetics that removes any individual claim of control. Instead, the poet is but one figure in the energetic exchange of forces metaphorically oriented by the image of a field as both aperture and entry, the interface where poets encounter events of the universe by way of the terms of their being.

For Olson, impoverished and increasingly isolated in Gloucester, "there is either Kaos or Kosmos(? / *disorder* / and confusion," as he says in letter 84. In part, Duncan is fed by Olson's chaotic energy, but as Olson turns now toward the remote interior of his soul, Duncan moves with a growing sense of sociality to support the publication of *The Opening of the Field*. The arrival later in 1960 of Allen's *New American Poetry* will provide other economic opportunities for them both as central figures (with Creeley) of a new poetic movement. Despite the external, public factors, the letters take on a growing sense of adventure that is also increasingly dogmatic. Those dogmas of creation are, for Olson, more and more advanced toward the creative imagination he confronts, while Duncan, in many ways, acts as shepherd to his friend, enlivening and tending the chaos. For outsiders looking in, at a distance of more than half a century, the terms of their correspondence can seem remote, even obscure at times. But the private debate and extension of personal narrative in the letters give insight into the public records of their poetry and the outer dimensions of their biographies. The letters in this part sound a cosmological reality for Olson, a sense of devotion to study as access to his soul. And Duncan meets the demands of the creative energies bestowed on him by his friend.

In part V, "'you must feed your heart, Mr. Olson' (1963–1969)," both men increasingly see themselves in a kind of creative union, though it is Duncan who tends the practical details of advancing their positions in poetry through conference organizing, and he is encouraged with the award of a Guggenheim prize. Duncan's domestic order and social appetite for travel conflict with Olson's withdrawal and increasingly localized social capacities. Nevertheless, on December 20, 1963, Duncan writes that he has had a dream about Olson, and he expresses regret for not finding greater opportunities for the two to connect in conversation at the Vancouver conference:

In the dream I had the great joy of seeing you, embracing, having some part of that *tête à tête* we did not have in Vancouver. I have affirmation of my life in you and being able at last to go to you seemd curative. At this last summer you calld for some "homeopathy"—but I couldn't think what homeopathy was.

Five months later, Duncan vows to dedicate a period of time each Friday to write Olson (letter 110); this dedication of time functions as a mnemonic, on his part, to maintain the correspondence, though Duncan's full domestic life and busy schedule frequently disrupt his intention. His self-acknowledged role as shepherd or "sheep dog" imposes on Duncan a sense of dutiful tendance, and on June 29, 1964, he writes:

> This writing to you, Charles, came as an inner imperative, an appointment
> with you for communication's sake. So that today when I was ready for
> it, the worrying was gone, as if it were the beastly alternative to my atten-
> dance. Goaded, driven, herded by what shepherd, but I feel the sheep dog
> more, only this direction of work going upon freedom. I have to use you as
> my communicant and have, I realize, to trust that: the contradicting voice,
> adversary to the work, argues "Why do you think he is interested in that?"
> "Oh, friend of my free spirit," today I answer easily, "and wherever I go
> towards what I have to do I go towards him."

Despite Duncan's strong affections for Olson as expressed in the letters, he walks out of the July 23, 1965, lecture Olson gives at the Berkeley Poetry Confer- ence. Olson's three-hour anti-performance drives away many of his old friends that evening, though to others he accomplishes an exemplary enactment of con- science in a setting of his own making, where the personal erupts to dislodge public ritual. Olson presses himself beyond the expectations of his audience to challenge social decorum and privilege by publicly insisting on what Nathaniel Mackey calls "a form of penance . . . [Olson's] way of sublimating or attempting to sabotage his birthright."[12] The evidence of the letters, however, shows that despite the public frustrations of the conference, the two men remained close, acknowledging the bond of their poetry and their love. Duncan certainly would have intimately recognized the complexity of Olson's public statement in Berke- ley, alert to the cosmological reaching forth by his friend to subvert his own implicated terms of social bearing. The social reality Olson confronted required self-risk and took a bodily toll. In December 1966, in a moment of physical and spiritual vulnerability, Olson writes from the Hotel Steinplatz in Berlin to acknowledge a sickness of body and spirit:

> (The problem is, I have had to 'rest' here. And very happily, actually. I had
> a 'turn' like they used to *say*, 10 days ago and a cardiogram led Herr Doktor
> Otto Mertens to conclude my heart needed to be fed, for the rest of my life!
> That was *his* words: you must feed your heart, Mr. Olson! Wow. Truth is the

month & I, the "Physician" [who once sd to you, Mr. Duncan, I have home-opathy, to offer you!

Despite Duncan's quick response on his birthday to offer expressions of sup-port, the letters between them slow down, though they see each other when Olson visits California in April 1967, a busy year for Duncan, who gives readings in nearly twenty American cities.[13] The men continue to exchange letters, often near the winter solstice, showing strong devotion and acknowledging each oth-er's publications; they also continue to advance ideas about poetry. At this point, Duncan and Olson's friendship becomes more expressively intimate regarding their mutual admiration and love; they acknowledge aspects of their feelings that had been present for decades but that are now articulated regarding the roles each took in the other's life. "I *usually* think of ourselves . . . with a great psy-chic aura," Duncan writes on January 19, 1968. "I swear we share in some fashion uniquely." Olson's quick response, in the penultimate letter, confirms the spiritual bond attested by his friend: "My dear Duncan, It is like the hoop and the circle, I must know nothing when I am not in touch with you (! Isn't it incroyable to be so slow & have known this powerful consciousness?" (letter 126).

A tumor is detected on Duncan's lung and in June 1969 he undergoes an inva-sive biopsy; six months later on January 2, 1970, he flies to New York City to be with Olson, who has been diagnosed with liver cancer.[14] A crowd of friends, poets, and other well-wishers gathers in the hospital hallway to pay respects to the dying man. Duncan is in and out of the hospital to visit the frail and now unconscious Olson, and returns on January 9 to San Francisco, where he receives news of Olson's death and records it in his notebook: "Charles dead, Friday night, Jan. 9th, as Creeley phoned Saturday."[15] Duncan remains an active advocate for Olson and his poetry, and presents nine lectures devoted to Olson and field poetics over the next two decades.[16] He survives his friend by eighteen years, dying on February 3, 1988.

The letters between Duncan and Olson provide a map of their early encoun-ters and document the shaping and promotion of their unique approaches to poetry as a form of life. The inner substance and outer measure of their con-cerns acknowledge both the risk and the love made possible by their adventure together among the company their conversations made possible.

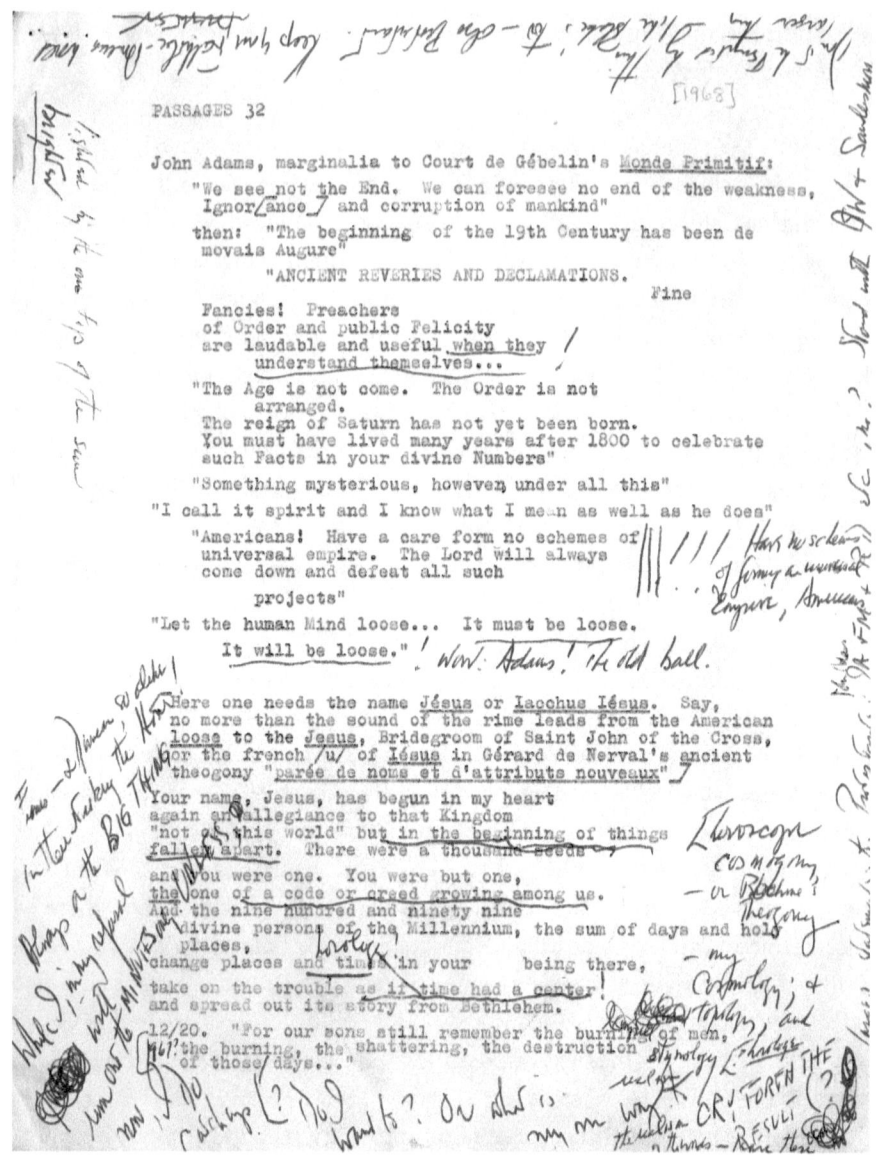

PASSAGES 32

John Adams, marginalia to Court de Gébelin's Monde Primitif:

"We see not the End. We can foresee no end of the weakness,
Ignor/ance_/ and corruption of mankind"

then: "The beginning of the 19th Century has been de
movais Augure"

"ANCIENT REVERIES AND DECLAMATIONS.
Fine

Fancies! Preachers
of Order and public Felicity
are laudable and useful when they /
understand themselves...

"The Age is not come. The Order is not
arranged.
The reign of Saturn has not yet been born.
You must have lived many years after 1800 to celebrate
such Facts in your divine Numbers"

"Something mysterious, however, under all this"

"I call it spirit and I know what I mean as well as he does"

"Americans! Have a care form no schemes of
universal empire. The Lord will always
come down and defeat all such

projects"

"Let the human Mind loose... It must be loose.
It will be loose."

Here one needs the name Jésus or Iacchus Iésus. Say,
no more than the sound of the rime leads from the American
loose to the Jesus, Bridegroom of Saint John of the Cross,
or the french /u/ of Iésus in Gérard de Nerval's ancient
theogony "parée de noms et d'attributs nouveaux"

Your name, Jesus, has begun in my heart
again and allegiance to that Kingdom
"not of this world" but in the beginning of things
fallen apart. There were a thousand seeds

and you were one. You were but one,
the one of a code or creed growing among us.
And the nine hundred and ninety nine
divine persons of the Millennium, the sum of days and holy
places,
change places and time in your being there,
take on the trouble as if time had a center
and spread out its story from Bethlehem.

12/20. "For our sons still remember the burning of men,
the burning, the shattering, the destruction
of those days..."

Manuscript of Passages 32 by Robert Duncan with handwritten notations by Charles Olson
(page 1), 1968, Charles Olson Research Collection, Box 151, Archives and Special Collections
at the Thomas J. Dodd Research Center, University of Connecticut.

Part One

"near-far Mister Olson"

(1947–1955)

1

Los Angeles, CA
September 9, 1947

Dear Duncan—

Christ & Robt Duncan will know whether the enclosed is of use.[1] Anyhow, felicitations.

I was back in San Fran one night last week & met Muriel Rukeyser. If you have not already, add her to yr. sponsors: she's warm abt you.

And advise if E{zra} P{ound} notion worked. A note right back to me (which you might do & reprieve me for delay) would catch me before I head east: c/o Sean, 673 Broadway, Venice.[2]

Remember me, & Constance,[3] to Jane, yr Niobe.[4] And beg to excuse no visit to Van Fraghs.[5] On the Tuesday I was to go I looked at travelers checks & saw the mene mene.[6] I am making fast for Washington, base.

Let me hear from you.
Yrs,
Olson

～

2

Los Angeles, CA
January 30, 1948

Robert,

I pulled away fast—broke. & this time I'm gone.

The last 5 days I carried yr black book back & forth SF to B{erkeley}. I took the freedom to leave it as most safe among the other historic transcripts, at the Bancroft. If you will call on Eleanor Bancroft herself, she has it.[7]

Read it all. At the moment haven't a thing to say, 'cept I think you are wonderful.

But that doesn't do you a bit of good. [Read Miss Stein on bomb.[8]

I shall compose you a letter. Do likewise.

Yrs.
Olson

～

3
Berkeley, CA?
Fall 1948?

Dear Ole Olson:

WHAT?!*.?[9] I keep an eye upon die Märchen;[10] to have the poem now quite occult—not with the meaning hidden as a jewel may be hidden in a box, but as the inside of a box may be hidden in a box. Are there "springs" in the language; anyway there are sources and mechanisms that we run across in the making, that lie in wait for us not in us. Is language Pound's sound element, stone in which for carving a sure hand? or is it that and other, a jungle or a storm in which we exist too: and we may need the bit of shelter of a story before this whirl is over.

It may be the authority of the *Cantos* that compels some but it's the imagination of the *Cantos* that persuades me/ and so I am at best a heretic Poundite; and no more than a Taoist (and even Confu{cius} observed the whirld) as bottomless; and not much less than a magicker to keep my own house warm at shallow show. We wright: to kik up the water so the pond don't git stale. A pun in place will save mine.

If as {Gustave} Flaubert has it "A Simple Heart": simple means single track, in a sense—and there is a duplicity not an ambiguity. What one reads is the unwitting verity reveald in the helpless effort to conceal the source and nature of the actual content.

Ambivalence—not imprecision—but a precision, a sense of language *at balance*. The sharper the definition and the keener the acknowledgment of the weight of one's words.

An ironical tone: the tone of the verbal scales. Then what we must picture is a complexity of weights in "balance" in suspension or equilibrium. An ironical tone: the verification of three or four or more factors: seeing the thing from all angles.

—After discussion on the "Infallibility of the Pope" at Mary Fabilli's: But what one *knows* is the utter fallibility of one's self, a saving grace: and the wondrous fallibility of the universe. "So many faces, forms, glances." Contradiction may render false to logic; but poetic dialectic comprehends contradiction. Experience insists upon the reality of contradiction.

It WUZ you who said something about storytelling. & rite now I wld like to stop over at this small house by the side of this sideroad. YOU throw a big rock in the water; I'll divert the course downstream to a meander. OR is the stream so sacred from its source that we can't play with it.

~

4
Berkeley, CA
November 24, 1948

A copy of the first issue of the *Berkeley Miscellany* has been sent to you some time ago.[11] We would appreciate knowing if you wish us to send you future copies of the magazine, and any comments you have to make about the contents of the magazine.

The magazine is financed by contributions and subscriptions. A minimum contribution-subscription for the next three issues (beginning with issue no. 2, which is now at press) will be 1.00. This is possible, if indeed it proves possible, only because the first issue was entirely paid for by contributors.

Robert Duncan
P.O. Box 3
Berkeley, California

~

5
Washington, DC
April 3, 1949

My dear Robt—

Thanks for BM/2.

Mary's garden is a delight & yrs.[12]

Yrs Olson

~

6
Black Mountain, NC
August 1951

my dear robert duncan

a good time ago i had sd to the editor of ORIGIN that of all those others, me, i took it duncan, was more of the thing, and that his work wld go there, properly[13]

now both corman (the editor, cid 51 jones avenue
dorchester, 24, mass)
and my running-mate, my tandem, robert creeley press me, where can duncan
be reached

an enemie of yrn now tells me, thru, {James} Broughton[14]

so please, if you get this, and you care, why don't you send the
best (as W{illiam} C{arlos} W{illiams} started me into it all by saying, why not
anything, you think, should be preserved)
to the above lad?
he awaits it
so be you, eh? how be you?

yrs,
charles olson

i still see in day dreams
yr wall, there, b, decorated
with rejection slips

~

7
Black Mountain, NC
November 25, 1951

My dear Duncan:
I ask yr pardon I have delayed to welcome your delightful
Song of Borderguard.[15] I waved it & read it to all i cld lay my hands on the day it
came, it is so clearly something fine, & a pleasure for us to publish.
Both Cernovich & I have slowed, in the doing of any of these Broadsides.[16]
None are out, or even on press. So, we shld welcome yr idea of yr friends designing yr poem for us, eh?
Let me enclose the details on size, etc. And as
soon as you both can conveniently get his design to us, fine: we shall move more
rapidly, I figure, in January
(it burns me up to give you all the sort of
delay you and i have to put up with from other editors & publishers, and I am
most chagrined: the thing is, i am not the "publisher," and i can only bull-whack
cernovich along, and he has to sweep, mop floors, dance some and manage his

way, broke. So you must not think we give you anytime the usual run-around. I have had enough of it myself (just lost the volume THE PRAISES by my own impatience/after a year and four months from shipping mss!)[17]

The whole fucking thing abt issuance of work burns my ass: one thing Corman has given (or did, at first) was some fast delivery service. But I'm afraid he too will begin to figure he has to spread the manure to get readers to come to his field—already he gives too much space to such bores as Bronk and Morse (#5 is all an essay of Morse's on Stevens—which is most late, & like the Hudson Review or some other drag-ass sheet):

one thing only has gladdened me, recently, vis Origin, that, #6, is to be yrs:[18] hold to that, and there is hope for the damned thing: in fact, for my money, if we can keep the thing concentrated by you & Creeley—

(in fact, i wld woo you to be my ally, and encourage Corman to concentrate, for by so doing we can carry on what Creeley started: he held Corman's hand, pushed him, for a good yr & a half past, and is now—just now—beginning to wear under it

> PUT THIS UNDER YR HAT, for i am working, at the moment, to
> keep the two together, simply, that, we have here a going biz, and
> you'll well know what drag there is to get another going

Crazy biz, tho, on other front: {John} Kasper (lad who got out the Fenollosa in 9 days) was here to fetch a "selected Olson," and I took the liberty to say I'd be willing if & when the house (Kasper & {David} Horton) was MAN STANDING BY HIS WORD[19]—read EZ on masthead, say—and had a shape to its list other than the old man's present conspiracy—and my idea of a shape (in addition to the restoration of other texts than merely {Louis} Agassiz, {Alexander} Del Mar etc) wld include a selected Duncan and collected stories of Creeley.

OK? May I get yr word to come ahead if the Gasp[20] can enlarge his spot the Old Man has him dancing on?

—

It is yr perception, moves me. This is yr weight, the beauty, even behind the verse, what beauty it hath is clear, perhaps too clear, it is so unstopped, man of my other sense of reality might say. But give over, olson, give over before the impeccability of, such singing, moving through such artifice, as, say, the giraffes, or, that, the secret of fucking, the dying man sd

—my lord, duncan, who, here, maketh such song—the rest of us are only
story-tellers
                              As story-teller; Artificer, {Guillaume} Apollinaire, Pound in the
posture, Eliot, in the American—
                                        the thing is, you have learnd, and what learning
I love is the learning
                              of yrself: o, this, Duncan,
                                                            you need not (I
myself of course—you will not understand it) say
                                                            it says, a giraffe[21]
speaks for you, a
skull
    (and so, the coda
    throw away
                          the bbbbbbbbbbbbbbb
                                              i learn from,
            most
                        (as before, footnotes, &
                        always, art-
                        ifice:

                              FACE
                        _____

Well-lit
man   PS#2: tell Jess Collins
              we can best handle
              silk screen or linoleum cut
              —& that best size   ok.   let me hear fr ya
                inside 9 × 12

                                              olson

                  Am making copies of yr poems Corman sent on to me
                  —to send to Creeley: he is editing an American issue
                      of Gerhardt's mag., FRAGMENTE—hope you will
                      care to stand in
                  there, if it is Creeley's pleasure.

~

8
Black Mountain, NC
December 9, 1951

RD:

fine. am abt to make copy of "Borderguard" to go to Creeley for possible use—*fragmente.*

> (the creel pissed off on corman, and pulled out—so, it is—to my
> liking—you & this lad now, there (& {Stuart} Perkoff, for what? not
> verse, yet, or say, the component "energy"—as {Jaime} d'angulo was,
> my impression—but somethin else ain't seen since A. Blok (exception,
> 'course, Chaplin), that that Dickens was, something having to do with
> non-poeticks & at same time not poetics/in the practisin sense—
> schmaltz, sans sentimentality (& certainly not schmerz, as, {Rainer}
> gerhardt has it {Saint-John} perse had:[22] shit-poet's pain, as poets, is
> not very interesting

> anyhow, Perkoff: what usually comes out communism, what in anarchists
> (romantic a, I hear the phrase now is—Kenneth {Rexroth}, say—either
> of em?—or those bloody soft unChristian Hinglish-men) is self-love
>   something, perhaps, is best
> in the movies—YES, is a spill over into verse, no doubt

as a romanticformalist, wld say so: ok.

the NEWS is, the Broadsides are moving, and yr news, that you are on top of yrs (it will be #2, thus, January–February), that you are sending, is good for Nick {Cernovich} & me to hear

                                                (if this gets to you before you get anything off, switch it to 217 Randolph Place NE, Washington 2 DC— that's my house or studio, there, and I leave for it tomorrow, to be based there (going also NY, NEgland) for a month—until January 7th.

(J{onathan} Williams promises to send you copy of #1—so, I'll save one, if you will take his/as also mine, to you, eh?

(at the same time i ask
you to be quite clear that, only BROADSIDE—among the
several proliferating—like corn cancer—"presses" here—
do I have anything to do with, act or approval)

Take you as cold to lights in (A): that there are as few readers one needs
as con-temp-o-rarities

& (B): i take it for granted i knows what i does
when i dud it

ok. this, to keep things moving—& please, keep on, eh?

yrs,

olson

Later *PS* BG {*The Song of the Border-guard*} copied—& very damned glad to
have it—try it, Robt, with two lines middle left out and tell me, eh? (The guards
No grt matter—merely, *moves* it all & locates it, more simply?
PS #2 Nick sez, you must not pay out anything—this project is supposed to pay
for itself—only—do send us list of bookstores, friends, etc for mailing, eh?
PS #5!: Robt—is there any *bookstore* SF, or Bay, might handle 25 (50?) of Broadside #1? If you cld let us have note on this directly. Wash.—fine—we will take
copies there & can ship immediately for Xmas sales, Ho-Ho!
P.S.

Have also sicked Jonathan Williams (here) on you as   black mt
1 of 4 present joes worth looking into—got any other   n c
ideas of men beside

yourself, Larry Richardson, Bill Merwin
hey Dunc!   *any* you are a believer in???

#1. Lad here designing & printing single poems (one out, design,
woodcut or linoleum or silk screen, & type)

1st, is Olson—bullfight

2nd, or 3rd, is Duncan—if
you will shoot me one—how about Africa Revisited? or one of the a. Genesis
pieces[23]

(I am editor)?

{in left margin} And do you want to do your own design? Or let Jess? Open shot, all the way (marketing still also open)

Any #2—Corman says, yet no mss—why?

Write

Charles

∼

9

Black Mountain, NC

January 21, 1952

dunk:

what wufs me some, is, that you have already laid in my hand a SELECTED DUNCAN. In this way: that i have no place for such YET. and pray nothing i sd misled you

that is, (1) creeley wanted to see as much as possible of you for his editing of an issue of *fragmente* on amurrikan po-etts; and i have kept carbons going to him

(2) corman is prepared to feature you in Origin #6 (July 15th), and i shall see he sees all you suggest for that gig

(3) we here *may* get to more than the Broadsides if cernovich & i are here in the fall (a selected Olson, if we can get the dough, is on the plan for this spring, and maybe a small go on shake-speare's punctuation: otherwise, or instead, we'll be lucky if we ham-mer the 6 Broadsides through)

& (4), THERE IS KASPER, to whom i tried to sell the idea of three selecteds: you, creeley, me—and i hope that possibil-ity is the one you have picked up on, to send me the SELECTED D

but Kasper is involved in an assault from me on his vices (actually, as much as on him, on that MAN STANDING BY HIS WORD lie of the present conspiracy his publishing house is)

and how far he will go with men like you, creeley, me (instead of with the Old man and his stooges—Horton, Simpy, et al—)[24] i don't yet know: he certainly aint been friendly to you, as rep-resented in, the Heavenly City, Earthly City:

he is innurant, & of course

this is the hook the Old Man has him on, that, be there a better eduka-
tor than, He?

until we can edge in uswise, he (K) is beholden

to, the Master

OK. Just so our wires are straight. want no chagrins for you. want otherwise:
things done, even if they start small, & go slow. OK?

As of THE SONG OF THE BORDERGUARD. It goes straight ahead as B #2.
ONLY: Cernovich, as boss of designs, takes it that Jess's job is "illustration." And
thanks god that you are planning to use a whole series of Jess's things side by
side with single poems—for he (and i) don't want you to have been to any loss
on that cut (recd Sat)

For the point of these Broadsides is to design, not in
the sense of an illustration; but, in the sense of the whole thing, from the poem
out to the paper, type face, shape & size of paper, what painting, woodblock,
whatever, to, the finished job—and each one done for itself, wholly

i hope, therefore, that you will be satisfied if cernovich goes ahead from
scratch here, by way of Cy Twombly, here, and himself:

i attach a rough sketch of what c{ernovich} & t{wombly} have already done,
and are close to production on (one c did for me for you)

(i have seen twombly's part of it, and it is beautiful: is parallelism, not
illustration—a method which we want to carry out for all these things:

the other two to follow you & me are a story of creeley's (THE
PARTY)[25] with the whole thing worked out from ground by him and Ashley
Bryant[26]

and a poem of Kitasono {Katue}'s—a queer one—on night
& sex—and very flatly both, including, the sweetheart's pubic hair!—the design
of which we haven't got to yet

i somewhat blame myself that i was not clear to you, & that Jess, or yrself, may
be p.o'd over his design not filling our needs: please wink at it, as, we were only
starting, and the problems only now begin

(allow, too, that, for cernovich, the only real act in such businesses
as these Broadsides, is, just such complete acts, from bottom out—and tha

{in Olson's hand} fucking t just

busted on this machine

OK. Just c/o keeps you on

(Cernovich is

mailing to you p.p. the 50 THISes you kindly offer to market for us there.

Yrs

Olson

~

10

San Francisco, CA

April 8, 1952

DEAR OLSON:[27] I've been waiting for a shipment of number one BROADSIDE
to peddle around here. And/or news about how two is coming along.
THO since it takes me a thousand years to get anything underweigh

I ain't asstarnishd AT not hearing frum you. My point about getting
number one is that I think if I have one issue to hand to each convert
I have a better chance of getting a check to cover the series. & why
begin with numero 2?

Or: if you want send number 2s and I'll see to it that know won gets a
copy without supscribing to the series. It's ruther important to stress
the series sins there is a grate inertia in these quarters about supscribing to enything. I myself am a stand-buyer/tho I know damn well it
don't do enybody eny good.

Wall, I just got a typing job done so I am parting with $2.50 to cover
the Broadsheets for this household. Do you know how to reach young
{Jonathan} Williams—I sent him my books & he hasn't sent the dough
... cld you suggest in a letter that he might send on the amount to
ORIGIN to cover a subscription there?

MEANWHILE we are starting a critical "four sheets" type format out here, a
journal for THE ARTIST'S VIEW, painters and poets writing on their work. It is
going to be done by a photolithographic process—quite cheap and anything can
be reproduced ... a page of handwriting, a typescript, a painting, etc. We'll have
extra copies of the Introductory Number to mail out—I'll send you one. Claire
Mahl who is engineering the project seems to be one of them people who actually can get something done. I will have an article in first issue[28] to give a send
off for poets (but most poets around here ain't adventuring—tho I hope to prod

{Philip} Lamantia into writing something about dope & poetry—he's sold on the Artificial Garden tradition and it IS an ancient tradition of the poet; & a realm of pure criminal activity of the spirit today. I think, at least, that Philip has some IDEA about what {Antonin} Artaud was trying to get over; and seen in the lite of the dope-addict {Charles} Baudelaire emerges as something more interesting than a sinner. Maybe I could get a few cryptic or tightend up statements from Sanders Russell.

Anyway I do want to hear even a card from you. One, thank gawd, and ORIGIN does get to keep up somewhat on what you are doing. I wish that I cld have a month or so direct exposure to your center of Action. . . . but travel is prohibitive.

Yrs
DUNCAN

1724 Baker Street
San Francisco, 15, California

∼

11
Black Mountain, NC
April 11, 1952

RD:
See!

(And rest—75, plus 50 #1's follow p.p.

Let us have yr impression, pronto!

Hope it will make up for de lay

(Crazy plus: time pushes a man to brink but still
sometimes a result
—back on,

Olson

∼

12

San Francisco, CA

ca. December 15, 1953

near-far Mister Olson![29]

I have two books on my table—*In Cold Hell in Thicket*—which has been a constant companion, increasing (as if it were possible) joy, and renewal to my intellectual heart's craving—and now *Maximus Poems/1–10* which {Kenneth} Patchen presented me with two days ago.[30] 'near' means everything indeed; a slowly increasing centerness of what you have been writing, retroactive and for several months now the excitement has been on. Say—early pieces came around the corner of the eye, spoke in the background of the ear, seemd incidental. Then a shifting of the sights and a tuning of the ears bring the Olson intellectual heart into range. These pieces in scatterd magazines and these books now are those "friends coming from far quarters" that Confucius finds one of three civilized pleasures.[31] It is the containd Effort—another of the three pleasures—the "constant perseverance and application" of young birds learning flying on the wing—and the perspective "containd"—the third that is everywhere and every thing.[32]

A very structure of act, a speech as learnd in the hand-ear-to-mouth as walking, an athletic language. Because all here is the purpose of the poet there is no discouragement: that you have such technical achievement compared to my often inadequacy there is every encouragement, heartening: to be free! an I am as I speak.

What more central love than the disturbance and trembling awakend by each new song; the calling up of one's own spirit in answer, the still center in the excitement that comes as the poems are comprehended. A challenge. But to the intoxicated mind a more marvellous alcohol—a nourishment. Of my own otherness. My entirely differentness. It's the coming back to the core of speech— that poetry might be a revelation of the language written by, created by Man—a closet of speech wherein one speaks with the vastest spirit—a revelation of language not personality. What more central love than the comradeship in devotion to the art?

Then, but it is not central yet, it is still coming into view, another devotion. The wisdom we seek. The counsels of the language. The purpose, the effort—is part of the wisdom. "One loves only form . . ."[33] or love, the sense of the form—a form itself—a created thing. "It is elements men stand in the midst of"[34]—what we are . . . "did you know, she sd., growing up there, / how rare it was?"[35] citizens of a language—"go sing"[36] "you who also wants"[37]

but why "come home a winner?"[38] yet one knows that the course one has been winning in the poem is not the race—is the course one has been running, winning not the course but the awareness of it, the revelation "as much of a labor / as to lift an arm / flawlessly"[39]—how that quickened my scents—the effort—but with flaw as without flaw . . . a wonder.

"to live our life quite properly in print"[40] over and against my "I write to exercise my faculties"[41] akin? "only eyes in each head"[42]
    digesting Maximus this
is like writing a poem, that kind
of listening to the words, almost catching them
but / throwing them into e-motion.

One sees the configuration of Gloucester: and qualities of men—self-contain, devoted "as mastheadsmen,"[43] in the element of an art—fishing—or staring at {Vincent} Ferrini's magazine cover, at all magazine covers in the Waiting Station—the demand for a poetry that can be tested by the measure of their living—a field of tansy. And it is the measure, the test for a poetry, the imaginary audience that one subscribes. One shld meet eye to eye—yes—so designd to be inspected. (But an imaginary audience of the lotophagoi? of sensation mongers? a trick—I am among the devious)

but
it is the Maximus who urges us.
"seeking too ready ears"[44] "who want to lie down in
Tiamat."[45]

    close to *Paterson*? yes—and there be a root
in the *Cantos*, in *Paterson* that is hardy stock
—a direction in poetry—

RD
San Francisco

∿

13

Black Mountain, NC
December 21, 1953

RD: the greatest. You'll know. Or how cld you, that your own, is, plus one, what has come in—and on both of the bks. So you can guess.

/// to say But—and how to say this—that it is you, both that sd it, and had it,—this is very damn important to me, having (since that Milton, there, Circle)[46] had what you have, by god, awarded me, in that bracket, that,—well, reverse it: since '47, it has been *your* technical achievement compared to my often very damned often inadequacy . . . {in left margin in Olson's hand: Yr one great differentness}

So: to have you say these things gives me *the* sense of having done the job, the sense of that comradeship, that central love.

Look: it's now three days since yr letter came. And that I waited this long (haven't even read yr own thing enclosed) may be sign of what food and water . . . and how i had to do nothing but savor it, falling back into that: enjoyment. Christ! That's walking up to a man, and giving him what damn little he gets, eh?

OK. Just foolish to try to say it.

Now: wld you, without at all feeling jumped, let me publish it, as it stands, as a review? For it does have its own damn form, as it stands. And is so beautiful (I'm sure, for another, as well as myself), that, if you wld let it stand as a review of Max, I shld be damn greatly spoken of.

The place: the first issue of what looks as tho it will be called the Black Mt. Quarterly is just these days beginning to be made up. With Creeley as editor. And it is there that I'd like to place this thing, if you will permit.

And leave it as signed, R.D. And leave it as it opens, near-far Mister Olson/

So far I've sent Creeley one thing, also a review, under pseudonym, called "The Name Is Smith,"—the name is Hines, actually—but it's a thing on John Smith, as of this new book on him by Brad S.[47]

I plan to send Creeley one of the Maxes fr the 2nd set, one i like, called "On First Looking Out of Juan de la Cosa's Eyes."[48] And may I urge you to send him all the verse you think the highest of (as W{illiam} C{arlos} W{illiams} sd, when he 1st put me in

touch with Creeley, when he was then, Littleton NH, proposing to do the magazine it now looks as tho he may actually get into print:[49] his address:

Divers Press, Bañalbufar, Mallorca, Spain

Question, on letter: is the ideogram "young birds learning flying in the wing" or
in the wind?????
        And might i change that bracket to read "(that he has such technical
achievement compared to my often inadequacy)"—this one change I think for-
malizes the whole matter—the only change necessary to do it.

And if you want to make sure you'd pass on it for public place, I'll send you a
copy. But do let me urge you that, as it stands, it is perfect. No man cld have
himself sd so finely—and richly.

                                      Very damn wonderful to have you

let me know   breach

                                              Nothing,

                            like it

                                        Olson

{on back of letter}
The beauty is, not that anything is durable
but that it
continues

Why we have it, or all these religious
Ginks, is
That wld you can do with it
—and it is enough, God damn well ENUF, is
Compose it
               —that it is
Composed.

{next page}
(later)

                    As for the wisdom isn't there—"yet," i read it you are saying,
in Maximus
                    that it is (1) friends, (2) the effort—you call this "part of the
wisdom"

but i take it confucius sez the 3rd is no more than perspective,
the 3rd that is every where and every thing

Which wld be enuf, for
me, if that cld be got in

That is, (tonight reading jung—wilhelm's golden flour,[50]
and protesting—there—j's having to be the White Knight—why i had it, in pencil,
away with curing, art does not heal, medicine does, art composes. And that's good
enough

and, last, reading yr "Artist's View":

u see, i don't at all take
it you are as balanced as those sentences up to the IT
downed
on u. NOR
manque.

neither.

That that's the trouble with wisdom. It isn't a measure.
And thus has to go, from language (not knowing abt
art)

Doesn't it honestly—to be flat—come to, to love? that all springs
up, there? And that what springs up is *energy*, with which to do anything, think
(which is to be wise), cut wood (& i mean for no other reason than to keep
warm), push something, ahead, make it different, etc., anything, all

that all the vocabulary—the words you
seek to make gnomic by doublet—are valid enuf as reductive (that is, that they
do analyze validly the worlds love opens one's eyes to,

that *light*
is reductive, and that . . .

but here i do go off, or must explain i think the classic
order of water, fire, light has to be changed, that light was before electronics.
And we are after. And so fire . . .

Sound
is fire. As
love is.

That is, *all*
is reductive except
fire. (Heat, to get rid of any paradox in the statement—U see, i think thinking is
analytical, and has to be severely single statement on single statement because
thinking is that way. Writing, isn't. But writing is not thinking. Writing is not

reductive. Writing is what love is (and again, to keep off aphorism, love is the heat which so reveals energies in and beyond us that, like the act of writing you testify to, things we did not intend happen—and we then, need light, to reduce what has been found out . . . why you say you do study what you have done as text. But the revision, is the next writing

One thing Jung got a hold of (but because he does not know form he knows nothing, only astrology, or some such description as Dr {J. B.} Rhine's) is, what is opposite to, the reductive: the *synchronistic*.[51]

This seems to me extremely useful, as a fact, say, of the writing of a, poem—that the most compelling fact abt sd act is, isn't it?, that it is simultaneous—that this is its homogeneity which tells us when it is done, that does bring in what comes in, that it is time (rhythm is time, no? "flow" i think *rhein*, the root, means "to flow" that "measure" is only late, Alexandrian, when the pedants . . .

but i (again) don't want to leave it at that word "time," i want to try to convince you of what you have proved to me in poems, that yr own experience/is orderd by a seizure in a poem ({Leo} Frobenius' *Ergriffen*)[52] not so much in time ({Edgar Allan} Poe's Poetic Principle) or by time (metric, measure) but of a characteristic *of* time which is most profound (and still most unattended to, that it is time, in this sense—and in all those other senses of the synchronous, how another person, how an image is forever in that moment impressed upon all men thereafter "absent thee from felicity," say . . .

This fact that time is a concrete continuum which the poet alone—i insist—alone practices the bending of

why this art is, than no other

that only also love is,
simultaneous

that this is why we invoke

And why—if we were ultimate (& i believe we are, when we do bend to the law: the law is,

/whatever is born or done this moment of time, has the qualities of
this moment
of time/

But you will not mind, having in mind two things: (1) that i am stuck with such particularism; and (2) have had the conviction, from things you have done, that they have had this moment of time—and so i do not think it is the same thing that you also have to trouble yrself abt how it is to become a child; or that you care to complete your pretensions with yr wit.

I want only to urge that those are measures. And that a poem
is not wise, even if it is—that any wisdom also is solely
a quality of the moment of time of that poem in which there are
wisdoms. There are obviously seizures which have nothing to do with wisdom
at all.
And they are very beautiful.

I guess i don't even believe it's beauty—that how Bill has it (in To A Dog Injured in the Street)[53] that he and Rene Char[54] believe in the power of beauty/to right all wrongs . . .
                         that this is partial, "social," wisdom
It is time (love) is difficult, Mister
{Aubrey} Beardsley

(Why you say the aesthete, will have a hell of a time with, what you have unse-lected—why you say yrself you have found out stuff you'd throw away, turns out later. . . .

How to get it all in (which is, i suppose, an
olsonism like you have picked it, "go sing"[55]

                              I'm so foolish. A song
is heat (not light—light, yes, but not the *state* of a poem: the state is the fever of
(and it is not feverish, is very cool, is—the eyes are—how did they get that way?

"He who controls
rhythm
controls"[56]

This wld seem to me to be the
END

Otherwise we are involved in
ourselves (which is demonstrably
not so very interesting, no

matter
who

> I think when you exercise your (faculties, it is in yr letter; facilities
> at large, you are altogether separate and more than even the way it
> means, to make
> love
>
> I pick out the para.: "Here I am, at last . . . at last."[57]

Well, haven't any idea what hour it is, but the cocks across the gully at the farm
are crowing as steadily as minutes. And I must quit and have more blue cheese,
before
turning in

　　　　　yrs,

　　　　　　　c.

(last, next day)
　　　　　i think wisdom, like style, is the man—that it is not extricable as
any sort of a statement, even (and there is the catch) though there be "wisdom,"
that is, that life can be shown to yield "truths."

　　　　　　　　　　　　　　But truths are
as mortal as the life in any of us, which we cannot, for sure, heave (as Cordelia
couldn't) her heart into her mouth.

　　　　　　　　　　I take it only sectaries can deal with wisdom
as tho it were thus disposable. And even they, then (and i don't think it is at all
persecution which makes them secret, but it is), symbols which they then make
use of. And symbols as signs (ex-ample, the *I Ching*).

　　In other words, I fall back again on a difference which I take it the poet at
least is crucially involved in: that *he* is not free to be any sect, that there are no
symbols to him, there are only his composed forms (and each one is the issue
of the time of the moment of its creation), he cannot traffick in any other sign
than his one, his self, this man. Otherwise God does rush in, and overwhelm art,
turns it into, like that, the other great force, religion (in the exact sense of the
religious experience.[58]

It was thinking abt an early eastern Westerner, Apollonius of Tyana,[59] which led me
to sit down to write this additional note to you. That insistence of his, that there is

always "the moment that suits wisdom best to give death battle." It is in this sense of something which is carried like a gun—like a man's own life—which I mean as what seems to me important, these days (when the wisdom of the East and the unwisdom of the West are like looked-for dispensations, by the right, and the right Right), that it is important to assert that wisdom is that same thing as the skin of one of us, which we lose only when we choose to, not pour out, as of any, moment.

> ((I don't know enuf Anglo Saxon to say, but if the noun "wise" (AS. *wise*) is the root of the adj. (AS. *wis*), then by the noun one is back at the sort of force I suggest the whole concept of wisdom properly rests on: "Way of being or acting" ex.: on the wise))

~

14
San Francisco, CA
January–February 1954

dear Olson—[60]

—There are some poems you *shld* have seen long before now—and Jonathan Williams's letter (writ two months ago, and "answerd" this morning) sez "I'll see Creeley and Olson late this week" which may mean you have seen by now the mss. I sent to Creeley—but that was to Majorca, a jump from Black Mountain. Enyways I will enclose said above pomes.

Meantime: A "Poetry Center" has been started at San Francisco State College—plannd on a fairly ambitious program. At the present time I am conducting a workshop (unpaid) which meets one evening a week for a two and half hour session. After two months it may have occurrd to some in said workshop that there ain't no iambs or dacktillies in the langwidge. That a sonnet mite be a form with an invariable syllabic structure (ten to the line) and a variable structure of weights. And it has begun to dawn that there be breaths. (?) My sense of the effort & its possible "getting across" wavers between the keenest sense of in-forming and the cruelest sense of doing little more than exhibiting.

It's all an affair of contagion. But there is superstition rife. A positive will to resist the actualities of a poem. And to revert to value judgments and appreciations. The world is lousy with sensitivities and empty of curiosity.

I think I started wrong way round now on the tonal end—that is—I am prone to vowel and consonant development by echoing affinities. But that is so easy to accept and obscures the vital composition by the affinities of dis-resemblance. One seems to be encouraging a hot-bed of rhymes, alliteration (full, reversed, partial etc.) as a virtue rather than a method. And now I have to stop up them riming ears and re-tune them to what happens when the poet sets about a "twelve-tone" that is non-repeating sequence.[61]

Had I re-read (as I did thus last week) the Projective Poetry piece of yrs.[62] I would have stuck to the syllable and not divorced tone from its actual place.

Issue right now—is to get into form some understanding of the physiology of poetry—I drew a blank when I asked where (head, hand, heart, lungs, nerves etc.) the process took place. How can you tell? They ask. Or (and the worst *does* come up) what has this to do with it? The rot and the rut of the persisting super-stition of the "spiritual" extra-existence of an event.

Well one ought to know what daemon by where the daemon sets his works and how many daemons (centers) can come into play.

I have observed in myself a curious double role in hearing. There is a previ-ous "hearing" out of which the lines (or from which—as in sketching from an object) are composed, written on the page. Then the central "hearing" is in the hand. The act of writing seems to hold back, rein, (Plato's image of the horse-man)[63]—listen (?). But the important thing is that "earing" only come as the eyes relay the words seen from the designing hand—

> the other "hearing" is a response
> nerve-wise   to sound.

It becomes obvious in the hand. Touching the sounding violin. But since it is a matter of vibrations that are proposed, and of movements (in time) the fingers can hear as well as the ears.

And "subjectivity" which I take it to mean viscerally—it is the heart that is most tensed to the operation, and (but we persist here in our "spiritual" superstition) the brain—but it seems to one that the feeling of intensity is an actual tone change in the brain, a sensible recircuiting of charges and organizations—

it is the breath (and you

Yours—for an example of old (by months) letter unfinished communiqué—and broken off mid passage as it is, yours yet—
February 6–7, 1954

postscript

Yrs of February 4 received this morning and I reply at least to say YES and that if I get that Minimum of sending copy of first essay at the *MAXIMUS*—as I hope I might—I'd have to go at giving some 'literary' account of it, and in turn some poetics of what this thing *literature* is viz. The *MAXIMUS*. But the challenge anyway to give some definition to my admiration etc., whets my appetite.

Love. Etc

R.D.

[PS]

Did you send complete file of B{lack} M{ountain} R{eview} to William Roth

100 Spencer St.

Sausalito, California

I will be seeing him in two weeks or so, and I want to go on with the possibility that he might aid BMR and MEASURE.

〜

15

Black Mountain, NC

February 4, 1954

My dear Duncan:

Thanks, for letters & Faust Foutu[64]—(which I haven't yet got to, simply, that for two weeks I've been taking to my bed & try to get some simplifications: work, & events were too all over the lot.

I don't, of course, know what Corman was up to, in postponing you in order to put me into print.

Though I may have flashed it by sending him a copy of yr opulence on Cold Hell/ Maximus.[65]

What happened was, Creeley turned it down, for the Black Mt gig figuring (and one can understand) that for us to have that friendship in the 1st issue of what is so patently a mag of all of us is pretty chummy.

But I regret it, simply, that where the hell do we have so many "homes?" And who are these snipes who care for us, eh?

But maybe *Origin* is that closer

(in case Corman does plan to use it).

I had another regret:

to go with yr words on me, I did a review of "Artist's View" (along the lines of my letter to you).[66] Hope it will sit all right with you, now that it sits there alone.

Will write soon. In any case, DO GET POEMS of yrs to Creeley for #2. (And hope you can read this: it is written in the dark, in bed.)

O

∼

16

San Francisco, CA

June 17, 1954

dear Olson/ I am driven by the need for correspondences to make (or attempt) for the first time a primitive allotment of the day—with its period (the early morning) for letters; it (the need) is backlog piling up, pushing against some months now. I had returned to typing-money-pleasures—America's own version of the slave camp; and for a year have sufferd under & in the self-destructive slop-drama. Today then (June 17) I have rudely disrupted that course—and the jam of logs is shifting (nerves shifting, eager for the current of speech).

Thus—to make my beginning. John Adams writes "I will rouse up my mind and fix my attention."[67] And had that task of arousing himself to do, with a rigor, before he find himself. In your "PROJECTIVE VERSE"—the drive toward a maximum energy—an exertion in the works of it, measured phrases to drive, the engine designd wise movement: instructive each time at a level vital within "what yare saying."

Writing the letter to you about your work and then seeing it again, as you suggested it, to be printed, I thot of it in the context. I was sure of a critical response to the Maximus letters. Now "they" must go back, it ran, to sum up, to sit up, to set up their guns. All for or against this. But we see now that the current runs underground; it does not decrease the excitement that these signs of new (re-newd) life in the language do not appear (tho be thrust in the faces of) upon the surfaces of this literary world of not-critical criticism.

All the academy that despised here my ardent consultation of the *Cantos* (as a breaking up into movement of the old log-piles) now address themselves to sorting, identifying, deifying the old log piles to spite the energy set thereabout to break it up.[68] Only {Gertrude} Stein remains freshly disrepute-full. And the "objectivists," "dadaist{s}" and "surrealists" (of the absolute order—{André}

Breton, {Tristan} Tzara, {René} Magritte, {Benjamin} Peret)[69] indigestible to the professional readers. They demand "the unique presence," the actuality: beyond/before the "image"—I don't have right at hand the files of *Origin* but someplace there-abouts you bolsterd up my growing adherence to thingness. This is a box with nothing inside but the inside inside. All the Pandora's woes and hopes—the glamours—to be let go; for the otherness.

Well. A Pandora's box-full of stagnant pre-occupation is to be cleared away; for the clear in-sight hear-say testimony in act to "raise up and fix." Williams's sight of Curie working at the muddle of pitchblend / one's apprehension of the secret energies of the speech.[70] To clear away one's own secrets [the miasma] toward the work at the source—all the contain human energies of the language.

The mythic content has been released to use—Freud, Joyce, Graves, Pound, {Benedetto} Croce,[71] Jane Harrison, Cassirer[72]—plenty of ready work done. {Wallace} Stevens' demonstrations of mythy construction. Then you prodded well at my "wisdom" (re. *Artist's View*) toward the act-ual sense (in Harrison's *Themis* the effort was to point back of the seem of the myth to the actual, the dromena—thing done).[73] Back of the reference to; to the taking place. And an observation re: energy inherent in her study—that the energy *is* in the thing done; appears as derived there from in the re-currences (the ritual reenactments), further derived (lessend) in the references there-to—the mythic constructions. But is embodied in the language—(Diff. between the act as contained (energy) in its words, as evoked by its words (a memory of that energy, seeming charged), as exploited in history (a reference to that energy). Thus; I ex-Pound. And you will allow my delight in calling up your presence/company (tenuous only when I reflect upon the alternative of your actual company). And talking to, at, (tenuous against a vividly with) you to release currents of my thot. It hardly stirs against, to break up—as I would—very old channels. I wld. seize at the least breach of its con-duct. To have a sight of Jerusalem.

As for instance—a flash-sight in/beyond E.P.'s old rut of *Social Credit* that the language is a social fund, an air, water, earth or fire, an elemental wealth in which we, any, all have a social credit: unbounded.[74] To claim. Inspiration (in breathing) currents, roots and light/heat.

What a mud—a pitchblend—those recalcitrant pamphlets are, a crisis where we are forced to all the damnd (the unmoving backlog) wall of his mind he drives in spite of against. But then toward? To? And everything not there springs up to mind. To

"tell you what any knowing man of your city might, a

letter carrier, say, or that doctor"—
but "if they dared afford to take the risk—"[75]

Our joy is that impending—here—we calld for it, it calls for us, that "dared afford" grows, increases, changes over is—a necessity. No other art but to "take the risk."

And E.P. (they kalld him a cracker-box filosofer) driven to the risk, unprepared. But it is not an occasion for accomplishment, but a necessity that drives him, I, the letter carrier to write the pamphlet. To do it "corony," to force the damn (nation) that the waters be released.

The task is there—beyond giving *Testimony* that I recognized,[76] at last, what you are about (given in the letter you forwarded to *Origin*)—to write out what these two books of yours point toward. And I mean "to rouse up my mind and fix my attention." Done, you tell and I'll tell Creeley this is not in your services (not an affair of the sheer camaraderie) but obviously (no one ain't taken no intrust) a necessity. A what are we doing here. Can't distinguish twixt a critical task and an "age-of-criticism cud-chewing cow-licking exercise, an old habit"[77]—it's a sad day a coming. If it is we is a literary movement with our fortunes to win I gladly default. My ever omnipotent laziness is healthy instructual recourse there. But if it is there might be, even if only in—as if accident—an accidence, a spark from that flinty task to arouse us, get a move on, it's to be done.

I have in mind mimeographing said summing up of your work—say circa 200 copies to be maild out to a critical "elite" of readers—I mean those letter carriers and doktors where we have come to recognize their readiness.

"In the third place the third capital is aroused"—Stein[78]

Yrs for a call to arms
R.D.

∽

17
San Francisco, CA
June 29, 1954

dear Olson—
I've let the writing on *Maximus* lie fallow. Meaning in part re-reading the pieces in issues of *Origin*—not that I mean to expand your literature on the issue of the

poem: but that the essay be conceived not as springing full armored from yr. thigh but that it be an address to: a conversation with you and myself as various proto- types of the imaginary reader. Not an introduction to nor advertisement of the *Maximus* but a discourse referring at root to the poem having been read. The irony of composition shld. lie in the supposition that "we know all about this *Max- imus* poem—what can we learn from this known thing about unknowable poetry."

The second part to move from the meanings of the poem as historical evi- dence (as one can ferret out certain forces at play in consummation in Dante and hence get a sense of the Middle Ages and the Renaissance) from the "signif- icance" of the poem toward a{n} explication of significance itself.

On the one hand to make clear how the poem seemd available to my own anarchist persuasions and on the other hand (thus against this: look at this foto, and on this) the poem moving thru its sympathies (ideals) toward its forces (reals).

"its stories
as good as any of us are"
stories[79]

      an ideal consciousness of a real power.

But I don't want to expand my attentions here in the direction of the notes on your work.

Rather: to relate and maybe to bring into focus in talking with you (the imagina- tion somehow? unreally? entertains the probabilities of your presence)—some notes on my own. There is the feeling, isn't there, in the Imagists, in Pound and Williams' early work that the poem is a directive toward seeing & feeling things, the objective; and in the surrealists—the objective again: a world restored. And as it is feeling as the objective the poem makes it clear. To define what can't be clarified.

But my excitement starts, I am aroused as I find myself referring to no feeling other than the feeling of writing. Let's say this is a necessary apprenticeship. But then it is to be gaind only as it is whole-hearted. Every admiration has its ghost of accusation in what I want to do. The divided allegiances

significance, passionate   utterance, otherness
involvement articulated, ←- -→-------←- -→ of language articulated
love affair with the world
(inner and outer)

Poetry leads me to poetry; words to words; talking concerns talking.

Everything that I admire in {Igor} Stravinsky of this—a music about music (that he is acclaimed as he fails in this; denied as he succeeds).[80] And all the voices of that public conflict are voices in private me. As if I were a crowd and not a person.

Fifteen years of Gertrude Stein has been the subversive element? Part of my conflict is the very unoriginality of the necessity. And originality (that the poem originate in itself) is an article of our conscience?

This only as a note, thrown off as I pass by, of a persuasion. And a perhaps needless indication that in the deeper sense I don't know what I am doing. Playing the fool (I mean as in Yeats; or even as in Stein) is the happier part; being the fool remains a disgrace.[81]

Yrs.

Duncan

~

18

San Francisco, CA

August 8, 1954

dear Olson—I picked up Black Mt. Review at the Pocket Book Shop and read the "Wisdom as Such" piece.[82] If it reprimands in part I ain't going to rise in defense of my bewilderings—this matter of clarification is too important and, if there were no other measure of it, I shld. say that it is the keener excitement in writing backs up your point.

But moral urgency, the hearty man-to-man gusto—might also dissemble? Anyway: the whole realm of spirit I distrust if it is not at play—and a play is a sleight-of-mind, dissembling in that sense—I wld. not disown it. Love, wisdom, suffering, foolishness, truth, false pleasures etc. etc. "I'm so foolish" you permit yourself to say. Arbitrary: we can lay claim to love, wisdom, suffering, foolishness, true and false pleasures at will. And that in part was the demonstration of the *Artist's View* pieces.[83]

item: Martin Seymour-Smith's comments on {Theodore} Roethke and his "importance" and on Dylan Thomas are not "ideas at play" but proceed "importantly" to talk about importance; to distinguish true from false importance.[84] So M.S.S. agrees with the other critics on the importance, and has only the virtue of seeing that he ain't importance—the virtue the more vicious for his disinterest in what Roethke or, or, or etc. actually is.

Is a titmouse bigger than a hellaphunt. or why shld. he be? or wld he save us if he were?

Now to get back to the starting point.
First to go on record:
Knowledge and control (don't mean domination) in actual life is subject to an unremitting clarification. For motion to be free and energies just here: the real must be distinguishd from the unreal. Things must be discriminated and acknowledged.

—Sects, religions, platonics etc. don't countenance it: wld. rather fuck a dream walking than actually fuck. And they lead to all kinds of clarifications about what it is like to fuck a dream but fewer about the act.

But in made-up things, in the imagination the will has range of a different kind. Words like genuine and false, truth and lie, up and down (where there is nor up nor down as it's named), great and small are anything and everything we design.

—item—when someone sez this is genuine marble, tap-tap, hammer, chip: genuine marble. It is or it ain't. If a man (equipped with standard apparatus) sez I'm a woman we can see if he "really" is or if he only "make-believe" is. If a line in a poem is ten syllables long we can see (hear) if it "really" is; also mit rhyme, breath groups, movement. We tell "really" with tongue, skin-touch, eyes, "sounding," ear etc. The mixing here correlates: the senses discover.

—item—when someone sez this is a genuine talent, poet, poem, artist, saint, lady, or some such realist assertion of the make believe, we must either agree or disagree. There is no data.

_____

The giant-bodied I may be the world
    but the actual world is the actual world including me.
Yr. "that any wisdom which gets into any poem is solely a quality of the moment
of time in which there might happen to be wisdom: . . ." clears the way in part I

think—for me: this is a mountain seen changing only in aspect as one regards it, walking around it. Mountain shows itself grand, small, ridiculous (a vast suggestion of a trivial resemblance, a frivolous head), austere, comfortable.

As in all these exhortations of yrs, the urgency disaffects but it also—and this, its *virtu.*—disrupts. Disjoins habitual attitudes. "That he is not free to be a part of, or to be any, sect"—there, as man, I am disaffected—and even "fierce about it" I demand whatever free range. But it is the *poem* that is not free to be part of sect, that is thereby vitiated. And I am as heartily for yr "no symbols" (*symbols* arise from violations of the mystery of *things* and you have elsewhere, again after my own sense of it, calld for the "thing") and "there are only his own composed form" yes and "each one solely the issue of the time of" yes yes and "not any ultimate" yeah man.

—Well, I have another section on notes on *Maximus* underway. I have to read the poem over and over again to re-focus each time. And since I'm trying to write about the view of man in the poem I have to weed about in my anarchist prejudiced mind to get back to the poem. Not anyway an unrewarding engagement.

But "a man-made continuum" will perhaps provide a new sight on the subject.

For my own response to Black Mt. Review—the thing is split in two. Items: LaCosa, Against Wisdom as Such; The Quay; Lacquerd Westmount Doll; The Search, The Assistance; René Laubiès: An introduction;—Laubiès work (tho half-tones miss one suspects all-important densities, and hence much of what is going on); A Fete; Round the Year Jazz; the John Smith piece, and C.C.'s (Corman's?) Yeats (for "that ridiculous hallucinatory cat, knocks it erratically around the parlor"—and the quote from Yeats on Lewis)—these all give rise to, seed, impulse to forms.[85] But there is another sort: of the worst. Martin Seymour-Smith, A.M. on Canadian poetry, none of these are concerned with what is happening—all all concernd with critical evaluation.

And ...

is the *Black Mountain Review* going to be concernd with whether or how Mr. Roethke, Mr. Steinbeck, Mr. Thomas are or are not legitimate literachure?[86] Is it really legitimate "to speak of Patchen himself," when it means no study of the writing at all.

I ain't interested in whether Patchen is good or bad writing. I want to know about it what is going on, how it is made. If Patchen's wreckd back reappears in the physiology of the poem (as for instance Miss Josephine Miles' wreckd body reappears in the physiology of hers—an all but incapable body out of which must look cunning eyes.)—then O.K. But as Creeley excites any interest in the "pain" it is sentimental.

My cross-eyedness, for instance has a lot to do with the physiology of my poetry—but I shld. be outraged (as regards the poetry) if some critic shld. care to commiserate for what my oculist refers to as the "cosmetic" handicap.

All of which belongs in a letter to Creeley.

So much studying out and calling attention to how a poetry is, can be, "ought to be" (that's your urgency), might be made. Redirections of the writer to such form, composition in time, melody, fragmentation, disruption, blockings, channelings, designs, decorations, arrangements, markings, machineries, periodic structures, relations of syllable, accent, breathing and forced groupings are needed that this ("I am among the devious") one given often to "false pleasures" can carry no compromise that far. These idea-less cerebrations are displeasures, be they false or true. But displeasure can be of greatest value—as displeasures disrupt into life of answering from sloth or habitual pleasures.

Point is dis or pleasure—"*Where is Mr. Roethke?*" is incompetent but more important it is so much not the affair of anyone faced with the task at hand. (You might get at the task by clearing the *Cantos*, *Paterson*, or *Maximus* or my own work at this point out of the way—but you won't find yrself anywhere I's going after clearing Roethke, or Thomas out of the way).

       Patchen or Rexroth are in my way.

       Right at the moment you are more in my way (as sympathies, identifications, common attitudes block the view) and hence struggling with *Maximus*.

   But Creeley takes Patchen for granted, clears no way beyond. Maybe Patchen is not blocking his (Creeley's view).

The kind of criticism needed is not "The Contribution of Mr. Pound in the *Cantos*" but "what we now see is needed after the *Cantos* have been committed."

   And then, one's own poetry is most in one's way.

   No question mark.

   Don't need ironical "possibility" to say what that said.

With that confidence that is a certain part of love that I may be understood.

                        Duncan

It has been the fullest reward of my services to the POETRY CENTER (where, unpaid, I conduct a workshop) that I may see you once more.

~

19
San Francisco, CA
August 19, 1954

dear Olson / Last night read *Max* thru for Jim Harmon[87] (I see some issue or other of *Inferno*[88]—a well-building pote) and Harold Hackett (bearded mistakal saint who's just been visiting sister lives in Annisquam)[89]: and followd

> [Harmon read Berdyaev[90] on "the spirit" and
> whale again as always newd insistents
> Hackett askd had Duncan read "Krishnamurti"[91] and possibly
> "facts" of Max are rearranging structures in my head
> there was one sin "wanting to talk and not to listen"
> "peltate" "totipalnate" "metaphrast" "ukase"]   upset
> the appeal cart.

Came to mind: "wisdom as such" is perhaps a digestive disorder? or of the digestive order. Internal, that is: the brain, lungs, stomach, intestines, heart, liver etc. a complex of equilibriums; the rhythmic interaction measures up or don't. Why it is not "what" is the head but the tone that tells. Self-improvement hence linked to breathing exercises, dietary disciplines, anti-
  sex or action or ex-pression or invention
  since these are external, active or digestive.
Writing: an affair of hand, eye, ear. O.K. I know you done said it already: "By ear, he sd." and "polis is / eyes."[92] Aye. And hand is suggested in carpenter—Hartley—etc.[93]

Zukofsky who has done some (New Directions 14) solid work on the eye might be brought into the discourse.[94]

Once language is ingested (known) "in the blood" I think Rilke sez (only he wants writing out of the "blood") an inter-
        action
of making with language (which is an exterior fact—an "in the airness" or "on the pageness" of language—hence reading out for a phrase etc.) subject to the brain's sympathies. Rhythmic "abilitys."

Writing on a too-full stomach, writing with a stomach ache, writing on an empty stomach.

The activity is of the hand, eye, ear hence or therein having "no end no more than their own" [95] hence "attention" and "care" count or discount.

This kind of disreputable physiological tack might divert Jonathan Williams's proposed collection on "Olson" from being as I hope will not be another *Examination of Erza Pound*. And hearing help us awl if tis another Hoppy rawk for Henry Miller. [96]

Duncan

This poetry is not—as Eliot wld have it—self-improvement.

∼

20
San Francisco, CA
September 1–2?, 1954

dear Olson—A note of exasperation; and to extend toward deeper questionings—? There has been something here I had not anticipated: a concerted action of {Norman} Macleod, {Leslie Woolf} Hedley and {Richard} Wirtz Emerson [97]— an actual demand, I take—that there be no Olson. There were intimations of the disaffection in the *Golden Goose* notice of *Maximus*. [98] But all this only underlines my own mistake and reinforces it for the new little magazine that is an outgrowth of literature classes where young Wirtz Emersons learnd that some modern literature came out of "little mags." And tied in to the kind of that re-separates writing into prose and poetry, that out of Williams and even Pound (as see Kenner) is busy setting up a new convention (and Williams double-speaking we even see/hear *Origin* underwriting "the valid reasons for what they are doing.") [99] This is the very muddle of the road. Liberal, fascist, communist, democratic, theocratic ideologies crowding out, superseding all contemplation, entertainment, invention of, sight of, forms, "polis." No wonder only the flame at the mere wick is left where once the blaze, the full ardour. And these fumey heads filld with "what about MacCarthy?" [100] Wyndham Lewis once said or something like it re: Time & the Western Man—"A man measured by his enemies." [101]

But more than this the association of "poets" is not true to the heart. The sense of kin so blurred as it is—but I am sure of it when I discover it. "I have a way of telling a Brancusi from a dipchitz" (or something like this is in *Kulchur*.[102] Distinctions of this kind can only be a made with the kin: where one recognizes the root nature of the work.

As one can't or doesn't choose to know a Hedley from an Emerson. Or a *Golden Gas* from an *Inferiorno*.

And I wonderd at the time whether your root criticisms wld. or cld. be brought into play in forum (as picturing having it out with Headless, Wirtz and an etc.). It is where our deepest sympathies lie that our differences can be articulated. Writing is measured by what one recognizes to be writing.

And here: one's own work is probably the *crux* of any illumination. Anyways as I see it poems by Olson, Levertov, {Paul} Blackburn, Creeley cast a light on the matter.

Meanwhile—reading *Maximus* whenever I have surmised a free ear; and expounding as I work on the notes the possibilities in theory and practice I have begun to uncover true readers.

It has a lot to do with whether someone is writing to get into print, writing to express themselves (these two types are dead beats) (beets) or writing. "Exploitation of my faculties" I think I said in *Artist's View* but cutting the aphoristic tone—"learning to use one's faculties."[103]

POSTSCRIPT 9/2/54:[104] This was a couple of weeks ago—the sorry Emerson-Hedley-Macleod ultimatum on subject Olson. And now references toward your reading here which were positive are becoming vaguer . . . postponed into the manyana.

But I keep hoeing away where it counts—at getting *Maximus* and *Hell Thicket* under the eyes of, at the ears of the ready readers. This in my own interests, for some realm of talk to bring to and forth ideas, a sounding board or practice range. There is a little gang of us stirs (what Ole Ez calls an élite), an enlightend bit of a mob that will be hounding said Poetry Center "We askd for Olson and you gave us {Allen} Tate" etc.[105] There is a vivid distinction between what bread a maker is asked for and what stone the pedagog furnishes.

. . . .

Sweeping all excrescences away.

At this point your student reads for heat: the condition of motion, nature of activity, to "be in heat" or the "now you're getting hot." The poem as trace of activity in language is testimony of, reveals, temper (as one may read "motion" "heat" in the crystal); but the poem (not as crystal, but as dance) as pattern of activity, read, is on a new level proposition of temper—may be re-lived. That is the heat of the act (the making of the poem) and the other heat of the poem as nucleus for reactions, for not previously existing temper in the original medium—the speech.

"that time is synchronistic and that a poem is the one example of a man-made continuum etc."[106] (Time just so has been the source of the new forces in painting . . . that they are conceived as continuum). A "pun" on time. In which identity "takes time."

Difficulty of "this moment of time" which like "this inch of ground" belongs to old structures of: you will endure I hope my stumbling around; hardly getting beyond parroting. The other side of these reasonings shld lead thru to free (that is, "to drive all nouns . . . back to process")[107] the act. If I repeat it is to get the feel of the ideas; to force the movement of them thru me recalcitrant brain. Ize zo fast Ize slow.

Yrs

Duncan

~

21

San Francisco, CA

November 26, 1954

dear Olson—

The lot of this is about a pseudo-event; I mean what one is not yet in, hasn't come about and so the actual events—what I wld. be finding in the writing is not the "news"—but the "news" is what I want to make real and so write it. Point is: overnight but that was a month back we decided to break camp and go to Europe. It cld somehow be done and then I have been set to it, set to myself, as if trying to shove aside a hill or set to building a house of pebbles. Picked up to accumulate a will. This is all now rooted in this domus—I'm a damnd vegetable not an animal. A repressive type anyway. And then once I admit it, urgency and disbelief are compounded: the inert hill. So it needs declaration. That, for what it is worth is [stet] the condition. And we both we own Pavlov and we own dog.

But sighgoulashy aside: it means to that February 1st or thereabouts until March 8th when ship sails for European scene, I'll be in the East and wld. crave audience. You'll get further trying to clear the air with me than in any round with Golden

Gaso or Headless.[108] Don't mean sage discourse but what I somewhat remember (I have at best only figments of even having been alive) is a perambulating discourse—and from that as much (as if this were what the talk was) sprawling on a hillside above the campus—or you and me & {William} Everson squatting down on the lawn. This anyway a solid job at—in its own time. An event.

What is it that happens? The writing tackling that: on my mind fresh up from Creeley's *Gold Diggers*. And this an immediate event: digging Creeley—I mean the absolution of his style. Like ain't nobody written since the 20's—ain't nobody set the new water mark after {D. H.} Lawrence, Mary Butts, D. H. Lawrence & {William Carlos} Williams and that was the old watermark. Brings my interest & excitement back into the short story: where it ain't been. And then I've been digging away with a will to get the touch of Creeley's work—to have it "come" like *Maximus* comes, comes thru. And to have more than appreciation, to have the recognition. Anyway dated as of Thanksgiving morning (yesterday) I got it: the station came thru and there was the sure feeling—I mean I cld. weigh these prose things now, the specific gravity; or do a dance accurately imitating the structural concept. What is happening. And then, everything reveals its orders of pleasure and displeasure.

Not without its cost—the tension and cost of crack-up in these stories is an accurate shock treatment. I've been two months exploiting a Romantic vein in notebooks, out of which some passages that show a possible form. How to design a machine that produces itself.

We're (Jess Collins & myself) trying to arrange for a place to stay in New York during February—however we can to do it, I'll want that month. And if we can rent room from someone cheap it will be it. Jonathan {Williams} thinks he can get us use of an apartment in Washington for a couple of nights (we want to see paintings and I want to pay my dues to E{zra} P{ound}—tho that path is now so pedagogue trod that I'm superstitious about it and may let the old man be). Then to N.Y.

What I want to know from you is what and where the chance is for me to see you. And I'll make it.

Yrs
R. Duncan

4724 Baker Street
San Francisco 15
Calif.

≈

22

Black Mountain, NC

January 17, 1955

My dear Duncan: I delayed to welcome your coming here, simply that—just because Dec thru March is *supposed* to be the time one is off—one figures & figures how to get out! But the dirty thing twice now is that just this period, for us, who have the charge of the bloody thing, is the filthiest, money-wise and plan-wise: all the future suddenly hangs over us, impends & all that, and we are dragged from week to week without heat or food and finally cash, until some fluke turns up (as it did last year) but this year, yet, god help us.

As it is at the moment, we are hung by a prospective buyer (for a piece), so the next two to three weeks (while sd buyer goes to his backers in New Orleans) is abt the only time I'll have a chance myself to get away. And i have just written to a Friend to see if he'll give me the money to help out, at the moment, and give me a chance to get north.

Point is, both Con{nie} and I would very much like to have you visit us here.—I can't lay my hands on yr letter, so don't have your dates at hand, but WHEN you are off from there, let us have a card saying what your plans are, where you are headed, and, say, what your address is in New York in case it happens that I am there at the same time.

I also feel very bad that your own mighty correspondence the past year and more got such a peep out of me, but I assure you to be a writing man in this damned place (at least for the past year and a half when i have, like a damned fool possibly, thrown in, to see if it cldn't be bred into something any or all of us cld have some vertu out of. . . .

And either way, if it does or it doesn't, I shall be better, have to be, or my own life will be wasted. And that I can't see doing, if i can manage not to!

I can tell you this: just to have you coming in as you did, riz me up. By god, to have you saying what you have said was my candy—instead of more work of my own, almost!

(Tho, that way, I don't feel so bad. That is, I have been digging below what was done, and have some little sense that the science of verse, as i find {Sidney} lanier[109] putting it (how they all had that bug, those years! It seems now as tho one must now say the Religion of Verse, yes?

Quantity, by god. One ought to scream it. I wish it were more, but i did get some part of a book on the late Shakespeare verse—which turned out to be both more us, and the other Elizabethans, especially {Thomas} Campion, than the master—done this fall.[110] But then it got hung, as i was just telling Jonathan {Williams} I am being busted each day right now trying to get ready for the mss of MAX II (sounds like either a godamned new car, now that they have taken over the military as well as the millinery as well as all images. . . .

Facts, & quantity, Enuf!

Let them be silk & guns and whatever.

OK. And please come! Yrs, O

The tel. here is
Black Mt 92541.

~

23
Fort Smith, AR
February 11, 1955

dear Olson—

I aint the Coronado type.[111] Bad enuf to motor thru here. East bound and shld. hit Black Mountain en route to New York about Sunday—maybe Sat?—not straining.

Me & Jess Collins and Harry Jacobus the latter two painters. This as a fore-warning, case we get there like we have to be put up for a night.

But it still won't be much of a visit—as we have to get on to New York—and I still hope you can find some transportation North. There is no proper leisure to a morning's visit or even a day's.

Yrs.
R. Duncan

~

24
New York City
February 1955

dear Olson/

This mad city—and then that I had in hand no real and sufficient certificate of birth (this is all the complications of being born Duncan & adopted which means I have to have papers for both names[112]—well, a Kafka-like rigamorale

which I handed back to my family to clear)—neither of these any "experience"—
no honey-source for this bee I mean. Tho arranged in time I might devise a
flower of. Rilke gets the honey-pot part (misses the rest via Chinese, in World
War II meaning of h.p.) but forgets to mention that poet is bee as invents his
own flowers. Even be it out of flowers. Streets, dirts, hurrys. And what of that,
honey?

Jonathan {Williams} sends on without comment/ (but I know he is abashed at,
not sure of how to take) Rexroth's Thomas pome.[113] And (because I know you
ain't "for it" as written) at the risk of making an apology—I mean to get it down,
commit it, that the poem is admirable. It's the authenticity of a work—that
speech is appropriate to the source & object / and here that is all as undigested
as the poem is—but digested in some other sense, so that there is energy and
direction. Rexroth don't fire (test) word by or even phrase by phrase. But he also
don't write without the fire (fuel for his going on for him).
　　And sure—when like you/me and a handful of contemporaries the heat is
both energy and object (a machine driven and refined *at once*). But to make the
art of a poem is individual.
　　And a larger central necessity of poetry to which my adherence must be
declared: yours I know—that it be speech only from the nexus of event. Things
that dismayd me in the poem now seem the best of it "I want to pour gasoline
down your chimneys"[114]—etc. And memorable discrimination "the vampire bat
at the couch head"[115] of rage.
　　OK.—it becomes once one gets these evident that rage don't bring to test all
utterances. Much of it "heating up" and not "hot"? Yes.

But I—when not "hot"—always lapse into the aesthetik. Which is an enemy of
poetry when it is divorced from the root, both of the quality and the quantity of
the line, word or whatever. Which is the "fire"—it's your insistence contra me in
Wisdom as Such—and the Rexroth poem on *Thomas* is excited and straight out.
Like Thomas himself isn't—the fire there used to fuse and glow thruout the poem.
　　And it is me aesthetik is abashed at R's pome.
　　No disAppointment re Denise {Levertov}. Whose beauty is all of a focus, that
she "lights up" and I am joyous with her, catching the eyes that dance "wherever
the speech focuses."[116] But speech is solitary / and since finding companions—at
this time, and that an eternity—the language becomes a conversation, a discourse, not a speech. I can go from your poetry to mine to hers as I go to poetry
at large as a continuum of discourse. Original in that it stirs the origins / that
language is the always coming into being of something.

That to convey the *esprit*—we "hit it off"—and then for inventory of {Edward} Dorn's reactions as you relays them.[117] Not toothless but gap-toothed, so that the horrified male sees female mouth back of smiling and hence teeth as teeth. Which accentuates the innocence of the woman.

But where in the hell did he get the idea of fat? That guy must have Harpys Bizarre fat wimmin in mind. I was prepared at least for hippy, bozoing female of {Gaston} Lachaise proportion; or at worst dumpy slattern. Maybe I met the wrong Denise? or lost wait since his departstour from the sitty?

She saw it all that he was dismayd by the city.

{Harry} Jacobus—who was so impatient to be off, to get the traveling done—now regrets that we didn't stay in Black Mountain. And what makes regrets irritate is that as turns out we could have stayd—the man to whom Harry was to deliver the car arrived in town only yesterday.

I is still too scatterd in brain to work—and since excitements to work have been rushing in, I is "charged"—Meet sleep like a blow on the head at the end of each day—But I will like J. Adams put myself to task one of these daze.

When I think it all out it looks unlikely that you wld. find the time much less the way to come hereabouts before we leave. But if the passport business is cleard in time I might try to come back to B{lack} M{ountain} C{ollege} before March 8th—My regards and thanks to Connie.

Yrs.

Duncan

Part Two

Duncan in Majorca

(1955–1956)

25
Banyalbufar, Majorca
May 17, 1955

Dear Olson/

Creeley is off (yesterday) to Paris; the Review being supposedly off the presses yesterday. & the next number is on our minds.[1] I hope that this idea of a journal may be a practicing grounds—what the review needs is to get off the ass of "Eliot and the etc." and to get into the dance. The journal (CORRESPONDENCES) will depend however on my finances and that means the first one cant come out until after July 1st.[2] And finances are so low that—since we want to get off this island once a year, and cld make it to London or Paris in the winter—there goes another year before another paper wld be sure.

I have been at work on the Maximus notes and have the "body" finishd, which will appear in the journal (I enclose a section thereof).[3]

Jonathan {Williams}writes "what abt Auntie Maxie Muse and the end of that Miscellanea bit???" and to Creeley he writes that he is hinging the publication to *Maximus 2* onto the projected miscellany and planning to bring them both out soon.[4] This "Auntie Maxie Muse" is a homo-colored jive talk for the Anti-Maximus which I told Jonathan would follow the politics and precede the apotheosis in my plannd composition: The Body, the Polis, the Anti-Maximus, the Apotheosis. Giving some dialectic so that move-ment and change of idea can take place. I am not sure he quite gets what an Anti-Maximus means, but it is clear, since he thinks to get it to order, that he dont know the cost or the possible failure of my mind—that is that I may not . . . well, that I am reading the thing, in the *process* I call dreading, and I'm not just making remarks. If the poem doesnt get me to its contradiction, I wont get there by thinking up one.

As it stands, if you are for this Miscellany, I've got this first section of my notes, and it's a creditable piece as is, after all, I've put myself to it. But I have been more and more uneasy about this Miscellany idea. We talkd about that anyway, and as I got it then, you too werent hot for it. But my distrust has grown. The poem is not completed. It is not in any way an obscure poem. So a Miscellany turns out to be a claque—and can it be any better than the one on Pound or {Edith} Sitwell or Joyce . . . might it be as disgusting as the one on {Henry} Miller? It is not the pleasantest thing about our time that it puts these tombstones on living men. The best thing in the context of the Miscellany for me is that I appear to be riding the bandwagon of the fact that you are "it." The worst is that we shld all be riding it and making it at the same time. And this loathsome bandwagon, this roundrobin of acclaim, this "Why isn't the *Maximus* acclaimed like *The Waste Land* or the *Cantos*?" But that is the worst of the trials of poor Pound, and one might hope that only "care and attention," not acclaim, however perceptive, might determine its readers.

The publisher of course, for him the book is a commodity—Or it may be a luxury item and then its having a small élite public like a Picasso or a Rolls Royce or a Frank Lloyd Wright house has is O.K.

But what if one aint writing for the $25 a volume, patron edition, boys? What if there is no longer anything that elegant, that rare, that clandestine, that expensive or exotic, left in one's purposes. The way I see it anyway if one honestly wanted this subscription it wld be not only elegantly bound and printed but obscenely illustrated and contain also a few choice and coveted secrets of the universe or a strange experience or two that no one else in the world cld provide—it might even be some speciality of style that cld be the caviar of the rich. Or something more than reality, illustrated by a great painter . . . like the French do it, the Picasso or the Matisse or even the Max Ernst, contain is worth the price of the edition. But Laubiès or Dan Rice aint in that class.[5]

You get my drift. And so if it should happen that you dont particularly want this Miscellany and should write me so, I will write to Williams that I cant make the essay and give some account of what the Miscellany seems a bad thing for me as it is much less for you.

Unless there is money in the pocket for the writer out of publishing I dont know what there is in it for him. It is as reader that one wants a book in print, the reader wants it. Before the invention of printing, if he wanted it he copied it out or had it copied. Now, every printed writer has gaind over that initial reader, a crowd of dilettante readers who would not copy it out but will read if no labor is involved, and, because of the publisher, a larger crowd of culturized readers who buy it and reluctantly read it in order to keep face (it is this crowd of readers that Jonathan seems to address himself to, alternately bullying them, accusing them, appealing to their consciences about good literature, begging from them and at best selling them the goods), beyond that is the vast horde of readers who do not read, the pure consumers. The publisher has to sell to those readers who in these differing degrees dont want it.

And the writer is damnd, utterly damnd, if he be writing, even for the first reader who wants it. He's got—you've provided for it—either to write for the self, or for the homo Maximus. For an abstraction!

Yrs.

Duncan

~

26

Black Mountain, NC

May 31 and June 12, 1955

My dear Duncan:

Thank you for yr letter—and for *homo Maximus* (the phrase itself is enough to have done what it did do, put me back on the rail—at least, in the midst of the misery of having put a solid year and a half into this place, I am grabbing days now to try to dispose myself anew to the seriality of occasions which is one way i find it possible to call the poem

the seriality of occasions,
the slow westward motion of

more than a man[6]

Did manage to set one yesterday—#30—and felt wonderful. Yet I haven't the strength these days (I have been culled) to satisfy myself by what I most need: a run of 'em. Want to invest a sequence you wouldn't, I think, yet have had the chance to know (tho you may have seen #29 in the Beloit Whitman issue??[7] It's a crazy spill out over the Alleghenies which I wasn't prepared for two years ago, and which threw me off badly until i did get 29 done. ((In passim: yr lecture to me when here abt the "unknown" a man better damn well allow also was a goad, like they say)). But one has to be so fresh, god damn it, to trust oneself into the unknown. At least i damn well do, having no obsession (not believing it's quite enuf—or at least that i don't know the method yet to make an obsession real . . . tho i have one crazy clue, and dare say if i were in lerma[8] or somewhere where i might be in that sense "free," i cld . . . balls, it's a dream, it can be done if i'd take myself as such: in any case, the day i make that method i shall despatch it to you!

Am so hungry to spend this trans-Allegheny sequence (it seems to go as far as Natchez, mind you!). And get back to Gloucester (or, rather, to go to England, and do the research I need badly to dig that ground in front of my house.—I even yesterday persuaded myself that, on the experience of this poem, I'd hazard the guess that the US had better be regarded as dividing itself into two parts:

part I, the Littoral of Europe—the Atlantic—the littoral of US east—the spill-over to the Mississippi (the latter all special cases, and defying Turner's frontier:[9] his is a middle colony middle culture theory, and there were sports who are the natural excess of the Atlantic-Atlantis push (saying that, you will know why I take it the Renaissance was pre-Part I and post-it, but that until the source and the excess of the Atlantican is put down, it will not be clear how "done" Europe-America has been for some time ((compare Webb on the Great Frontier,[10] in which he also errs—he is doing, now, by the way, a History of the West—in taking it that the Metropolis has beaten the Frontier

((knocked off to damn well write a note to Webb and

ask him for something for the Review!))

Part II, it strikes me, is exactly that the "West," as we use the word in the States, is something entirely different. And is a series which only takes off from the "East" as it (the Atlantican) did from the littoral of Europe. It ends up, as I guess I have sd before, only on the coast of Asia.

I don't know whether this throws any light except for myself, but it sure does for me. When I met you in Berkeley, I was as lost as I have been since, just on this point. There I was trying to find out what exactly was {John} Sutter, and damn well cldn't, for the life of me, until yesterday, make sure where homo Maximus had to go. Now, maybe, I guess I do!

But to get back to you and your text. Jonathan {Williams} was here, and tho I again ducked this question of the Miscellany, I have this impression: that it will fall of its own cost to print. I told J you had sent this the piece, and my impression was you wanted to use it in the newspaper. He sd, why not, he can use it twice, he says, maybe, he says, the newspaper cld be a Maximus issue! wld be sign he is wavering on putting money into the miscellany.

I follow you on it (as I followed Robt {Creeley} on it likewise). As, indeed, you both follow my own difficulty with same.

Not that Maximus won't complete itself! The more so that you keep me on to it! But that, like you say, it's only, so far, 10 poems! And who the hell shld be crowing abt that

(By the way did i tell you how damn well impressed I am that you seem to me singular in having maintained a 32 page poem, the Venice Poem[11]—what a lovely imperishable thing it is. I have all the characters here digging same. And by the way: did you ever put into the book that Milton poem i so rode up on when it was in Circle??[12]

Ok. Great to hear from you. And please write again. Best to Jess. How's it going there? And forgive me for not getting back to you in NY—you shld have just come. I was then, and still am, surrounded daily by the snarls and terrors of getting this place on its own, & away. And so I am apt to be unable to live a continuous and fruitful life. But you will know the spirit, etc.

(Jonathan showed his pictures of you both)

As of IIIm how to dance sitting down:[13]

(1) yr 'muscular realization of language': I can't still get away from my amazements of how the stance necessary is so crazy phylogenetic that one can, today, see man as only differentiated from nature by the development of his gray matter, and all of it communication, speech: that the "old brain" (which Jung makes so much of as an analogy of the unconscious)[14] was suddenly surrounded by a yellow crown of getting it across—that finding out for yrself (history) only cld become history by speech.

I was even suggesting the other night (over E{zra} P{ound}'s 85th) that you can't catch his form there if you aren't capable of standing, as to man, at the point man suddenly was so differentiated!

(2) as of {James} Joyce, just this organic (instead of historic) direction he turned is, of course, why I find him a totalizer of the previous civilization, not therefore so pertinent as those Americans you list (including, I'd say, of course, that Taos Man, {D. H.} Lawrence). But you are generous, and give me the game vis-a-vis Joyce!

(3) I am, of course, at this point, going through just that fire of "energy," or, as you have it rightly, the 'emergence from vitality of faculties.' Even the future in the phrase is what I have been in hell over: to get rid of future. To have it, now. To put it down truly active. (I think that it will come out that 1–23 are the 'future' of the poem. And that thereafter the injunctive

(the shift is on

the point of 'honor,' curiously enough)

gives way to the faculties

(the ear) in action there and then in the poem

(myself, #9 must

have been decisive. For fr abt 21 on, there is this 'celtic' image of the poet's act: stopping the battle,[15] to get it down.

And I am only now

again finding out what that means—christ, what a goddamn idea anyhow, holding up one's hand, and everybody suddenly ceasing what they are doing, and lending ear!

(4) You are quite on the ball, by the way, in—in footnote 1—insisting that the ontogenetic recaps the phylogenetic. Only—did you know that geneticists now restate Haeckel's law to include the fact that the ontogenetic sometimes creates the phylogenetic![16] This, of course, sends me, as, sufficient evidence of what we know.

arete = fish-bone, skeleton of the fish.   Who then swims

(5) It is crazy, the day, May 31, 1955, thus: that the carpenter is so much on my mind this day, that my alternative to writing you was to try to write the unwritten poem I there promise on this sd carpenter!

((((Interruption: one damn thing abt this work of yrs on max is,
              that it is made for the poet himself! And I am sitting here
              putting down my thanks by just damn well showing you
              what don't I know that, by telling me, you are giving me
              power over the poem by)))))))

Wild, what you sent me on to with yr *makaris*.[17] Didn't myself know that "poet" holds in itself as a name the same thing from Greek as the maker does from Old Teutonic: *poietes*, fr *poieu*, to make—made, wrought, done finished, effected; assumed, adopted; artificial, fictitious; supplemental additional; or, the noun, a maker, framer, artist; founder, builder; a doer performer, actor, player; an author, composer, poet.
                              (I shld guess, here, one is
opposing something "old" to the something new something blue of EP's, *techne*[18] (that, no matter how you cut it, technicism, no matter how much you breathe on it and polish and quote and ideograph it, it's one-half it, at least)
((((BY GOD: I just damn well did it. By god, My thanks to you. For giving me a leg up. And over a stile which, cld be, is THE BREAK, in two years! Damn well just now wrote THE CARPENTER POEM I—for it will take another, when I know the facts, to do the II. (And you will note I acknowledge you even in the form of the title. It is Max #33, but like the "Songs" & "Tyrian Biznesses,"[19] will stand as The *CP*.[20] Great. Thanks. God And how. It's long—2 1/2 pages—and you'll know one doesn't want to copy after a go. But it's yourn. I must say.))))

June 12, 1955

Santa Torpesa.[21] This place: how much, ten days, two weeks I have been drug away fr this letter, fr its concerns, fr yourself. Please pardon, & believe it only has to do with cause: that is, if one cld catch this place on the upswing, then, one cld kiss it off. Ok.

Back. (I haven't looked at the Carpenter poem since then. And I don't suppose I cld do it again. But it sits alright—dove sta memora—[22]

My craving today (of which my ability is not the equal . . . yet) is to write an altogether new poem. New, I mean, in the sense of brand new, getting it all in, that desire which I suppose accounts for the fact that I am always envious of those who do it the other way. Not envious, but desirous, actually. That it does seem as tho they seem able to take it they have done something! Like Kenneth {Rexroth}, whose gruesome Thomas thing Jonathan left with me yesterday.[23] Or W S Merwin's sad Sapphire (what a grocery after yr impeccable Saf-fire in the V{enice} P{oem}), whom some joker publishes next after Bill's Asphodel.[24] But Bill's A too . . . how pat his relatively stable foot makes his thought, loses him that opacity EP sd truly was his vertu, deprives Bill of that stumbling which kept his pack/ now only a knot of the poem will yield, and the knots are now flowers instead of a bag of a man on the International Bridge. But then. Who can ever say a word against anything Bill does, just that he does what his querulous diverse nature misleads him to do?

Ok. Back, I sd. Even tho I wld rather, for today, be Horace Walpole, or some silly Goncourt bro.,[25] or some very light commentator on coup d'etats (tho that sounds impossible now that radio . . .)—it wld be so pleasant, a bright cool day, to be without the heavy desire (like limbs) for form!

Looking into a depth of green woods this morning, at the back of which leaves the light was on the smallest farthest of them in the perspective, I thought, with the jump away of the attention-muscles-risus, it isn't for me to paint.—And again stone came. The desire to set down. (Is it true that Hesiod's text was written on lead plates???? What is this?

Or just to go see the Trace. The Trace. That's it. The Trace.[26] (What, even, does it mean? I feel it all palpably. And see it. Don't hear so much. Hear silences. Words are so rarely apt. It is very difficult for the word itself to be alone the same. And especially if one sets oneself loose from the manner. (I don't believe Bill when he says that the manner, not the matter, is the lesson of the ages.[27] I don't believe he thinks so. Or does, only, by a default. Or that, for him, it is at once manner-matter (sounds like a new indian name for same: Mannamatta,[28] I won't go there any more!

I won't. It isn't. It is Mayflower doughnots. And boys with Princeton arsis. And girls with Princeton farses.

The Mannamatta is not the Trace, I told Walter Prescott Webb. And he didn't, of course, know what I was talking about.

It is such a thorough question, what one wants to do. And I go crazy, I need so much to do it with—{Wesley} Huss did the Trachis Friday night.[29] And it put me in a roar. I guess it's not Pound, but Sophocles. I abhor Sophocles. Think he is manner. And manner is forever a reflection of a worst time, Athens, after Aeschylus and before Euripides. The play, anyhow, is technically Euripip. And so why it, instead of Hercules Furens, the Bacchae, or the Cyclops? Sophocles was the damndest adjuster to whatever was just at that moment the smart thing. Don't believe him at all. Social. A fucking Irish American Catholic parish priest of Athens: shld have coached soccer. Or run the Lady's Sodality. And stayed to hell away from myths.

| EP likewise | Please write. And all thanks (Heard your Pindar[30] |
| Or now. | Creeley writes back: what goes? |

Love
Olson

~

27
Banyalbufar, Majorca
June 19, 1955

dear Olson—

Shld. be a preamble to the enclosed—this is not a scientific study but a picture of what I mean.[31] Whatever else it might do the ideogrammic method allows the mind to build without having to seem reasonable. Some of this stuff is so schematic—(all that section wrenching at and forcing Pound's "there are three modes of poetry"[32]—already a prescription—towards ones own conclusions. But that is saved as being a section of a picture that, if it came out, shld be various, contradictory enuf to include section II and to restore it to the level of suggestion.

Well. This typescript is just hot off the pages of my journal—and I plan to mine mine mind eagerly, to lay bare the veins along this *Maximus* line. I can afford my excess; and more importantly *Maximus* can afford them. It is solidly enuf itself, your writing here, that it don't tempt me to push it aside into glory with a "greatest poem in the language since. . . . ."

2 kinds of getting-on-the-scent, running off after the farthest & worst recalci-trant idea (not even sure if it's to be got at) and then finding myself back in home-ground; with just that farthest idea shown in the home-ground (the Max-imus). And (2) uncovering coherences in the home-ground.

After all this burrowing around, throwing up earthworks, and digging out a few specimins is exhausted—it shld. give a matter from which to proceed. This is very much the stage of discovering what one is making as one is making it; I mean to speculate; out of the "notes" I might be able to shape up a baedeker guyd[33] to the historic landmark—

R.D.

~

28
Banyalbufar, Majorca
June 19 and 21, 1955

Dear Olson: We arrived this afternoon after two magnificent & miserable days in Barcelona—magnificent because of Gaudi and the Catalan museum,[34] somehow I was unprepared for what the fact that all of Pedret and Tahull were there would mean[35]—these churches aren't the product of Medieval princely wealth, like the pure splendid gothic cathedral of Palma, but of native imagination—the frescos, fragments of which, or amazingly all there of which, rescued from country (and then *pagan*), mountain churches, from their ruins. Romanesque then, but *pagan*. Repeat the word and set the eye for what the world-contempt, terror, and giantism means. Faces hunger. Or where there are smiles, Madonnas that are idiots, with Child, face emptied into?; and on capitals, the starkest terror I have ever seen, in a sacrifice of Isaac and then as one changes, walking around the capital, a terrible jubilation. The Scapegoat! But the animal is in the first tableau, innocent, before the idea of sacrificing him. Isaac lives, because his innocence is sacrificed. Give up the innocent animal, and save the man! And then out of that what We all are.

And in Gaudi again, which is 19th century neo-gothic, this time not pagan but the other outlander, ourselves—or in the sense that we might be like {Stéphane} Mallarmé, and Darwin, and {Henri} Bergson, outlanders. And I've begun to get some notes done on Gaudi from that trip. Oh yes, and "miserable," that was the fact that to do even this we have to budget it, count it out, allow for it, and then exceed visible what we can afford; and then we had open deck passage and it raind the day, and turnd just at evening so that relieved we could make it.—The Creeleys are here for this week, and then, too soon, he will be gone.

6/21

How does this business of kind and kin go? I write FOR A MUSE MEANT as a letter to Denny {Levertov}[36] because it was through her work that I was seeing that the mastery of walking lay in the mastery of stumbling and then how to fall! upon which it was all built (as only a dancer, thru an art, learns to fall): and receive a wounded cry that I am ridiculing her work. Then, out there, Corman writing to you that the poem was ridiculing your work, or a satire, or a parody; and your letter to Creeley with me there biting at the heels. It's how this business of kind and kin goes that dogging my own heels (who else is it that includes H.D., Stein, Zukofsky, and dada in the pot—a reading of the text might have cleard up who the particular was); but of the kin that Denny or you were unprepared for it. As Addenda Denny's letter to me, my reply to her, and your letter to R. Creeley illuminate the poem, and poem illuminates them. It would be this that would make it all clear. And back to kind and kin that the work gets under the skin, bites, demands no easy realization. So, my reading notes of *Maximus*, are propositions for the poet, and from this, for me and then you write "it is made for the poet himself!" and the particular is then you. But a poem, like a map, or the record of a science (read, Harvey's *Circulation of the Blood*), or the witness of a religious man (the accuracies of St John de la Cruz) are written for the man who is concernd. The hot air of "the critical era" as the critics call it, is that these Schnorers and So Fharts suck up to everything that doesnt concern them. Men pawing over Lawrence and Blake, professors I.B.M.ing Pound—that breed!—who have no regard for the process. What can they verify? They see the pome like the real estate dealers see a map. By what analogy can they read at all.

Let's set against that, and then to see it, your record of discovery thru Melville,[37] or Lawrence's *American Literature*.[38] Then back to these letters, as I takes sights on Creeley's prose, or you and Denny takes sights on "For a Muse Meant." . . it's not our understandings, or discriminations that makes it: but the adherence.

Well, then here is our goddamnd language, or the Anglo-Saxon way of hiding his concern with it, keeping it "unsaid," or surrounded by words pointing without distinguishing: "kin." But we are left with "love" and "in love" to say it out with. What is the verb of "eros?" Only the way of talking shows it, then by mimesis not by naming, and no verb, the language must move as the passion of it does. The word "love" is anyway demagogy of the Xtians. And it is in service to Love that loving is realized—a *virtu*, not a virtue; just as it is in service of the Poem, the Conception, that making or conceiving is realized. Your poem *LOVE* relates to *POEM*—the sense of the appropriate, create and/or avoid, is of measure.

The joy for me of Charles Olson, or Robert Creeley, or Denise Levertov is the joy of the work and its visibility, which we also call the work. Old Whitman wld call us companions. Here's where we will re-see the Christians, that there was the idea that "The Church" was a commune (those who communed??). What is shared is voluntary, a voluntary.

But there it is—a kind of "love." Or the friendship of the Friends. The "thee" belongs to it; the "thee" which the English, and then the Americans, hide away, or tremble before. (I feel even here, trying to keep my distance, that to speak of it is to trample all over it). But without this kinship a man's life is hell. The particular hell that Lawrence's life was, he who wrought all friendship not to the test of work shared but to the test of sexual coherence, to the touch. But how the hell was his "self" to be touchd without those parox-ysms of outrage, those "noli me tangere"s,[39] that necessity, that must go on to exceed this line of tensions to oblivion. To over-come the nervous irritations and convulsions of "knowing." Consider the difference between the sufferings of Melville as it comes to us as we love him thru the Work, they flower in the being embodied, in The Work ((And it seems to me that the love between man and woman is likewise when it is embodied in the Child—the companionship there in which the pleasure or pain is not all redeems. As Lawrence who wanted the Coming to redeem—who does not conceive of the Child—suffers the intensest sense of the Otherness of the woman. Unintelligible emotional pain takes the place of the intelligible pains of labor. Give birth to me! give birth to me! he cries to Frieda. Thou shalt give birth to no other.[40]

But this Child I am talking about is, like the Poem or the Love, a desire, a vision, of whom the child is the persona. "The Love," "The Love," "The Love" it is all the dramatic embodyment for celibates, homosexuals, and for lovers, who live for themselves or for each other; or for world sufferers who live for others. What can they address? for the Second Coming.))

Well, then the differences between the Melville in his work; and the Melville as he tried to tell {Nathaniel} Hawthorne about him Self, or as he sufferd his domestic scene. (How did I circumnavigate that parenthesis.)

A man pleading to be understood, or proud to be recognized, or guarding his secret. And so covering his sexual organs that sex might be his secret. And thus must speak of love.

The whole process is a lie, Williams sez, unless, crowned by excess, it break forcefully, one way or another, from its confinement.

What goes with Creeley you ask? I see it anyway like that—that its got to do with Ann,[41] and with, is it a process or a confinement.

———

———

Well, old continent straddler, I'm trying to get at something. And no matter how I goes about it it sounds like I'm putting someone down or setting someone up. But I means these, Melville, Lawrence as exempla. Of what it was like. And when Creeley comes in, it's because it was his story as he told it to me that, or as he has told it clearly in *The Gold Diggers*, or the poems, that brings What Is This Thing Calld Love,[42] as the song goes, into mind. And there it goes chugging away at it. It needs a novelist to put this sort of thing straight out, complete, clear. Poetry, or short story, tackle another thing about it.

Old Man Mose you are with your stone tablets.
For me, the desired extreme is that the form be made in the air, or delivered up to a forgetting ear, or written, at best, on paper on its way to the fire. I mean, if I went mad, this might be my madness. A lucid sense of what the word is made actual.

This after an evening arriba at the Creeley house in which talk of what's up went in circles. There is only one established factor = Ann is going to America in October or November in order to settle into more of her estate. And there is a dual variable factor: she wants a separation, or maybe she won't. In case of Creeley solo he has no money to make it here; and he faces the problem of where and how to get a job and take hold. In case of Creeley familia, it must go as she allows or as she wills. A snarled yarn of economic, domestic, amorous, erotic, sexual, ego, aesthetic, etc. etc. motives and conflicts of motive. And dont ask this tired old psycollegeizer to turn on his wisdom as such. Smother a sphinx in goodwill butter? Cut the life-line lest it be an umbilical cord? Drag the rich man thru the eye of his needhole? Me? R. Bovary Duncan, fix the old foot with instructions from home?

Yrs

Robert

And yrself about ready to, if only etc., get up from out under the old Black Mt. Vulture, Mr. Prometheus, lineman?

≈

29
Banyalbufar, Majorca
August 14, 1955

dear Olson /

Stevens is dead, the news comes.[43] Well, it's the Stevens and back of him the shadowy {Stéphane} Mallarmé that seems to me to haunt my work, Keres from his world scuttering in to attend the seance of each poem.[44] The poem anyway being not only made but heard, so that one is listening, the line comes to one, as much as one is inventing, as cuts, or measures into the line. I just spent a week in Barcelona—which meant four hours again going over the Catalan romanesque frescos and sculptures, and another four at the archeological museum—and beginning, just beginning, to get the feel of a world emerging (as this world here emerges little by little as one learns its language . . . will only be there I know when I have got the worlds (words), the contour of, into my system). There are two interlapping pictures from these two collections: the one extending from cave scratchings, flints and wood charrings, lion, bear, hyena, horse and elephant jaws, thru megalithic cultures (the dolmen makers not only swept down thru Spain but invaded Mallorca, leaving Stonehenges and cairns), grave remains where the most elegant Carthaginian beads and blue-glaze amulets of Bast accompany primitive native pottery. Ibiza was a Carthaginian colony and the ceramic figures from this period are magnificent. This goddess crownd with the walld imperishable city clutches in one hand to her breast a miniature lamb—in time we see her again holding the miniature child-lamb. What have any of us who aint sheepherds got to do with this thing? Something, some insistent thing, because the images bring back ¿out of what memory? the sheep. As the lion, bear, hyena, horse and elephant rise up into feeling from their jawbones. (On a stone from the cave world, over and over again scratchd horse and elephant; on a stone lintel from XIIth century graphite it shows scratchd horses and knights, city walls and buildings—which have not yet emerged in the frescos).

But it is in the masterpieces of the medieval culture that an epiphany comes
12th century San Roman de las Bons[45] shows
apostles
their eyes obsessd with sight
ears obsessd with the word   as: 1123 circa

> the great apse of Santa Maria de Tahull
>   Christ Pantokrator holds
>   the book   the Word
>   the world then
>   enthroned: *ego sum lux mundi*
>   the A & w[46]   the throne
>   the book   the light
>   surounded by evangelical beasts &
>   great wingd many-eyed seraphim

—but the epiphany (mine) is that just here a complex iconography (where all images are signs) is brought into a complex plastic knowledge (where the two dimensions of the fresco, and the symbolic many dimensions of what is represented, and the three dimensions of the architecture—the apse is semicircular—provide spatial counter-points with the advancing and recedings of forms and colors). You see at a glance a created space, which being drawn, draws. And—the exhilaration of the maker is so keen—see the created time of a poem and that as the plastic feeling be complex there, then needs—for this exhilaration—a like wise complex iconography.

Wherever the spatial knowledge does not exist, the iconography does not exist. The images are not signs and with the "renaissance" everything is lost of the order; the icons are humanize{d} and became idols; the terror and majesty of the romanesque is superceded by piety and luxury; the painter at Tahull finds in the robes an agency of color and movement—so that draperies swirl to make new spaces / the robes in the 15th century chapel of Lluis Dalmau[47] (who paints after the Flemish model) reveal shine and glow of their expense.

¿"the giant bodied spirit I"?[48] the thing as I see it between you, me, Bob {Creeley} and this Pantokrator, lux mundi / is just that the forms—the meanings—lux, mundi, pan—have changed. What we believe them to be as surely as the painter of this Christ enthroned upon the world globe believed this to be the cosmos. The created thing then, as now, emerges from the thing seen (the painter's necessary book), the thing embodied as a sign in the thing seen/heard (the book, the word, and the letters—the world emerges from vowels and consonants), and the thing as heard (the musician's necessary book—and hence here the trumpet, the harps and lutes).

But insist upon the central picture, that one hold in one hand as this christ the open book, and the other hand raised in benediction. This excess of feeling lasted, even here—when in these country churches it flowerd—only two hundred years; the real fine exhilaration is only there in a generation of painters at the beginning of the 12th century. Works up to this giantism. And then ennuie, humanism, and "proportion" have their run. Revelation is followd by illustration or description.

In 1920 Stravinsky composed his *Symphonies of Wind Instruments* in homage to Debussy upon his death (as Manuel de Falla did at that time).[49] A composer could have done a funeral piece / but the appropriate homage is a demonstration—in Stravinsky's case he anticipated 12 tone construction. It is that the work not be *about* the addressd master but that it be a demonstration *for* his spirit. And in this sense I would design a piece for Stevens. It gives me at least the challenge of the invention. If I can do it—to attempt however it goes—two theoretical inventions! to measure silences in the time of composition, and to work from an arbitrary series of points in the time of composition rather than "beginning at the beginning."

Gradually recent work is coming into book shape. Once I had the title LETTERS, it was clear.[50] From the Letter to Denise Levertov (but I mean to remove the "letter" aspect, any dedications, in order to make clear the letters vowels and consonants of it) thru to a projected second letter to Denise. Much of the work for the book will appear if ORIGIN continues in an issue, granted again that {Cid} Corman means what he sez. It's this book anyway that will be for Jonathan {Williams} if he manages to perform his other announcements.

with old affections,

Robert

[ask Bob, what about using my notes on *Maximus* as stet for the *Books & Comment* section of #6? I am sending your *Anecdotes of the Late War* to Jonathan as requested in his postcard of this week.

～

30
Black Mountain, NC
August 19, 1955

My dear Robt—This started as an acknowledgement of yr letter, for which many many thanks. Because it did come out this way I make it the letter. (God, keep me on: what you are getting there is what I might, and I can share: wild how you pick up where I have, those great things . . . get to Italy and see the Duccios, Giotto, and my lad Giovanni di Paulo (Siena).[51] Or it doesn't matter: you have it right, the 12th. And after, the "Queen Mary,"[52] only that displacement of so much water!

Wild. Keep me on. (Things rough here.
No money, and all of us broke. But it will have to close bust or make it by sale of
property. Then we might. Otherwise, over the hill: (where? If i cld redeem anything, i'd head for Yucatan, I suppose, but I'd rather see this thing go first. And
the Review. Well. . . .

Best to Jess. And come back

O

~

31
Black Mountain, NC
August 21, 1955

ON DUNCAN ON
THE PANTOKRATOR   *ego sum lux mundi*

(1)

a city is a sign of that
the many have it too

polis is a happening
to be together to avert

(1a) Sticks/ and against which sprays
from the myrtle bough:

avert.

And produce. These
are the injunctions, the hand
held up.

The cornucopia,
the great bodied spirit I

She eats the young
by preference

and the riddle is late.
The first thing is,

there isn't any answer.
The trouble with a sheep

(1b) "This goddess crownd with the walld
imperishable city clutches in one hand to her breast a miniature lamb—in time
we see her again holding the miniature child-lamb. What have any of us who aint
shepherds got to do with this thing? Something, some insistent thing, because
the images bring back? out of memory? the sheep"[53]

is that we aint allowed to be

(1c) "as the lion, bear, hyena, horse
and elephant rise up into feeling from their jawbones"[54]

She has a sister.
The sister went down into hell.
She was stripped of her garments piece by piece, stage by stage
of her passage. When she was admitted to the last hall, seven
old men looked at her naked. And her sister
sneered. She packed her off back to earth with all diseases
after her. Woman is two.

(2)
luz
es fuerza

          (2a) ".........the throne
there is measurably   the book the light"
no good other than
that we would   grit keres bacilli fistula:

        the pipe or reed from which the
        infection comes

             what terms?
        what *terms*?
        "great wingd many-eyed seraphim"?

I believe
in the distraction. The meanings
have not changed—the strength
of all / the polis / the light.
The things have.

In the fistula
is the music, is where I stand
on the seventh sphere, look

(look! she is there!

At the Pillars,
Mendes hidden in the thigh
like a fish-hook,

and the proud
flesh

(3)   No book.
We have no book.
We can sit as he does,
and spread our knees.
But there's nothing on it.

A word is a speed
which fuerza hath,
happen the great bodied spirit is

The book
is what we make

(3a) "a like wise complex iconography"

That is: (1) *animals* (surely you are right that sheep are
not for us non-shepherds; and I'd guess that what the images bring back is not
the Lamb for you but

(2) *earlier sizes of oneself*, exactly, *bambino*: that
you put the sheep & the City Madam together is where giantism first asserted
itself *literally* on any one of us ((it is of course very boring, once one knows that
another discrepancy of size is more interesting: Troilus, on the 7th sphere—or
those fat thin long stupid swelling retina images which over-come one before
sleep once in a while, that vertigo

(((A Note at this point: why animals? I don't much take

phylogeny here, except in the sense that in the psychic you move the whole system of Haeckel's law forward, that is, the phylogeny is the history of the individual as his own limited species; and ontogeny is the present stage of the movement of sd individual (in the sense that each new instant is a form of birth or development of the further organism: Whitehead's "actual occasion,"[55] to reinforce the point, that the past-future-present is no more than the matter & total of, at the outside, 1/10th of a second.)

Animals, like flowers, are the only possible companions size-wise when one is small. I had a guy Cabbage (of Mephisto Freud!). Etc. Anyone fill in their "companion."

But that don't end it. That's the recalled picture. The *action*. Think of it! The owl howls in the night. The dog bites. The automobile drives you into the gutter. A red flower. The sour-grass you eat. What a population is being bred for the city. . . .

And ma (and pa?) govern, sd city. Are kings and queens. Are Pantokrators!

You will note I avoid or evade all later transformations. Again, I suppose, the reductive process: find out what the objects are on which the words run to place a name, and to which experience runs to set the place, to see here is where he she it (each man gives his noun, until he knows the proper noun!)

I take it we cannot miss the proper noun (the likewise complex iconography) once the world (mundi) (urbe) is re-inhabited, is constantly (permanently) inhabited: no distraction. Experience is not distraction it is the amassment of the materials of recognition: one does not know a new thing one knows what one knows. This is very difficult.

((((I am cribbing, here, from yr wonderful statement in yr letter to Creeley this week on having it all,[56] not as ego, but as man, having it as wide and handsome as you damn well can: to recognize, I dare say.

I am struck (or stuck) by the cluster: that all later experience goes home, is centripetal in the sense that it bombards these hidden clutched *earlier* animals & selves

to release them

And that size

(later permanent formal size, the pressure—of the eyes, in Giotto, of the sitting, in yr Pantokrators (the "terror & majesty") which no "piety or luxury" can throw down, can dethrone)

comes when those creatures are

named & placed.

Ok. I begin to repeat myself. It is stupid. You and I have no argument. You *reduce*, willy-nilly. And produce, what is more. It's wonderful.

My love & admiration,

Olson

~

32

Black Mountain, NC

August 24, 1955

Robt (Sunday)—thinking more abt yr letter, & the partiality of my answer as poem.

That is: was able last night to confront the poem with a psychological examination of it (and, incidentally, as a result, though I didn't look back at the text, the Against Wisdom thing, especially the speech is fire stuff).

And tho I value such an examination as no more nor less than any other technical aspect of a done thing, I was led to see that again I was pressing on you (as I had in the Wisdom letter & piece) the reductive process as one to be held to so that a "like wise complex iconography" may come to all of us ((such as certainly you marvelously achieve in the Venice Poem—St William Shakespeare!)).

What struck me in yr letter, was the way the prose sentences on the two interlapping waves of the Barcelona things (the City Madam and the graffiti of the animals as the object of the hunt, whether paleolithic or 12th century scratchings of knights & horses) was, in fact, reductive: that is, that what invoked you was those energies (fuerza) which you at that moment are.

And that the lovely lines pivoting on the two churches (La Bons and Tahull), and the Pantokrator, are productive, by displaced rhythmic activity as well as displaced iconography (using displaced in both instances in no pejorative sense at all, au contraire, as transformations.

But my question persists: when is a transformation possible to the reductive materials????

Ok. Just to say it that flatly, to further the investigation (mine perhaps, not necessarily yours at all, but we are such damn brothers, or at least i know you are brother of mine, so vividly and surely do you so often invoke me, and, by resistance, a person stands up inside me like the eidolon of Patroclus over Patroclus himself, his chariot and his grave![57]

And to see this image (idol). . . . have you noticed, by the way, the crazy etymology of yr word icon and this one idol? That they are both the thing seen, the sign ("you will see a sign.")

And the sign as image not symbol (I again battle that modern word, and cry that symbology is when the form has stiffened, and that only image-icon-idol is intensive, only when the things seen are presented in that first vividness does one have form, that asymmetrical classical thing.

Ok. Excuse, please, the last aestheticism. Not at all interesting. I come back to that damned word reductive. Makes sense. Break it down. Get the pieces. Work from them. Have no intention but oneself as the possible source of the transformation: that if one *honestly* (wow!) tries to make the picture, the picture will be iconographic—will be whatever is the polarity of reductive: (productive? reproductive?

You will now see (as I do! why I make as much of *eidos* as you do of *eikon*:

it's crazy, because it comes out the exact opposite of what you are so exact that 12th century had, giantism.

I guess I am arguing that the little, parvo, eidolon (the brother) is what we are made up of: that is, that the person has size (the Pantokrator) as any one of us *is* an assemblage of the essential little persons we are made up of.—(It is apposite to a sense of kin or tribes you may have seen me also refer to. I take it, of course, that what {José} Ortega y Gasset called life as no more than preoccupation with itself is a fucking intellectual statement which leaves out its activeness: that preoccupation must lead to the dynamic of *recognitions*

(naming, like the poet sd

(& locus, or placing, as I keep adding:

what,

& where?

ubi, et

qui[58]

And I need not labor to you of all, that these places & persons as things & spots are all inside any one of us, that the whole world & all experience is, no matter how real, only a system of metaphor for the allegory (Keats called it) a man's life is.

What I don't think is sufficiently known (as anciently it appears certainly to have been) is how *limited* (& thus how big) is what we *have* to *recognize*. (Why I speak of kin: that the circle of the bee-hive or omphalos of any one of us is a closed circle which opens solely when the inhabitants are *known*, that there is no *out* until the *in* is done.

And that the *practice* (I use it in the religious sense) is permanent (both as to duration & to intensity, that is, that the very persons & places sought, are *permanents* too, that the matter & the means are one, and are in both time and space.

I dare say that is why I no longer fear the static: that stasis is not the lack of movement, it is on the contrary the recognition of movement as it is molecular or atomic (to speak as in the 20th century) in the comparable sense to which an agricultural people spoke of the Year, and divided it into two, the Pankarpia was it and the Panspermia or something, the spring & the fall:[59]

(((((I have the urge to tell Robt, in the pile-on of his troublings over Ann[60] etc., it takes a year, Robt, it takes a year at least! &! Imagine!))) Such agri-

. . . . culturalism!

"a standing still": "To stand."

There is a Pantokrator (Byzantium?) in which a huge giot-tesque Christ as father holds a Christ as son-baby (also giottesque) on his lap (no book, I think)—and on this chest is an amulet (3rd dimension) of the Holy Ghost (as dove, I remember): an exact displacement of the feminine. And size (gained? at least *got*.

And you know what I think of the Omaha,[61] and the practice of the signature animal from the adolescent dream (yr lion, hyena, elephant, horse.

I am puzzled as to how much I take it the psychic is also recapitulatory. I think i take it very much, if the 20th century's revision of Haeckel's law is let in: that ontogeny can just as well *create* phylogeny.

∽

33
Banyalbufar, Majorca
August 28, 1955

dear Charles /

The established iconography—what Dodds in *The Greeks and the Irrational* calls the conglomerate,[62] or for a psychological view the gestalt—as you have it instructs to avert (as a city it seemd to me when we talkd together so many years ago is it now—is to hold back the dark and not just the dark, an expanded cave fire, fear-full anyway) and to produce. And I found myself puzzling as you puzzled and came up with a distinction between those things at La Bons and Tahull that had seemd to speak to me as another world speaks; to instruct me again what this mystery of making might be: and those *things* (I dont have no library here to locate where but you've said out much of this business of the *thing*), traces from whose spoor the life of the making, what kind of a life it was, leaps to us. It's no choice between the two—the difference is so wide. Or it's inside and outside. And here you are in the letter which arrived today with the best I could be waiting for, well, with what unlocks thought—that the religious thing is this *practice* of the outside and the inside / to learn, as surely as we learn to walk (which is simultaneously by a practice of the inside and the outside, of the ear-organ of equilibrium i.e.) to dare to exist.

But what I've got in mind in conversation with you is a note to my enthusiasm for the hierarchically arranged thing. I dont get to it in the notes so far on *Maximus*, but I heartedly, by heart, agree with you that "There are no hierarchies"[63] or it could come as an agonized cry from this man glamorized, in love with the great wheels of cultures "There are only hierarchies!" And we've both of us, got Grandpa {Ezra Pound} to thank for our way station of the ideogram (which allows for movement as the iconography doesnt, for individual discovery). I'm now in mind to have done with the glamors of history or of arrangements, but now I begin to see that while how to arrange to release powers is a vital struggle when my organism was new (and actually struggling toward a definite arrangement), the struggle now is to disrupt the inertias that fall into place. The fight begins to be to "release them," to release the configurations from name and place (and hence I, tho there are other reasons, pursue {Gertrude} Stein); the dynamics of the making needs as much incoherence (incorporation of natural inability, corrupt flesh etc.) as it needs coherence (genius, skeleton etc).

The picture that I gave of Tahull came from my centering with awe upon the achievement of the apse, the hierarchic, the arranged thing. But reconstructed, the church had another movement, figures as large as to be contradictory to the giantism of the iconographic thing—that is men dying, devourd by animals, or witnessing, or fighting (the plough excluded?).

{in left margin} The thing or things I'm after is to chase down the celtic and germanic art—there's lots in Spain—hinterlands of 500 BC–500 AD—with Scythian overtones.

    The important thing for me is in these "masterpieces" just that, that they are masters to me in learning the art; and that now I begin to see too that they are a comfort too, because I read in them that there have been others who would have been makers. It's not the only human appetite, certainly not a universal or very common human appetite, but we've got it, thee and me and our small company; and as surely as men have handed down the "secret" of fire, or of how to work the soil, this how to work the life or the living is handed down. Well, what I have in mind is that that hand to avert and to produce as it signs, signs also a benediction, and that the benediction I feel is the maker-to-maker (and since they were enthroning, the King is a Maker). There's a Hell of a lot of art that doesnt bless like this, that curses the sights out of the initiate, or that even thinks of itself, of making as a sin. There are periods when all trace of the "brotherhood" seems lost. And then you have things like the way the Brontës thought out the structure of the novel, and the great fraternity of novelists in the 19th century (and extending thru Virginia Woolf, Dorothy Richardson, James Joyce, in the 20th)—Or there's the other certainty of being able to read thru from Hawthorne, Melville, Emerson, Thoreau to the Jameses and to Dewey with a continuity. Or there's Yeats at his séance table calling up Swift and Blake; or Joyce, likewise, these Irish, calling up {Giambattista} Vico and {Giordano} Bruno and Dr. {Lucien} Levy-Bruhl—for a conversation.

    Without a feeling of his craft brotherhood, and recognition of his masters, a man falls away from an art unless driven thereto mightily. But I have already seen painters and poets dwindle away into professors and magazine editors, or run away from their arts, precisely because they were *theirs*.

All this—with the interruption in which I was deep in a summer cold, lying in a sweat and taking some cure in reading again Cantos 85, 86, 87 and realizing that some of these ideograms are coming into my language. Then a friend from Berkeley sends a clipping from the E{zra} P{ound} Newsletter with note that in the next issue they will have letters for his 70th birthday & would I send some.[64]

But I've a question as to whether the Newsletter is the appropriate place and time; I think I would rather send directly to him myself.

{Michael} Rumaker's stuff arrived; and I'm a bit uninformed as to what exactly I am to do. In what form to send an o.k. as examiner, I mean; because I don't see why not that. But then, as I shall be writing Bob {Creeley} and at more length— these pieces give me a slim idea of his mind. Isn't there something more important than the O.K. for graduating or passing or whatever? There's the does he know the first thing, or his first thing about his art? I'd want to know what he thought writing was about, as well as who did he think did it well enough to be his particular masters. And then too, if he thought something was happening or needed to be happening in this short story form; and if not, why write etc.

yrs. etc.

Duncan

∾

34
Banyalbufar, Majorca
October 6 and 7, 1955

Dear Charles: For both of you as it might be of an evening to talk of Dear Bob: what concerns us three here as we go. A letter to accompany my letter of recommendation on {Michael} Rumaker and how I see the questions I had about that occasion when you, Bob, first sent his work. I knew quite clearly and delighted in the qualities that Rumaker shows, and by "knew quite clearly" I mean that I imagine, whether he realizes it that way, a Rumaker universe. Then I had other tasks on my mind, other prose that Rumaker isn't going to write, that maybe nobody isn't going to write; and there for the moment I wanted to exclaim, "But does this young writer know this business of writing as the frontier of something, as a part of a science as well as an art." But I meant "the way I do" and was, I was aware but didn't want to see it out, impatient with the way he does. With having it go along as he, as any of us, will have it unfold for us. And it's that adventure, the finding the way of it, that's the thing. So, my bon voyage to Rumaker. It's a bon voyage not unhaunted by the wreckage of F. Scott Fitzgerald nor without its promise from the trials of Mark Twain. I think the thing that eats away at me is the difference between writing like this having a "level, 'educationally' speaking," between the "does he write as competently, and as potentially well, as the average graduate from the usual college"—which he more than does—and something else. O hell, the difference between what the colleges and universities are and the Learning, between literacy and the spirit of letters. And in the Learning, you and I are all students. But Pound is RIGHT that once it is the Learning one is at and not the college graduation or the teaching profession—a Kultur appears to challenge one. The challenge is not to conquer or to inherit (as I am often minded—and there is something to this inheritance business along the line of the "cultural conglomerate" as Dodds has it, or the "increment of association" as Pound's Social Credit has it),[65] but to discover your Maximus, Charles. As I see it right now anyway, my "wisdom" is to do with this inheritance business, this more or less ness, and your "against wisdom as such" is the man who comes to be able to converse with Shakespeare or further back into time, with Homer or Plato. To be engaged that is. And this IS learning, seeking out. "I sought you out." The thing is I'm driving at that just so he converses with rocks, birds, and energy: a complex in which the "Brother Fire" of Saint Francis has a place and makes him a legendary poet, and the lore of physics, "heat is disorderd energy," has a place and makes of the "scientist" who comes to such a *make*, who says this, a *makaris*.

==========10/7==

         "that I am so by the grace of technique, and work, and being able to give myself an absolute accounting of, what it is, a poem."[66] (Lorca comes saying this thru {Paul} Blackburn to me out of this ORIGIN that arrived yesterday) and I'll go back to it—that the grace, the work, the absolute accounting of, what it is, the Effort for me, that first of Kung's listed three joys, or roots of joy. I think that's the beginning of the *Analects*.[67] And then that poem is engaged in just this, this effort, this absolute grace, work and accounting. And the story. And that you, Bob, have got this; and that Rumaker hasn't got it yet—clear—is a difference of kind before any measure. Yet nothing is clearer than that while "technique" may be taught, grace of technique can't, can't, can't. This other word associated with grace of technique, "vocation," calling. Is exact. For the way the writer has to listen for a calling out of the language; is nothing until he can hear again; has to be in tune, tuned in like a radio. Exacto. And just there, where he gets it, not passive at all, but alert, at the struggle with his energy pitted to discriminate and make tell this energy of the language. What a specialty! The Rumaker case! the Rumaker case! Let's take it—it's not far out of the question that he takes it straight, along the line of the fact that he can do it, get into a story with gusto, has his keen sense of how they talk, and how they are, has this engagement with the time of living, and writes it. Sit down with the volume of Ring Lardner. This is what I have in mind. Or say, not as grim as Lardner but a step over to William Saroyan with an easy does it, difficult falls sense of being a writer. Part of this picture is a living, money coming in, and repute rewards, disrepute or no repute punishes. How well he knows life! the reader is moved to exclaim, where he is moved. But say a disturbance begins—a disturbance of time sense; and he begins to move out not from the journalistic center, the center of dailiness or rather of today. Say he finds himself as he is, not in his life but, in his race's life or—he is already then on the brink—in man's life. Everything changes and "Can you tell the down from the up?" Pound asks.[68]

It needs a great innocence to live a lifetime without need of the Learning. And all about Rumaker I can see the wreckage of the break of innocence—of those like Hemingway who couldn't write eventually, or of those like Fitzgerald who drove the car wild like the innocents do in Rumaker's story.[69] The point is that when innocence is out, then one really has to know or crash. There is no renigging on a question of a grace. A man's work is like his marriage, his friendships, his pleasures—he's got to know it for sure when he ain't innocent and then he has to search out the facts, the sphinx of it, to face them—or he goes back into that other thing of innocence—ignorance; lives in a wishes he didn't or hadn't, or a what he could have. It's in this absence of innocence in writing that the man has to tackle, take under and over the job as it appears once the journalistic, the daily, gives way to larger areas of time. Then he's got to go to just those works which have opend up this time; he's got to learn out of them how to live in time and how to keep at it—as we have learnd it out of Pound or Shakespeare, however we can. Hence some sort of a list of a beginning of what a story writer might have to know in order to give an absolute accounting.

But I am aware that as this innocence thing came to me, I was picturing it as being lost and then the time sense needed to keep going—but it's just this being innocent that's kept, as one comes to know the journalistic day one moves into a larger area to keep the very "day," the now, in its freshness. Moves out of what one takes for granted about it, to what one doesn't know about it. And this is the frontier of the science, the MAKE IT NEW of just coming to know, fighting with one's innocence to win a new place for it—as your Maximus, Charles, must move out in space.

The thing I found to my dismay in *The Plumed Serpent* is that {D. H.} Lawrence throwing up fantasies and sceneries was in the very slough of journalism, trying to make real by working it up, by pumping juice into it, his tired knowledge and worldliness. Damn it, I kept saying, freshen up your eyes, man, let me see this thing that you're taking for granted. What Lawrence wanted was not to move on in time and in space, but to regain his innocence at his journalistic level; he wanted to "be" innocent, and hated working innocently which meant moving on thru knowledge; which meant the cultural conglomerate, which meant increment of association.

And then a man has, no matter how far he goes in time or toward what world, such vast areas of immediate innocence. As {William Carlos} Williams is innocent for cats and wheelbarrows, but not for "Beautiful Thing"[70] which is charging thru so much knowing toward the borderline of innocence—of something he does not yet know. As Pound seems to be innocent about every damnd thing—about documents, about {Constantin} Brancusi's[71] sculpture, about Chinese—always just about just coming to SEE what it is all about. As Lawrence was always innocent about flowers and animals.

Ah! we say, the letter is at an end and I must part company again. Friends, again the very thot of your being there/here with me excites me to these things of myself. And who would have known I had "innocence somehow on my mind?"

Love,

Duncan

~

35
New York
February 16, 1956

Dear Robt:

Letter in fr Robt {Creeley} just now gives me the welcome news that you & Jess may have to return in March—and it comes pat to the hope I had voiced to {Wesley} Huss in a letter which crossed Robt's, which is this:

that you wld "suceed" Robt & I as teacher of writing at Black Mt.

This then is to invite you officially no less. And to ask you to write me as soon as you can 1) if you will accept & 2) when you can get there.

Robt sez you are fixed for the Poetry Center as of Sept. Thus I suppose, if you did accept, we could count on you for the Spring Quarter (opening last week of March) and Summer Quarter (closing Labor Day), each 11 weeks long.

BUT the sooner, immediately, the better. That is, Robt has already gone. I return today, but wld like to have the writing in some one else's hands as soon as possible. In any case, if you cld arrive sooner than the 4th week in March, the better for me. In fact it wld ease things mightily to know that you were coming whenever, so that students cld be promised Etc.

Now as to what it wld amount to: an apartment for you & Jess, if he too wanted to be there, plus utilities taken care of by the College. A food allowance. And the pitiful salary (half-salary, actually). I think you cld figure on an income of something around 115 or more a month (if it is crucial to know the exact amt I can have Wes send it to you (Huss, the Treasurer)

Ok. I hope you can. Beyond any statement. For the three of us, you know. And to have you there wld make it for me.

So I shall hold everything until I hear from you. And like I say, if you cld come straight there, it wld {be} the greatest (by the way, there is a week's break between the Quarter now on and the Spring Qu{arter}, so if you did want to take in the sights of Ny, maybe you cld get to B{lack} M{ountain} C{ollege} 1st, and then come back for that holiday!)

Ok. Not to press you, like they say! Wow. It's a dream.

Yrs. with love,
Charles

~

36
Banyalbufar, Majorca
February 20, 1956

Dear Charles/   Yr letter arrived just before I was about to sit down to ask if there wld be any crack in the bulwark of Black Mountain that wld allow for my taking root & flowering as I might until September when the San Francisco thing begins. The business of overlap between the end of the Black Mountain job as you outline it and the beginning of the San Francisco thing I think will not be difficult—I have an idea that the Poetry Center will begin its new program when I get there; and that preliminary work can be done by letter.

Jess and I have to return as Paris and London ate up all funds. Meeting Gael Turnbull was worth the effort of London—the seeing the Blakes and Turners at the Tate (to bolster up my galloping adherence to romance) gave me a turn or two.

This is a letter of acceptance, that might have been a letter of enquiry. I had already sent letters to Tangier to see if they could get cheaper passage back; and my mother had sent money for fares. Tomorrow in Palma we will not only be mailing this letter but getting boat information—and I hope soon to reassure you as to dates. It will be as soon as I can make it. It can't be much colder where you are than where I am here in Bañalbufar—where it is the coldest in eighty years as the radio sez. And I am in bed with frozen fingers pounding these keys.

I hopes that you might be around Black Mountain (it aint clear from your letter whether I relieves you from "righting coarses" or from the vicinity); but I has a little plot in mind about you and me and Creeley sneaking up on some kind of grant to do a Grammar of Poetic Form (a kind of scholarly research job to go over the work of the last fifty years and show what has happend in it. Sich & sich a line is two syllabubs long, etc. And also to give some account of what is the "body of poetic beliefs—." . . . warrant it wont be just Graves's W{hite} G{oddess}.[72]

Some of this work I have got to do anyway for my own information. And we might prepare the scene for an assault on the give-away 1957 programs in the Spring.?? American Poetic Form is what I has in mind. With such inviting sub-titilations as the Greek Revival in England ({James} Frazer, {Gilbert} Murray, {Jane} Harrison, {E. R.} Dodds) and the Americans; the "Melting Pot" America and amalgamations of languages in American poetry . . . etc. but it begins to sound like all the criticism of the last 25 years—a grewsome outline could be made for hacktivities which might support the three of us for a year to turn out with collective efforts a real book on poetics.

Above: sidelites.

> I'm dreaming anyway like you say. This offer you
>   make is divine (I mean it raises the roof here)
>   (I mean it stretches the limb on which to be way
>   out on)

love

Robert Duncan

Jess and I will be having mail sent on to Black Mountain College from the second week in March on.

If you reply within a couple of days try me at this address. But we plan now to leave here on the 5th for Lisbon where we will get a boat sometime the week of the 10th—so any later correspondence send to me

> Robert Duncan
> c/o Virginia Admiral
> 219 West 14th Street
> New York City, New York

Part Three

"Haven't you, from of 'Wisdom as Such' on, given me myself"

(1956–1957)

37
San Francisco, CA
September 1956

Dear Charles:[1] Here I am indeed in Ginsbergenlandt according to Herr {Richard} Eberhart tho it looks like my own San Francisco and not like the suburb of Brooklyn that as scene of the Affair Ginsberg it would be.[2] We finally found an apartment and move in next Saturday—well, partially in, since it is unfurnishd and there will be the degree by degree moved inness of adding furniture. But I will be "here" enuf to declare it. Tho the city is so familiar that having been away at all is most unreal. And this week or so, magnificent! September everywhere is of such blue and sunlight? {Kenneth} Rexroth I have seen, of course. He keeps at Marthe[3] relentlessly and insufferably (even for a visitor)—so relishes the atmosphere of accusation, taunt, sentimental indulgence etc. that the wonder is she stays an hour. His accusations of Creeley are wild, and even to someone who has no idea who the "object" might be, these obsessions would be clearly of the fantastic. Those sexual phantasms which gave Rexroth's humor its audacity—when renderd serious show up the worst disorders . . . there *is* an order of a man that has its black, colors, white, its phantasmas as well as its realities. But here Rexroth does not own up to his content—and so is a disorderd witness. All passionate reality is demoded. There: for the flaw.

Tom Field[4] arrived the day after I arrived; and I judge had decided (partly by the fact that he didn't make a fortune at fishing) to stay on this coast and go to work. Jess and I went out to dinner with Tom and Paul {Alexander}[5] Saturday at a Basque hotel—with such wine and food as we spent much time at B{lack} M{ountain} C{ollege} dreaming of.
* * * *

The prospects of the Poetry Center are both better (for it does not take the time at all that I had feard) and not so good (for it will take insistence to get a good program for Spring). I found out what was Ruth {Witt-Diamant}'s evasion in regard to our commitment with you; and that, not from her, but by reading thru the files—which gives me an upper hand. And I'll use the upper hand. {Robert} Heilman at the University of Washington (which seems to have "control" of the Northwest bookings) when Ruth wrote our schedule specified that you had read there and had been "objectionable" whatever that one stands for. Roethke had read here and had been more than "objectionable"[6]—this is part of the luck of the situation—and we had long established that to work at all with any poets who were poets would be in the soup . . . I have to see {Thomas} Parkinson in Berkeley to arrange if possible U.C.'s scheduling a reading, which with State and the Center would be circa $300. This would be for February which is the best time here—January being split up by changes in semester at these institutions. That gives us time. Thing is: the Rockefeller grant covers my salary and Ida Hodes—but doesn't expand the Center's plan for travelling funds for poets. If I can I want to get a commitment for funds for your travelling. But, if I am not successful there—given Mr. Heilman's disrecommendation—travelling would come out of the fees and leave you about 0-0-0-0 from the basic $300. Ugh! I will check thru correspondence files with data on previous travelling funds in mind. But right now I want to open up the attack: if we could feel out and get some itinerary of readings in the Midwest etc. circumventing Mr. Heilman's heavy hand (what gets me is that his hitting out at you was gratuitous since he had written in relation to {Stephen} Spender that at the University of Washington they did not have the money to hear a poet twice) . . . Jonathan {Williams} if he makes a circuit on his way West might be interested in helping prepare an Olson tour de force. And MiGawd do we need some FORCE in this weak season as far as Guest Stars goes. I arrive on the season for a fall program of JAMES MERRILL, RANDALL JARRELL, JEAN GARRIGUE, RICHARD WILBUR. . . . and Creeley read in the Junior league here.

The plans for an Institute in February for the *Special View of History* I think will go O.K. And if workd out shld make that extra $ that would make your trip worth it. Jess and I will guest you—so there would be no expense for room and board.

If you are still at the College—I haven't received my trunk here yet; but I think I left the Tolkien *Lord of the Rings* Vol. I behind; and any other mail etc. forward to Robert Duncan 1137 DeHaro, San Francisco 10, California.

If you are all at the shore; bon voyage
   and love
     Duncan

          ~

38
San Francisco, CA
December 1956

Caresse Crosby[7] is to be in S.F.
late in February—(maybe you
synchronize?)

dear Charles/   We have sent our year's end greetings—and now in the official green ink of this office our unofficial letter. You have an enthusiastic follow-ing (no, I mean in quality not numbers) here; and thereby the anim-adversion of Kenneth Rexroth who is going full blast on his spite campaign—but which functions since it does as much if not more than my preaching the gospel out of Olson. In the six months–like four months I have been back, my feelings for Kenneth have shriveld under impact of his actuality until it is hard to recall friendly sentiments (as, for instance, that he still is a "character").

This job at the Poetry Center gives some economic stability ($150 a month) but it requires eclectic arbitrations in a field where I have convictions. Luckily with my bargain to have you as a condition of the job and with my getting at least two poets for the academic circuit that I too read ({Robert} Lowell and Marianne Moore) I am not too unhappy. I am just subverted, innocuously out-raged for the price of admission. Where do our commitments lie? Well, I am now arguing with myself that I should resign as of the end of my first year and regain some public truth.

I've got in mind a subscription for a series of eight lectures (your design) at five bucks a head and/or (your choice) a class at a dollar a class (or eight bucks a head—fewer enrolld) which should supplement the money the Poetry Center can supply. Either way, I will personally guarantee a hundred dollars supplement and anything over that guarantee if we make it will be that much better for you.

You know that if you and Betty and Charles Peter[8] were to plan to come for a California "period," it will be the very best for us. I am in the thick of the second Medea play working twice a week with Wes {Huss} and from our old cast—Don {Mixon}, Eloise {Mixon}, Anne {Ann Simone} and Erik {Weir}: I've just finishd the first act, and the first of the year I will be back at it.[9] We would have hopes of having a new play for you to see when you arrive.

Medea Part One is to go into production thru the *Playhouse* with Wes directing (but I wrote in specifications for the bloody murder) during the same period.[10]

Well, Charles—there have been trying aspects to the last four months; and then there has been every best aspect to the town—and we found a fine apartment on Potrero hill (now Don and Eloise live just up the street from us); and all are eager for Spring.

Love
Robert

39
San Francisco, CA
December 20, 1956

Dear Charles:[11]

Will you be able to read for us between the 20th and the 28th of February? There would be two readings for the poetry center itself, one on campus at S.F. State and one probably at the S.F. Museum of Art each paying $100. The Universities on our usual circuit cut you short ({Robert} Heilman at the University of Washington specified that they didn't want you—and I will have now to work independently of the Northwest Colleges Association with not too much hope to try for a reading at Reed College); {Thomas} Parkinson at U.C. wants you there, but he has to go on English Department funds since the Extension isn't interested—which means about $65 for a reading. Much depends upon correspondence during the first two weeks of January—pretty close: and I will have notes on your work to send out to associated campuses by that time.

But what we need from you right now is a formal letter of acceptance to corroborate our vocal agreement last Summer. And, after so long a silence, I shall try to get into this same mail a personal letter to catch you up with prospects and events. If you should have any leads yourself as to readings en route, or out here; either make inquiries yourself or pass them on to me to make from here.

Yours, as ever

ROBERT DUNCAN
Assistant Director
THE POETRY CENTER

◿

40
Black Mountain, NC
December 31, 1956

Robt:[12] I just sent the formal acceptance to the Poetry Center. And now to get down to the deeds. It is very great news, and I shall do my best. What I wld like fr you is yr sense of any difference in those two readings—that is, yr sense of what poems to read at which places. As well any third difference the Parkinson reading might well have (?)

In the other note I sd I wasn't sure how I'd come, thus when, and let me mull that over at the same time you go ahead with any readings you come up with (if any additional, such as Reed {College}. It's a question of two things: (a) my present concern to have this place *clean* for spring sale; and (b) getting down to one's own work *again*. Actually I *hope* a month more at both will give me a real sense of springing free. In which case I'd drive out, with Bet and Pete,[13] and not *rush* back—that is, take a couple of weeks there, and give say 9 or 10 days each way, with a stop-over in Albu{querque} to see Robt for a day or so.[14] But if time's on my back (as it still is) I may do it by plane, say (which I don't like) or train.

In other words I'm right, ain't I, to figure, at present, on a take of $265 as set: 200 fr center, & 65 fr Parkinson, in other words three *readings* definite?

Whc brings the other, and tougher one: the lecture/ or classes I tell you what: I'd like very much to use the six weeks to prepare *anew* the "Special View," but *just* at the moment, whether I can do that (in the face of the work of the place *and* the necessary *drift* so far as my own work goes—in the face of five years of too much of every concentration) I don't honestly know.

Why don't you give me a further sense of what you think the traffic will bear, in so far as those "lectures" go? In any case, as you'd know, I'd enjoy very much doing *any* sort of after-reading or meetings any person or persons might ask for. Or might come out of anything. But if we did formalize the "lectures" (I think they are preferable to "classes," even tho mss. discussion I shld certainly enter into, yes?), if you thought there was a group who wanted something set, I'd want to have solid text: no shooting off of the mouth.

Ok. I hope this makes sense.

So far as any readings en route, J{onathan} W{illiams}, it appears, isn't getting off himself until March 1st.

This then to get it all pushed another step, and to let you know how very great it is you pushed it across. (Wow. Shall I expect hecklers?

Love to Jess, and thanks to you both for my Xmas poem, dream, drawing. Tho I have purposely laid low on the holiday, I want to greet you both for the coming year, and Bet and I have you so much in our minds and talk. It made last year to have you, and now this year we have you there, or I do anyhow. (I did think, at one point, it might be quieter and cagier to do the lectures *next* year, that is, let the readings work this time, and come back a year from now with one of those Institutes we are always talking abt, and if funds are available from the College's sale, set it for

San Francisco. What I had in mind is a series of lectures in Pre-Homeric Texts, with myself say giving the whole thing its frame (thus using the "special view" in its aspect of the ancient as present, literally) and coming in with Kramer on the Sumerian texts, Guterboch on the Hittite,[15] and a third other (if there is one) on the Phoenician—say something covering eight weeks, 2 lectures a week, I doing first three weeks, Kramer 4th, Guterboch 5th, Phoenician 6th, and I winding the thing up in 7th and 8th.

Well. I throw it out to you. It cld of course be a retake, but it might be wise to make it a ball, for the first time *all* of it. (Cld be rather handsome, what?

I very much hope the new Medea as well as the reproduction of the Maidenhead[16] do get shown so I can see them. I am so happy it is working out that the set-up keeps the play coming out of your hand—wonderful. Surely it will do what you are: the thing the town is, as it never was able to be without you. Lovely as it is. It is a very strong sense, how you are it.

> Who slays the Spanish sun[17]
> the Russian hill, makes born
> what Monterey was the farthest (Larkin[18]
> all that the American has been there until)
> Duncan
>
> (sutters basques[19] or my friend Facci[20]
> driven out, as a newspaper man,
> by Mussolini gangs: the dull radical-
> ism of the town as dull as the local-
> ismish way San Franciscans reduce
> everything to their size except their
> streetcars
>
> On Potrero Hill a wisp of a girl cries
> "Mother" who will kill
> her father her husband her children. Is a flower
> the streets
> did not sprout until
> Duncan broke through the curtains
>
> The infestation the sun

does not breed, what you can't put down,
San Francisco, washing
your hands. And
your minds. What he won't let you
wash

Nor enlarge
Or sell. Who teaches you what
to enjoy what he got there
out of your clean clothes. Cruel
was your loveliness until your loveliness
fell into his cruel hands, his aimed
aimlessness, his love

    who slew the Spanish exotic
    indulgent North Beach, was shrewder
    than the Sacramento Irish man (none got further)
    than Larkin
    until now

Well. Nice feeling, any how!

Love—& soon
Charles

∽

41
Asheville, NC
January 11, 1957

WESTERN UNION
TELEGRAM

LAST THREE DAYS THE BEGINNING OF LECTURES ON HISTORY COME
INTO HAND. WITHOUT UPPING FOR IT ABSOLUTELY I TAKE IT YOU
COULD PROCEED SLOWLY IN THAT DIRECTION IF YOU ARE OF A
MIND TO. WILL LET YOU KNOW DEFINITELY AS SOON AS MORE IS
CLEAR LOVE
  O SIGNATURE O

∽

42

San Francisco, CA
January 21, 1957

dear Charles—

I have promised for today my program notes on one Charles Olson; and after a
morning at Eloise {Mixon}'s talking about the new play I have the whole second
act churning in my head and jumping up from heart and guts. . . . So it's a letter
to you that comes first. After a bleak spell, broken yesterday by the first poem in
two weeks, but I've been stoking the fire-box with A. Merritt[21] and Heraclitus,
with a memoir of the Pre-Raphaelites and a new record of Marianne Moore's
proprieties.[22] This town needs and is eager for A Special View of History—for
a dare to enlarge response abilities of the poem. It would be a joy for me if any
will take a new measure there. You stretch me, and tho I know that abounding
appetite is rare and an affair of the root not the graft I hope even if vainly for
nearer at hand challengers, ... realistically I know the View will be more likely
a discovery of what this Charles Olson is than a discovery of what the hearer
might be. For me what the View is enlarges my demand. *MEASURES* I think
I would title a book of speculations—and I want to do one—less and less and
I contemplate an exposition of rime and metric divorced from (as if they were
merely techniques—or as if techniques were not intimations of, creators of, reality) a special VIEW. A particular structure of the language; then, the interrela-
tion of making, projection, and reality; swing (back?) to nature (to expose the
recent occurrences of the words "nature" and "natural" in notes and poems of
mine); the image; and finally a concept of theater. To give your *Special View of
History* a contemporary. "The Sun is God, my dear" the painter said with his
dying breath.[23] An exclamation for the day, and for—as always when on the
brink of work—a swift thot of you.

love

Robert

∽

43

Black Mountain, NC
January 23, 1957

Robertino:[24]

Enuf is done to say (you willing)—5 "Lectures, with

discussion" on "The Special View of History"; and it wld seem that the 2nd week, say, 5 *successive evenings* {in right margin} or 2 1st week, & 3 2nd [I am assuming 2 readings 1st week in SF & The U of C reading 2nd week]

Well, to give you the go ahead. (No further word yet received from you, as of this writing.)

Which then makes it possible to thank you for yr "generous" "guarantee" of sd lectures. I hope 5 @ 5 doesn't seem too little, but I think 2 weeks is all I ought to be there.

––––––––––––––––––––––––

Now, as to two other possible readings. One, the Reed {College} thing: Jonathan {Williams} reminds me K. O. Hanson[25] is there in Eng. Dept, and wld be a warm one.

When {Stuart} Perkoff asked {about} an LA reading, Jonathan sez, Lawrence Clark Powell![26] Wld you, as you suggested, be willing to write Powell on Poetry Center stationery? I shld think such an additional trip & date would only be worth it if, say, 200 or 250 was the fee   ?
{in left margin} Powell is sd to be an Olsonite.

I shall enclose a picture-sheet of sd "Special View" which I sort of had in mind to (like) pass out at opening session, maybe. Or something. But I send it along in case it might be "bait," like we say? Any way you want to use it.

Hope you & Jess are in the best (by the way Jess's *Ma* has written me asking where her student son of Baroque Art is—

Please have him tell me what he wants me to do? (mind you, I do have to say something to her officially!)

Love fr us all—&—it looks as if we will all see you
Charles

≈

44
San Francisco, CA
January 25, 1957

dear Charles/
O.K. on plan for five successive evenings. Re. Reed {College} I will write directly to Kenneth O. Hanson at Reed today; I have already written to Lawrence Clark Powell preparatory to a tour of the south Witt-Diamant and I are making first week of February. $150 is fee paid in past by L.A. institutions—I wld. take it if

I could get two readings south at that price it would be worth it (particularly if you were planning going back by way of Albuquerque).

The plan of lectures is a challenge. I will run off copies to send with invitations to series. I want the attendance at lectures to be *right*—that is a basic twenty which will clear the hundred dollars and then allow for public attending (for those possible right ones I know nothing of)— But audience designd so that the literate will know at least what this Olson has to say.

Here in San Francisco you will be housed & dined at Ruth Witt Diamant's. She has often been attachd to poets by a cord tenacious: both taking said poets every where and accompanying poets every where. There is, however, a private "club"—The Maidens—of Jess, myself, James Broughton, Madeline Gleason, Helen Adam and Eve Triem: designated by six art-nouveau buttons of a Maidens head—whose guest you wld be one of the evenings you are here.

Jess has tried to cut his mother off [in an unmodified sense]. Sorry this has involved you—tho you might in reply to her say that Jess was not enrolld in the college etc. was a visitor during the spring and that the college has forwarded his mail to my address since he was my guest there. Jess will write her from here and tell her not to write again. I hope Jess's re-action doesn't—but all reaction does—bring the feard thing on ten-fold.

Duncan

∾

45
Black Mountain, NC
April 6, 1957

Dear Roberto:[27]

Such legalisms!   OK

The College has closed, as you may know, and is in the process of liquidating its assets.

It will, therefore, pay the contingent salaries of all 33 persons involved as the means become available to do that, distributing said means when and as it comes in and dividing it among all in proportion to each person's total amount.

If anyone has any questions please write to me and please confirm your address if there should be any difference or change from the one here used.

> Cordially,
> Charles

So.

Love

Please write

> Charles Olson,
> Trustee for
> the College

∼

46
San Francisco, CA
April 15, 1957

dear Charles/ The Evergreen Review did not take "From These Strands Becoming."[28] I send a copy on: it is not an occasional piece, and shld have its place when false biography has been done and it's time for the true. It is important now to tell a life from its in-forming. It is the false biographers who wonder why Beatrice quickened Dante or Mr. Edward King gave rise to lament in Milton. And these same minds know not that "influences" are life-lines. The vegetable me uses every source to thrive. The animal me sets up four (¿grandparent-wise?) (coignes of the vegetative field) (determinants of the that-which-animates). I follow it here—that this locus is provision for the emergence of the animal's powers out of the vegetative. And remains the WORD, for me the emergence out of the animative into the protean relationship between the individual and the universe. The follow up on *Becoming* wld be *Taking Hold*. Picture it as Man's particular mutual being with kosmos. Toward the interpenetration of fact and feeling.

•

Right now I am reading thru {Walt} Whitman—after dipping into the work here and there and getting the sur-charge. Am I incorrigibly transcendental? But here is a beauty I find William James quoting from R. L. Stevenson: "The ground of a man's joy is often hard to hit. It may hinge at times on a mere accessory, like the lantern; it may reside in the mysterious inwards of psychology. . . . it has so little bonds with externals. . . . that it may even touch them not, and the man's true life, for which he consents to live, lie together in the field of fancy. . . . in such a case the poetry runs underground. The observer (poor soul! with his documents) is all aboard."[29] What happens in the *Structure of Rime* pieces (which are to appear 1 thru 7) in Evergreen Review and in the performance piece *On Blasphemy* I send herewith leaves me uneasy—the excitement spreads out, over-reaches everywhere.[30] The Japanese mediums cross their eyes to look into the "other" world. ¿Over-looking? It is a metier of mine: but it sends me back now dissatisfied, the more unprepared, to focus—it *is* the specific that satisfies. Grove {Press} was quite excited about {Michael} Rumaker's story and have askd after a book.[31] Which has Mike on the brink. He demands more of himself than what he has done. There's a contagious excitement (no, not in his personal manner which is excit*ed* rather than exciting) but in the impatience in back of it—to push thru, to establish a new claim. Mike ain't like me so I am the more sure of what strikes me as vivid in his work. He insists upon reality.

And does not, as {Michael} McClure these days, try to rest the work in its reference to a feeling previously claimd. I am bored I find by just the reclaiming of emotion (and with the definite boredom one has for being askd to share what a poet takes for granted)—its discovery, not recovery that touches the living thing for me. And that there are these two—means false biography (the thing that happend) and the true biography (the thing that moves happening).

•

We visited the Tylers[32] on their farm near Healdsburg and had our hand in setting in leek sprouts and weeding. With a bit of news I may have heard before but because it was present there—suddenly counted. That the wine—when the sap begins to rise in the vine—"rises"—even on the high seas and reaches a (sympathetic) crisis. How it gets thru the season of the Vine, the leafing—determines the quality of the wine. It can be decanted from its barrels once the parent-stem is established.

Note → I seem to have lost the check for $5 you gave me at the bus. If it has not been cashed to date *would you cancel it and write a check for five dollars to send on my behalf to Wieners for the magazine?*

And return, o return the Jane Harrison books (*The Reminiscences of a Student Life* and *The Book of the Bear*.[33] We went "bear" hunting the other evening and were at a loss.

•

A strange occurrence in which Black Mountain plays its part: I was on a panel of poets for the California Writers Conference this weekend. The affair was out of the way enuf—preceded by a banquet, with the panel in poetry filling out a picture of writing centerd in the interests of the *Readers Digest, Good House Keeping, Saturday Evening Post,* sponsord by The Chamber of Commerce and the Oakland Tribune: a pure world of Sinclair Lewis (and how triumphantly he got the nature of that world). Eve Triem and I had accepted the request from two enthusiastic ladies at your reading. In the panel aroused by the stupidities of the main-speaker-of-the-day preceding the panel (who had committed all the unforgiveable short-sighted pedantries about "modern" poetry and how it offended the inability to understand etc.) I rose as the first speaker on the panel and follwd thru Whitman "Do you not know O speech how the buds beneath you are folded?"[34] to find myself thundering forth upon the real hidden thing, even as I remember—in speaking, to ask and to you so much that there is no secret in life or death hidden? and back to the word in which and thru which *spirit* acts (is)— Then back to Whitman's *Sail Out for Good, Eidolon Yacht!* and from there to read the Ra-Set boat passage (with "Miss Tudor" and Drake) from *Canto 91.*

At intermission Eve Triem and I fled thru a door marked *EXIT* and found ourselves on a flight of stairs. She remained at the landing, but I (as if moved by a sense of the scene to come) descended seven steps and stood [posed] looking up from below (from depths) as we talkd: When the door was flung open and followd by a somewhat perturbed companion, a dwarf woman enterd, her face (set in the hump of her back) set too in a luminous, beaming triumph, and said: *Here he is.* The whole—the having descended, the looking up, and then the unusual passion of her entrance and the grotesque radiance—renderd a tableau so that I was unsure it had happend. Eve and I waited and the dwarf with all the luminosity, the beaming, the triumph interchangeably her face—her eyes turnd full upon me said—it is you I want to speak to. I ascended and stood looking down at her. Then the rapturous middle-European (that I always think Austrian—but she was a Miss Luba Lowinsky ¿Russian then? ¿Polish? And I could not be sure why I thot, not Jewish) Black Mountain geist. Ten years ago she had been there—her brother—a musicologist now at U.C. Berkeley—had been at Black Mountain as early as 1940. But the urgency was all, I knew, the eagerness for the depths. As I had been aroused to hurl up the depths at the pedant—I had been careless and was surrounded now by the female powers.

As I found when we returnd to the auditorium and I struggled my way thru aridity after aridity. Ancient women trembling with it, their eyes glistening, and women driven by energies, regular bank vaults of self-invested power. God, I thot, if it weren't for the men fucking women we would be crowded out of the field by these accumulations of female demonic. "This way, come youth, along my thread and I'll show you the man with the bull's head that stamps and rages in the hidden place."[35]

/Robert

The *STRANDS* I'll send later; I find I have only one copy and will have to type it anew.

Jonathan sent—arrived in this morning's mail an absolutely lousy book by Patchen.[36] O my dear God! It cast the fear of the lord in me for them, self-indulgences that so barely hide an insolence toward the orders of the art. That *damnd* HURRAH is written with a so-what toward the heart. One poem [p. 60] had grace. Jess equally or more so loathed the volume [as his painter's eye verifies me sense that the book springs from contempt]—above page I tore out of the book—and threw the surroundings out of the house. I wish Jonathan wldn't send these things as gifts he knows we don't want. Like the {Stefan} Wolpe record for Xmas two years ago.[37]

Amen. RD

≈

47
Black Mountain, NC
April 22, 1957

Dear Robt:[38]

As you know, several members of the faculty brought suit against Black Mountain College for so-called contingent salary claims, and a judgment was entered permitting these contested claims to be filed upon the conditions set forth in the enclosed proof of claim.

As a result, the undersigned, who has been appointed Assignee for the benefit of creditors of Black Mountain College, will recommend acceptance of a claim by you under the same conditions which are in the enclosed proof of claim, but will not accept a claim under any other conditions.

Therefore, I recommend that you send to me your claim on the enclosed proof.

For your information, the Trust Deed recorded in Book 785 at page 36, assigns to Robert R. Williams, Jr., a portion, but not all, of the proceeds from the sale of certain land to George Pickering to pay Paul Williams and Mary Fiore for money which they loaned to keep the College going and a fee to Williams and Williams.[39] Attorneys, for legal services. The deed of Trust in Book No. 559 at page 184, is a mortgage to secure accrued and unpaid salaries amounting to approximately $9380.00, but the land which is mortgaged is worth many times that amount, and there will be a large sum to be applied on all unsecured claims.

It is necessary to file your claim promptly and, therefore, we recommend that you sign and return to me the enclosed proof of claim at once.

Charles Olson
Assignee for Benefit of Creditors

Such a Gescheft!
This ought to end it!
Will write when free for such!

∼

48
San Francisco, CA
April 30, 1957

Dear Charles:[40]

Here's a tribute sent by one Peggy Pond Church . . . you who "speaks as a bear might who has swallowed a Harvard professor." Why is it that it's these old girls of poetry these actual "poetesses" who can respond right out without worrying about how their posteur (or posterior) looks. And get good things, facts (like the pink tongue) and the breaking into the hive, right things. O! those! shoes! just bought! "for a bear to come out of the woods with." Bears is my animals.

Sending same, gives me chance here at work for a little note to you. To say hellow, and I will soon get a copy made as promised of FROM THESE STRANDS BECOMING. I'm chewing away still at Whitehead's PROCESS AND REALITY . . . with some illuminations, more ruminations.

Love

Duncan

THE POET AS BIG AS A BEAR

Sits behind the table shuffling his feet in
shiny new shoes that might have been just bought
for a bear to come out of the woods with.
His enormous round innocent face
is hairy as a bear's except for the bald manskull.
His hands curve
inward like a stuffed bear's paws. He reminds me of

megatherium a little,
 "an extinct group of
very large sloth-like plant-eating animals
classified as edentate whose remains have been found in
Pleistocene America."
He speaks as a bear might who has swallowed a Harvard professor.
His clothes hang
wrinkled as though he had just crawled out of hibernation.

A strange den for poetry to inhabit I think as
out of the round pink cave of his mouth
surrounded by beard like thickets of underbrush
the words came, the
images crept and flew and
jostled one another as though a
bee's hive had been broken into
or as though an infant blew sounds like bubbles from
the tip of its pink tongue.
The words swarmed from the womb of his mouth like
creatures that had been hatched there, or
as though he were making an omelet and
seldom got past the stage of opening
the eggs one after another to
show us what was inside.
Many of them were infertile, but
some spread marvelous wings and flew forth
in the direction of Mexico.
Others hid among the rafters
of our baffled minds and for all our coaxing
could not be enticed down till long after the hall was emptied.

Oh poetry! set free like the birds of Montezuma
when the willow cages were burnt down,
no longer will sing dutiful on the tame wrist
like the mechanical nightingale.
The poet, as big as a bear, has come out of the wild woods
like Samson with his riddles,
his hands already
have loosened a little the pillar of these temples.

Peggy Pond Church
765 San Luis Rd.
Berkeley 7, California

~

49
Black Mountain, NC
May 6, 1957

Robt:

Preparing B{lack} M{ountain} Rev. records & accts—
De Boer has recently returned 41 copies of #6.[41] I find in yr Notebook that 250
were shipped to him; am I right I shld now bill him for 209 copies??? And do you
know *what* % he takes of the price of an issue???

I hope you wont mind if I trouble you with ?s on the file & notebook until we
are squared away for #7's arrival

---

1. *Bear* (Harrison) to be shipped to you tomorrow: more shipped for both [sent
Recollections 10 days ago], and please excuse delay, but all this other bizness
kept me from her!

2. The Poetess's appreciation rec'd today—wow, his clothes! & shoes!

3. sent $5 check in yr name to Wieners

Love to you, & back on to better things *soon* (I hope!)

Jess/Love
Charles

~

50
San Francisco, CA
May 13, 1957

Charles/

By gasp and whee!   Hurrah!
Writes Grove Press to me today that in addition to a *Selected Duncan*: "Barney
{Rosset} and I want to consider bringing out a volume of Charles Olson's poems.

I know little of his work beyond *In Cold Hell in Thicket* and *Maximus* and some single poems I've seen. I'd like to suggest that he send us a volume of poems, including *In Cold Hell* or some of it, as he pleases, plus other poems. Can you give him this invitation to submit work, or shall I write him separately? His address?"—from Don Allen, 59 West 9th St. New York // ←

re: Review—I cant remember the particulars on De Boer. I'm sure tho he got 250 of the review*—he was supposed to deposit returns with Cernovich at Orientalia.[42]   Amen.

I think I can get the money from {William} Roth for B{lack} M{ountain} R{eview} #8   At least, last week at dinner he was in a generous mood and is going to consider same. He's off to Europe for two months and I'll be on the button when he returns.

love

Duncan

*Go ahead and bill De Boers at 40% discount (forty per cent) and let him correct the bill

∿

51

Black Mountain, NC

May 17, 1957

WESTERN UNION

TELEGRAM

WHAT NEWS. WOULD YOU BE OF A MIND TO MAKE SUCH A SELECTION? AND PRESENTED TO THEM? IT WOULD MAKE ME FEEL FINE, AND GIVE ME MORE HOPE, AND I AM SHY, TIED UP HERE AND AWAY FROM MY TRADE. IN ANY CASE, THE GREATEST. AND BLESS YOU:

CHARLES

∿

52
San Francisco, CA
June 4, 1957

dear Charles/ I am still of the mind I was when—now it seems so long ago—I got your telegram re. my "selecting" your poems for the Grove ms. Said mind being: that the event here lies in your own proposition. I am among your most ardent readers i.e. am "sent" forward toward necessity by each made thing poem you show forth. And this *book* idea is, as I see it, potentially a proposition in itself, can be demanding beyond its parts. I need the sending forth that you might present in imagining the book.

This is certainly my own struggle here—first typing up all the mss for poems which as yet have not seen book publication—then seeing that the solid core here is not a "selection" but contains potentialities of a book: that is another in the series of my own proposals. As I see it—in a book the poet can place there poems from their own place—where into a new "arrangement," make a place calld book from which, out of and into which is the before unrealized event. [Critics for instance see the author as some particular world-man in each book: and when an author like Patchen or Rexroth devotes all or a major part of the use of a book to *identity*, tries that is to be Mr. *The* World Man—we get a sameness thru voiding the intensity of the event.] [Patchen finally in becoming a general world-man reaches Hurray For Anything or Everything in which identity-stereotype—vacuity-idiocy (viz Greek root) are united.]

But (and with such economy of language as {Piet} Mondrian uses) if poet is not using the act of making poem or book in order to make "identity"—a who I am—then they might, primarily, be events in themselves. . . .

Well, and it's this Event of a possible book of yours that is the flower that I keep watching this green plant for. Don't we break into freaks of foliage and lures of root stem stamen and petal, don't the words send up aromas and tremblings and colors, at the very hope that there is other blossoming joins on? That it is the Season! It's our natural generosity toward the life that will thrive on our having enterd life even for a moment.

It's not much blossoming that's going on around here to give me any whiff of my own species. And as I'm no self fertilizing bush I grow lonely, looking far forward to *Measure* to supply evidences. Hovering over Whitehead's *Process and Reality*, which yields, where it yields at all, excitations of "greym altar."[43] That the torpid stuff of the brain acknowledge the green tips of the fingers. I need exercise right now of the virtue of dwelling in the palm of the hand. To be a flatness upon table—or here to dwell in the cramp—pinch of fingers on pen writes ("I'm all the way down to and including the pen to feel the paper at the tip").[44]

[And as this feeling extends to the green edge of saying,

: states a mark: as a station

I don't feel either a "tradition" (as viz. {T. S.} Eliot or E{zra P{ound} do) nor a personal, ¿personified? intensity, an "individuality" (as viz. {D. H.} Lawrence or {James} Joyce) adequate. Reading Joyce's *Letters*, I notice him searching, in the form of reading and coercing reviewers, for where was any reaction to his work. Just beyond that feeling, is there any response? is another feeling of a nonindividual significance to the act. The poem, book, thing made after all states more about "making" than it does about any ιδιοτης.[45] The beautiful thing for me is that I can take these certain uses of language, concrete in poems, as my own uses. I can, in a sense, have written *Maximus*, as much as I wrote "The Venice Poem"—The idea perhaps contained in my habitual confusion between writing and reading. Saying I wrote so-and-so for I read so-and-so.

{Bartolomeo} Vanzetti wanted a voluntary community.[46] There is one in this elective correspondence. As, I take it, if you mistakenly address a poem to X, it is not the same thing as writing a poem that reaches X.

In less than a month now, by July 1, I will be released to no sure income, but no inappropriate allegiances [as Poetry Center offerd no sinecure without sin]. I want to begin my book on *Poetics*—The time (my time) is ripe. And the beat quickens at the thot of breaking up into a movement my rudimentary grasp of the "essay"—

Fondest thots thru these months of dogwood and trilium (trillium) and for both of us to get at least one flower to fill the nite air.

Love

Robert

∽

53
San Francisco, CA
June 20, 1957

Dear Charles Olson:[47]

We are at present preparing copy for the Fall 1957 brochure of the

Poetry Center. Could you send us a quote that could be used in the section "The Poets Endorse The Poetry Center"? Copy has to be in the hands of the printer by mid-July. We will be most grateful for your contribution if you have time.

Sincerely yours,

RD

ROBERT DUNCAN

Assistant Director

THE POETRY CENTER

ETC ETC. and off the carbon . . . I am on my last ten days with the poetry c{enter} and then my mind free I am back on the prowl for mss to type, lawns to mow etc. Back, on the etceterer. I am filling out forms for grants of whatever kind to go ahead with a book of essays, a Poetics . . . by that as expansively to include all reaches. And I am eager to get into new notebooks, a divorce made with community culture and all improvements—to address the birds and bees, practice indolence, exacerbation, and joyful celebration. But then Jess says be anti-"ation"s. Those Roman vices. I want to dig in the language garden for stones and turn-ups. And brood good and bad thots over the lettusses. What!"?% about the Olson book? did Don Allen follow up my letter? My own drive thru to put together the book I might want is going slow—by the factor of typing mss; Allen is to be here in San Francisco next month and I will have it done ready for conferences with him by then. But I hear rumors that EVERGREEN #3 is to have Williams and Olson in it[48]—this from Wieners, not from Allen.

~

54

Black Mountain, NC

June 25, 1957

My good Robt—

Wot a request!

But see if the attached is of any use. If not, & you scrap it as frivolous, make me do it again! I'd certainly like to oblige!

Love (& the *end* soon! So then I can
be one of you again
Love to all
& Jess
Charles

Such as the Poetry Center (S.F) is the chief form of publication the poet has left. People at least pay to hear us! We are troubadours, when there (at the PC). And it's live (not that swollen or goggleyed tape or tellalesion). It gives you a life. I'm for it.

The only thing is, we ought to go on tour. There ought to be such in every town, so we can spread it, that hard-working, not the dolled-up personal appearance.

Get good at it.

What's nice of course is when a poem makes it, in that curious situation in which one is one's own mouthpiece—publishing by mouth. Wow, it puts you back!

It's also a great strain

Signed: The cat who swallowed his tongue
and not who ate the canary—Olson

≈

55
San Francisco, CA
August 24, 1957

dear Charles/

Your "Variations" continue to inform.[49] And now in print, and in company. I've written {John} Wieners and {Robin} Blaser what a solid body there is there in Marshall, Dorn, Eigner[50]—these because the work was moving / and what three could be *more* individuated each from any other? allied by their respect for, responsibility in the poem. Then, because here I am surrounded by the pusillanimous, who would avoid reading at any cost I set about to dig at "One," "The rick of green wood," and "Brink"—with the idea that I would type at least nine (in 3 rounds) copies of the notes resulting and place them where they might be used to hand to fools who say there's nothing in it. Going at the poems again,[51] particularly at the Eigner where I found myself right there in the deep water and me liking to swim but—what was there to explicate? that did not fall short of the challenge.

I'm sad about the Gavin Douglas piece.[52] I had meant to encourage a direction, but I find the writing so untrue. Damn this shuffling off—of "But fuck it" and "like sometimes I think I. . . ." it vitiates at the source of any feeling. Where "fuck" ceases to mean fuck, and "think" ceases to mean think. And all the beautiful care Lawrence or Joyce or Pound had to bring that good verb fuck into the language, these cowards throw it out with their rubbish into that batterd old can, the psycho-anal-hissts ear.

And fighting mad about the {Jack} Spicer thing. What, I started at him in a group gatherd here to read Blaser's work, do you think you are doing? How in what hell did "Call'd a custodian" get to be a line? Where does "American translator of Rilke" send you?[53] And mad at Wieners too, who had written me:

(May 21)

There is no excitement in form. His Song for Bird in Measure I is the most boring of all, in fact, none other bore, even {Frank} O'Hara in his chi-chi, has a quality (you'll see) but Spicer lays on the page, no care, it aint ideas he thrills to, I feel its feelings only, where he has participated HIMSELF in like feelings . . . etc.

But I am such a careless reader of letters. It is typing this out that I discover what this says is that this bilge was to appear in *Measure*. Not that Wieners aint mixed up. What is an "idear" and what is a "feeling." If Spicer etc. had botherd to demand a "feeling" of the line, to call even one little receptor into action: but the hysteric has the one route, convention may contain emotion—but the break-loose is only unconventional. He has no freedom and can not articulate. Enuf.

MEASURE, the fine corps of it where the charge lies—tunes me up. As your presence (presents) here demanded out of me the "Propositions." And those five evenings provided a ferment that has given me, gives inexhaustibility, directions. Tho I thought you were in a knot, a tangle . . . it was always of the central thread. This one needs that knot, that all but inarticulate—to accuse easier clarities, easier articulations. Sure, I knows that the loveliest pome comes easy, and would have been a "cultured man" had it been in my nature. [See "Rappel a l'Ordre" in Pound's *Kulchur*, pp. 134–135: "The defects inherent in a record of struggle"]. It's one of the blessings of the language is that ever as we must struggle to keep it, it will [a gift!] suddenly provide us ease. Such "ease" is of the sacred. And I am not one to fiddle the sacred objects or wallow around a ravaging tourist in the pools of the taboo. Let these be separated from our use. I am ready enough when the easy demands its use of me.

That beautiful tradition, precinct, of the English lyric. Take {Walter} Raleigh's "Pilgrimage" or {George} Herbert's "Discipline" as prototype. Such rhyme is holy. And H.D. or Marianne Moore [in "Rosemary"] venture there priestesses; must *mistrust* every word (as we must mistrust the divine or be swept away, garbled by it.

{Duncan inserted a transcription of Moore's poem "Rosemary" here.}[54]

The lyric needs nerve, and a heightend sense of the "brink," the danger of rhyme. {Robert} Creeley has it—he likes to take the dare. and he dont under

———————————

estimate the powers.

———————————

After writing on Dorn's poem, I got this pome:

> By stress and syllable
> by change-rhyme and contour,
> we let the long line pace even awkward to its period.
>
> The short line
> we refine
> and keep for candour.
>
> This we remember
> ember of the fire
> catches the word, if it be heard.
> "We must understand what is happening"
> and springs to desire, a bird-right light
> sound.
> This is the Yule-log that warms December.
> This is the new grass that springs from the ground.

RE: Your book, Grove, etc. It's begun to seep into their comprehension that your work gives us all measure, that you move to excel what you have accomplished, and I've dinnd it into Mr. {Donald} Allen's skull that every published work from you is a necessity for anybody seriously at the work. What comes out of his skull is that this Olson thing is a loaded literary event. O.K. if that gets more in circulation.

I take it that he wants to "launch" you—and try not to shudder visibly. What I urge is that you get into print a solid collection (including *Cold Hell* poems) (and *Y&X*) of the work extra-Maximus = this for the book. For *Evergreen Review* a group of Maximus cantos, with a prose piece will illustrate the scene. Allen wants an essay on your work—and I am preparing (most of the text is already in notebooks) the second section of my essay on *Maximus*. It's three years or so that have elapsed, and my attention shld be refurbished with *some* new idears. And even, page Wieners, feelings. I haven't been asleep.

But make *Evergreen* toe the line, demand and get exactly what you want. The time is ripe or maybe it's an iron that's hot. If it's the heat of iron, we have to hammer the sword again.

Let's say *Y&X* and *In Cold Hell, in Thicket* these two to catch the laggards up on what happend: and give us companions a third, the news. It'll take the page-dimension that can handle, deliver, the long line.

I hope you are already in *Gloucester*. "In a shower of rain" and all. Tho, consulting my *Oxford Dicker of Nursery Rimes*[55] I find it is all a foul wish. And will retract. But their learned notes tell me Dr. Foster was once Dr. Faustus. Fiddle Dee dee, Dr. Dee. # With love, and a couple of recent poems—how tall is Charles Peter running about? and tell Betty she remains one of my beautiful women/ who give the heart measure.

re *Measure* 1. it shld take *writing* as center. An editor will know no more
about "poetry" than he knows his prose.
2. it lacks the woman; and hence lacks the manly.

Robert[56]

~

56
San Francisco, CA
August 29, 1957

dear Charles/[57]
That {Edward} Marshall needs a certain intellectual responsibility: in that sequence from Anselm to Hollywood.[58] A reader who is certain (this one, not totally unaware of the medieval man) wants that grounded: at least in the popularly known thing, the "I do not seek to know in order that I may believe; but I believe, that I may know." In these orders of effort it's Whitehead that is in sequence. A poet's concern is in the scales whenever he designs sequence. The important thing for me is not that Marshall needs the responsibility—but that brought to order he is most capable of it.

~

57
San Francisco, CA
September 1 and 29, 1957

dear Charles/ After a session with Don Allen today: I gather in that the news has got out that full steam ahead on Olson will start a real thing. He spoke of in addition to a selected (or collected) or (projected) etc. pomes, getting Maximuses 1–22 into reprint and circulation CIRCULATION {Duncan draws two intersecting rings}; and then encouraging for me, he said he would keep at {Larry} Eigner's work tho he can't yet see it, sez he. But I think I got it straight that he will keep at it, and he seemd today more receptive to my speaking again of what I thot was going on there. It's just that Eigner obviously has a lot that anything right now of his interests me especially in the stories that his independence of the time flow, his always being just there where he is makes for an inconsequential form: I mean here he can keep his (then our) attention, establish the "story" and then does not need {a} "point" to have his stand. The "why" of his story is simply that it is.

A group of {Edward} Dorn's poems has arrived just this week (or Allen had got at them just this week) with Allen's eye tuned up by my two weeks running to date {Edward} Marshall, Dorn, Eigner notes. That, those notes, have carried me to labels, handles and pidgeon Holes: the epistle, the song, the poem-as-agency-of-feeling. As I get it—these reviews is like zoos if you tells the publishers that there animal is a MOUSE they will put it on exhibit?

September 29, 1957

Today when I wanted to write to you—here this month-old beginning of a letter was at hand and so I got on from here. Over the accumulated litter of a month; and a wretched hangover "you who think you will get through hell in a hurry";[59] and a drenched atmosphere for several days with heat and downpour out of it. You know here we have the autumnal thing on faith, but I get announcements of it out of the air.

I'm applying for a Guggenheim and will be giving you as a reference. I was going to make it on the plan for the *POETICS*—but I want the money however best to get it and am persuaded that the better chance is to ask for it for creative writing in poetry. It seems too likely that there would be prejudice against a non-academic learning.

{Kenneth} Rexroth's loud mouthings and obscuring clouds of "avant-garde" and "disaffiliated" are a miserable association.[60] He should have been shot a year ago, and saved us all from the big noise.

—For the Guggenheim:
If you would have any suggestions as to anyone who unbeknownst to me at this point might be interested in my writing—and carry some weight, I would be grateful. I plan so far on you, {Louis} Zukofsky, {Muriel} Rukeyser, {Robin} Blaser, {Robert} Creeley, Denise {Levertov}, {Thomas} Parkinson, {Jack} Spicer. M. C. Richards?[61]

We get news indirectly of you.   I wld. like to be brought up to date con-densare as to the Olson saga—wheres and whens of you.

I enclose a new song—rudimentary signs of work on that English lyric. . . . yes, it's an actual song, not a poem and I've got Ida Hodes singing it.[62] In mind—a group of songs to be sung of an evening about any fireside—

Love
Robert

~

58
New York City
September 23, 1957?

My dear Robt
Sitting here in a train, crossing Hell Gate[63] (just at this minute) & altogether *lifted* by first reading & reading the final section (5) of yr Measure poem[64]

so satisfying
& delighting, the
claim
of it

Love it very deeply, & wanted to tell you I pray I am one of yr kin you name!

On way to final out of Blck Mt {Black Mountain College}—I hope!

All set on all you set up with {Donald} Allen—& his visit flew me forward.

4 new Maxies, to please my ear & longing

Love yrs
Charles

~

59
San Francisco, CA
October 5 and 8, 1957

You are, dear Charles, first of my sense of the kin. Ken ye the kin? That Max Pulver piece on *Jesus' Round Dance* gives me lines out of St. John of Ephesus: "If you have not enterd the Dance, you mistake the event"; "For until you call yourself my own, I shall not be what I am"; and "Not as I have said I was but as thou, being akin to me, knowest me."[65]

Eight years ago in a poem this passage came in a poem

> Thirty years have brought me,
> chaind bear, to no
>   consoling six foot teddy-bear lover
>   I waited for,
>
>   but to the dance
>   of the totems of an heroic race
>   after the dying away of their creators.[66]

and at a point in my life when only longing for that dance (which appeard as a certainty of my being at the beginning of it) was known. Haven't you, from of "Wisdom as Such" on, given me myself; and certainly as I came to find that the dance had been, was, is there: "came to" in the midst of, your hand was there in the round. And, this last year, uplifting again the heart—you gave that news of the primordial out of Whitehead's *Process and Reality*.

In return I can only give the poem, myself, to the Dance itself. And, as in "Upon Taking Hold" or "Light Song" or these "Propositions" sometimes give it, as part of the inscription in your name.[67] I have this certainty; that you, like me, thrive upon, spring up from a community not of imitation but of volition. It's into life we'll have will or no our initiations; not into the kind.

Send me a new Maxie and I send a song. Keep me anyway—in the news.

A young composer here, Pauline Oliveros, had set the Spider Song and wanted to do a group for the Composer's Forum concerts[68]—so off she went around with my seal in the depraved wave, Creeley's "Venus"—and Maxie's sixth song. The which last she sent us a week ago and if all comes about there will be, all of a flash, a beautiful you almost hear it, shortest lieder in existence.[69]

In the mail with your letter came a check for a hundred dollars and a notification that the group of poems in *Poetry* had been awarded "our Union League Civic and Arts Foundation Prize"[70]—with the first installment from Black Mountain it has saved the month.

I'm enclosing a copy [This will come later. Right now I'm up to my neck in preparing the Guggenheim application Oct. 8, 1957 etc.] of the open letter on 3 pomes from MEASURE.[71] {John} Wieners sd you didn't have a copy—I thot I had sent it. If this shld be extra, pass the previous one on where it might do some good.

                                   love
                                   Robert

~

60

San Francisco, CA
ca. October 15, 1957

dear Charles—here's a poem I sent off to Ezra {Pound} with instructions same was not for his bandwagon,[72] but wld appear in my "The Opening of the Field" as it is—as a verification that the question of a just exchange relates to the poet's concern. I gave some note that I mistrusted much of his writing—yet had found even therein where it was clear, open and above-ground—substance.

Well, I send it to you because it shows my beginning struggle with a lyric verse and even full-rhyme. It is after all where in relates to E.P. a remembrance. Where it relates to you, as I send it—a correspondence.

Spicer has prodded me into, and got under way, a weekly meeting at Joe Dunn's where we can all sharpen our demands and tackle one poem a-fresh. Spicer is all for a solid pursuit of measure: and I (not unrelated) have got on my mind the objectivization of thot/feeling in the poem; locating the image. I wish you'd been there last Sunday. Spicer had asked the *Larousse* {dictionary} (which M. L. R. James in "The Ash-Tree" informed me reading today is calld "drawing the *sortes*")[73] what would be the subject of the poetry at the first meeting—this the evening before and known only to Jack Spicer, Joe Dunn and {Ebbe} Borregaard: the reference was "metallurgy" and the counter reference in the I Ching: that below ground brought to the surface. Which occasiond a revelation when— the last to read, I read the first draft of this new gold poem.

I am in reaction to Jung (well, I have never liked his ponderous lack of *condensare*,[74] nor that he finds models of *clarity* as source material and proceeds to muddled commentary). What sticks in my craw is that them archetypes are not of the unconscious but belong to the conscious storehouse all of them—as they are manifest: and as he seeks to establish them are an ideology.

The beautiful mystery I find in the morphology, the physical source. That the central intelligence is of skeleton, nerves and sinews whole, the extra-conscious. Personality (and then the individuation process) I take as that which we entertain. An ideational universe. It's your universe of discourse (what could be more discursive than five hundred pages of cognition supplementing the concrete information of the life cycle of the unicorn?) that, I agree, we have rightly to attack where it usurps the actual.

But that angel of death's message to {Victor} Hugo stays by me. That there are two works: l'oeuvre du vivant and l'oeuvre du fantôme. We've not finally to neglect either; but to be courageous in both. And who are WE? Spicer says that will be the place of my vulnerability—that I risk it to be "wrong" to assert we are only attendants, as far as the art of poetry goes, upon the language. Perhaps I am coming rapidly to the turn where this will be so convincing (a groove into which un-wary I slips) that I must be about discarding the obsession. Will find it splitting apart to make way for some green necessity. Hail the stubborn blade that cracks the granite conviction.

A mind too often content with mere rapture. With the giddy tickling of an amorous idear.

hey! hey! I have constantly to remind myself that I am no more than—and p'haps this season must feed at old books, even while I suspect I needs the discipline of listening and looking at larks and lunar effects.

Marianne Moore here was your witness, and voicing her predilection for those spring variations verified her concern for reciting verses thereof.[75]

love

Robert

∽

61

Gloucester, MA

November 2, 1957

My dear Robt: Thank you for yr beautiful poem and yr news. As yr correspondent I am not yet in any shape to give you back as good as I got. Like a fool instead of plunging into words when I landed back here I went into local research. And have spent myself, like an idiot (hungry, after all these years, to find out facts abt my place—instead of doing what is wiser, contemplating through a glass darkly, wasn't it Wisdom who sd?

The best I can do is this leetle one:

Beauty
is to lay hold of Love
is the leave
to

Which i guess is finger exercises. I crave to sit down some swollen morning and let go from down under (like the sortes predicted you wld . . . tho what is Larousse? Larousse? the dictionary used as the bundle and liver? For the toss?

(Don Allen asked me if I'd do something on the Tarot—a book, I believe he meant; but it is to me like Wieners asking, for his Numero 2: magic? It is so clearly true all one can say is, to those who care to practice it, be as good as. I took another course seven years ago. Conceivably I shld now go about a bit (come about, is the technical phrase). But I am too far gone after.

I will soon try to get you some of the songs I got done due to the impetus of Don Allen's coming with such gifts, and sitting in front of the Tavern reading Letter 5 to Robin {Blaser} and Allen. But it broke off, coming from Black Mt, and now I am out of touch with it, even tho I had big ideas and read {Thomas} Campion's essay in Black Mt (shoved by those poems of yrs I hope you finally got the misaddressed letter about

The Campion disappointed me[76]

Poor Jonathan {Williams} got the bowels of the th-oughts. I was all hot I cld say what a music of quantity might be! (Watching man, Russian included, trying to lift such heavy weights into the mesosphere, it is urgent to reveal by song what powers vacuum hath! Cf. my latest 'master,' {Henri} Coanda[77] ((note: ask Jess to give me any critique he has to offer on that "effect," if he wld, it wld be enlightening to me:

mebbe I think the magic of the open road and the hermetic are just about met (?)

yes. And isn't it a delight to contemplate? Down with materials, and moving parts. Up praxis!

Love, and please, whenever you can, drop me a line—and poems. I am hungry to be one thing once again.

Love (and fr Bet: Charles
Peter thinks the word wheel
is the most; and that the moon
disappears behind a cloud!

Part Four

Projecting Verse, Opening the Field

(1958–1961)

62
San Francisco, CA
January 8, 1958

dear Charles/

Wotz going on out there? With yesterday I enterd my fortieth year which some-how {is} more impressive than being 39. And found myself in quandary areas of my field. Doz you dig your roots or go there on yr own backwash? My backwash is lush—p'haps soggy; hence the engineering when a call to order comes. Got to test those underpinnings, fancy & coated riggings, drive a steel (steal) pylon into the sludge to terra firma. Does the granite intrude? I do get it now, going back into it, that thot/response passive to rhythmic pulsation without the intrusion of the wilfull act sways thru revolutions. (This is dancing: the gliding unarticulated pantheism of ladies and gents in Greek nighties dependent upon their raptures that suffer no ruptures, the Isadorian mode).[1] Then where the foot pounds the earth, a simplistic measure, the rest of the body passive by attention (tension) to the active foot tum ti ti ti tum tum ti tum tum klop klictyty klop klop klip klip klop klip klop.

What sets me off on this is that I find myself in the current poem in The Field back below the level of the foot in the "wave" state and might posit:[2] measure in thot (the orders of justice) is co-equal with measure in composition. Focus (claritas) = accurate count. (As access to granite concept below the solid con-sciousness = access to numbers beyond (above?) the conscious mathematics).

Also, as far as I see diffuse emotional character is as everlasting as focussd emo-tional character. The definitive distance between {Allen} Ginsberg and {Edward} Marshall (both having hysterical tone) is that between diffuseness and focus.

{Walt} Whitman is not diffuse. In a section of the poem I am on, going back to Whitman I find what I produce is more like {William} Blake (who is some outer boundary of the poet surviving in the diffuse). I hit inertia after thirty-four lines; where Blake could go spread out his charge as to go on at the edge of inertia for books. No goal! Inertia = loss of appetite to go on the way you is going.

In diffusion the image cannot define object, and an habitual inner whirl of appearances—may be luminous or dim—takes the place of perception. One sees as vaguely as a polyp.

As in the foot, one sees as a dog does who must walk back and forth in order to achieve decisions in seeing. So's how to dance sitting down—how to see with the eye.[3]

Ideals belong to the diffuse order; insights to the active focus. In one level one exceeds by swinging wide; in the other by over-reaching.

A report for the New Year from the back-tracker to his dearest border-rider. Keep a coon-skin cap furry for me when I come West Kit Olson.[4] The Indians here are all on reservations, on the interior warpath. Is it true that there are red-skinnd nations beyond the Rockies? Kinfolk of animal spirits?

The cats here are all on reservation since giant adoration of death first raised Giza Kitty spectre. The woman that sez ugh! from the hearthstone of civilization.[5]

Love

Robert

∼

63

Gloucester, MA

January 17, 1958

A LITANY, FOR DUNCAN

IN JANUARY

Birdhead Thoth[6]

be over us

Hold us, as brew

outstretched

in his hand

Love

Chas

∼

64

San Francisco, CA

February 5, 1958

dear Charles

S.O.S.

re: income tax reports. Was income tax taken out of the $59 received from B{lack} M{ountain} C{ollege} corporation??? Or do I have to pay on it?

_____

and for yr. Valentine, the concluding parts of the "Pindar" pome.

    With love in distraction
    yrs. trying to straighten out the exorbitant tax on no income
                                                love to distraction
to Betty & Charles Peter & all

                                                Duncan

                                ∼

                                                        65
                                            Gloucester, MA
                                            February 6, 1958
Roberto!

    God damn it, it *wasn't* taken out (you are the sticker in the whole
    deal—because you come after all that bug up over Contingent etc)

    so please pay it (alas) in case I ever do get involved with Justice over
    the whole matter: you see, what I did do was assume I was now

    (or since last April) only a "receiver" for a "bankrupt" matter: thus it
    wasn't any longer 'salary' but "Debts"—and so I *hope*

    other payments to others wld be regarded, if ever put to the test. Yrs,
    then is, the One out of the PIX

    OK? Regard it in other words as one which shld go to the
    USG{overnment}

    Very Sorry. But. So

                            And above all thanks for my valentine and
                            just to hear fr you, mon!

                                        Love (and be back:

                            this, to answer your SOS
                                            Charles

                                ∼

66
Gloucester, MA
March 6, 1958

Robt:

Like one sez—sitting here, thinking *of* you. (Off my own pace, after some sort of a run—much song (the music wander) but too early to be certain it says what I am altogether committed to (yes?—*want* it to?—But you'd understand it's something to be at it (very busy on *materials* too. And was happy getting them.

Busted somewhat I take it by engaging to do a review of a new Macbeth book for the *Chicago Review*. And find it, as always, too much for me: hate the area of a review (shld know better than to have taken it. But was all fired up for years on Mr. {Herman} Melville,—who is my poet . . . however much I suddenly found one poem of {Walt} Whitman's which is way out/in: do you know it? "Darest Then Now My Soul?"[7] Can you put me on to any other like it?

The success of yr "Pindar" comes back to me fr correspondence. It is magnificent, as you know. (Told Robt {Creeley} abt it. Maybe you'd send him a copy.) It's so *steady*—and I'm very happy to be in it, I'll say: me & the Presidents. (What delights me, of course, is that you have got them in there—wow, *Hoover*! Man, he should cut you off a swag; he's *lucky*! ((Did you read him/at Valley Forge?[8]

Tell Jess how very lovely I think his cover for Denise's book[9] is (isn't it his? The one with the choo-choo train for "by"? Delicious "recall," the drawing has—& that angel wisdom in the lines (via topologicals ((like his dream—didn't I see it was published somewhere?))

Charles Peter gets real gamey and his ma blooms: she's "Aunt Betty" for some reason—& I'm "Pop" (by God!

Had a wonderful time, by the way, doing you up for the Guggenheim—but I pray I didn't do you *in*, for I can't speak of you calmly (as I suspect executives etc—: you know "Chaucer" (as of the long poem)—supporting you on the *compositional* character of "Open Field") and "Ben Jonson" (as of the play) etc—Too much! Pray they have sense enuf to come across: if they do it is of yr own making, the way your "career" just now ought damn well to force me.

(This paper one can buy in blocks from the A&P—for 19¢ So don't be concerned that I go on and on!)

Love to you—& please tell all out there I do think of them (& appreciate, tell Joe {Dunn}, receiving the last White Rabbit)

(Our fondest to Jess/ Love
Charles

∾

67
San Francisco, CA
Late Winter/Spring 1958?

"This is precisely what you are to do. You will thus inform the people that will live in the future; you will tell them seriously. Then they will not be lost."

from the *Owl Sacred Park* of Fox Indians, Bureau of Am. Eth., Bull. 72.[10]

∾

68
San Francisco, CA
March 10, 1958

dear Charles/

Here I was just putting the enclosed copy of Pauline Oliveros's *Maxy's Sixth Song*[11] which may be the world's shortest lieder and setting myself down to write you a ladder when your missle arrived; so I picture you as surviving the cauld which is the cold covering and direct me (without searching around for any particular Whitman—tho it's those poems out of his old age that I am drawn to and companion to "Darest Thou Now My Soul" is "Sail Out for Good, Eidólon Yacht!"[12]—where {D. H.} Lawrence must first have found his soul-boat) to what was on my mind before! there you were![13]

It's this anthology bizness. First Jonathan {Williams} announces a {Kenneth} Rexroth approach; and now I hears {Donald} Allen & {Barney} Rosset want a "Beat Generation" anthology—"from Olson to {John} Wieners" as {Michael} Rumaker writes to John. Both ideas give a distorted picture in my mind: obscure just where there shld be clarity. The basis for either Rexroth or for the House of Grove with its specialty being *attitude* won't be process.

Take is just there. The job would be, not to bring together samples of a group of writers. But to present PROCESS in collection

1. Establish key texts
2. let interaction of texts (form/content) be the design; eschew categories [yr. pigeon holes] directives to be possible for intelligent reader once he sees said texts in juxtaposition.
3. present a constellation

take your work, mine, Creeley's as
the configuration: we get an
insistent design of determinants
and derivations, & relations
              Dante (Rossetti)
historical verse (Browning) Whitman

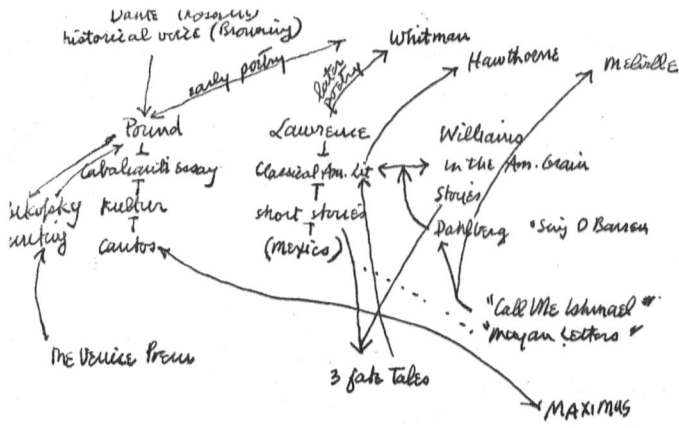

Which only shows that the mind has to read to it—and needs correlation of data. Say—to begin with you, Creeley and I sketch out [to be exchanged] what texts we think wld form the basic material. Above, for instance I tend to think of persons (influences) and not texts, bases.

And I specifically don't want to come at you right now with the—with more than the suggestion.

If we could get something in line we'ld have an answer to the pictures conveyed by "Beat Generation" talk, "San Francisco Scene" blarney etc.

I declined Grove's approach to do a *Selected Poems* (selected by brothers Allen & Rosset) instead of a volume of my own volition.

                    to Charles Peter, Aunt Betty, and Pop himself
                    love

                    Duncan

69

Gloucester, MA

March 30, 1958

Easter Monday wrote a

cover

My dear Robt

Again a fan letter. This time it's about that bunch at the back of Origin? (featuring {Irving} Layton)—Love Poem/ Salvages. Noon/

Friedl / Conversion / Jews[14]

&—Dar Ling

WOT A SET

You sure had yr nose in the grass, in them

And if I was answering you on this *anthology* question (in yr last) I'd start with these half dozen poems. In fact why not? Each of us an anthology of *the poems* I believe make truth—the pure poems, say of the last 10 years, viz:

starting there, Love

Friedl Conversion etc.

Some of Robts/Denise's Love[15] (is a crack

fr the scalp to the crotch,

wasn't it (in Origin

Ezra's 85th[16] / WCW's Burden of Loveliness,[17] rather than any poem of his/ Marshall's 1st in BMR[18] Ginzy's Xbalba, possibly[19]

and of Phil Walen's *Takeout*[20]

Etc. That way!

poem "Holy Saturday night the tide" which (if I had made *my* voice had

possessions you had in

these beauties I stumbled

on again this morning (preparing

a "Selected,"

for Grove)

Love, & hope the steam

stays in yr boiler

forever

Charles

{in right margin, upside down} John Wieners has one new one (for Measure) I'd enjoy your seeing / on Descartes & Boston, it opens actual title (not on the copy as John has it) is "Stiffening in the Master Founders' Wills."[21]

~

70
Gloucester, MA
May 20, 1958

My dear Robt—

I got so goddamned angry to discover today you didn't get a Guggenheim I spent an hour analyzing their list to see if there isn't some basis to do something about it—that of course there is any way to right it for you, except for you (and please do if you possibly can) *but come back on them until they are forced to yield* (whoever is their literary adviser, alas—This is the X of course, which hangs one, as far as reaching in there to accomplish anything.

—My own guess is only the search for some wealth to create a genuine tested exposed judgment system in the arts, is anything like an answer, the academicism of the basic jury leading inevitably (Wright,[22] {Carl} Sauer, Wilson etc—including {Henri} Peyre, who we (as well as Wright know the ghostliness of) to their dependence on some anomymous s.o.b. who can be who? Who? It once was Edmund Wilson, for example. It cld just as well as not be Harry Levin,[23] today!

Judging fr the awards it's someone more commercially involved—like J{ames} Donald Adams![24]

({James} Purdy![25] or a study of Ezra's verse *up to The Cantos*! Or the novel believe as, *since* World War II. Or {Alfred} Kazin.[26] Shit.

I note only 3 poetry awards (1% out of all, & by god 10% of all in the arts, in other words poetry 1/10th of the arts! {Katherine} Hoskins we know.[27] I don't know either Philip Booth[28] or Edgar Bowers,[29] but my 1st instinct was to get their work & analyze it point by point against yours for {Henry Allen} Moe.[30]

Anyway to share my common irritation to you and—& burn, that you should not have the advantage of it *right now*.

More power of course to you—That you join the elect. Those who were not chosen. Wot better pleasure that is, as against the bucks!

Love,
& let me hear fr you,
when you can
Chas

{at the right margin} They will of course be awarding Guggenheim one day for someone to study your work!

{at the left margin} All goes ahead—but behind schedule and somewhat frighteningly.

∾

71
Stinson Beach, CA
November 3, 1958

dear Charles/

Latest break here has been a WRITER'S THEATER that started out with a Broughton enthusiast who had money;[31] was nursed in secrecy of darkest Mt Ida by same Broughton; and now, out from undercover, promises at least that the MEDEA will go on the boards here, rehearsals starting in December for a February performance. And Broughton wants all three plays of the trilogy; so I've to get at it.

And *The Opening of the Field* with forty-five poems completed has only five to go and a preface to meet the projectile of my 40th birthday in January. Then I plan slowly issuing from my typewriter copies of the mss for my few readers. Shld *LETTERS* by some freak of the fates find recognition, and a publisher appear who will respect the intention of the book, and would undertake the *Field*, I would be joyful. But as the conception of the book begins to take on the exactness of placing tesserae in a large work, the where and how—the relation of the parts—is needed for justice.

What gets, on the Black Mountain Review front? Tho I suppose I shld ask Bob {Creeley} the question. Point being that if somebody wld write me quoting estimates on how much #8 will cost to be printed I could enquire in certain quarters about financial aid.

But Jonathan {Williams} don't keep records and wldn't trust money going thru his hands to get to magazine publishing. The open maw of Jargon is always more immediate to income. Have you-all any idea anyway how at this point BMR financing is set up?

As, it's the handling of monies, that puts me off of *MEASURE*. And too bad: Wieners has editorial responsibility and liveliness; mit managerial impulses at the borrow today and pay back? when the bills come due level.

San Francisco's North Beach flares out with open-air café, and a nite-life these days more and more a simulation of Paris, Italian style. As according to news reports the old metropolis is psycho-psity of the nation.

And I'm back on the Guggenheim application wheel. Tho I hopes that the old letters of recommendation can stand, and you won't be requested to re-recommend. Bad enuf to write out a new application. Especially this time with the Field to be finishd—having to propose a new book.

{Gael} Turnbull due here the end of November, from Seattle. He writes: "If I can get some sort of lucrative medical job in the S.F. area, this would be our first choice. But it may be over-run with doctors."[32]

—

At the close of The Field, what I anticipate is a need, shift to natural elements. Tho in a year here I have yet to "enter in," get the profusion of simplicities [piecing together the sky map necessary before casting it anew] to take in the scene. And learn to read a briar patch. Cow pads.

—

I've just finished a close reading of *Prometheus Unbound* {by Percy Bysshe Shelley}. Even in his own terms there's too much dross. Certain imitations glower up at one thru murky verse. And he's almost sure to be off when he end rimes [in this pome at least just don't compare in end-riming to Yeats or E{zra} P{ound} who at times are in the same vein]. But lovely when in a "blank verse" he lets the rime dance in its impulsive measures.

Reflections in water wld. seem for Shelley true vision.

> "but by the light
> of wave-reflected flowers, and floating odours"
> or again
> "All things had out their evil natur<u>e</u> <u>off</u>
> I cannot tell my joy, when <u>o</u>'er a <u>lake</u>
> Upon a drooping bough with night sh<u>ade</u> <u>twined</u>,
> I saw two azure halcyons clinging <u>downward</u>
> And thinning one bright bunch of am<u>ber</u> *berries*
> With quick long beaks, and in the deep *there* <u>lay</u>
> Those lovely forms imaged in <u>a</u> sky[33]   I take it a<u>I</u> not <u>^</u>[34]

or   "as the sharp stars pierce winter's crystal air
            And glare upon themselves within the sea."[35]

Striking because here, the Pacific is too disturbed to reflect images. Casts back dazzle. Well, these few notes must do for yr. request dear old corporation etc.[36]

Love

Robert

∼

72

Stinson Beach, CA

December 1, 1958

dear Charles,

Bobbie Creeley has just written me:

"The writers Bob feels most concern for, and the two friends he misses most are you and Charles Olson. I would like to give him a tape with you reading on one side and Charles Olson on the other, dedicated to him in a personal way. It would come as an immense pleasure, I know, and act as an amulet against Professors Pierce, Wicker and Friedman (who says John Cheever is the greatest American writer and writes short stories which surpass Henry James' because Cheever gets his characters into bed) (with each other, let it be known)."[37]

She's sending a tape to me and in the letter encloses a check to cover mailing to you etc. Which I will send on to you at the time I send the tapes; since there won't be any expense here on making the tape. The idea of the conjunction with you lifts my spirits, where that conjunction has its place in Creeley's heart. And shining eye. This being Orion's splendid season, where he swings above the coastal hills.

I'm at work on *The Opening of the Field*, defining the text. And I find that my close reading of {Percy Bysshe} Shelley's *Prometheus* sharpend my (own) sense in reading my own work of a certain kind of writing that is "likely poetry": in the long "MASTURBATION" poem [#21 of the *Field*], the propositions were not like the propositions in the poem in *MEASURE*, not that is operative, but argumentative and the verse remains expository.[38] I junked all but two centers of concentration in which something happens.

As certain passages of Prometheus are "created" but the form is continued. Where I keep after the form [as in "PROPOSITIONS" or the *Pindar* Poem], and all content, theme, development is rooted in and constricted to the necessities (laws) of the made-thing: then the long poem rings true. But the key to something being wrong was that I had no formal directive in the #21; and could see thru Shelley's magnificent mis-take that the burden of writing that does not spring from obedience to form (in creating the master work—the work that makes the writer its servant) is a bore.

{Lawrence} Ferlinghetti has proposed terms for a Selection of Poems that I can meet and am preparing a manuscript for.

First: there will be a formal contract, stating terms of royalty, price of book, minimal description of contents etc.

Second: he will keep the book in print.

Third: I will select the contents and write preface.

The title CERTAIN SELECTED POEMS. From the work 1942–1950. The minimal contents to include:

1942:	Toward an African Elegy
	King Haydn of Miami Beach
1947:	Medieval Scenes (entire)
	The Temple of the Animals
1948:	Homage to the Brothers Grimm (The Robber Moon,
	Strawberries Under the Snow)
	The Venice Poem (entire)[39]

Ferlinghetti thinks he can get out a book for $1 that would cover that! It will bring back into print *Medieval Scenes* and into an edition that will have distribution "The Venice Poem."

It will get me out of the deluxe editions class. And since Ferlinghetti hasn't the slightest *idea* of doing me a personal favor or helping me along in this world, I can ask for guarantee on a cash basis.

———————

I've written Jonathan {Williams} off the books. The deal of doubling the announced price on *LETTERS* was more than I could stomach. I gave that text the closest of care, and between {Claude} Fredericks and me reading proofs and arguing points of notation[40]—the book represents a demanding labor. Then to have J.W.'s off-hand expansive make-shift publishing take over. With the possible readers of the trade-edition askd to pay for his poor management and blatant incompetence in planning the deluxe edition! to the tune of $8!

In wry anticipation and criticism of the fact the original *LETTERS* was to have its Jargon vanity special copies I had connoisseurs of éditions de grande luxe off to join the Legions of the Dead with Hitler, the psychoanalysts, the gourmets and labor unions. And Jonathan knows damn him that I objected strongly to his original plans to have the book fine printed and charge $4. The deceit of his whole procedure is rotten. I did—when he announced that he had raised the price—ask for an account of costs and an explanation. Which was not forthcoming.

So, Mr. Williams joins Ruth Witt-Diamant, Bern Porter, and Don Allen. A particular corner of hell that bakes in the heat of the work of art as commodity, a "hot" tip, the culture pushers and poetry lovers clambake. Those "in the know"—the know being the level of shit "the latest thing" "dig those waves" etc. up to and enclosing.

My true readers will not be the crowd at Jargon's cocktail party to "dig Duncan, {Mina} Loy and {Henry} Miller." Not this imaginary reader who must, like I do, hunt out his texts second-hand, and budget them against Boehme's *Six Theosophic Points* marked down to a dollar, and Harrison's *PROLEGOMENA* at $1.29. Test, as I do in writing, against inspired impatience with culture. Hunt out that which will move the heart from old ways.

Nor will my ideal reader, that other "poetry lover" who has a Jeanne D'Orge[41] grand baby ego and lives immediate to forest and household, who has "known life," she won't be there.

Not the poets I rejoice in thinking of. {Larry} Eigner—but I doubt he finds the light in my work I find in his—Well, Denny {Levertov}will be there, but won't she have a reservation about "digging Duncan." I'm trying to ring poems here against stars, mountains and that old sea!

Jess has a show coming up in January[42]—and there is ready for it a magnificent group of paintings: that have their indebtedness to certain shared mysteries of 19th century romanticists. He's taken the illustration back into the fulcrum of the oil painting [as it was for {Eugène} Delacroix or earlier for {Hieronymus} Bosch] and projected a series of showings forth where the personal, social and religious vision appears fused.

As, for instance, in a small canvas finishd last week the Hay Wain [that in

Bosch we saw close-up and was the temporal world of Christian belief, the harvest of this world with its dancers][43] appears central (but in the far distance at the upper left corner) on the crest of a rise in the road, broken down, against a white glare. It's only a truck, with a man changing the tire. And all forward is an illuminated dark, where a man sleeps in the hay mound upon a forward bank.

   Evocative, not representational.

—

And that we all need a nexus at this point.
Yrs.

love
Robert

∾

73
Stinson Beach, CA
December 11, 1958

{in upper margin} p.s. that check from BMC.
saved the sinking ship

dear Charles/

  A note to accompanying recording tape. One side is filld with me recording at 7 1/2 ips: and as indicated in last letter the other side is open for you to turn to gold.

  Enclosed a check Bobbie sent to me in case you need it for postage etc.

  I managed to get some good passages on this tape—The "Pindar" poem is there and some recent things if you have time to listen before you send it off to Bobbie. At the address below, by the way:

  Bobbie Creeley—But damn it!! I can't find her letter and she wants the tape to be sent to her mother so it will be a surprise.!!!! I hope she's written to you direct.

  This has to go right off in order to get in the mail.

with love,
etc.
and hello to Betty and Peter
Robert

~

74

Stinson Beach, CA
February 7, 1959

dear Charles/ Enclosed is Master Copy of the third set of *The Field* (in which the title appears there for the first time, and there have still been adjustments of the text to get the structure of statement I want). It's also the first set that is done after all fifty poems were finishd. The first two (to Denise {Levertov} and {Robert} Creeley) went off with 48, 49 and 50 still to be added. Each set with 3 carbons, and after five sets I'll have distributed 20 copies: I figure if I have twenty readers that's a good beginning.

To be independent of publishers! I'm going thru the business now with {Lawrence} Ferlinghetti: when he askd for a "Selected Poems" he was all agreement with my proviso that I would set a minimum text in which contents there would be no change [of 72 pages] and indicate a maximum text in case he could afford a larger book. Since the text has been finishd [a month ago] he is enthusiastic but still writes: "isn't there anything you could use since 1950? Think it over." This after my most adamant, short of threatening resistance on behalf of the integrity of the contents. As stands *The Selected Poems (1942–1950)*—but Ferlinghetti don't want to have them dates—is a solid necessary item, it brings into print poems that were not in volumes before, shows by selection in *Medieval Scenes* and by returning to primary manuscript for text my critical estimate here, and includes in its entirety "The Venice Poem." I've to set my jaw and my temper until I see it done.

And J. Williams who stuck me in the first place with $14 freight costs (C.O.D.) on the limited edition of *LETTERS*; and now that I've got the first group of books finishd (which means end paper drawings (2 each volume) and on the special limiteds colord ink paintings and notified him there is he won't send postage to have them sent to him!!! I had canceld the $14 paid out by ordering a copy of the limited edition and taking the rest in credit toward the next *Maximus*. To top it all none of the subscribers to the regular edition have received their copies. I've supplied them all from my own lot.

Adding to this my disgust with Evergreen-Grove gang, and the result is this here plan for typescript distribution.

This is probably my morning coffee temper and I've got to nurse this grievance in order to keep it with me.

Is it not to be found a) a publisher who will keep the integrity of the book [no trouble there with Jonathan] and b) will match the care the author has taken in his end of the deal in production [care of costs and price] and distribution! Well, Ferling has the b) down pat, and offers a clear contract to keep the book in print, etc, with 8% royalties on the first edition, 9% on the second and 10% upwards [The book at $1].

Jess's show at Gump's elicited only one sale [and now we find we have to wait until the end of the month to be paid], a round of critic's fusillade all the way from one oaf's "dubious mysticism" and "lugubrious color" thru another who reprovd the tendency to illustration [all the paintings were accompanied by texts from Goethe, {George} MacDonald, Mallarmé, Dostoievsky, Hawthorne etc.], and a couple of guarded acclaims as a Romantic painter in the 20th century. It's the visual legend Jess has been striving for; and that the eye can see the Other that the word waits upon. Goya of the black house and Bosch away among the Masters of this art. A return of the iconographic in an all but fanatically iconoclastic period: especially if one takes into account that much that is representational is iconoclastic; and that the non-representational is not necessary agin' ikon.

We are both bearded. Jess has initiated the move when he was reading a life of George MacDonald[44] and was won in part by the romance-doctrine of the natural man [the lion with sun-mane], rays of my beard, and in part I think by the determination needed in the first half of the 19th century to have a beard against public proprieties. Ebbe Borregaard told me he was persuaded to his beard by the doctrine of natural man out of D. H. Lawrence.

On my part the beard celebrates a rite de passage of my fortieth year [Jan. 7, 1959], having come to that celebrated forest *nel mezzo del cammin di nostra vita. . . . per una selva oscura*[45] that in Dante's day was 35 yrs. surely in ours is 40, we being more prolongd and postponed in our resolution and search for the goods. Having no more than our statement of resolve. And what an eye-opener it be when a poet he do set down to listing 1, 2, 3, 4, 5, them gods, even with an old Chinese model, as E{zra} P{ound} he do. And gets at beats *Food is the root. Feed the people.*[46] Which has memorable rime.

Now that *The Field* is done [and there's 6 years come to one effort; a continuity of structure twixt *LETTERS* and *THE FIELD*], I am restless to break the hold of this way of working language, the anticipation and recuperation interlocking of elements. And to strive for serial time, an axis of form in the immediate solidity that asks no reference. And do away with that *that* and the *it is* and see what me mind is forced to.

P'haps some of the activity of line has been transferrd from activity of them verbs. Keeping a consistent equation [equilibrium] of activity to structure. But for my taste (appetite) whetted by this work I have done both *LETTERS* and *THE FIELD* seem too rigid, constrained in measure [I wld. seem unable to let go of them reins] and not rough enuf to be beautiful. At least, this reader is feeling the accomplishment of control thruout, of *performance*, has in his recognition that he knows his business in this verse making the further longing for a new inability. There's a lovely quote from {Paul} Valery who god knows ought to have known clear thru how over-finished one's hand at the game can come to be: "an explosive incapacity that surpasses the *necessary* and *sufficient* capacity." [47] Well, damn his frenchy literary neatness—he's using that phrase to distinguish poetry (and the metaphor specifically) from prose: when that pushing the language to an explosive incapacity is the crux of writing at all. . . . where it gets wired up for sound, heat and light.

Is there any route for some responsible party to take over the financial management of *MEASURE*, and to get Wieners back into operation. He's a first rate editor among the new generation [he don't gang up like Ginsberg and crowd; but goes after a text]? Richard Duerden's got a printing press here and is at work on a issue of new mag *FOOT*, with the Pindar Poem for ballast. *The Big Table* I'll leave to Ginsberg and gang. {Paul} Carroll forwarded a request for material to Spicer and me thru {Michael} McClure: but as I get it the effect of Ginsberg's campaign is as damaging to the cause of a sound concept of what a poem is as is the academe's literature.

Where the conventional and the unconventional are one force [Ginsberg supplying what most English professors believe would happen if you kicked over the traces].

vs. FORM, critical structure. I'd be out of place at that *Big Table* talking about the law I love[48] while the pariah generation shootz the joy-juice into their frantic nerves and stands on their hands for the daily press.

> love
> Robert

~

75
Gloucester, MA
April 24, 1959

Bro Robt: bro Robt in today with April Poetry, & this is to exclaim to you over yr {Edward} Dahlberg rev., as the only time, since DHL{awrence}, that the truth has been placed upon him.[49] And admiration for you, knowing the tangle of it as a task—to say it at all! (I killed my own chance to do it, on Flea of Sodom,[50] because only a reductive method—an examination of the resident/physiology in him, of contra nature—wld satisfy; and that was direct assault in public place.) You have given field to it, and got the flexible altogether, even to the glittering eye. A first rate and first value thing. Very straight.

This gives me the chance to beg you to allow my failure yet to write you abt FIELD—it awaits as it came in my time to read it, simply that I am still stuck in months of research. Also please thank Jess for my O'Ryan.[51]

Love to you both, fr us all

Charles

~

76

Stinson Beach, CA

May 2, 1959

dear Charles/

I thot maybe you was Hibernating, and I were waiting for warm weather to come in on Gloucester. "When does it thaw in New England?," I've been asking Easterners who didn't know what wuz on my mind. But I'm glad you're waiting until you can tackle *THE FIELD* straight on as a whole; and maybe by the time you are ready for that I will have the "Preface" ready.

And that you read the Dahlberg review as you do reassures me that the struggle to clear away obfuscations was to some extent won. You can guess how many letters flattering, whining, prodding and inflating I received from that mistaken old Man,[52] pouring praise upon my reviewing head and bemoaning the conspiracy of critics over years: so that I was tempted thruout to start a *real* conspiracy of critics and treat the book with an ill will. Amen. I wish I could have got into form the observations about the meaning of style that Dahlberg calld up; but the account involved too much for the proportions of a review. But E.D. has a direct relation to mannerists like Nathanael West, and this guy Burrows where their style is their hatred.[53] [A paralyzed man has a style of walking]—and it's turnd upon grace. As for the rest of us we've got to keep our style alive, as we don't want to deny our hatred (I mean even our hatred that flares up or insinuates itself toward the good), but we seek grace, an inclusion that allows for hell and heaven to exist. As {Michael} McClure pickd up on your

"but hell now

is not exterior, is not to be got out of, is

> the coat of your own self, the beasts
> emblazoned on you—"[54]

but I don't think I got thru to him that correlative is heaven is not to be got out of: that we find ourselves out of place when we try to take one and deny the other. Or throw it away. Better throw both away and live in Aristotle's likely mean, than choose good or ill demon and call the other twin power a fake and a lie. I will probably come thundering in one of these days on what angels are and aren't: a warning to enthusiasts. But so far it's in my own counsels that such warning seems pertinent.

95% of the population today is Trimmers[55] and know nor hell nor heaven nor the common life.

I'm working away at {Jacob} Boehme. There's 6 *Theosophic Points* in pocket books (Ann Arbor 2); and one on the Adam from the library—*Of the Incarnation of Jesus Christ*,[56] where I find agreements on light and dark of it. And a doctrine of *Magic* that wins me.

Love

Robert

∾

77

Gloucester, MA

May 21, 1959

My dear Robert—Thank you for yr beautiful letter (which I read to all & sundry who came in here, especially C {the following letters were erased}.

The pt. to write today is that interview (sd *Time* sd week): and how wrong they still get it, 1948 circum & thereabouts (the Bay) *not tallying U* (ok: we'll live long—I hope). He's abt as beat as my asshole (which is strictly non-Burroughs). "Pre-beat" my ass![57] What he is {below line: was} is a "*pre-clear* seeking that hopeless state (status) to be {in left margin: nothing to/ do/ until/ *Claritas*} clear (short for comfort station). The verse therefore is [stays] Euclidian—& Christ (or the devil) is *Lost*. Terrible lines on the Cross hope to stop long enuf soon [my God catch my breath]?

Don't miss it actually having wonderful time breaking my wind—(pipe & general organism getting down the (to)—spring is beautiful too.

Love Olson

{at top edge of envelope} best to those you see whom you value & I know
{at top of envelope} the cosmos / Kosmos de Sitter / spelt it / best / down to / owl / hair on our / heads / in / it
{in middle of envelope} The dark shape / flew by me / last night on / my perch, over / the harbor was / a gull /—another / night-owl / like myself
{at bottom of envelope} I left *that* out of the new "Whipperwill" Poem I wrote last night I want you to see some day soon.[58]

~

78
Stinson Beach, CA
November 10, 1959

dear Charles/

mystery #1—the sudden appearance of the enclosed check in the pocket of the coat of a suit I got at Next-to-New a month ago at about 1:30 pm yesterday Nov. 9th. I put hand in pocket to get bus transfer and felt a check the enclosed. No year date, and I can't remember what you sent it for?? But if it is in order, fill in the year and return it.

mystery #2—but not a "mystery," rather a near simultaneity in constellation of images. Don Allen sent me in thermofax your old Zeus young Augustus poem[59] where given "theme" of love—there are striking correlations with my "Dream Data" [from a Lammas tide dream, poem circa August 3rd]:[60]

So the distances are Galatea	There was, did she say, an aesthetic stronger than sex?
torso on torso in either direction	tanks or cribs in each which male torsos
Sons go there hopefully as tho there was a secret, the object to undo distance?	the Prince [the young Japanese son] in his laboratory, assisted by the boy experimented in sensations

/but it's not this kind of piecing out that shows the mystery—the two poems are haunted by two different appearances of the same event.

And I find from your poem the gift of your sight that opens up anew dimensions of the thing I had seen. What I don't account for in the poem was the Japanese son's Samurai uncle, the "military camp" of your information. The dream itself I have recorded and if a reader wanted to find out what is going on, what's the score, what music them instruments is playing tonite—said devout hunter-out could find more complete evidence—could put together a picture of how I still don't manage to bring the record into its form as fully as you do. And that, for instance, Galatea is a specific, a focus for the mind that "aesthetic" ain't.

> And you set free then
> "the girl who makes you weep, and keep the corpse live by all
> your arts"

Where I cannot go beyond the initial horror—I woke in that damnd dream with just the one point from which to view it, the one thing true, in which all else was true and then false: there was only the vistas of corpses. And lying in bed in the dark of the morning I could only face the disclosure as if it renderd false all but some calculating but bungling mutilator of bodies in me.

But what a joy it is when I have a new poem of yours to go at. Would you put an extra carbon on the typewriter for me sometimes and send me a present of the day? Your lines are directives.

love
Robert

⁓

79
Gloucester, MA
November–December 1959

My dear
My beloved
Dunk
The enclosed carries its own explanation—Only, did you *buy* back yr own suit, fr the Good Will?

(the Good Will—wow I shld say—

& likewise as of the

Happy Time of our two Poems: events
                                          in the cosmos
                                          are as the crystals
                                          in the gene
                                          the tree
                                          which emerges
                                          is the multifoliate
                                          rose
                                          Love
                                          is
                                          God

{at right} God suffers the failures only of the [above] Prepared Pictures [below] (Images) of his love
{at top} We suffer too because we don't make those Pictures: when we do we don't suffer. He meant nothing not to bring its self to be.
{at left} The law of creation The law of creation is *tale quels* be (to speak in Hiawatha-talk, of love
{at bottom} LOVE TO YOU BOTH from me and Bet—all goes well at the moment.

                                                              Chas

                              ∾

                                                                      80
                                                          Gloucester, MA
                                                      December 23, 1959

My beloved Dunk:
    I was offering the right stuff—but I knew nothing *nothing* about it
                        in San Francisco, 3 yrs ago come Feb;
                        and Black Mountain, the spring before[61]

    The ANCIENTS (meaning still the world outside and before
Christianity—with ONE EXCEPTION? [Augustine?] *inside* it: circa 1200 AD,
among Arabs,

                            as well as English (Scandinavian?)
                            Gothic Dante Giotto—*JAVA*
                                    (a *padma* these, date
                                        c 1220)

the '*ANCIENTS*' (including Alchemie, both
European and Tibetan (? *or* China?)

knew the *NECESSITIES*
of the soul *IN*
And *OF* the   And *FOR* the
KOSMOS

my own soul has been bereft
all these years
of such simple rites
as   *AGGREGATION*

&

SEGREGATION

Don't even *know*
what they mean
except
the *experience*
of their need: I am speaking
of their formal existence
(allowance / action (presence)
in ancient circular life—

the *admission*
that one is living
in the presence
of a larger
life: BUT *FACT* [PRAXIS]—what I take it has been

MISSING

_____

The *desire*, anyway, this date 4 days before
my own birthday (*birth time* is *more*
important) to salute you, fellow
goat-out-of-the snail shell

Love to Jess at Jesus-time too

My love to you, Robert Duncan,   Charles Olson

∼

81
Stinson Beach, CA
January 4, 1960

dear Charles/

Yr aggregate / segregate vs integrate? "integrity" and "integration" any ways round mean whatever and however victory of person over the One any one is. Some place among those legends of Hassids was that Victory is always victory over truth. It does occur to me that where I've got integrity (and living close into the middle-class household ways integrity is part of my middling hubris) it is conquering life or being prepared against life. And to that poet, he'd always drive the word straight as he can into peril. In *Faust Foutu* that dear Mrs. Patchitt-Wildebeest said that's what life was "the peril of souls"[62] and being a realist she says straight out *sin* or *shame*, truth or consequences, are preferable to *that*.

As feebleness, inconsequence, failure of wits are all perils. The boldness and fierceness of E{zra} P{ound} in *Thrones* to charge ahead, the bright brigade himself and musn't he have trust to the last that he and we [who have *trust* as the full zest of reading] will finally put that ghost of integration in his place, house, time [a time for integration and a time to disintegrate] and time ourselves to the full scale of an aggregate of cantos? Creeley, writing to me of *Maximus*:—but now I come to look for it, it weren't in a letter but in that "Preface" that appeard in Gael {Turnbull}'s *Migrant*[63] ["I do not want to drift"[64] wander, migrate etc.] but letters that come from some beloved part of my being strike HOME, for I've made a home to strike, or be struck in. Not a center but a place among places. Celts were (migrants) no, but held courts that always were not there where they were. Is shifting different from drifting? Yas, well, old Hermes were shifty not drifty.

And later, organized, as the State appears (ie becomes subject to inte-disintegration) the court has progresses. In arts progressions and variations which now we've to put in its place.

Well—I'm with you that the old feeling of kinship with like spirit is my good versus the evil of Xtian universal brotherhood. ie short of the Adamic species as whole [which ain't less than all].

[handwritten diagram:]

here concept / is needed

here inspiration / from which / derived or / to which / referring / a melos

notes [facts] → units / given or seized / sound / possibilities as / in

scale / which put / Schönberg we / conceive of as / a reference / that may/is / re-made each / (instante)(melos)(unit) / of a / (melody)

↑ mind

feelings of melody, / out spinning of the / spider

co-ordinations of sensory / and visceral being

the poem / or made-thing / soundshape / and / meanings / a new [act / note.

postscript Jan. 21/60

   The check I'm enclosing as returnd—with only the thot that if funds ever come into the account you might keep this on record. NOT to be kept as a personal debt.
   My planz for touring the Eastern bastions begin to take on time-shape:
April 6th—read at Illinois College
                ↓

                    Yale reading—no date yet
                    Institute of Contemporary Arts—no date yet

                    April 24 read at Honors College, Wesleyan U.
                    following week at College of Letters

May 20th read for *Big Table* with Creeley

Which all means I will have enuf money to get around—and come to see you in yr homegrounds—

verso

Cld. you put a word in for me and/or negotiate a Canadian reading while I am East? I'd like to see the country—and also I've got to get to Canada within the year to cash a money order for circa $5.
   Any idea about readings and or such? Grove Press is now at work to get me more appearances.

And here's a foto of me caught in the act of writing by one Patty Topalian a huntress with camera.[65]

Our always love—and only two 1/2 months away that we'll [rex Duncan] see thee

RD

~

82
Gloucester, MA
February 4, 1960

Robt:

Very good news that we will see you again that soon (keep me on to schedules and such, and if there is anything I can do East here to forward any of that— Vincent (Ferrini) and I plan to have a gig for you here, but there is no audience other than ourselves, and you'll be free—at that stage of yr travels, and tiredness, to choose to have it or leave it as you will (as it stands, just to have you here, will be the delight

A quick note simply to *levy you*—and on the *Maximus Poems*: I have given your name to the Guggenheim people. My situation is this: I'll be busted in a couple of months—for sure, and for good (that is, borrowed on a hell of a solid future to stay this additional year). I had only this 'long shot,' that conceivably, those people *might* entertain an extension on that renewal of 10 yrs ago! (One does have to find out, doesn't one?

> In any case my desire is solely to be spoken for by those who have in print spoke up for me!

> The request is specifically "to continue the Maximus and to enable me to stay in Gloucester to do that"

((My other press to go in there this year is solely that once broken out of here that part of it is over—and if I cld manage to hang on some time more I'd cash in, so to speak, on the accumulated 2 ½years))

If you wanted to do anymore than throw them the "Notes on Poetics etc—Maximus"—as yr speech—that wld sit fine with me ((I am aware you haven't seen the '3rd volume' (which is due out in March, and I have written to Jonathan {Williams}, asking if possibly we can get proofs—when they are ready—to you.

Anything in short which you are prompted etc—and it is a pleasure to think of it!

Love, and be back on soon/
Charles

best to Jess and those you love ((you may have already spoken up for
Creeley this year—I thot much be-
for going in there because he was
in But my conclusion was we were in
different departments (I am assuming
a 'renewal' is) So I shldn't think
you need feel there'd be collision

In any case just what you wld choose yrself anyway
{on recto} Sorry about this wordy check. Will send a new one that will work! as soon as I can check check book.

Charles

∼

83
San Francisco, CA
February 6, 1960

dear Charles,

I've kept yr at Jesus-time letter by, with the strongest things there NECES-SITIES of the Soul and then "my own soul has been bereft" and even "all these years" [66]

with that *in*, *of* and *for* the κοσμος. [67]

rites of aggregation you had in line of insistence when you were here: your "not only but also . . ." which allowd a net to form in place of the old teeter-totter, allowd to "not only the teeter-totter but also . . . and also etc."

And am ready now to write as I want to—for I'm in the midst of a poem again, projecting a construct of five sections that allows me to come alive, with the nodes—nodes of illumination for the course of the making.

> "I was offering the right stuff"
> and [in the enclosed pome]
> "flames of beauty on old stuff rage" [68]

Well, for me there's first the elemental life—what your ancients meant by "elements" and settled finally as earth air water and fire. There seems to be only an atomic reality in the table of elements—there's the thing we know more about now, then, the atomic reality / and the old thing, the elemental life. Harvey's *Circulation of the Blood* or Paracelsus{'s} the Doctrine of Correspondences and the Alchemie have to do with the elemental life and see man as an elemental being.

And doesn't the adventure into the Kosmos[69]—the atomic reality make man *not the center*—This is anyway my dissatisfaction, some times an outrage at the Jungian concept of *integration* and of a *mandala* view of the universe. It literally circumscribes the spirit from much of what it already *knows*.

Where your Whitehead—that now translates into my Whitehead—where we are *events*; and that "we" may be extend{ed} as a sum of a progression of imagined *events*:

atomic   within which is the borderlines of the unobservable the uncertainty principle where time or place are *void*—   where there can be no observable flux

elemental   it's here that I return often via the cults of the elements; that we were born out of the Sun; and are so much of water we are shaped by the moon and the planet orders; and to elemental powers and their attendants; fairies, nixies, goblins etc.
alchemie and catalyst operate here; and medicines [Asclepius advised in dreams walking barefoot on the earth]—

But as we realize that on Mars, Venus or planets even nearer our own in composition—*at the elemental level*—man can not be a *forma maxima* but node among nodes [and among mammals I find it difficult to think of man as a *mammalia maxima*, for he is clearly a contemporary instance or possibility (actual) of what a mammal can be along with elefunts and rats.] And this is still the elemental world for as long as we think of life on Venus or Mars or in the system of Betelgeuse. We are still thinking of elements and how life will or might appear in different compositions (alchemical universes)—and beyond that the Kosmic [in *Process and Reality* Whitehead speaks of our particular Kosmos as atomic; and doesn't he open the imagination then beyond Nicholas of Cusa's plurality of worlds to a plurality of Kosmos.][70] It's what I meant in "Structure of Rime" by the stars going out to enter a new universe. There is anyway in Whitehead's scheme an unknowable unknown. And when I work in a poem, the order of the poem arises from two relations:

a. a universe—your everything can be known—that a whole poem is a whole poem, as we are at any moment a whole event

b. a kosmos or order or harmony, that includes a void, and *cannot possibly be a wholeness*, but is a mathematical incomplete [our own versions of harmony, our own scales, are always incomplete and what had been dis-cord is being added]

 Don't we like the cosmos throw out melodic lines from ourselves (nets) that are entering a new universe? And whose spirits must be bereft for the Kosmos is. Mrs. Patchitt-Wildebeest says of Faust Foutu: "The peril of souls?"[71]

I find that *soul* seems to me a thing of the visceral elemental aspect. It's one node, one event: atomicly, there's a body or substance as an aggregate of atomic events.

Elementally there's the soul and kosmicly what we call spirit = breath/but these are not three persons or three beings but three appearances of a node that might well be a plurality of appearances.

What we are that is a kosmic event I can't think of as a *soul* for my soul appears to me as a man. My *spirit*, my "I" can appear as a planet or number or a bird.

Not *any* planet or number or bird. In my magic my "I" cannot be anything but that "I," might have an elemental universe with Charles Olson (by sympathy) (has what I call kindred soulship) but spiritually is a node, a Note in an harmonic order or net that is bereft, includes a void, ie, in some parts of which were it a whole "I" would be excluded.

Heraklitus:

XLVII   The invisible attunement is better than the visible[72]
LIX   Couples are whole and not wholes; what agrees disagrees, the concordant is discordant

And his observation you put here as man is estranged from what is most familiar[73]

It seems to me that the "peril" and yr. *admission* [that one is living in the presence of a larger life ⌊FACT (PRAXIS)⌋[74] are one with those apprehensions
                            DESIRE,
of "love"—in peril

of such simple rites
as the tying of knots,
or threads interwoven
to show design in lives
and what do we imitate
where we must cut,

                    knots the thread for love—

I know it *is* for something missing that the line of the poem goes out and must refer to

                        Love,

                        Robert

postscript
    Yrs of February 4 received this morning and I reply at least to say YES
and that if I get that minimum of sending copy of first essay at the
MAXIMUS—as I hope I might—I'd have to go at giving some 'literary' account
of it, and in turn some poetics of what this thing literature is viz. the MAXIMUS.
But the challenge anyway to give some definition to my admiration etc. whets
my appetite.
                            love. etc
                            R.D.

                        ∾

84
Gloucester, MA
February 8–9, 1960

Robt: Your letter and poem are a joy.[75] I walked right out of the house into
the sun and onto the beach which fronts the city to the harbor and the sand
is brown and fresh from the winter's storms, and wrinkled like desert sand
from the north wind of the past day and until the bitterness of the wind at the
sluice near the Tavern turned me up Beach Court and to the gas station (to
cash a check to get some breakfast) it was all one thought: the beauty of your
own thought, come to me across from a beach on that other ocean—and I am
still happy of the thought of your life speaking to me as for some months now
Ibn'Arabi has since 1220[76]—same same marvel of *being*, that, we are here and
can seek to see it truly

being, Robt: I felt so strongly
reading yr letter (yr poem is because poem so free from anything but its own
beauty the mother toad in the muck true sight forever for man, and placed in
like Ibn's bezels—o love of God

being being being—and God,
the Creator

{handwritten insertion}: There is no void/by
existence of/ Creator (?
There is either Kaos or Kosmos(?
disorder
and confusion
what I don't think you by *void* is *future*: what any of us brings
in to *being* is the furtherance of the will (*bould*-feminine) of GOD
this sweetens all atomic fact, and is love's burning that love burns
forward
o Creator/who waits on man

{handwritten at left} XAOS   XA- *Tiamat*?

((I crib from Whitehead perhaps the wording
of the experience of our own novelty—but like you say love's own concern for
the loss of itself of its beloved is merely a worry: of it itself it breeds only the

future of the life of one's self, that that self may be more beautiful because love has been able to get in

> alright: I am all new from your poem and letter and ready for anything!

> (The other thought I had was that the cosmos is time and that all these fools of the present—even Whitehead's vision of the difference of other epochs than the electromagnetic, is time

time, & being in

creation[77]   eternity is more interesting than infinity
—like you and Ibn Araqui and Jess and I are and all whom
we love, and what, are *now*: space isn't objects ain't, like the Hopi say!

> I am yours forever in love,

> Charles

{crossed out in blue pencil on recto}
Time is {unreadable four lines}
But do, because we are not
Any other than
This   'peril
of the soul' & the impossible(?) completion
of Creation that times itself is
    Form?

Tuesday, February 9, 1960

Robt:

    thot you'd be amused and interested, that the night before last, during the night—in other words the night *before* your letter & poem came—I had this dream/ It had waked me, and i had written it down, and only long after I had written to you last night, when making the bed, did I see it. Reads:

> "Mistress Employment
>   "   Unemployment
> & Mme Sentence
> at—East 40th Street
>   (Duncan's

address
in the metropolis
a large city"

Charles

～

85
Stinson Beach, CA
February 19 or 20, 1960

Dear Charles,[78] Yesterday brought good news from New York—that the Living Theater plans a reading plus "a performance of one or two acts of your play directed by Nick Cernovich."[79]

As the day before brought most certainly the rejection of my book by Grove in their sending a substitute cover for the design Jess did.[80] When a condition from the first has been *their* acceptance of cover design as integral to the book.

Love,
Robert

Dear Charles,

I could not go about writing this without clearing the way of that pesty discriminating anonymous judge (most schoolmarmy to my mind) who has not so far shown much sympathy etc. for what I've had to say quite forcefully and clearly re- Creeley and Rumaker. Not to overlook the further case of my own exploitations when I was working on *The Opening of the Field*. Are!

I was never without a fury in writing at the thought that *The Maximus Poems* will be dropd like a hot potato by the Guggenheim advisers. I have this faith in them, I find, that I expect the rejection of your appeal.

～

86
Gloucester, MA
end of February 1960

My dear Ro-Bare,[81]

I have guided myself (throughout the year—unsuccessfully so far!) by your own observation of how many weeks a man can appear except as he has a 24 hour after 24 hour life of his own.

Thereby hangs my present winter-time. I have, and I hope you will have all reason, and none otherwise to speak up for me on one or more applications for gain when you do hear from any or all of these dispensaries.

Unfortunately plump on the table still more of the ele{e}mosynary things produces without either your argument or mine on my

∾

87
Stinson Beach, CA
March 7, 1960

dear Charles/

Did I write that the Grove deal is kaputt? They wouldn't take Jess's design for the cover. Which they'd had in December; then three weeks ago sent me a design by their staff artist [as {Richard} Seaver,[82] when pressed wrote: one "attempting to incorporate the spirit and at the same time not betray the type of cover design of the Evergreen line"]. Which was even in commercial terms a sloppy job, hideous as all commodity-mind must be [untouched by human hands, feet, eyes, mind, soul etc]—but more to the point one could see the antipathetic hack at work "using" elements of cover-design he hated, cursing the job as he went at it.

But I am the more in love with that book by my having stood by it. I should say by my not being able to "use" it; for *The Opening of the Field* has more resistance to being carelessly published than I have. I myself felt I had lost an opportunity "to be in print" [me to be in print, not the book] and had a couple of dour days. Meanwhiles, or as Jess collages it in Tricky Cad "Whinemeals": herewith a new movement of Apprehensions.[83] What I "apprehend" for the fourth movement is a new STRUCTURE OF RIME (XIV), and then the closing (fifth movement) will need what I can't at the moment feel up to—some sweeping utterance. Anyway I sketch it out as? That excavation must "after all" be not only a grave or a well but an excavation for a building.

My progress of the far East to include Gloucester races nearer if I am looking the other way; creeps if I am waiting.

love
Robert

∾

88
Boston, MA?
May 4, 1960

dear Charles,

Scrawling this here before taking train to Dartmouth. From which institution I will depart Friday May 6 morning to arrive in Boston at 9:25 AM.

Any chance you cld come down and we could get Wieners and Eigner seen Friday? And me visit you. Or—maybe I shld take week-end when Stone and Klinà[84] are home for Boston and we can have Mon. 9th and Tues. 10th up til train time for return to New York for Gloucester?

I can't manage to fit my time into these schedules.

Love in all times and to all those Olsons.

R.D.

∾

89
Gloucester, MA
Fall 1960

Dear RD:

the day, the year—and the Platonic month. These seem now to be the ones which count, so long as one treats three great sets of 2000 years as carrying—and, as you know, somewhere I still feel Pleistocene, has to be counted, though it isn't—or maybe it is—as necessarily habitual as the other three terms. Yes, I believe it is (and different from other 'outside' frames such as Neolithic, or absurd surds like Maya—or geologic etc—because it was directly *before* the sequence we are a party of

but except for that shift of 'French' Man Spanish Man Shadow Man African, I get to believe firmly that the organic does lie in Day Year and 2000; and that they have a common, which is simply that one, that one feels them as holding a like experience, and giving a different effect

suddenly then (like that time I wrote you that letter about 1220 AD or thereabouts) history like they used to call it gets already very accurate; and one has some fun out of it: I shld imagine Herodotus got a good belt like this when visiting those priests up the Nile

one other thing: one does want to say we are now so thoroughly over the dam and into that lapse of aeons—Fish almost done, and the New One andsoforth—that I should think our sensitiveness to these character{s} of time wld be particularly high—

and too I don't
believe it ever occurred (even though it obviously did three times in those sets—
once at the Amuq, then when Egypt was in such a helter Hyksos could come in,
and last previously as St Paul said) this same way except once previously *outside*
the system

that is, that it *was* that previous
time of Pleistocene which was as species-ridden as men now are, not among
animals but among themselves {the following lines were crossed out by Olson:
planets, maybe. No. Just machines. And anyway fuck that reference. It isn't the
experience, and the Basques anyway feel closer, isn't that the point, than those
at Stinson Beach}

{A line was crossed out above the word "Love": [Hope all goes well]}

Love,

Charles

∼

90

San Francisco, CA

ca. November 15, 1960

dear Charles, I've got another letter hereabouts, I wanted to catch as it went
along my dimmest sense and sensation of the new *Maximus* poems.[85] From a
kind of Neanderthal reading. As: even the dimmest sense of things is susceptible
to the full impact of that hymn to the drowned at sea, that comes in along the
line of universal acknowledgments—of sea and death, of men and wreaths—to
inform. Where, elsewhere, if we could be informed we must come across ourselves, go after the particulars. "Go to Gloucester."

But here I'm writing straight off because this young Gerrit Lansing has written me a letter about his *SET*—and it's the first proposition of a new magazine
that awakens my concern. I'd given up the possibility that there might be an
agency, or vehicle, or boat that would revive our hearts, and bring our songs
and dreams back into the Way and out of the market. And here is that Mercurial
agent, if I read a-right!

This morning, contemplating the program as Lansing presented it a poem
began: and there Set, Osiris and Isis began.[86] Have I a begrudging heart, dearest
Charles—for whenever a poem seems most realized, or some pressure moves in

a passage of a poem, my thought flies to you, as if to dedicate it to your honors. Yet I withhold from sending some scribbled note. But this scribbled note, this morning, to send you the poem I have just finished . . . along with a typescript of the work I've done since the *Field* was finishd.[87]

Boy! when I saw them words: "its character will be dual, *historical* & magical, the emphasized characters of Time"[88] I saw it was time to wake up and get a move on.

love,

Robert

∿

91

Gloucester, MA

March 10, 1961

Robt: forgive me. I'm just an old mope: I think yr book (Opening of the Field) is so beautiful and I haven't *yet* got beyond *one poem* I read St Valentine's Day, the wondrous big steady song in Capitals (in sixers, and a wondrous couplet burden?)[89] I read it to Gerrit {Lansing} in his kitch{en} while {he} and Bet were making supper and was still going on abt it last night at Brandeis[90]—reading some poems but actually billed as Lewisohn Lecture #1 (for this season, that is—{Robert} Lowell of course has been there before! the goyim, to spread a little the immense and increasing ignorance of phylo-Semitism!

Love to you and to Jess and don't think for a minute your name and work is out of my mouth like holy seeds for a moment: including the Zoharism of same images I do believe yes? (Mine I mean, testing, against yr Self

Abt what I got was a girl saying why do you use such unknown words as thyrsus and of course I sd you know which to look for sympathy?

and a lovely poem of {Thomas} Carew's I never heard of(!) on the death of John Donne ("Thy Giant phansie." . . and those "*Libertines*" who won't be able to pile it on as You Have etc[91]

best and please write me when-

ever you are minded to

and many thousand million
thanks for the new poems
sent

love,
Chas

Please: in a hand-written letter
        abt a year or more ago—on the 13th Century
        what was the literal date I
        used, to you?   1220 or more precise?

∽

92
San Francisco, CA
March 15, 1961

dear Charles,

Writ on blank pages from an old notebook of my father's in which were correspondence course studies in Astrology and Hermetic philosophy (Rosy crooshian style)—in which I saw him earnest as he was and dutiful, even to those mistaken lessons.

I'm trying myself a budget of three letters today, and then to the "Little Day Book" central section for the H.D. Book.[92]

Was you the "Charles" who once corresponded from the Pound environs with her?[93] Comes briefly into her *End of Torment* memoir of Ezra kept during the period of his release.[94] Verification everywhere of the "Opus" interpretation of our work. That Poetry is one of the Opera in the Alchemical sense, of the spirit. Us'ns being cells of said body.

And having all kinds of parts of that opus to do then, as cells of heart, liver, lung, intestines and *the daily shed skin have.*

Last Thursday I lectured on one Charles Olson, his Poesie critique and his *Maximus*[95]—and I got, grabbd out of the air where it had been waiting, or grabbd out of my heart where it had been wanted.

Maximus as a magic opus—not as magical or imagination
but as a recipe that has to be followed, paced out to a locus as in *Letter, May 2,*
1959
    this line goes finally straight
or as in *The Record*, depending upon just these ingredients—
    to get thru the winter
where cost too matters
And in the gospel of Charles Olson
        how small the news was
        a permanent change had come[96]

So! I was just readied to write you how I got this gospel and how my spirit would
be a child in Gloucester—![97]

When yr letter comes.

But read so, as all that involvement with the instructions that is *in the Shaman-*
ism of alchemy and of witchcraft—[98]

I read "From Dogtown"[99] as a warning the Earth gives

warning↔yearning

about this same "shooting the bull" or "throwing the bull" we call it, where
Merry[100] has raised Him

as Olson wld raise thru Maximus this "how small the news" until

    didn't Merry notice

    the deadly power of her?

But I think—it's possible—I got some of the contagious fever of the possibility,
disturbed the mind of Ron Loewinsohn that time. To be a real lion's son.

I don't know. Otherwise, he wants to write with no bull.

Distances has only that disappointment—that we all need a collection to date.

Given that, that every scrap of [error and truth] is needed to ransack, for us to go through. . . .

It's a lovely book.

And in which, I dig, for the first time it seems, the to Gerhart. "Among Europe's Things."[101] Having come some long way round to be ready for the digging.[102]

> how to handle the bric-a-brac
> what did you eat when you was
>   took bad? Lad?
> how to keep the great man going,
>   or the fire or the yeast . . .

raise the roof from the shoulder-line—

Mon.
Feb. 8/60   I find from your letter:
"as for some months now Ibn'Arabi has since 1220—same same marvel of *being*"

Dec. 23/59: (in hand):
"The ANCIENTS (meaning still the world outside, and before [Christianity—with one exception (?) [St. Augustine?] *inside* it:
circum 1200 AD among
Arabs, as well as English
(Scandinavian?) Gothic
Dante Giotto—*Java*
        (a *padma* there, date
            c 1220)"

And then yre (my) "our" beautiful only blessings

"the NECESSITIES
of the soul *in*
and *of* the   and *FOR* the
KOSMOS"

In this *End to Torment* H.D. says:[103]

"I can not *take* Aztec and Aztlan, though I wait feverishly for news. . . ." [as Ezra, off to Europe, left La Martinelli who headed for Mexico][104]

And: following a scene with Sylvia Beach who evokes the E.P. the terrible old man—fascist—anti-Semite bogey—

  "It seems that a great deal will be resurrected or re-born once Ezra is free. Consciously or unconsciously, it seems that we have been bound with him, bound up with him and his fate"

And then, after the "scandal" of his interviews upon release:

May 8, Thurs. "It runs thru all the poets, really, of the world. One of *us* had been trapped. Now, one of *us* is free. But we, the partisans of world-thought, of the myth, shiver apprehensively. What now?"[105]

Work now, however. And love to Betty. What makes with Gerrit {Lansing}'s plans for *SET*?

Robert

∾

93
Gloucester, MA
ca. April 15, 1961

Dear Robt

  You will of course know what happiness your letter brought

  Also power. Or at least I wrote a Maximus that day which (if I can get it finished) goes to Don {Allen} for Evergreen R{eview}—& has for title for Robt Duncan etc (1st time, I do believe, the directly personal has fitted[106]

  (Also last night by the way carried O'Ryan Poems to the Castle here,[107] & Jess may enjoy the fact that this Jack Hammond (who owns same) spoke particularly of the handsomeness of the book itself [and, like, he's hung up on stars? Venus in particular?

  It did me much service to have those letters of mine to chew on again—but actually the quotes from H.D. were of such use I shipped one right off to Michael Shayer[108] in England (who needs encouragement, to realize that the mind of man is busier now than ever!

Love to you both,
& whenever:

Charles

∾

94
San Francisco, CA
ca. May 1961

Dear Charles/ This is an opening essay at study of what Form can mean.[109]
I hope to follow with a study of organic and cosmic forms. And there could
remain the idea of a linguistic and artistic form (as inherent in the material?)

with love,
Robert

This copy for the man who most demands of me the effort that awakes radiance
in life. Whose "Projective Verse" essay still challenges and can not be taken for
granted in my thought. Each time I understand it anew.

With, this year, my larger endebtedness after grammarology and physiology
of human spirit in The Floating Bear.[110]

∾

95
San Francisco, CA
August 20, 1961

dear Charles/

The I.C.A. askd me to read next Spring; and I accepted.[111] Following the
which I received a letter from the Poetry Center in New York (Elizabeth Kray,
YMHA, etc.) and accepted there—the two making it possible for both Jess and
me to make the trip.[112]

YMHA has this damnable policy of double-billing and at first has proposed
Creeley to which I joyfully replied—only to find he is for the Fall. Then I proposed you and got this reply: "I value the appropriateness of Charles Olson
reading, too, and can imagine how dashed I felt when he refused to read here
this year, sweetly, politely, but firmly asking for postponement" etc. Any remote
chance of your reconsidering some—to join me in April 1962?

love
Robert

∾

96
Gloucester, MA
November 6, 1961

Robert

Thank you, thank you very much. I can't tell you how *valuable* it is to me *today*—right now. Please go on.

Love,

Charles

Love to Jess

∾

97
San Francisco, CA
December 18, 1961

dear Charles/

With the arrival of *SET*, and yr beautiful shot to hail the equinoxes' wheel:[113] only this perspective makes a locus where intelligence is empty enuf to be full-filld and, if sounded, ring true. With our two weeks of birthdays after the solstice: with you right in there; {John} Wieners and me at the terminus.[114] Children of Capricorn—well, I was raised as *that*: so, my parents' old-wisdom had gone into the cultsure as the editorial in SET labels it,[115] and conventions, the oc-cult-sure. But children of the winter solstice, of the return of the sun.

"Economics" and "history of prehist." of the list of elementaries need to be calld anew, don't they? These words have been so loaded and taken over by the cult-sure? As—Marx, for any example, just where he had a lead to find out the operations, what was going on (what orders we can give, given the orders we are), was trackd into the cultsure, for sure, by trying to picture a humane order as an economy. How to manage a household—and him calling up that specter of the Industrial Worker and his other counter pactsong and singer the Boss—with society—as if in such a name a household might be found! And calling it all the economic man. Yet some specter, and even that one, *is* essential to holding the house at all.

If, anyway, we take it, *economics* is elementary; then the ordering of a house-hold is. With the Old Man under the hearth, and the First Born, headdown, under the threshold.

But "history"?—couldn't we throw that word out and establish

histology: the tissue and structure, weaving, of what {it} is we
know.

story: what we know from the questions we askd. This
thing is made-up, or an answer—but is, also, the only thing
we knew to answer: oracle or sphinx-demand.

That: we *do* hold by histology and story having to do with one *gnosis*. And the
art, the story, seeks out histology or lapses into the cult-sure. Just as there
is a "science"of the cult-sure, that sets itself against story. The science seeks
out story or lapses into the availabilities of the cult-sure.[116]

So, in this *physics* vs. humanities we got the Work vs. the works or
working-man etc.

I've got to take a look, after some twenty years, at *Das Capital*: as to what does
the man tell us about the histology and the story.

Yr. "America, you are the end of three months of man" gives
the histological story—[117]

Had America not fought against England, Blake had it in 1793: "Earth had lost
another portion of the infinite"

"But all rush together in the night in wrath and raging fire."[118]

As, now, vainly,—the men of the establishment, in universities and govern-
ments, in whatever is instituted, offer *humanities* to put down the wrath; or
diplomacy; or even threat of power. Men without households (Jacqueline Bou-
vier Kennedy interior decorating the White House—a householder would build
a Black House).

As shown in *Les Heures de Rohan* (early 15th century) Aquarius is the
Star (dubbd Temperance) of the Tarot—She-Who-Mixes or Exchanges-the
Waters.[119] But in *Les Heures de Rohan*, from the two water-jars she pours out
or empties thro streams over the Earth. Below, the magics is a-cold; holds his
mittend hands over this fire: above which the (magic?)—the brew.[120]

These "things of the story" having been told or drawn being now actual (acting) (or traces of the action?) tissue of the histology—form (what happend or
creation-created).

A Christmas (for Mittrea the Fisher-Fish Man) card for the old and a New Year's
card (as rightly we picture ourselves putting away that Old Man and taking on,
over and over going at it, the new "year") for you from me with love (recalling

to the heart how you get in this *Across Space and Time*): "*the affectiones* to cause all of it to swarm."[121]

Robert

≈

98
Gloucester, MA
December 22, 1961 (the turn
hath come

Robt:

Delicious letter (as well as such a lovely card from you and Jess) and I am wholly prepared to accept your division of that wild word history into histology and story: I never could force that verb istorin on even myself![122] (My only problem remains that old stubborness, abt story, that I still like to let it lie—like song the feller said—in the fact itself—like; but then I'm learning: did a Christmas play[123] for a Catholic college for girls outside of Manhattan—Manhattanville. And that larned me a little. —Not that I don't dig what you mean by story—and indeed seek more and more to universalize!

Love and quickly to come to you
both around and about the
Nativity—BECAUSE BECAUSE
it is *our* time of the Year

love and bounty
Chas

Part Five

"you must feed your heart, Mr. Olson!"

(1963–1969)

99
San Francisco, CA
January 9, 1963

dear Charles,   The sun in progress again thru the brain-labyrinth of the Horse-
Man (and whose arrow is let fly back towards where we were before) time for
long creative tribute: for how you keep the line moving, and how your attentions
can always excite my own (likely, without being calld to order, to succumb to my
pleasure in word feeling), for how these gists of yours challenge my own sight.
When Creeley was here (in October (?) he had new tapes of you reading—that
"Gulf of Maine"[1] that made (thinking of my own going at it along a literary
voice) me feel like a lapsed Catholic before the way you get the story told—that
lovely

>   So. The night
>   was growley
>   the waves
>   were high the high built pinnas
>   tossed the winds down
>   pressed
>   and the drowning
>   where their heads
>   below the water
>   filled and shoes
>   and coats pulled down

So let me get the record down here this year when the culture mongers are com-
mending me for richness and mysticism and humanism and what all: that I ain't
lost me senses, and can recognize where and what the good art is, what's fit—for
what. Having—just this morning (and it now short of noon)—copied for myself
the "Bibliography on America for Ed Dorn"[2] (the which ms. I've had in keeping
since {Richard} Duerden's default; initially, to copy the diagram in ink so's it could
be reproduced—but I knew at the time he was ridding himself of the thing—¿this
is three years back?) (as that Horse-man's arrow points) preparing to send you
your ms. (Don Allen having his typescript for use with publishers)! Key in with
those concerns we commit ourselves to, you and I, "attention," "person," "process," throwing Kulcher overboard (and I mean here the high culture, cultivating
the ground) is digging. As I've always to keep at it—but then I do consume and
not cultivate. I sweat bad stinks when it don't belong to what me nature is.

And at one point: the "continuation-of-millennia-by-acts-of-migration-as-arising-directly-from-fierce-penetration-of-all-past-persons, places, things and actions-as data (objects)." I am so *with* you, or you are so with me, you strike the dinner gong for me.

Where I do see I have neglected *quantity* and hence (for all of getting, for instance, that Set and Isis boat thing right, I think) miss on *millennia*.

The art or care remains / of meanings (that the man working strives to realize, i.e. locate what he is working: make it fit, sound), hence measures. In *this* poet, the orders above must contend with a tendency to let pleasure float spread out or blurred. In vegetative terms I'm likely to luxuriate; not, here, to go beyond my roots, for I put out roots as richly as I put out branches: but to go outside of my *seed*.

Hence: that etymologies for me are important as *form* = nature.

And poetry, the making, then specifically to in-form in making.

Here, the keeping-form is not all, but yr novelty, in-novation, in-spiration that I'll take to come in our sense of where/when the form ("we") are (Whitehead: event).

But what now the accident boys have made of that word "event." What they just happen to be doing. Shitting on the rug or reading a poem backwards (the *inversion* warning you give: deliberately "processing" one's nature again' the turn of it). As, now, here,—{Jack} Spicer leads a re-action, preaching a poetry of attack: a deviation from Calvinist-anti-materialism "gnostic" or pseudo-gnostic: hatred of what is the matter. So he is (in his *Heads of the Town*)[3] concerned with poems as inversions of meaning.

And has no sight at all of the poems as inspiration of meaning (i.e. seeing as old Hairy Klytus sees it: the resonance, in what we do). Isn't Harry's reproof to Hesiod that "he did not understand day and night" and the following XXVI "God is day and night, winter and summer, war and peace, surfeit and hunger" counterpoint of yr questioning?

O.K. the "how how how" to do it. But where is the "what is going on," knowing what yr doing? Not in his-story: this thing as makers we know in the feel of what is being made. That can be faild; that, evilly, can be twisted against the feel; that can be carelessly (lost, done at haste) approximated. Is the what in yr *quantity?* [As I get it the feel is quantitative: has to do with work energy⟵⟶space-and-time of the object] so that "full" and "fit" have something to do with it; sound and accuracy.

As, doesn't {Allen} Ginsberg in *Howl* and *Kaddish,* given that force, mess up his particulars? Or {Michael} McClure, in his now characteristic FUCK SHIT CUNT shouts drown out the fit meaning of fuck, shit, cunt. (So as we become involved with McClure's own noise about these things—and a noise remote from—for all of the projected images of {McClure's} *Dark Brown*—the process. Well, as in "Revolt," McClure has the good of his language,[4] i.e. he can follow immediate to his thought; but he cannot write yet immediate to his bodily process without a great surcharge of feeling-effort in which words get blared out of any sound sense.

—What a lovely thing for me it has been sitting here; writing to you, with you almost here in the doing-so. With that love, I'd send it—off to the post office now/
　　　　Robert

～

100

Gloucester, MA
ca. January 10, 1963

My dear Robt:

　　Am so happy to hear from you, and to have that mss. back (which I now see deserved to circulate as it did—and no more: I guess millennia, of all said there, I do still believe is worth breaking down; or that that still occupies the fore-mind—or hasn't grounded to my satisfaction yet. Until about a week ago was still bullishly shoving at it still like a fence. And though I don't know that I won't, once more, return to it again, did have such a sense of some beginning of relief from it I thought to myself that if I should get time some time in the decade I would like to learn Greek—in order to write in it! Which seemed a satisfaction, of the sort which doesn't sound like much to have come to out of 'millennia.' I don't really know that that says anything, except that the only thing I've done so far today (beside the pleasure of reading to the full your own letter) has been to check the vowel sounds of eta (why *prey,* if it is long why not *pea.* Prey is a diphthong as I hear American. Etc. All sorts of exasperating ignorances passed on like even in my Greek book, as though that was the way it is. And omicron and omega both ō

Fortunately there is a very gifted Greek boy here, Peter Anastas,[5] who is a pleasure on Dante and Italian anyway, and is just back from two years in Florence and Greece. And he comes in and I can get out of him sometimes disappointing results to my own use of Greek—like finding out by asking that a word I had built a poem on, was really pronounced *fine as thigh* when I had it *phain as thai* (solid ignorance of that diphthong!

Ok. Just to give you some sense of life here. Think so often of you and Jess and life in yr house etc and it is a comfort, like they say, I can tell you. And to have you in the world to hear from you when you do write is about like having the bull-s-eye come to the target. Which sounds crazy. But so was yr wonderful shot today of Himself-on-a-Horse-shooting-backward-at-you-and-me. I even got out my elegant Duc of Berry is its Zodiac (Time Magazine's printing)[6]—to see which way he did face! Though I get you two at (the more, that last night, thank the lord, I delivered myself finally of a good kick-in-the-face to that dying year anyway.

Will write again, this is just to tell you how good it was to hear,

Charles

∾

101
San Francisco, CA
March 9, 1963

dear Charles,

Some time sequences that I've just begun to see in articulating the story of my "H.D. Book." Pose first that each our "spirit" and "consciousness" is born within (takes its form, using as a material—) the egg or surrounding of the human hive itself. Then phases of history will have a distinctive "tone" in which we may ourselves be defined or to which we belong.

1. There is a difference in type between Gertrude Stein (b. 1872)[7] and the "Imagist" generation (b. 1883 {William Carlos} Williams) to 1888 ({T. S.} Eliot the youngest you could be and still be an "Imagist"))—that marks within a decade an historical shift. [i.e. Stein belongs to the naturalistic or realistic psychology of the sentence—still related to Henry James]—no gods, no luminous extase—states—no "vision"—

2. This "Imagist" thing has its childhood between (taking the age 10 as ultimate limit of "child") between 1885–6 (at which point we imagine Williams no longer a "baby" but entering the learnd realm of walking and talking) and 1890 (at which point Eliot learns walking and talking). And its boyhood or girlhood between— no, I see what I've missed here. Let me graph it and the gist will be surer. You'll see what I see. {There is a blank space here in the letter before Duncan picks up again, apparently mid-thought.} graph of "conception" (i.e. the world-tone in which the parents of the given poet were "conceiving" the child—I use rather than "fucking" because this fucking also involves unconscious *concept*)

babyhood (i.e. the world-tone in which the poet is nursed, surrounded by the language of his nurses which is here his "food" and not his own instrument)

childhood (first initiation: learning to walk and talk).

boyhood-girlhood (development in delayed sexual consciousness: not the same as sexual unconsciousness—but I am busted here. It is development in delayed sexual permission).

Manhood-womanhood (the individual creative identity). Stein in *The Making of Americans* observd that Americans were often twenty-eight before they knew what they were doing. That which I remember because I was that age when I wrote *Medieval Scenes* which is the first point at which I *knew*. [As I was thirty before I knew how to do what I knew I was doing.] But here is what I saw more simply—given that there was a creative wave "before the War"—in which the Imagists came into their manhood and womanhood: and the impetus of that wave was towards a world-mind or world-poem.

1882 ({James} Joyce conceived ➜ born)   germinal
1883 (Williams conceived ➜ born)   time area
1885 (Ezra {Pound} conceived ➜ born)   #1
1886 (H.D. conceived—born)
1888 (Eliot conceived—born)   1882–1888
          [which may be taken as a germinal not only to the
              "Imagists" but to the *First World War*?]

Time map #2 1902–1914 "the pre-war Era" in the world-consciousness of this
          period the particular type of poem was germinating of "the

poem incorporating history"), a syncretic world-poem where locality and field are crucial. Time & space.

The Cantos	(begun 1912?)	World War 1
The Waste Land	(peripheral—1921)[8]	
Ulysses	(begun circa 1914)	

Finnegans Wake	(1920–1938)	post-War and Depression

The War Trilogy[9]	(1942–1944)	World War 2
Pisan Cantos	(1945)[10]	
Paterson	(1945–1958)	[now it is clear that a long state of War has set in]
Maximus	(1951?—the first *Origin*)	

But why, how did *Maximus* come into this type series?

Born in 1910, sd. Charles Olson was conceived, born, and nursed; but also initiated into childhood—learned to walk and talk "before the war" the last possible member of a creative family that we now sketch as having its *time* from 1882–1914: and its *type* in the poem that organizes time and space to "include history," where the line is conceived of as "free" and the spirit can move freely in time and space.

[Where, when I include time and space I compose symphonically and by theme. I seem to have no vital impulse for "free" movement.]

But *Maximus* is not only like the world-poem it is also the first of a different type. i.e. Maximus as closely related to *The Distances*.

There is another time area I get—the area 1919–1929 post War, pre-Depression.

O.K. You	1910–1914	"pre-war"
↓	1914–1918	FIRST WORLD WAR
me	1919–1929	the "illusion" of peace and prosperity
Denise Levertov		
Creeley	1930–1940	the disillusion of depression and war-preparation
↓		
	1940–1945	SECOND WORLD WAR

1945–on

the state of war economy with
the idea of world destruction

Creeley is the youngest one could have been to have been a "child" in the 1919–1929 period. Born in 1926 he was conceived, born, nursed, and then learned to walk and talk in this period.

You were the oldest one could have been (a boy of 9 to 10) to have also {been} a child in the period 1919–1929.

A picture of how we *do* have our own tribal initiations and correlating these successive "lives" with phases in the larger commune—how these "lives" have character.

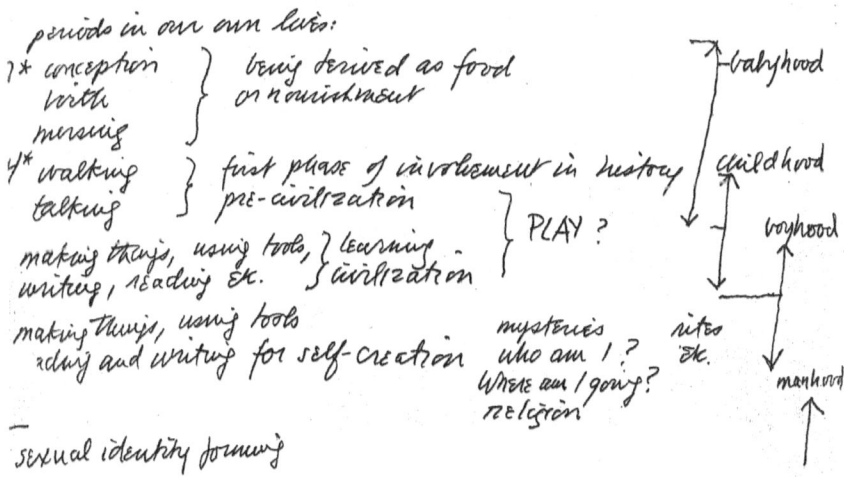

I'm not concernd here with development but with a gauge for reading evidence of what is going on in the human conglomerate and in the individual.

{Federico García} Lorca, for instance, learned to talk when he was four. The eldest I've heard of 'em being nursed,

Yrs etc
Robert
mit love.
Spring times

102

Gloucester, MA

March 11, 1963

My dear Robert:

There is either one or two 'hystorys' which count: that remarkable one, of the Christian theologians, that Christ created history (by, to spell it out) because God did create Adam, and Christ by giving his life away—like Melville misled said—routed life back into victory. Death / lost her sweat—'his' sweat, ever-loving death, calm easeful death.

(I was prompted to say this much after my eye swept your letter—in today—and I will read soon.

The above may have nothing to do with yr letter but only my own thought recently, or at least following from writing you previously that 1-2-3, which gave me a leading sense, of day year and 'age' ((did you notice Pope John's interesting remark abt error how easily it gets dispelled by an 'age' arriving at a later point?[11] I felt he was talking sort of in links of ages of 5 years but that at least that is also true and the best thing about it was that some anti-taxonomy other than Marx (or Hegel's—not to speak of those miserable American personalish-ishes about each their own lives, simply because they have names and faces and can make a living) had entered the public place.

(((The non-holy life/ Miss {Margaret} Avison, whom we will see together in Van's Corner Bar and Eatery this summer is a person who deserves support in her own maidenhood here. She is a very sensitive human being who shows recognitions in the out-epoch area but doesn't guess (beyond Samuel Johnson, and the delicacies of physical actions springing from genuine tenderness—but her tendernesses only known in the constraint of the Scapa Flow[12] of her two parents, now old and living a bungalow life 50 miles north of Toronto, where they have placed themselves, precisely on the snow-line—where the Arctic shows its rigidity formally and stays put like a nailed down table or chair aboard a yacht. She is a real person, and I told Creeley I thought it was one of the 'happiest' aspects of the World Congress of Poets he has arranged, that she should be invited. God knows how there is anything you can say directly which works but there isn't any doubt in my mind that shots ((like, she was reading S. Johnson's Lives of the Poets when I was there last winter) give her 'relief.'

How are you and Jess? I hope as full as your lives make me sense you both well can be. I have lived much of this winter with your own thought flashing on the boards for me like the returns of the pari-mutual. Love, and please write me whenever you are promted to

(I have this damned flu—not the fever one—from the East Wind blowing to over come the West Wind—but the West's own virus; and I've never had it so long or bad, in the vitals; and the new chemical medicines—and doctors—are all made to service the 'manly' types who go to work each day and keep this economy and State in 'health.' They don't relieve a sedentary worker like myself at all—as a matter of fact I don't mind at all except to the stupid business of feeling 'sick.'

The winter here has been delicious not at all stopping up the days and nights and being up to now very well behaved, only doing one thing, and a new thing, going cold severely about six sudden sharp nights—probably our side of that wild weather-front or mountain which has been sitting up out over the Atlantic and choking East-West movement so much Europe has had Siberian weather all winter—almost as though the paleolithic had re-obtained in the Saone.[13] Around here it is so different that there hasn't been any of the usual 'length' of the months; and though I am hot out this March it feels somewhat 'safe' that the calendar has got this 'far.'

May your lives be 'fortunate' (like if I knew Greek I cld be sure why their word blessed (blest, better) seems to be interchangeable with fortune; and I *believe* in their word-corners, they were—WHEN HELLADIC at least and surely THROUGH HESIOD (with no derogation to Aeschylus Sophocles Herodotus and Euripides but otherwise—with almost no exception I can bring in to my mind—misleaders all, especially (again) now for me joining the other two more and more as having split what counts into that wretched ethia[14]

(Hygeia also is a skinny 'disease')

and Scientia: Aristotle. (As fine old W'h {Whitehead} made clear for us—he didn't expose it as sharply as he did the Semitic notion of transcendence—he says in so many words what 'damage' (gamage) A. did "because he did not distinguish between extensive quantity and intensive quantity."

(How Aquinas Aristotle and {Robert} Grosseteste combined to give us the mt. of all mountains in a bungled truth

Well see you Love (the god Eros—"fairest of the
deathless gods"

Charles

{in Olson's hand at top of final page} the Helladic Greeks were fortunately intonal; and the mistakes start with Socrates—or Pindar probably

{in Olson's hand around the final lines and signature, referring to a drawing at left margin} I can't make the flopping hat the way you did down the garden path or gathering flowers while she did

{at left in Olson's hand} Your Omnivorous & loving reader

~

103
Gloucester, MA
ca. March 1963

My dear Dunk: we have got to make that place between the 'University' (you proposed that day we drove back from visiting Wieners when he was in that 'Biddeford' of present social non-Hell) and my suggestion then, that you and I take steps to find wealth to create a Crankcase standing up (with octets or 12 men's work flying off their own piazzas, each maybe wherever they are but a way of living starting at least with money)

I'm probably not going to be able to effect it here simply that my Milliardaire is not a King of Hell but solely a stupid selfish grease-ball;[15] but I did want to lay-out quickly to you the way it falls out today, simply that I believe you also have the sense that somewhere we do have the chance

{Olson draws a slanted line with the words "administrative unit" typed above it}

	And at least here is the
theater	not performance in that dumb
film	sense but *publication*
publishing	
& dogma	(painting music and poetry left wherever it is)
epistemology	(ex-"Science"—and "Learning"
theology	(ex-humanistic study
politics	(ex-politics history govt and that stuff

{signed in the left margin}Charles

~

104

San Francisco, CA
April 26, 1963

dear Charles/

I wrote off to the Yale birds some congratulations on their taking hold of *Maximus*.[16] It comes as a rare hope and maybe dawn does come, crack the shell and start in how to live. As they got me right in seeing it was art for life's sake and not for Arthur's. (Arthur too, King Day Dream, for life's sake).[17] Before setting myself to the typewriter this morning I want this prime bonus of writing to you and that brings you right in here around me. A Gloucester morning—which in that one sample I had I had in sun and fog. Sun this morning, but bird-blue heaven and Pippa is passing[18] his/her (how that W{illiam} C{arlos} W{illiams} always thinking with his anima which done showd his animus—or the other way round, berated me cause he said in The Venice Pome he cldnt tell hises from hers) greetings! When at last there is evidence that this {David} Schaff got Maximus right side up and without fretting over cracking all the nuts on the tree (the scientific method) knows and can testify that the meat is sweet, the good of intelligence. And may even in Yale come to suspect that intelligence is alive at the surface of things. He does quote

> I have this sense,
> that I am one
> with my skin[19]

—but looking that up I see it's in one of the selections published in the thing. The sparks of possible light are encouraging in such a clearly collegiate scene.

And I owe you the copy of my spring song—"The Continent" the which I include—for your "Christ created history. . . . routed life back into victory" along with an article in the *Scientific American* on continental drift and Earth currents set me off.[20] As I found midway in the work and got the lift of.

Along with this news that I got a Guggenheim—it's $4000 for this coming year, which sets Jess and me in gear (clear) with that other $145 a month from my mother's trust that saves us from the toils of where does the rent come from? {Cid} Corman, for once, sees something: these grants, awards etc are not kindly. But seeing that, and in these last couple of years being meself more kindly in relation to Cid (*For In-stance* came thru as real), I'm glad the luck, any strike like this, is not kindly.

What comes to me in your "God did create Adam" is that creature I am in the works of evolution where every "Man" is a cause of god's / and in this hidden; fig leaf and all. And in the second Person; that Christ creates there in His Passion—life.

The time it takes for shifts of continents haunts me, but right now this round-of-the-sun time, the north-south-north swing of earth that brings me back to day (and in Vancouver this summer to long-day) is my patron. And comes kindly.

Will Betty and Charles Peter[21]—who must be seven? eight?—be able to come with you this summer? Jess always has to leave work to travel (and he's in the works of painting these days; I am eager for your seeing) but I think he will be coming to Vancouver. The plans are made anyway for that.[22]

My "H.D." book is coming into its shape now—it gives me my area, a range that must be "unexplored," for there are breakthrus. Country that ain't already litterd with our uses. And I've set a mode where what's wrong will be apparent I've hopes and what's going on will be clear. When it's there the "H" "D" will be initials in the title (as she used that signature in *Hermetic Definitions*—her last long poem).[23] And I will have given boundaries "one / with my skin"[24] to those damnd words "mystic" and "occult" that don't work.

O.K., for celebration, now a little anthology of poems—and if you were here I'd be reading them to you as a concert for the day's sake.[25]

love

Robert

$\sim$

105
Gloucester, MA
ca. May 18, 1963

My dear Dunk

Have had this idea for some time, to get those short pieces (inc "Grammar a Book," which I hope you saw [in *Floating Bear*]) into a very little book with title of 1st piece PROPRIOCEPTION—running from that piece [*Kulchur*], I think, along with "Logography," and probably inc "Theory of Society" (originally in *Yugen*)—and ending with "A Work," that 'Hesiod' is matter (abt a year ago).[26]

Now Wilenz (Totem-Corinth)[27] has suddenly lighted up & want to do it (in hard cover mind you, 1st!) and Leroi {LeRoi Jones} says they also welcome my other idea to ask if you wld want to do the book a pre-face or as long as you want to: it has been such an attractive thought to be there together in print if it at all fitted yr own present plans—and that particular body of things seemed 'fit' to you. Does it at all sound like anything?

Delighted to hear you have that Guggenheim—breaks that whole freeze there up, maybe—or maybe they finally caught on, and *had* to, in your case. But anyway, delightful.

And also very happy to have your letter and the poems

Love to Jess

& will be back soon—

Yrs

Charles

Saturday May 18th
PS/ If you discussed nothing but 2nd person and I responded with Middle Voice

Libet[28] (it pleases
(itself) love

Love Charles

~

106
San Francisco, CA
May 28, 1963

dear Charles,
1)) post August 16th—which I take as the terminus of the UBC summit conference. It's open as follows for you to swing down to San Francisco for a second front and/or a visit without great furor. A) Parkinson has cleard it for a U.C. reading (fee $100); at this point you've to write

Dorothea Jensen
Committee on Arts and Lectures
University of California
Berkeley 4, California

and decline or accept: in the latter case name your date between August 19th and August 30th. (I suggest Friday Aug. 23rd).

B) Marthe Schön (once Marthe Rexroth) will be writing—she wants you and Betty and Charles Peter to stay at their house—it's a big (three floors) place and comfortable—besides, between the 16th and the 30th of August they are going to be away on vacation so you'd have every ease of the house.

2) Hope you can go along with this—and that this gets to you Friday or Saturday. The time is ripe (as it was for Creeley's reading this last fall), and the stay here might go along the line too of your reviving that question of how education outside of institutions. I've no more confidence in millionaires I've met being worth the effort than you have (and I've faild in the past, whenever I wanted any use of them)—but one brought up, the idea is back with me. I'll admit it.

3)) Your asking me to cooperate re. the "Preface" (and LeRoi {Jones} next day with a letter asking me to contribute to the scenes; also {Robin} Blaser) lifts my spirit I'd want the contents: ie which pieces of work already publishd round any unpublishd bits to be included—well, I'll go at what I've got now on hand and be in correspondence in a few days. Right now me mentis is floating away with thots of your visiting (us in locale, scene Duncan-Collins; for all that we'll both be at UBC), and around a glass of beer, and some guy outside planning a board, blue sky—at random.

with love,
Robert

~

107
San Francisco, CA
July 8, 1963

dear Charles,

Just a salute towards Vancouver at the end of this month. I am keeping that "Preface" cooking with 2nd person, something about gists and directives and homage to thee—what a teacher means. I plan to get to Vancouver on the 25th. Jess and I have an apartment reserved thru the rest of the session.

Even if you don't come to S.F. afterwards, we'll have almost a month. Which is the best part of it for me.

love
Robert

~

108
San Francisco, CA
December 20, 1963

dear Charles,

I'd been thinking yesterday "its natural enuf, I've been retrograding for half a year." In the dream last night the woman in the cloche said "Oh yes, Mars has been retrograde since 1926." The impossibility left the number—since 1926, when I was seven? On a slip of paper I found after my mother's death, a chronology drawn up for her astrologer, there was "1926—Robert very nervous"; or was it when I was 26 (19 to 26?). In 1945 I returnd to California, had had a near psychotic episode after three days of my Aunt Fay{e}, and Mother had offerd to provide for me if I would sign papers and go to a sanatorium.[29]

In the dream I had the great joy of seeing you, embracing, having some part of that *tête à tête* we did not have in Vancouver. I have affirmation of my life in you and being able at last to go to you seemd curative. At this last summer you calld for some "homeopathy"—but I couldn't think what homeopathy was. Yet since that session, exposure to {Allen} Ginsberg's and Bob {Creeley}'s various impossibilities, I have been in a like sickness of refusing to work, as if demanding to be able to live without it? Malaise de Guggenheim? Study has continued, and for four months I have been at your work from *Y&X* on, piecing out working materials and again and again trying without getting start—or getting the start—the inner command—and refusing it.

Flying home—and with a continent to cross to get back to my home-body—I was lost in the problem of avoiding the fire—the threat of high-tension wires—I could not gain altitude without passing thru that zone.

•

Late in August or early in September I had what Jung calls a big dream. It presented a trial which, in rank cowardice, I faild, and then instructions which again I faild—I was to relate the happening to you and only now "too late" for obedience, having received absolution in the dream, I come thru with it. I had a gift for you and refused the giving: which now in this time of gift I release.

In the time of refusal the details have been lost—does some telling fragment of the message I was to pass on to you remain? I was surrounded by pillars of silver light—the Mothers of Muses—moon angels, great women (my mothers, my high school teacher Miss {Edna} Keough,[30] and H.D. were among them) teachers who had come to present to me the Kelipah,[31] the waste of creation, and I had an instant of seeing (almost a sight of) scutterring dusty or dirty off-castings in interstices of planes that appeared in space. (The Zohar calls these *shells* or bark; but the things in the dream were dead leaves of the tree. The dream did agree with my studies that shit is of this kind).

I refused to look (and the demand that I look was greater than it had been in the dream of the jewel or crawling thing in the pit). Then my teachers, now very clearly moon angels, were protectresses: so that, magically assured, my refusal of the command was the more abject.

When I woke I knew that I was to relate the dream to you, and pronto, right then. Four months ago Jess had wakend, hearing me cry, and attended with the surety that I must go thru the dream.

Just now Jess has returnd and supplied another passage of the dream he remembers me telling: in a phase following the instructions I had gone thru a doorway of white light into some "past" life, a battlefield where a horse was dying in agony. A dream of Pegasus? But now, in my recalcitrance, I do not remember the significant facts of this.

This last week I have got the "Preface" under way, and that I hope to have in the mail to you in another week. Starting work is the starting of the tide—in its low I seemd so removed from you and yet, in reading, so close. Tomorrow the sun will be at the turn of the south. I take heart in his return. (This is our coldest winter in San Francisco since 1954—Jess and I faced a colder in London 1955).[32]

Now that plans go ahead for my reading in Buffalo I look forward myself to realizing in waking what I realized in dream—to have some time with you. My thought is that I will not leave Buffalo until the 15th (the day before the N.Y. reading April 16th); and that en route returning I might visit again. Will you have room for a house guest come the last of March, for Easter, and the actual resurrection of the sun?

love

Robert

≈

109

Warsaw, NY

January 21, 1964

WESTERN UNION

TELEGRAM

JUST TRIED TO CALL YOU. HAD PROMISED MYSELF THAT I WOULD
REACH YOU THE {S}PLIT SECOND I HAD FINISHED WHAT HAD BEEN
HOLDING ME UP. LOVE TO YOU. WILL WRITE IMMEDIATELY I HOPE.
LET ME HEAR FROM YOU AND A MILLION THANKS FOR YOUR LET-
TER OF DEC 20TH LOVE AND LETS GO.
    CHARLES

∾

110

San Francisco, CA

May 29, 1964

dearest Charles,

Let me give you Friday mornings. Whatever. However. In the course of my
thots and things. Our beginning of summer morning, fog overcast, almost cold.
How my spirit moves about objects of a household, Jess's assemblages of found
things, indoors plants, vases . . . a clutter of instances. Kept things, like kept
promises to living. (As reading can also be keeping a book, that way).

I've sent off to *Matter* an essay from my notebooks last October[33]—a previous
approach to *memory*, to questions of "seeing"—thinking of the tangle I got into
addressing your seminar in poetics. The Havelock book,[34] of course, cleard up
how specifically remembered content and reread content can be distinguisht.
"Recited" and written.

Well, I did get in how at Buffalo I was cornerd on the score of sleight-of-
tongue ling-wistics. Damn it! {Stan} Brakhage has so overdone what otherwise
might have been playful, I wince, embarrasst in the mid-air of writing something like "ling-wistics." Like a whole room of badly made would-be chairs and
tables, might end all home crafts. And does. The arts-and-crafts pottery such a
contempt for the inworking, the responsiblity in making. Who takes thought in
creation that he might say that *it was good.*

And I got in how you calld me on that word "hallucination"; which sent me
searching the word out.

Enclosed work on "Passages," since I last saw you. Correction: Passages are, not
is. A number of passages; not parts of a thing calld passages. Enclosed some
more Passages.[35] 7—I'll type up for you, allowing that it may or may not be there.
As is.

It strikes me that let's say Passages 5, any *thing* can (as in a dream) be an instance of itself, and does not have to do with sequence. So that passage 5 may reoccur again (after say passage 10), and given it was felt to be, created to be Passage 5, would rightly be.

Or, passages might belong to a passage larger than the writer saw at a time. Returning to that quarter of the sky I saw it anew.

In that drop of water given micro-vision I saw. . . . Where the drop-shape was exchanged for a watery-medium of other shapes.

Jess is at work on a series of "copies," most exact, and exacting translations into color and mass of engravings and photographs: experimental apparatus, repro-ductions of demoded paintings (the heretical sensual-phantasy academic paint-ing of the 19th century), and photographs of people and scenes.[36]

Well, right now, with the light clouded over, he is at work on galley proofs for *Roots and Branches*, the which is in process at Scribner's (we are to expect page-proofs in another week or two, and enter our corrections from the galleys on the page proofs—they are going ahead that fast).

There's a possibility the H.D. book may go ahead too with Scribners—as auto-biography or something side-stepping the literary essay issue.

Might you really come West? Once we find a house with guest room I shall be begging, but as it is, tho we have no room, there is ready a guest room at Barbara Joseph's in Berkeley,[37] and a room at Ida Hodes' in San Francisco. You need, I need, anyone needs that ease of it.

love
Robert

∿

111
Wyoming, NY
June 15, 1964

It's crazy: *here* your face is on *Wesleyan's* magazine[38]—) & wait until U SEE *THE REVIEW NIAGARA FRONTIER!*[39] & altogether thank you for your Friday letter [I thought you were going to write to me one every Friday

Love—& to Jess—Charles

∿

112
San Francisco, CA
June 18, 1964

dear Charles,

This THURSDAY is every Friday. Your day. As Jess said, "You promised yrself you wld." And today yr card came. So you are in Wyoming.[40] I hope with a leafy quiet now and again. My own longings going towards house and garden. With the line knocking at the door "to house my longings" or bring them home.

These opening "Passages" I send you herewithin still have a ways to go before I get going what I'd move towards.[41] It may be the whole will be freer if each "Passage" is (as in *Leaves*) titled, not numberd. As in *Maximus* you let numbers play where they will / the sureness that a series or sequence does appear.

PASSAGES OF A THURSDAY
TOWARDS CHARLES'S FRIDAYS

Tuesday we got the page proofs for *Roots & Branches* off to Scribner's. With the book announced for September. And they've taken an option on the H.D. Book, with an agreement that I'll deliver the whole by next Feb. We need tables cleard.

There should he, anyway, a news from me to you today before
tomorrow.

Did I write that I did manage a song and hymn for FUCK YOU'S GOD issue?[42] This week I've been scanning Goodenough's essay on Egyptian fluids and phallics[43]—and find how right I was about that white milk. Where had I come across the hint in my researches before?

You want any chapters from the H.D. book for the Niagara Frontier later?

love,
Robert

∽

113
San Francisco, CA
June 29, 1964

dear Charles/
From the library three days ago Jung's *Memories, Dreams, Reflections* which

has come for reading at a time ripe for it. The 1926 dream in which he is informed that he is "caught in the seventeenth century." "Resignedly I thought, 'Well, that's that'! But what is there to do about it? Now we shall be caught for years." [44] Then the consoling thought came to me: "Someday, years from now, I shall get out again." He came to see the dream as referring to his life-long—"condemned" he calls it—necessity to study alchemy.

In Africa an English squatter tells him: (1925) "You know, mister, this here country is not man's country, it's god's country. So if anything should happen, just sit down and don't worry." Which would mean take it easy, yes, but also mean don't worry about it, but attend.

His marriage in 1926 may have, *must* have, closed in on him, closing him "in the seventeenth century," his "life" having so arrived at an enclosure. Jung seems to believe the *Unconscious* so much a thing in itself that he never reflects upon *correspondences*; so no account of what happens in the dream as it happens in sexual life, or in household life, tho he does see how it happens in *work*. But here he registers "getting out again" in relation to his marriage: "After my wife's death in 1955, I felt an inner obligation to become what I myself am. To put it in the language of the Bollingen house, I suddenly realized that the small central section which crouched so low, so hidden, was myself!" [45] This central section he does not relate to his 1926 dream, but it was added along with the 'paternal' tower in 1927.

The whole chapter "The Tower," or "the language of the Bollingen house" as he calls it wins me completely to him. Here, at last, in the building he is making something—"space for the spaceless kingdom of the world's and the psyche's hinterland" [46] he names it again. A language! A space! Or time for the seventeenth century to get moving in?

With "Passages 8" my own yearning for a house, *the* house (and I got it at the time, the 6th of this month as "a house for my spirit, to house my spirit"—. Something different from home). Where the "Passages 1" proposes a nomadic house. [As surely I remember there your "having a home in movement"—these quotes again just my memory of it in those Proprioception essays, as I've appropriated it]. The architect being the Father having that further reality for me that my father was an architect (as my blood-father listed as "day-laborer" in Oakland City Directories of the 1920s may, I can interpret, have been a building-laborer).

Water was primary for Jung, his first thought in thinking of the place. It's light that comes first for me, the day at the window. And then the rain at the window. The night and the star at the window.

As now, the day at the window is the grey glare of summer fog, a corner by the window at the round kitchen table. A clearing in which to work. This writing to you, Charles, came as an inner imperative, an appointment with you for communication's sake. So that today when I was ready for it, the worrying was gone, as if it were the beastly alternative to my attendance. Goaded, driven, herded by what shepherd, but I feel the sheep dog more, only this direction of work going upon freedom. I have to use you as my communicant and have, I realize, to trust that: the contradicting voice, adversary to the work, argues "Why do you think he is interested in that?" "Oh, friend of my free spirit," today I answer easily, "and wherever I go towards what I have to do I go towards him."

I remember your sense of being caught in this period of having to, committing yourself to "profess" is it that the professor, professional does—and Denise {Levertov} writes: "The fact is I *don't* feel my life as a poet is threatened, *even though* I *worry* so about these publishing-type things I've gotten mixed up in. God knows I didn't seek them out, they came at me. I could have said no, it's true: but I have a compulsion to meet the challenges. *For every such thing I've turned down, in the last 2 years, 2 others have sprung up—like dragon's teeth.* . . . At the same time I feel, here & now, creative and alive, not drained by extraneous concerns. The only trouble is, one can't just say 'Well, if at any time it gets to be too much, I will just drop it—because one involves the hopes of so many others more & more as one goes on: like the *Nation*; I can't quit suddenly, ever, but must if I decide to quit) plan months & months ahead so as to see into print all accepted poems first." [47]

And the same week (June 24) Bob {Creeley} writes: "In one sense I seem again to be putting various jobs in front of me, rather than tackle those I clearly have now. . . ." Where I have balked, avoided, worryd, this inner commitment {to} Charles's Friday letter (this "Friday" being a Monday). "Your" tune does not arrive on such a "Friday" schedule; there are times in which writing-to-you starts in my soul, a voice dictating in my thought, and I've let it go, disobeyed. The first command I have circumvented—*was* to write on Fridays. Now I would follow what obedience I can and these two imperatives come to the one proposed.

That opening chapter of the *Analects* {by Confucius} returns to mind. Where the two components of a house: 1 the effort,[48] the study

<table>
<tr><td></td><td>the wings exercised
learning to fly</td><td>gathering in one
co-ordination</td></tr>
<tr><td>the study</td><td></td><td></td></tr>
</table>

which I get from {James} Legge: (carrying a burden)
the rapid and repeated
effort of the wings of a
bird . . .

and 2. friends: "properly *fellow students*";
        Legge notes "but, generally, individuals of the same class. . . .
        like minded."
the

guest   coming from distant quarters!

room

From my distant quarters I would come to you anyway, Charles, and in this same communication exercise wings in the flight. As somehow, along with the H.D. book I have committed myself to complete (the building of a house), I am abroad in another poetry—the whole open proposition of these passages. The title "Passages" will certainly be the next book. And these passages now numbered as if in a sequence I may title individually, to lift them as free as I can from the idea of consequence, the consecutive, that numbering gives.

The task Denise has taken is that she is *the* [not *a*] editor of a new venture to publish poetry at Norton (whose only previous poet, I think, is {Rainer Maria} Rilke). Four books a year, and the possibility of (responsibility of) getting young poets into regular publishing.

Creeley's big one now is the proposed *Reader* of your work at New Directions. I've already got a first letter to him in response to his query—urging "La Preface" from *Y & X* (for the definition there of open parentheses), "The K" (for the coordination there of life-time, inheritance, and the full circle/tide); and the beginnings of mapping out my own trek thru your works, as preparatory to that Preface I was some six months at it reading.

love

Robert

~

114
San Francisco, CA
July 3, 1964

dear Charles,

These two Passages, 12 and 13,[49] came on yesterday, and kept me working straight thru, in a rushet of the poem (tho the two configurations or ideograms— one, the components of a childhood scene, building a harbor at a stream for leaf boats; the other a quaternary that kept insisting later that night—came the day before). Very much meant for you, and as that Orphic theogony started playing into my hands, lifting me in its wind-rush (and what mistrust too we have in that *wind*, that can be our own body's gasses, or a puff of vanity: and the Wind-Child a misconception).

Here, just, your letter has found its time on a Friday. I'm battling a perversity in myself, a wicked-step-brother-me always ready to take over, against the Work: and the other process becomes more demanding. What is it so welcome that one sees in lights and shadows in the depth of water? The flickering activity in the medium, the stream a poem can be, fascinates. And as I begin to have to do with house—and in my own wish, with thoughts of a house—Bob {Creeley} writes of building in Placitas "the foundation and floor of the large hall, and then a much larger room that swings out to the road with round walls in part" aliterating and riming. . . .[50]

Give my high regards and best to LeRoi {Jones} and {Robert} Kelly, and {Edward} Dorn whom I've never met—

love,
Robert

∼

115
Gloucester, MA
August 18, 1964

My dear Dunk—just so you know your letters *were* appreciated; and that that last enclosure—the "Passages 12"—certainly called for the quickest rejoinder. It is so beautiful.

Please, if you can or will write do; & accept my miserable apologies. All better almost that I write to you.

Yrs with love
Charles

~

116
San Francisco, CA
January 22, 1965

dear Charles,

Have you left Buffalo? Postmark Gloucester and applying for grants wld seem so. I'm sending this to Fort Square address. I await inquiries from money-givers and will write as impressively as I can to same. You are the hot issue still with the growing number of conservative (which means thems as wants to appreciate with no digging) readers who are beginning to allow for me or Bob {Creeley} or Denise {Levertov}. The ones as kant hear the sound of words and the way they move in anything but a w-a-l-t-z or dithyrambic canter; the ones who cant cope with whatever content that ain't poetic. . . . We (the above now beginning to be admitted to exist) all have sufficient reference to poems previously seen in anthologies (said author including enuf roses, lilies of the field, lilacs and rhododendrons to be recognized as gardens and not ecologies)—to be allowd. Anyways, I've heard enuf and read too much of such literary palaver that I hope to cut thru some of it and maybe direct some Santa Claus's eye to your virtues without his being scared of not knowing what's going on.

What about Niagara Frontier {Review}??? Will you still keep a hand in there?

This has been a good year for poems—with the "Passages" series in motion; and right now I'm behind the eight ball on the H.D. (promised for next month— I've askt for an extension), just crawld up out of a November-December-January hole which wld have been O.K., lying around in a funk reading day in day out with it raining out and dark in; except I had the specter of work undone.

Your essays must be coming out one of these days which is a happy thought; and in Berkeley yesterday I saw yr. Oyez broadsheet which they haven't sent me yet.[51]

We heard from David Tudor that M. C. {Richards} has been having a hard year, losing a lover and then, after a series of tests finding that she has a uterine cancer. (The more tricky since her prose is so uterine).

Which does remind me to tell you that Jess and I are both in good health. He is to be in a Museum of Modern Art Show of 14 American collagists* this summer, and he's painting a series of some eighteen "copies" or "translations" from photographs and line-cuts into color and mass—of which he has completed five and at work on four.

→Richard Baker at U.C. Extension is trying to plan a Poetry session either this coming summer or next Fall. I had lunch with him yesterday, to learn to my dismay that they don't have the kind of money Vancouver had. I explained to him that U.B.C. offerd $1000 for you, Bob, and Allen {Ginsberg} teaching the course and then $300 for me, Denise, {Margaret} Avison reading—with traveling expenses paid. At this point his prospect is $200 for a reading, plus all expenses travel and room and board. He would like to have you, me and Bob—I urged LeRoi {Jones} and (to break the *New American Poetry* set) Jackson MacLow's "collage" poems I heard on a tape at Yale.[52] All this is most embryonic. But cld it be used to get you out here. Vancouver leaves data of uses and misuses.

love

Robert

{Duncan's asterisk} *including his illustrations for Joe Dunn's *Dream House*

～

117
San Francisco, CA
February 19, 1965

dear Charles/ Passages 21, "The Multiversity" enclosed. After you've per-used which, lend it to the Wahs[53] and John {Clarke} to read.

A form letter received this morning informed me that Maryanne Raphael is planning "an encyclopedic anthology" of poetry, and listed one "Robert Duncan" among poets to be represented.[54] This is just to tell you the listing was unauthorized and has now been protested.

I don't want to get a rigid rule to cover when and when not I will participate in an anthology. In general; if the editor is a poet whose view of poetry interests me (i.e. so that an anthology would have meaning as a statement of the range of that view), I will go along with it. Where the inclusion or exclusion of my work would be a definite part not of said poet's *taste* but of his statement. [I rejected {Robert} Kelly's anthology, because Paris Leary's coediting has garbled any such statement,[55] and Kelly had the idea of broadening the view to cover all kinds; lumping together poets regardless of ecology].

I've taken a part-time job at S.F. State—one class a week, two hours on Tues— advanced Poetry writing—/and Scribner's has extended my time on The H.D. Book still not completed. Our weather has been clear now for over a week, and my year looks up. (As came "Benefit" or "Benefice?").[56]

love
Robert

~

118
Gloucester, MA
March 29, 1966?

The sign of *the* Time: ∑

My dear Dunk:

I wrote you, and Jess, long and lovely letters last night but what is more as the snows of yester year than yesterday's news?

So instead without ado I greet you, & ask you to believe I said *all*—&

Will you my love admiration with you, & Jess, wld be sure to take care of you—& believe me Zeus P'romezeus plus

plus

per pee

O.

PS.
But the men *were* chopping ice off the Captain (on the foredeck) as she passed by, all while, out my bedroom window. So it was (cold out there also. In other words All's well on the Atlantic side. How's Pacific-Side?

→To greet you with 17 degrees of *spring* here—silly spring. And a ship just came in flying ICE like Theseus' wrong-flag (from St John's New Foundland.

~

119
Gloucester, MA
May 22, 1966

My dear Dunk, I just now starting to shave after writing a letter of some moment to myself to Robert in Como[57] thought how much I do now write & believe in it like an old woman so *please* let me remove & assign to the right person that grandmother thing must have seemed to impose itself on you.

In any case love & respect & all the best in the world for yourself and your life,

Charles at
>   28 Fort Square—his front room too finally May
>   by now
>   God help me—1966

⁓

120
Gloucester, MA
May 22, 1966

Letter

#1

By the way {Stan} Brakhage was here and (in another communication) reminded me of yr apercu that angels no more than humans like to give what is asked. So please (as of enclosed) feel entirely—free.

>   Love,
>   O

⁓

121
San Francisco, CA
September 15, 1966

dear Charles,

Enclosed two recent "Passages" (27 & 28) with a #29 already crowding in on me with half-messages and false leads I so far am holding out against. But what *fits* or is having a fit to convince me it fits, is a concert of how ridiculous my own little Cao-daïst temple of mixt masters is; the guy—an apologist for Johnson policy in Viet-Nam—whom I first read on the Cao-Daï finding them so self-evidently contemptible he did not load on further attitude of his own.[58] The tenacity of a papier-mâché be-Jesus to hold (belong to or fit) its locality (authentic) of the universe. A cozy sentiment to last, say, from Dickens to me. More vivid in lasting, the "plot" demanding that deceits and hypocrisies be shown up for what they are.

Things are going fine for Jess and me. He's deep at work in his series of "translation" paintings, which involves various excursions into accompanying studys.

Particularly towards the long plannd, some two or three years ahead at least, painting {Albrecht} Dürer's *Melencolia*. And I have still pending to do my introduction to Vaughan.[59]

How beautiful your acclaim of me (poet) sent to Oyez is! The "Orphic" touches my deepest spirit.[60]

And the N.E.T. piece brought your very presence and prophecy into our room. "We need only Heaven and Earth" the first given . . .[61]

love

Robert

∾

122

Berlin, Germany

December 30, 1966

My Dearest Robert:[62] This is to greet you & Jess with the Newest Year.—I am shocked that I have not yet sent you your own inscribed copy of "West" [of which you are as even at least with Crazy Horse, & Red Cloud the heroes, of my poem.[63] And it is absurd that still my copies to you & my daughter {Kate} (hers, was hand selected by herself, & is 'purple' on Barry Hall's superb "screen" of Red Cloud in a mad rotogravure section quite separate, skillfully, [B.H.] from the poem(s).[64]

Please don't overmind. Other than the purple copy [which is my own favorite, too, and along, for reading from, so still not Kate's] the five I have are in Lady Grady's house,[65] Mount Street, London where I hope they are safe & from which I can recover them. (The problem is, I have had to 'rest' here. And very happily, actually. I had a 'turn' like they used to *say*, 10 days ago and a cardiogram led Herr Doktor Otto Mertens to conclude my heart needed to be fed, for the rest of my life! That was *his* words: you must feed your heart, Mr. Olson! Wow. Truth is the month & I, the "Physician" [who once sd to you, Mr. Duncan, I have homeopathy, to offer you!

Well dearest friend, life's long path has uneven Sioux hills after 50—& as you'll well know, being Capricorns too, I was 56 God save the figures 3 days ago. My dear heart hasn't had enough loving ever since that prized & precious Christmas card from you both [made I assume of that wonderful artist of all our childhoods—neither of you probably remember the lilac the card was set on, or it—Maxfield Parrish, possibly, either. But it was Christmas, 1963–4, & I was so happy I keep it where it sat [if I lived there still, & you had stayed there] on a delightful bed-side table at Wyoming {in New York}.

So time also has its bumps, horribly, & unhappily, and I have never recovered from the last one, alas. Perhaps change—& being this near the East [as in fact Renate Gerhardt tells me the Berliners themselves speak of Berlin as being the corner of East—[66]

I had mentioned my sense, the taxicab driver looked like Radoslovich, my Yugoslav brother-in-law

Lucy della Picola or something,[67] guide near the Italian frontier on the RR {railroad} Ljubljana to Trieste

—I am only *hoping* now that I *do* have *some* return of my own medicine (as well as 'Theirs') and propose, possibly, to go for the East (certainly South a little, at least to see some of those green things my own *mind* has fed on; Linear A,[68] say and possibly a church by a lake in say Armenia something like that little stupid things which probably wld take traveling I'll not relish enough—at present I am now in this room here three to four weeks. [I am advised to hole up another fortnight]

In any case blessings on your own valued life & like we were Indian chiefs, [I learn they called the "older" men but they do mean the boss chiefs! the Big Bellies, at least it was Hunkpatilas talk,[69] to call them that I learn]. I send across from the good air of Berlin my love to you & hope myself that the Moon of Popping Trees will favor you more than

Ever,

Charles

Friday December 30th [next to the last day of 1966]

~

123
San Francisco, CA
January 7, 1967

dear Charles,

Your Xmas card 1966-7 is still sitting on the buffet where I had written "c/o Ed Dorn" and then been unsure you wld still be there. Now with this letter it goes off to you. In later copying, I changed "the human store of Kingship, Magic and Wisdom" to "the human *story* of";[70] for reading Bultmann's *Theology of the*

New Testament, especially ripening as he gets to Paul, I am the more aware that it is the "story" (just what was sent the new theology demythologizing) that I most mine, go back to, search out. And it's the truth in the story that draws me.

And I am hungrily looking forward to your 'West' saga of; I wrote to {Tom} Raworth and he is sending in all events a regular copy. "The West ain't seen *West*" I wrote him. Which was true. And I had sunk into an inertia, as if it wld be out of order to order it just when, because, or whatever I most wanted it.

So now there is the added joy to know there is a personal copy from you to me sitting there at Lady {Panna} Grady's waiting its Day-dee. (Sorry, that was irresistible. Which great added joy already is hearing from you, for all of my sense of how I have myself withheld from you the fund of my love for you, Charles, which love is one of those facts that shore up my sanity, seligkeit,[71] in this world; and I am that Indian Older Man, Big Belly, type I would keep just that inscribed round stone hidden in its Maori box on my desk.

Well, here I am today forty-eight and the sun has decided to shine bright for it all. And a hero of Olson's *West*; as you in the dream were a worker of the East. Along with me. And once it was clear it wasn't Einstein or grandaddy Freud and you were the Doktor, as I remember it you and I were equally having to work (and not having more than the *need* to go by) the shaman's task to release those springs. And they can be too the springs of my own heart, and I will have always the joy that you are with me "to feed the heart."

_____

I've received a National Foundation for Arts and Humanities (in the time of this national administration of fharts and inhumanities) grant for $10,000. Which is twice as much money as I've ever had come my way before. It is coming just at the time Jess and I are buying a house—a huge expansion of "our" space (in which any *time* expands). As if a year too now has three floors, twelve rooms and a basement with a garden and workshed out back. It will mean guest room and bath, where "room" really is room for, some area that can be a gift.

And my first poems volume is just out with Oyez. The hardback edition due the 10th {Robert} Hawley[72] writes me—

Love Robert

∾

124
San Francisco, CA
January 8 and 17, 1968

dear Charles,

The Mayans of the Chilam Balam have come into "Passages" as,[73] I take it, some identification of who *we* are: at once children of the book we write and children of the land we love (your Mayan outrage in Berkeley that in Gloucester they began to cash in on the land;[74] as the American thing is to cash in on the book—to seize the opportunity, Placer mine the vein of the sentence;[75] for *vein* read rubble. In the first "Passages" that came to me the people of the poem were Scythians.

Once Indians have come into it I see I am getting into your 'West'—where for Blaser's Mountain Meadow Massacre,[76] for me there is my great grandmother's friendship with Captain Jack (whose necklace is still in the inheritance of my ancient Aunt Fay{e}) which story I will have to get clear—as they remember it—and as whatever history has it. All yours, as one would write also in signing, truly. And in stages like this the closeness, Charles, so the inspiration of your poetry (how readily I get instruction from your example) comes, as always, with the happiness of being *with* your mind and spirit; fearfully too for just here, where we map what could be taken as the same territories I can feel (anticipate) as I project the heresy of my views.

The Modocs will have to come into it.[77]

. . . . . .

Just having completed my forty-ninth year, I am one day six hours out of my fifth decade—My family cult would measure by sevens, not tens—where the completion of seven sevens (seven growings out of oneself). I realize that our whole civilization (with them Greek gods opting for eternal youth) *has unprepared us for getting at what is going on*—at the series of body initiations. As I have for the past two years or more been having to *learn* a new body—how *it* wants to move,[78] how *it measures its day and night*. Old appetites, habitual uses, forced out of line.

And in counterpoint to the series of bodies. Taking sevens 54–60, 61–68—the continuity of life work, claims staked for complex patterning, i.e. keeping the world alive (alive to the world).[79]

I think of you here too, for the trials of your fifth decade, eighth body, (and I think too of the trials H.D. Pound, Williams went thru in that passage) give forewarnings in my own life.

In January of last year we found and bought a house that promised to provide and has the life-space we've needed for some time. Not only the ampleness of such room (three floors, above a full basement), but the beauty of it, fitting to our uses. With that 10,000 from the National Foundation and a mortgage from Barbara Joseph, we've made it thru this first year—that has involved another five thousand above our initial downpayment. We are still much concerned with the project of the household. Right at the present moment Jess is painting parts of the front stairs to the door, as Ivan Rainer (a craftsmanly carpenter from the old anarchist days of the 1945–1948 meetings) is completing his proud revival of the former set that had been in ruin from neglect and rot. The happy sound of hammering punctuates my thought.

Of the whole lot of us poets, I seem to be the only throwback to the nineteenth century middle class householder. I can find myself in Charles Dickens. At least, our age challenges the vices of such a scene. Your affectionate Duncan a trot-moc in *West*, fringed frontiers man outfit and all, who must also, since it came to you to specify "not Peter Rabbit"—be Peter Rabbit: is at least first cousin to our own Duncan (when I am also affectionate towards myself) setting up household in the "West"—as that great-grandmother set up household out of the wagon in the Modoc territory of Oregon country in 1864; or my grandmother as a young girl of sixteen in 1880 in Alturas. [But I see that Rabbit house under the tree roots, to which the disobediently adventuresome—(and me too led on by promise of food) Peter Robert must happily be at his retreat] . . .

January 17

A letter from Bob {Creeley} includes that "Charles was asking for you, i.e. how things were, when we saw him in Boston about a month ago"[80] and gets me back to this letter that does, I hope, give some of the "how things were." I'll to me typewriter and type up Passages 31 and 32 to date which will give you more specifics on how that goes.

We all much need the new book of *Maximus* poems (difficult how a title can give boundaries and even bind an open composition: yr Preface to 'West' "lets the Mind Loose").[81]—Nowadays I meet more and more young men who know much more about the Maximus to date than I do. Not more than I know about where I have dug. But they go at the job of collecting it all together from scatterd publications.

Time—the calendar and the divisions of the play; the continent; and the cast the persons of the drama
set into movement, having to get a move on by the
challenge of the actual time of day, place and inhabitants
[as once I wrote you "near/far" and shld have meant "dear" with the meaning of cost there]

We still have, a story to tell—and in that the root intuition or *feel* of what happens when who comes into that story, of the directions (directives) in the where of that story in this *myth* makers over against psychoanalysts of stories, reciters of stories, reporters of stories so that:

I remain your comrade in arms (but these arms are the "chants of battles" Whitman declared for in *Leaves* of 1871:

 ... *war, and a longer and greater one than any*) the force of that story in what is happening,

in this my love, Charles—

Robert

⁓

125
Gloucester, MA
January 19, 1968

My dear Robert—

It is *remarkable*, how much my soul correlates to such temporal matters as your mind & thought both supply me with [as here, in your delicious welcome letter (of your 1st house of 50th year) of 7's [it is like that letter I wrote you once years ago & boldly, out of the blue, sd something like 1224, I have yet no reason to change that sense, by sitting down & writing to you I established a time-in-the-world. I am still finding enough to do to find out what it is—and this *beautiful* thing you place in my hands, of the error of eternal youth so marks my soul in my own present striving to be able to succeed in living, I hasten to acknowledge it—before even continuing to read your letter.—It is remarkable, in that sense that the 'clash' of our souls [I was thinking of that musical instrument] on this matter of time: again I think of your own apercu of 1904 I think it was—or 1903 (1907) [what in fact you *probably* raised *The Maiden* matter on.[82] But I got from a lecture or piece of writing by you on the 20th Century writing—Miss {Gertrude} Stein as a chronological Fox.[83]

I *usually* think of ourselves (or write of you, as in *West*,) with a great psychic aura and yet when it comes right down on the track it isn't the substantive experience (alone at least) it is also this wild crazy time-thing I almost must dry-up about without such sudden in-ways or out breaks (to you) of this pattern of time. I swear we share in some fashion uniquely. (It is like when I used to do the Tarot cards—*not the same at all* I only mean the *mathematics* that I am speaking of in the extraordinarily *new* thing to me, your life by sevens. Wow it's snake-body skin-shedding truth! And of course what *frees* me like in fact 1st reading or coming on to Cabeza de Vaca,[84] is the region abt the heart: there certainly is love [in time] which is mathematical—fore-sight whatever a whole series of qualities we cld spell out, I only [again here] want to specify rather the Mysterium of/that it is yourself whose soul causes my own to awaken & spit, practically, the same "truths" of when a fire-crackers.

A squealing or screaming kitchen-maid the Germans have a fantastic 'solute' I fired myself a year ago New Years Eve at & from Renate Gerhardt's apartment right near the {Berlin} Wall! Screaming kitchen-maid was the translation of this wonderful fire-works.

And love to you, & excuse please this *scribble* to get back to you as soon as (ought practically thanks, both for writing & so far already for your grand formula of—living life's out living on-living itself

Charles   (Friday January

19th [1968]

And to Jess—& will he be to (I hope directly

And GREETINGS OF COURSE HAVE BEEN 7 X 7—And ON ON OUR God help us!

~

126

Gloucester, MA

January 23, 1968

My dear Duncan, It is like the hoop and the circle, I must know nothing when I am not in touch with you (! Isn't it incroyable to be so slow & have known this powerful {"affect" is crossed out} consciousness?

Love

O

PS (further things, on same

PS 2 Ya might even, make me a *poet* again, it is so beautiful to read the "Passages" you have sent me, I am ready now (too, in the midst of them.

Charles

PS 3 Oh God yes. I had myself only two weeks ago read again those words of Chilam Balam! Isn't that madness? Wow.

My God—PS 4: *horloge*—of *COURSE! Now And I Hands on the LOCK'S* Face
FACE!!!!

{on the front of envelope at top left corner}
Hail your lines,   You do find yourself learning to
believing everything Isn't so
beautiful?   Charles Olson
              28 Fort Square Gloucester
              Massachusetts

∾

127
San Francisco, CA
March 7, 1968 {1966?}

dear Charles,

Thanking you for the letters that were and are. Gnosis or news. And this just
to imagine a letter from me to you arriving in Gloucester whatever or however. I
am marking that kind of time that creeps in racing, me contending with writing
I mean to do or have to do against the just writing—and hung up too on the
hooks of making out my damnd income tax statement. Yet Pacific Side has, I am
sure, its all's well as yet unclaimed by me.

Intermittently studying towards a Preface for Vaughan's *Alchemical Works*[85]—
and as a picture of the chemical operations begins to be gatherd, I think I will
have an illumination or two of the spiritual experience and the fiction of spirit
involved. Jess won't allow a chemical laboratory in the basement—where he
would see me in my first curiosities releasing deadly fumes or catastrophic
explosions. . . .

And numbers are still on my mind, the nature of and the five digits. (And
Creeley's new "number" poems, informed by the count.[86]

love,
Robert

∾

128
Gloucester, MA
April 8, 1968 {1966?}

My dear Robert You make me sound like your grandmother but I should care it is such a pleasure to read what you've got to say anyway. Your news of your doing Vaughan's Alchemical Works, which I know nothing of, sounds so attractive and so well within your own swell swell I am engaged—that fiction of the spirit you so say.

Hope all continues anything you wish & this is thoroughly to bait you more to write me when you can. I miss your spirit in my life, and got part of it reading your fair piece (on Dante[87]—half-way through, so far [had *only* 'cause the night I read it something stopped me part way and I've got it right beside me now.

Also, don't know a thing of these new Creeleys you do mention. Wow, I *must* catch up!

My best to Jess & do old friend keep up that Friday promise if you might—

Love & all angels
on your side, yours
Yours

∾

129
San Francisco, CA
December 1968

a new leaf to turn over for 1969.[88] The calendar from Jess's translation-illustrations of {Christian} Morgenstern's Galgenlieder.

This time of year I think of you frozen in the Ice Age and would send you long distance another log for the fire, from me in the Astral Realm post 1885 to you-all in the Pleistocene pre 1975. As I get your drift (amidst your heavings out and heavings-ho of what seems always to be in your way), you are working to break away the wrappings of warm-weather culture (i.e. his humanity) and restore man to his species? Or is it to awake to the roots our humanity has in the species? The pamphlet *does* stir up queries.

I'm looking forward to the Maximus new installments.

Robert

~

130
San Francisco, CA
December 18, 1969

dear Charles,   It was a great disappointment to miss seeing you which was a
happy expectation for me as far as the Austin congregation went.[89] Well, {Louis}
Zuk{ofsky} was in fine, even amazing form, and Bob {Creeley} did beautifully.
The conference was one of the very best. And meeting Octavio Paz[90] was for me
the beginning I hope of a friendship.

This has been a lean year for me as far as poems go. Not that I don't feel the
things stir in me, urging and urging. But I've also got a store of refusal. And I
think I see what it (the refusal) wants. Towards which, a transition of some kind,
but also what thinking of the lives of poets I have seen as a doldrums of the
fifties, I have begun keeping dreams, fragments if that be all, and going into my
private counsels. I have the idea that I might bring myself to the discipline of the
dream as actual [where Norman O Brown, who in yesterday morning's dream
was howling and trying to get me to admit that conscience was the matter of
a knife and a sheep and what every man says and does with that and knowing
that and howling with it, is Normal O Brown]. So much so that seeing the late
afternoon papers yesterday about a girl's coat MISSING GIRL'S COAT found in
Santa Cruz, I thot that's what he was telling me about!

The actual and literal dream, and whatever analyses—the dream's analyses.

This not with the sense that the pump will be primed, or the primal pumpt—
but with the sense that biologically I might tune in on the function of this entering into the body of old age. I am convinced it is a counterpart of adolescent
years, the embodying of something: what we call *age*. Surely how much now science wants now to *prevent* aging, after blowing up the works the leading human-
istic wish, the dread of ages shld. give a warning of how important a stage of
being it is we are persuaded to avoid.

I had begun several months ago to work on translations (it was the only way
to read the stuff, {J. B.} Leishman's "translations" don't translatio anything—he
aims at "style" and throws structure and content away with contempt) of Rilke's
Neue Gedichte, getting thru the first seven that week or so of going at it. This
period is Rilke's push to take the form of the poem to be a hive into which the
content is stored (well, at least not as honey alone, but content as *wax*). I work
against my distrust and distastes for the presumptions but in the faith that even
in this perversity Rilke is too primal a {poet} to be only "winning" thru the

struggle. Reading old notebooks, preparing them for deposit at U.C., I realized that it had been Rilke's inspiration and direct instruction for the *Duino Elegies* which had implanted the commandment "not to rewrite." The imperative could only have come on that strong with a man who had gone into some depth of forcing conventional (covenant) form to its crisis.

Charles, one of the questions I would have had had you been in Austin would have been to pin down the rumors that the new Maximus volume with its blank pages frequently—which *could* be taken as spawnings or tunings—and since the form is always *present*, happening, as I get it, in that presence—the lapse is not a defect *from* form or meaning.

But, if you would—(and I know very well indeed how for me it needs the right moment now to get a letter going) could you tell me if there is a defect in the edition: i.e., what blank pages shld occur? I'll write off to the publishers anyway on this, Charles, but right now I *am* writing to you. And it's been months and I've not got a letter off to Barry Hall. . . .

If'n I didn't write hot off that first week when I got my Maximus from *The Tenth Muse*,[91] and it won't hurt to write from rereadings later, it is a beautiful music for these here ears, and a music that is thruout, a melody of idears (as vision we hear must be).

A recent rear-view of *Bending the Bow* seeks to wield as a club over me pretentious head the admonitions of your "*Against Wisdom as Such*" with the puzzling assumption that I could use, abuse and present as a ruse the same without heeding them.[92]

Our best wishes for this coming year. Your health and work is still very much of what a new "year" is for us.

love Robert

Guggenheim Letters

Charles Olson on Robert Duncan,
Robert Duncan on Charles Olson

January 30, 1957

(Except for Robert Creeley) there is not another writer I would sooner—if I were a member of the Selection Committee—grant a Guggenheim to, than Robert Duncan. In fact, he is today *the* most active one of all, in the field of original creation, in verse, critique and playwrighting. (It is a very exciting moment, both in creation and in the life of this man, who has, in his forty years, moved conceivably more than anyone, he was so much at 16, and since 1948–9, has done three or four such distinct advances—in poem play and conception—to be almost if not the front-runner of them (of us) all.

I'll spoil his chances with you, if I go on like this. It is the difficulty, with any presentation of Duncan's claim on your attention or for that matter (so far as I am aware, though, the recent awards to him by *Poetry* magazine begin to suggest that Duncan's achievement is now beginning to get seen for what it is.

For example: his "Venice Poem," written 1948–50, that long ago. To this day not one poet (including such modern masters of the art as Marianne Moore, Wm Carlos Wms and Ezra Pound—Mr Eliot excepted, who actually has done a "long poem," but it is as {John} Dryden might have, it is at heart a "dramatic" achievement, "Ash Wednesday" or "The Waste Land") none has done a poem of one 33 page length sustained in subjectivity and sensibility as Duncan did in the "Venice Poem." In itself it is an accomplishment like unto (in our tradition) only Chaucer however different Duncan's ends and successes are from Chaucer's. (You see what I mean, how one will damn him, because to praise Duncan involves one only in what must seem, to one outside the practice, too large comparisons. They aren't actually. He is a worker of prime intent and powers. He goes for the center—or the fence, if you like. He is what one of my peers has called a "serious man," of which there are never many—my peer only could count three, in a lifetime; Duncan is one of mine: I can think of another.

Yet I must use these measures on him, if you will try to go with me. For it is not praise I am indulging. It is my own experience of his work. I first saw a poem by a man named Duncan in the magazine *Circle* from Berkeley in 1946. It was on Milton, and I know; now its title was "The Years as Catches." I mention it only to make sure how work such as his does catch another who writes. There this poem was—and I knew, the moment I read it, that here was one man who was at his job and after the thing we would all wish to be able to do. It is not today one of the poems of Duncan's work one would say single out—as one does "The Venice Poem." But that's the point: his work, across the board, is alive with the dedication to the job, no matter what it comes out. (There is, with few exceptions—and they are mostly now men in their twenties, men who will be applying for Guggenheims, I imagine, in the years ahead—I can think of five right now even in addition to Mr {Michael} Rumaker, who has applied this year—Duncan, at 40, stands alone as such a prime worker.

All right. Let me try to single out the things he has done since "The Venice Poem" which make him so much our lessoner. In his Statement of Plans, he points out one himself: the discovery of how to make a book of poems compose itself as a poem does. In other words, by a law of form to cause poems themselves to get written. This is much more than a mere invention, or device, to pump the work out. It is as powerful an imaginative advance as "The Venice Poem." (The fascinating thing about Duncan is, that, where the rest of us are ready in mainstreams of advance from the American masters of the first half of the century, say—the serial, or the "epic" poem, for example; or the non-subjective lyric, say (mostly from Wm Carlos Wms)—Duncan is pressing a front forward which is distinct from any of these inheritances. (One can see its issue, by the way, in what he also lists as a purpose of a Guggenheim year—his Medea play; which I want to come to.) Here I wish only to support him in his indicating to you that his volume of poems, *The Opening of the Field*, is as original an idea of the creative at this point of time as his "Venice Poem" was eight or nine years ago (noticed then, so far as I am aware, by no one of us, though I believe Hilda Doolittle did sense it, at the time).

Let me grab on then by what excites me personally the most of Duncan's work in the last four years. I mean his plays. I suppose some time must elapse before it will tell, but I have seen both his *Faust Foutu* and his first *Medea* produced—and he is already demonstrably a playwright of the same mysterious power as Ben

Jonson. The thing reads as tho it were a "literary" achievement, but it plays like silk and reality—most beautiful incisive dramaturgy. Not at all dramatic, in the more usual sense; no problems like contemporary theater. But wild and full and dense and clear, like happening. It is the most.

So I fear I have hurt him altogether with you with superlatives. Forgive me, both you and him. I don't know how to stop long enough to put it another way. Or I could. But it is so much one of the pleasures of Duncan's existence, like he says in his wonderful "Notebooks," to go free of any posse—as he felt he had, of the critical posse: to be a man in his own front room. He very much is. It would keep us all supplied to have him, under Guggenheim at full time work!
19/20 February 1960

~

TO THE JOHN SIMON GUGGENHEIM MEMORIAL FOUNDATION

In 1925 Ezra Pound wrote to Simon Guggenheim congratulating him on the terms in which his Memorial Foundation was announced and suggesting T. S. Eliot and Marianne Moore as candidates for fellowships: "I have in my eye and have had for some time, flagrant cases of men of unusual ability hampered, infamously hamperd, by financial stress, while hundreds of mediocrities swallowed up America's heavy endowments. In the case of T. S. Eliot it may be too late to intervene. I don't know that the man's mind has been killed; he is fairly tough; but for ten years he has been entirely held off from research (that after full academic equipment and post grad. work). And his literary production has been reduced to a minimum, and that not of his best potentiality, from fatigue. . . . I take it Marianne Moore of New York is another case where subsidy would be repaid."

"Unusual ability," "financial stress," and a work of the order that demands specialized research and conditions: these three factors of Charles Olson's situation give a certain urgency to my report to you. In your request you specify a CONFIDENTIAL REPORT ON CANDIDATE FOR FELLOWSHIP—but confidence rests upon a relation that is mutual. You see, Mr. Anonymous or Mrs. Hidden "Confidential" Adviser or Miss Secret Arbiter (for I am aware that the Foundation is an institution and cannot read, that I must be writing to a person or particular persons somewhere), when I bear witness here I have a responsibility in signing my name that we do not share. When I write I write for my true readers—those akin in spirit and understanding—and they may be posited in the general public (as the general public will include you too) in a way they may not be posited in whatever particular Star Chambers of the literary world. It is my purpose then in making this report that it be available at any time for publication, for I have no private convictions that are not subject to public scrutiny.

"Unusual ability": As a leader in the art of poetry he has establishd a new mode, described as "composition by field" (see "Projective Verse," 1950), incorporating earlier disparate theories of Pound (the ideogram method) or Williams (objectivism) in formal principles related to Olson's wider knowledge of contemporary cosmic theory (Whitehead in *Process and Reality*), linguistic advance ({Benjamin} Whorf), and investigations of psychic projection in myth and history (from Jane Harrison to Jung), and related, more importantly perhaps, to Olson's demand throughout for his own research and experience. Imagination in *The Maximus Poems* is everywhere responsible to what is known: he has documentary care for dream, for daily event, for the written word; at every level there is locus and time. Not only in his theory but in my constant and close reading of his poetry over the last eight years, I have been led to a deeper, more various, involvement in life. "Unusual," rare, superior, these are terms for such men that have given consciousness new substance and spirit new strength. Olson's *Maximus Poems* demand, if we are to grasp them at all, that we search in the poem not for conventional patterns but for form; and in turn that we understand that form is not a matter of habitual usage but of meaning. He redirects our attentions from what is calld literature to what is process. Poetry might then be a question of vitalities; making might be a matter of creation. As a moral leader, he has increased the responsibilities of the poet.

"Leader" I use here in the sense of the man with a direction. He leads toward the fullness of his leading—an imagined fulfilling of the mode he participates in creating. As Olson in poetic theory, in philosophical and historical concept, and in moral urgency, as in his practice as a poet, leads continually toward a poem that may be pictured as *The Maximus Poems*. I do not believe that "leaders" significantly lead men. They lead toward what they make—whether it be a political or social nexus or a work of art in history.

But doesn't "unusual ability" include too Olson's resonance; the sense he has everywhere in his actual work, in phrasing and design of line, in sequence of stanzas, and of song within song, of a movement that is a melodic and has ready affinities to dance and to song (to those actual feet that the stresses pick up from; to those actual tones that the vowels vibrate to). {Igor} Stravinsky tells us in his POETICS OF MUSIC that the feel of the melos is a *gift*—so Olson has abilities then in the sense of gifts. Well, the sad thing here is that "ears" are not given to everybody, and you, dear reader, must go to the text and be able to hear before you will know what I am talking about. It is part of the grace of what is divine that you may recognize where you are ready in spirit (this is the magic of likeness in what we like) to love; but you cannot be won by argument to experience what is beautiful. {Arnold} Schönberg and {Anton} Webern are such rare music that few today venture far into their melodic secrets, though the mode they establishd is in every school.

"financial stress": Olson in writing to me asking if I would consent to making this report put it plain. "My situation is this: I'll be busted in a couple of months." He has just this crisis impending, in the middle of his work, of how to make a living versus the fact that he has brought *The Maximus Poems* with all the difficulties of the last years, up to the point where the whole form comes into operation. (One wonders what *The Cantos* would have been had at any point in his life Pound been given substantial aid. But this digression is off the point: for the *Maximus Poems* have actual definitions of locus that *The Cantos* do not). The point is the financial stress is there and has real bearing upon the fatigue, potentialities, etc. of the poet.

"I Maximus of Gloucester, to You" *The Maximus Poems* begin. Maximus then is the person of the poet and the real creator of these songs. He has this place, Gloucester, and this being, Charles Olson (as in *The Aims of Education* Whitehead writes: "The communion of saints is a great and inspiring assemblage, but it has only one possible hall of meeting, and that is, the present"). Maximus is the *presence* of the poem, the presence that this man Olson comes to create, to realize, is there. This Maximus is an imagined (created) speaker of the poem who speaks for Olson too (as in *The Tempest* we rightly feel Prospero speaks for Shakespeare, yet that he is The Magician). He is also *homo Maximus*; he speaks from a wholeness and directs toward health:

> one loves only form
> and form only comes
> into existence when
> the thing is born

>> born of yourself, born
>> of hay and cotton struts
>> of street-pickings, wharves, weeds
>> you carry in, my bird

But I do not mean to explicate the poem; only to show that it is of this order: has such levels constantly present as need the largest being (the *homo Maximus* or divine manhood in man); which is for *The Maximus Poems* "that which will last" (cosmic in-motion or eternal intent). There are two other levels of movement in the poem: "that which matters" (emotion or psychic intent) and "that which insists" (physical motion as intent). Feelings, Knowings, and Faiths.

And the city Gloucester is, like Maximus, such an event. This is a vital aspect of Olson's awareness in the poem. There can be "my people" as there can be a *homo Maximus*: Gloucester is in the eternal, a community of men; that must have presence in the city of Gloucester as Maximus must have presence through the person of Charles Olson.

> where polis
> still thrives

Because there is actual measure, a locus and a present (so that there can be present the eternal), where

> a peak of the ocean's floor he knew so well (the care
> he gave his trade, his listening
> at 17 to Callaghan (as Callaghan,
> at 17, to Bohlen,
> Bohlen to Smith)

a man "could set his dories out / as a landsman sows his fields"

> and reap such halibut
> it was to walk the streets of Gloucester different

There is too a confidence between Maximus and Charles Olson, an exchange. I take it anyway that in "The Twist" ("Maximus 18") Olson can write for Maximus, have his presence there. As in turn, through Gloucester the voice of the poem speaks for something like an *American Maximus* or rather a *Maximus* of the Western world. What history is in the poem is what it is in Whitehead's *Aims of Education* an actual content of the present, a condition of the form.

Notes

Introduction

1.   "Company," from the late Latin *companio*, "one who breaks bread with you," is a word Robert Creeley employs frequently in conversation and writing. He invokes the human resonance of the word in many places, especially at the end of his *Autobiography*. In reflecting on the beloved writers he knew, including Duncan and Olson, he attests: "One had the company" (Clark, *Robert Creeley and the Genius of the American Common Place*, 144). And in a poem, "The Company," he writes:

> Recorders ages hence will look for us
> not only in books, one hopes, nor only under rocks
> but in some common places of feeling,
> small enough.
> (Creeley, *Windows*, 26–27)

2.   There are notable gaps in the Olson-Creeley correspondence as well, so it is possible to infer that Olson was not fastidious about keeping track of the letters with his correspondents. Omissions in the epistolary record, therefore, cannot be entirely attributed to any drop-off in communication, though the evidence of the extant archives suggests a noticeable decline of exchange at certain times.

3.   We are indebted to biographies of Duncan and Olson in the construction of the brief life outlines in this introduction. For fuller accounts of the poets' lives, see Jarnot, *Robert Duncan*; and Clark, *Charles Olson*. Peter Quartermain's "Introduction: Disturbing Poetics" in *Collected Early Poems and Plays* (hereafter *CEPP*) also provided insight into Duncan's early biographical narrative.

4.   See *The H.D. Book* and *CEPP*, xxii, for a full description of Duncan's early encounters with modernist texts.

5.   See Clark, *Charles Olson*, 76–89, for a highly informative description of this period of Olson's life.

6.   Such debates and competitive assertions were not uncommon among poets struggling to define the terms of their poetic practice; Duncan's confrontation with Denise Levertov over the uses of poetry during a period of political upheaval is one example of this type

of competitive exchange. See Bertholf and Gelpi, *The Letters of Robert Duncan and Denise Levertov*.

7.   Jarnot, *Robert Duncan*, draws out the significance of Duncan's encounter with Kantorowicz, with emphasis on his sense of "style as a teacher, thinker, and conversationalist" (110). Duncan, Robin Blaser, and other students at Berkeley at the time were impressed by Kantorowicz's "sophisticated knowledge of theology and history" (109), and religion and politics intertwined for students in the larger architectures of community. Kantorowicz also introduced important work on Greek culture and religion by Jane Harrison and E. R. Dodds, two authors significant in the ongoing conversations in this volume. See the opening pages of "The Venice Poem" in Jarnot, *Robert Duncan*, 106–7.

8.   See Clark, *Charles Olson*, 254–59; Jarnot, *Robert Duncan*, 138–41; and "Charles Olson and Black Mountain College," in Duncan, *A Poet's Mind*, 238–54, for substantive discussions of Duncan's time at Black Mountain College.

9.   O'Leary, "Previews and Supplements: Peter O'Leary on Robert Duncan's *The Origins of Old Son*."

10.   See Duncan, *Letters*, 37–44.

11.   See Bertholf and Gelpi, *The Letters of Robert Duncan and Denise Levertov*.

12.   Mackey is quoted at length in Alcalay's *A Little History*, 138:

> The sense of poetry as something like a form of penance makes it a matter of conscience, his way of sublimating or attempting to sabotage his birthright, the complex of privileges and guilts we can, with Amiri Baraka, call white karma. At the Berkeley conference Olson makes an interesting remark: "I'm the white man. I'm that famous thing, the white man. The ultimate paleface. The noncorruptible, the good. The thing that runs this country, or that is this country. And thank God—And in fact the only advantage I have is that I didn't." His righteousness, what here he calls his "advantage," consists only of abstention, of writing poetry in place of running the country.

For more on Olson at the Berkeley conference, see Alcalay, *A Little History*, 119, 136–42, 163.

13.   Jarnot, *Robert Duncan*, 252.

14.   Ibid., 259.

15.   Ibid., 262. Duncan recorded the wrong date in his notebook. Olson actually died less than two hours into January 10, at 1:45 in the morning.

16.   See Bertholf and Smith, *Imagining Persons*.

Part One

Letter 1 (September 1947)

1.   In 1947, Duncan applied to the Bender Foundation of San Francisco for financial support to continue writing. Olson wrote a recommendation in support of his application.

2.   Louis Sean was married to Olson's wife's sister, Barbara. Olson stayed with them when he visited Hollywood in September 1947.

3.   Constance was Olson's wife.

4.   Jane O'Neill was the wife of Hugh O'Neill. They lived at 2029 Hearst Street, where Duncan and Richard (Dick) Brown also roomed. Duncan was then taking care of Jane and her new baby, so the reference to Niobe indicates that she was the center and the cause of

the stability in Duncan's domestic life. Jack Spicer was a frequent visitor to the house. Duncan had written his *Medieval Scenes*, his initial contribution to the serial poem, in February 1947 at the Hearst Street address.

5.   This person has not been identified.

6.   This phrase comes from Daniel 5:25: "mene, mene tekel, upharsin." These words appeared on Belshazzar's wall and are the origin of the phrase "the handwriting on the wall."

Letter 2 (January 1948)

7.   Eleanor Ashley Bancroft at the time of the letter was an assistant to Herbert Eugene Bolten, the director of the Bancroft Library.

8.   Gertrude Stein's article "Reflections on the Atomic Bomb" appeared in the *Yale Poetry Review* in 1947.

Letter 3 (Fall 1948?)

9.   This typed letter was not finished and not mailed. It was written in the year of Mary Fabilli's conversion to the Roman Catholic Church and about the time of the composition of Duncan's "The Venice Poem," which is quoted, "So many faces, forms, glances" (*Collected Early Poems and Plays*, [hereafter *CEPP*], 224).

10.   Duncan probably means *das Märchen*, which is German for "the fairy tale."

Letter 4 (November 1948)

11.   This was a postcard Duncan mailed to solicit subscriptions to *Berkeley Miscellany*.

Letter 5 (April 1949)

12.   *Berkeley Miscellany* (1949) contained a story by Mary Fabilli titled "The Garden." Duncan's contribution was "3 Poems in Homage to the Brothers Grimm: The Robber Moon–The Strawberries under the Snow–The Dinner Table of Harlequin" (*CEPP*, 241–44).

Letter 6 (August 1951)

13.   Olson wrote to Cid Corman in a letter dated August 12, 1951: "(by the way, i have found out from Larry Hat, Rob't Duncan's friends' address, and have written Duncan to send you something." See Evans, *Charles Olson and Cid Corman: Complete Correspondence*, 1:188.

14.   The "enemie" has not been identified.

Letter 7 (November 1951)

15.   Duncan's poem was published in 1952 as *The Song of the Border-guard* (and then as "Song of the Borderguard," *CEPP*, 379–81), the second of a projected series of broadsides from Black Mountain College. Olson's *This* was the first broadside, published in 1952, and Duncan's was the second and last. Jess's illustration for Duncan's broadside was lost.

16.   Nicola (Nick) Cernovich printed the broadsides with the assistance of Joel Oppenheimer, a poet and journalist who studied under Olson at Black Mountain College from 1950 to 1953.

17.   Olson prepared a manuscript of his early poems under the title "The Praises" and submitted it to Richard Wirtz Emerson at Golden Goose Press. The book was not published.

See Olson's letter to Robert Creeley of April 28, 1951, in Butterick, *Charles Olson and Robert Creeley: The Complete Correspondence*, 6:23. Olson wrote to Cid Corman in a letter dated November 24, 1951: "Also, yesterday, the end of 'The Praises'—Emerson finally, in answer to two registered letters, showed his hand—what I cal{l}ed him on, exactly a year ago Thanksgiving, that did he really want to publish me or did he want to do just the opposite, tie up my verse, as long as he did" (Evans, *Charles Olson and Cid Corman: Complete Correspondence*, 1:220).

18.   Duncan was featured in *Origin* (Summer 1952). Seven of his poems appeared, along with William Carlos Williams's "The Desert Music."

19.   "Man standing by his word" is a reference to the short essay "Some Notes by a Very Ignorant Man": "Man and word, man standing by his word, man of his word, truth, sincere, unwavering" (47).

20.   "The Gasp" is probably a pun on John Kasper's name.

21.   The references to giraffes here and above and the string of b's below are to Duncan's poem "Africa Revisited," which appeared in *Origin* (Summer 1952): 80–86 (*CEPP*, 367–74).

Letter 8 (December 1951)

22.   Gerhardt published Saint-John Perse in the fourth issue of *Fragmente* with Henry Miller and others.

23.   The references are to Duncan's poems "Africa Revisited" (*CEPP*, 367–74) and "Toward an African Elegy" (*CEPP*, 42–45).

Letter 9 (January 1952)

24.   The "Old man" refers to Ezra Pound, Horton is T. David Horton, and Simpy is Dallam Simpson.

25.   Robert Creeley's "The Party" was not published in the broadside series.

26.   He means Ashley F. Bryan.

Letter 10 (April 1952)

27.   Duncan's poem "An About Face," dedicated to Claire Mahl (*CEPP*, 428), accompanied this letter.

28.   Duncan, "A Little Freedom for Poets, Please."

Letter 12 (December 1953)

29.   This letter was published in *Origin* (Spring 1954): 210–11, and is reprinted from there.

30.   The references are to *In Cold Hell, in Thicket* and *The Maximus Poems 1–10*.

31.   "Friends coming from far quarters" is a quotation from Pound's translation of Confucius (Pound, *Confucius: The Great Digest*, 195).

32.   Duncan is referring to his poem "The Effort," which was written in 1949–50 and not published until after his death. In "The Effort," Duncan translates a Chinese character as "'the rapid and frequent / motion of wings' a bird / learning to fly; / an effort" (*CEPP*, 283), while Pound in "Canto LXXIV" writes: "To study with the white wings of time passing / is not that our delight / to have friends come from far countries / is not that pleasure / not to care that we are untrumpeted?" (*Cantos*, 451). "The Effort" was published in Peck, *The Green Tradition*, 263–79 (*CEPP*, 281–97).

33. Olson, "I, Maximus of Gloucester, to You" (*Maximus Poems* [hereafter *MP*], 7).

34. Olson, "Maximus, to Gloucester" (*MP*, 10).

35. Olson, "Letter 3" (*MP*, 14).

36. Olson, "The Songs of Maximus: Song 3" (*MP*, 19).

37. Olson, "The Songs of Maximus: Song 6" (*MP*, 20).

38. Olson, "Letter 5" (*MP*, 26).

39. Ibid., 27.

40. Ibid., 28.

41. Duncan, "Pages from a Notebook" (*Collected Essays and Other Prose* [hereafter *Essays*], 43).

42. Olson, "Letter 6" (*MP*, 33). The line is actually "There are only / eyes in all heads, / to be looked out of."

43. Ibid., 32.

44. Olson, "Letter 7" (*MP*, 38).

45. Olson, "Tyrian Business" (*MP*, 39).

Letter 13 (December 1953)

46. Olson is confusing Duncan's poem "Variations upon Phrases from Milton's the Reason of Church Government" (*CEPP*, 35–37) with either Duncan's "The Years as Catches" (*CEPP*, 45–48) or "Toward an African Elegy" (*CEPP*, 42–45).

47. The review was signed "Olson" and published as "*Captain John Smith, His Life and Legend* by Bradford Smith" (*Collected Prose* [hereafter *CPR*], 318–21).

48. The poem was published as "On First Looking Out of La Cosa's Eyes" in 1954 (*MP*, 81–85).

49. When Creeley was living in Littleton, New Hampshire, and Jack Leed was living in Lititz, Pennsylvania, they planned to start a magazine called the *Lititz Review*. Problems with the printing press stopped the project; the gathered materials were sent to Cid Corman and used in the early issues of *Origin*. See Leed, "Robert Creeley and the *Lititz Review*."

50. Jung, *Secret of the Golden Flower*.

51. Rhine's book *Extra-Sensory Perception* (1935) was widely read. See also Jung, *Synchronicity*.

52. Leo Frobenius was a German ethnologist who advanced a three-stage theory of cultural evolution: *Ergriffenheit*, emotional involvement, youth; *Ausdruck*, expression, maturity; *Anwendung*, application, age. Ezra Pound drew from his theories of culture and economics in *The Cantos* and corresponded with him beginning in 1930. See Frobenius and Fox, *African Genesis*; and Bush, *The Correspondence of Ezra Pound and the Frobenius Institute, 1930–1959* (forthcoming).

53. "To a Dog Injured in the Street" is a poem by William Carlos Williams that first appeared in Humphries, *New Poems by American Poets*, 165–66.

54. René Char was an admired poet who joined the French Resistance in 1940. In *The Linguistic Moment: From Wordsworth to Stevens*, J. Hillis Miller identifies a "return to immediacy" (360) in Char as well as in the works of William Carlos Williams, Olson, and Creeley. In this letter, Olson quotes from his essay "Against Wisdom as Such," referring to Williams's address to Char in "The Desert Music": "René Char / you are a poet who believes / in the power of beauty to right all wrongs. / I believe it also" (*Collected Poems*, 2:257).

55. "Go sing" is from "The Songs of Maximus: Song 3" (*MP*, 19).

56. Olson, "Against Wisdom as Such" (*CPR*, 264).

57.   Duncan, "Pages from a Notebook" (*Selected Prose*, 20). The passage Olson identifies reads:

> Here I am, at last, I said. Why who cares now, not I, that I imitate or pretend, or sit a great frog in the mighty puddle of my own front room. Here I need not be mature. I can be, as Virginia Admiral used to accuse, wet behind the ears, adolescent indeed. I shall live out my life in this small world, with my imaginary genius, doing as I please, as fancy will; all pretension and with my wits at an end at last.

58.   Olson is referring to his essay "Against Wisdom as Such" (*CPR*, 261–62).

59.   Apollonius of Tyana was a Greek philosopher born in what today is the central coast of Turkey. "Apollonius of Tyana" is also the title of Olson's play written for Nicola Cernovich at Black Mountain College. It appeared in *Origin* (Summer 1952): 90–110. Olson mentions Apollonius in "Against Wisdom as Such" just before the line "the moment that suits wisdom best to give death battle" (*CPR*, 262).

Letter 14 (January–February 1954)

60.   This letter was written in January but not mailed until the postscript of February 6 or 7 was added after Duncan received Olson's letter of February 4.

61.   The twelve-tone technique is a method of musical composition devised by Arnold Schönberg around 1920. See Perle and Lansky, "Twelve-Tone Composition."

62.   Olson, "Projective Verse" (*CPR*, 239–49).

63.   "Plato's image of the horseman" refers to the charioteer and horses in Plato's *Phaedrus*.

Letter 15 (February 1954)

64.   Duncan's play *Faust Foutu* (*CEPP*, 529–90) was published by Duncan himself in an edition of one hundred.

65.   *Origin*, 1st ser., 8 (1953) was devoted to Olson's poems and titled *In Cold Hell, in Thicket*. Duncan responded in the letter dated circa December 15, 1953, and Olson mailed that letter to Cid Corman. Corman wrote to Duncan on January 22, 1954, to ask if Duncan's poems, which were set to appear in *Origin* 12, could be held over for *Origin* 13: "Because Olson sent me some magnificent new work late (new MAXIMUS poems), I had had to edit the issue differently than originally figured. . . . I think they should have immediate issuance, as they are of the most current issue actually and, I think, important, to those who write and otherwise are creative in act." Corman then suggested: "If you are agreeable, I'd like to use your letter as a kind of intro to those two new poems." (Corman's letter is in the Robert Duncan Collection in the Poetry Collection of the University Libraries, University at Buffalo, State University of New York.) Duncan agreed, and his letter was printed in *Origin* 12 before Olson's poems "Letter 13" and "Letter 17." Duncan's poems did not appear until *Origin* 14.

66.   Olson is referring to his letter of December 21, 1953. The review appeared as "Against Wisdom as Such" (*CPR*, 260–64).

Letter 16 (June 1954)

67.   Adams, *Works of John Adams*, 2:23. The quotation is taken from the diary entry for July 21, 1756: "I will rouse up my mind and fix my attention; I will stand collected within

myself, and think upon what I read and what I see: I will strive, with all my soul, to be something more than persons who have had less advantage than myself."

68.   The reference is to Edwards and Vasse, *Annotated Index to the Cantos of Ezra Pound*. Duncan was part of the original group of students who contributed to this volume.

69.   Breton was a French surrealist poet and artist; Tzara was a French Dadaist writer; Magritte was a Belgian surrealist painter; Péret was a French surrealist writer.

70.   The reference is to Marie Curie in William Carlos Williams's *Paterson*: "a luminosity of elements, the / current leaping! Pitchblend from Austria" (174).

71.   Croce was an Italian philosopher. His book of importance here is *Aesthetic as Science of Expression and General Linguistic*.

72.   The first volume of Ernst Cassirer's *The Philosophy of Symbolic Forms* appeared in 1953, and the remaining two volumes appeared in 1955 and 1957.

73.   *Dromena*, literally "things enacted," was an aspect of the rites performed in the Eleusinian Mysteries of ancient Greece, associated with a dramatic encounter with the Demeter/Persephone myth. It forms a part of a dramatized sacred show, theatrical performance, or public spectacle of these rites.

74.   Clifford Hugh Douglas developed the economic theory of "social credit," a proposal for correlating purchasing power with production through a process of price reductions and the issuance of debt-free credit to all citizens. Pound enthusiastically embraced Douglas's economics and reviewed his major work *Economic Democracy* in the *Little Review*. See Kenner, *The Pound Era*, 301–317.

75.   The reference is to Olson's poem "Letter 3" (*MP*, 16). Olson's father, Charles Joseph Olson, was a letter carrier.

76.   Duncan, *As Testimony*.

77.   Duncan distinguishes critical inquiry based on projective principles from the historicist or New Critical academic paradigms of the period. New Criticism particularly privileged the text over the larger social and, for Duncan and Olson, cosmic realities through which poems derive their active forms. In "Ideas of the Meaning of Form," Duncan observes: "Form, to the mind obsessed by convention, is significant insofar as it shows control. . . . It is a matter of rules and conformities, taste, rationalization, and sense. . . . Poets, who once had dreams and epiphanies, now admit only to devices and ornaments" (*Essays*, 69–70).

78.   Gertrude Stein, "Capitals, Capitals."

Letter 17 (June 1954)

79.   The reference is to Olson's poem "Letter 5" (*MP*, 23).

80.   Duncan was devoted to Stravinsky's music and at one point claimed to own every commercial recording Stravinsky had produced.

81.   A typescript of Duncan's poem "True to Life" (*CEPP*, 659–60) accompanied this letter (*Letters*, no. 13).

Letter 18 (August 1954)

82.   Olson, "Against Wisdom as Such" (*CPR*, 260–64), which is quoted later in this letter.

83.   Duncan, "Pages from a Notebook" (*Essays*, 37–43).

84.   Seymour-Smith, "Where Is Mr. Roethke," is a review of Roethke's book *The Waking*.

Because it appeared in the *Black Mountain Review*, Kenneth Rexroth removed himself from the masthead of the journal.

85.   The references are to work that appeared in *Black Mountain Review* 1 (Spring 1954): Olson, "On First Looking Out of La Cosa's Eyes," 3–7; Olson, "Against Wisdom as Such," 35–39; Robert Hellman, "The Quay," 8–17; Irving Layton, "Lacquered Westmount Doll," 19; Paul Blackburn, "The Search" and "The Assistance," 20–21; René Laubiès, "Eight Reproductions," 25–32; Larry Eigner "A Fete," 33; William Bronk, "Round the Year Jazz," 34; Olson, review of *Captain John Smith, His Life and Legend*, by Bradford Smith," 54–57; Cid Corman, review of "*W. B. Yeats and Sturge Moore, Their Correspondence 1901–1937*, edited by Ursula Bridge," 48–51.

Letter 19 (August 1954)

86.   Also in *Black Mountain Review* 1 (Spring 1954): A.M. [Robert Creeley] reviewed the magazine *Cerberus*, published by Contact Press, featuring Irving Layton, Raymond Souster, and Louis Dudek: *Twenty-Four Poems* by Dudek, *The Black Huntsman* and *Love the Conqueror Worm* by Irving Layton, and the Contact Press anthology *Canadian Poems 1850–1952* (51–54); M[artin] S[eymour-Smith] reviewed Dylan Thomas, *Collected Poems 1934–53* (57–58); L[arry] E[igner] reviewed John Steinbeck, *East of Eden* (59–63).

87.   Harmon is a San Francisco poet; he was the editor of the magazine *Ark*.

88.   Six poems by James Harmon—"For Dance," "For Henry Miller," "On Leaving for Prison," "Love," "Barb," "An Ineluctable Modality"—appeared in *Inferno* (1952).

89.   Harold Hackett has not been identified.

90.   Nikolay Aleksandrovich Berdyaev was a critic of Marxist policies who was expelled from Russia in 1922.

91.   Jiddu Krishnamurti was an Indian Hindu philosopher. One of his books is *Education and the Significance of Life*.

92.   The references are to Olson's poems "I, Maximus of Gloucester, to You" (*MP*, 6) and "Letter 6" (*MP*, 30).

93.   Marsden Hartley was an American painter and poet. Olson's poem "Letter 7" begins: "(Marsden Hartley's / eyes—as Stein's / eyes" (*MP*, 34). Duncan may also have been thinking of Edward Carpenter, the British socialist and mystic whose writing on creativity and sexuality at the turn of the twentieth century influenced Hartley. See Henderson, "Mysticism as the 'Tie That Binds.'"

94.   "Bottom: Essay on Shakespeare" by Louis Zukofsky appeared in Laughlin, *New Directions in Prose and Poetry* 14, 288–307.

95.   Olson, "Letter 9" (*MP*, 48).

96.   Duncan is making a pun on Porter, *The Happy Rock: A Book about Henry Miller*.

Letter 20 (September 1954)

97.   Macleod was an American poet and novelist; Hedley was a California poet and the editor of the magazine *Inferno* (Duncan makes a pun on the magazine's title later in this letter); Emerson is an American poet and editor.

98.   The notice Duncan refers to appeared in *Golden Goose* 7 (April 1954): 135, under the heading "Sound and Sense." It reads in part: "Some critics have, with no real basis, lumped the work of Creeley and Charles Olson together. Creeley's direction is that charted by Williams, whereas Olson's is that first explored by Pound. . . . Olson's work has fine musical

qualities, but compared with the delicate nuances of sound that both the master and the disciple Creeley have produced, it sometimes has the hollow and slightly pompous ring of oratory." It also says that Olson shows "a willingness to sacrifice sound to sense."

99.   Kenner, *The Poetry of Ezra Pound*, 4.

100.   Duncan probably refers to Senator Joseph McCarthy. The Army-McCarthy hearings were televised between April and June 1954.

101.   The exact quotation has not been found. Lewis's "Editorial" in *Enemy* (1927) is very much in the vein of this passage. That issue of the *Enemy* also contained "The Revolutionary Simpleton," which became book 1 of Lewis's *Time and Western Man*.

102.   Ezra Pound's *Guide to Kulchur* covers 2,500 years of "cultural action" in which he contrasts culture as so many subjects to be studied with Leo Frobenius's understanding of a *paideuma*, "the tangle or complex of the inrooted ideas of any period" (*Guide to Kulchur*, 58). Pound's antidisciplinary approach appealed to Duncan and Olson, and informed their own far-reaching revision of cultural history, emphasizing the intersections of energy and life practices over the appreciation of cultural periods.

103.   This is a reference to *Artist's View* (1953): [2–4].

104.   The letter was mailed September 4, 1954, though it was written earlier, as the September 2 postscript indicates.

105.   Tate was an influential, conservative poet and critic and a member of the Fugitives and the Southern Agrarian writers who extended the influence of T. S. Eliot through the New Criticism. In many ways, Tate represented one advance of modernism's conservative and reactionary cultural tendencies, which Duncan and Olson vigorously refused.

106.   Olson, "Against Wisdom as Such" (*CPR*, 263).

107.   Ibid.

Letter 21 (November 1954)

108.   Duncan is punning on *Golden Goose* and Leslie Woolf Hedley.

Letter 22 (January 1955)

109.   This refers to Lanier's *The Science of English*.

110.   Olson's essay was published as "Quantity in Verse, and Shakespeare's Late Plays," in *Human Universe*, 81–94 (*CPR*, 270–82). The essay came together through research Olson conducted for an unpublished study of Shakespeare, the 1954 typescripts of which are collected in ten chapters in the Charles Olson Research Collection, Archives and Special Collections at the Thomas J. Dodd Research Center, Storrs, Connecticut.

Letter 23 (February 1955)

111.   Francisco Vazquez de Coronado discovered the Grand Canyon.

Letter 24 (February 1955)

112.   Duncan's adopted name was Robert Edward Symmes. He took the name of his birth, Duncan, in 1941. See the introduction to this volume for more information.

113.   Rexroth, "Lament for Dylan Thomas."

114.   Rexroth, "Thou Shalt Not Kill" (*Collected Shorter Poems*, 274).

115.   Ibid., 269.

116.   The exact quote cannot be identified. Duncan may have in mind Olson's essay "Projective Verse" (*CRP*, 244):

> Because breath allows *all* the speech-force of language back in (speech is the "solid" of verse, is the secret of a poem's energy), because, now, a poem has, by speech, solidity, everything in it can now be treated as solids, objects, things; and, though insisting upon the absolute difference of the reality of verse from that other dispersed and distributed thing, yet each of these elements of a poem can be allowed to have the play of their separate energies and can be allowed, once the poem is well composed, to keep, as those other objects do, their proper confusions.

117.   In 1957 Duncan wrote an essay about Dorn's poem "The Rick of Green Wood," Larry Eigner's poem "Brink," and Edward Marshall's poem "One." Although the review was unpublished, it reveals Duncan's sense of musicality and "tonal pattern"; he holds in high regard Dorn's rendering of "actual things . . . simple exellencies that come from complex attentions." For a partial transcription of the review, see Clark's *Edward Dorn*, 343.

Part Two

Letter 25 (May 1955)

1.   *Black Mountain Review* 5 (Summer 1955). The journal was printed in Palma, Majorca.

2.   Duncan proposed to begin a journal of his own, *Correspondences*. In a letter dated April 17, 1955, he wrote to Jonathan Williams: "Among cookd up while staying at Creeley's to put out an open Journal. Have already correspondence there for from Olson. Wld welcome correspondence from you-all. Articles, rearviews, pomes etc. Put out nudespaper style with all variety of things. Inclewd Childrens Page with story by Robit Creeley and Collins pome; if possible Dick Tracy comics." (The letter is in the Robert Duncan Collection in the Poetry Collection, University Libraries, University at Buffalo, State University of New York.) The journal did not appear.

3.   Duncan's article appeared with the title "Notes on Poetics Regarding Olson's 'Maximus'" (*Collected Essays and Other Prose* [hereafter *Essays*], 47–54). Two typed pages of that essay accompanied this letter.

4.   The letter from Jonathan Williams to Duncan quoted here is dated May 4, 1955. (The letter is in the Robert Duncan Collection in the Poetry Collection, University Libraries, University at Buffalo, State University of New York.)

5.   René Laubiès and Dan Rice were students and artists at Black Mountain College. Other notable visual artists who studied at the college include Robert Rauschenberg, Cy Twombly, John Chamberlain, and Robert De Niro Sr.

Letter 26 (May–June 1955)

6.   Olson deleted two lines that followed "man": "((more than one man? / more than I am??"

7.   "Letter #29."

8.   Lerma is a city in central Mexico where Olson lived from about February 9 to July 1951 while studying the Maya civilization. Olson's letters from Mexico to Robert Creeley were published as *Mayan Letters*. See "Passages 32," a typescript at Storrs (written on

extensively by Olson), for an illustration of the reaction of Olson to a Duncan poem. It is reproduced in this book before the beginning of part I.

9.   Turner, *The Frontier in American History*.

10.   Webb, along with Henry Nash Smith, Frederick Merk (Olson's mentor at Harvard), Frederick Turner, and Carl O. Sauer, informed Olson's outlook on the American frontier. Webb in *Great Frontier* places particular emphasis on the relationship of the physical reality of the historical landscape and its determination of human actions in it, along with the lasting effects of the early frontier encounters on modern modes of inhabiting the land.

11.   Duncan's "The Venice Poem" appeared in its completed form in his *Poems, 1948–49* (and then in *Collected Early Poems and Plays* [hereafter *CEPP*], 211–40).

12.   Olson is confusing Duncan's poem "The Years as Catches" (*CEPP*, 45–48) with Duncan's "Variations upon Phrases from Milton's the Reason of Church Government" (*CEPP*, 35–37).

13.   The reference is to Olson's poem "Tyrian Business": "how to dance / sitting down" (*Maximus Poems* [hereafter *MP*], 39).

14.   In his discussions of the "old brain" in *Archetypes and the Collective Unconscious*, C. G. Jung identifies the place in the brain where reflex responses start and where repetitive routines and emotional responses are remembered. It is the home for instincts. The "old brain" plays a role in the appearance and recognition of archetypes and patterns.

15.   "Stopping the battle" is a reference to Olson's poem "Letter 22"—"And what I write / is stopping the battle, / to get down, right in the middle of / the deeds" (*MP*, 101)—and also to "Maximus to Gloucester, Letter 27 [withheld]": "this, / Greeks, is the stopping / of the battle" (*MP*, 184).

16.   In the five numbered sections in this letter, Olson comments on Duncan's essay "Notes on Poetics Regarding Olson's 'Maximus'" (*Essays*, 47–54). Duncan's essay has no "footnote 1," but it does have a section titled "RECAPITULATON," in which he refers to Haeckel indirectly in a discussion of the birth of language in a child. In *The H.D. Book* (hereafter *HDB*; 153),, he refers to Haeckel directly and expresses the same point that he does in the essay on Olson:

> The O.E.D. gives 1873 as the earliest English use of the word [ecology] in our language, appearing in the translation of Haeckel's *History of Creation*: "the great series of phenomena of comparative anatomy and ontogeny . . . oecology." The very form of man has no longer the isolation of a superior paradigm but is involved in its morphology in the cooperative design of all living things, in the life of everything, everywhere. We go now to the bushman, the child, or the ape, who were once considered primitive, not to read there what we once were but to read what we are.

17.   "Makar" (which now means "poet") is a term with particular connections to fifteenth- and sixteenth-century Scotland. Duncan uses the plural "makaris" in his preface to *Caesar's Gate* (*CEPP*, 323), probably in reference to William Dunbar's "Lament for the Makaris." Makar, like the Greek etymological root for poet that Olson explores a bit later in this letter, comes from the word "maker." See Whiteman, "A Search in Obedience," for a discussion of makaris and "making" in Duncan's work.

18.   Olson typed over the first two letters of a word ending in *chne*, rendering it difficult to transcribe here. Given the context I believe *techne*, particularly as it relates to Pound's treatment of the technical aspects of poetry via melopoeia, phanopoeia, and logopoeia, is

correct. Robert Bertholf, however, originally transcribed the word as *ch'ên*, the temporal state of "the present," which is found in "Canto 85," first published in the *Hudson Review* ([1954]–1955) around the time this letter was written. The term can be seen in *The Cantos*, 545 and 547.

19.   The reference is to Olson's poem "Tyrian Business" (*MP*, 39–44).

20.   Olson, "The Carpenter Poem 1 (Letter 33)." In "Letter 7" Olson writes: "That carpenter is much on my mind: / I think he was the first Maximus" (*MP*, 35).

21.   This is presumably Saint Torpes of Pisa, who suffered under Nero and died circa 65 CE.

22.   "Dove sta memora" means "where memory lives." This is a reference to Pound's "Canto LXXVI": "And the sun high over horizon hidden in cloud bank / lit saffron the cloud edge / dove sta memora" (*The Cantos*, 466).

23.   The "gruesome Thomas thing" is a reference to Rexroth's *Thou Shalt Not Kill: A Memorial for Dylan Thomas*.

24.   Merwin's poem "The Sapphire" and William Carlos Williams's poem "Of Asphodel: Coda" both appeared in *Poetry* (1954).

25.   Walpole was an English art historian, belletrist, and Whig politician. Edmond de Goncourt and Jules de Goncourt were brothers who were French literary and art critics and novelists. Olson jokingly alludes to a desired sense of literary power and recognition embodied by these eighteenth- and nineteenth-century cultural figures.

26.   Olson's poem "In Cold Hell, in Thicket" contains the lines: "In hell it is not easy / to know the traceries, the markings" (*Collected Poems* [hereafter *CP*], 155); "how turn this unbidden place / how trace and arch again / the necessary goddess?" (*CP*, 156); "And archings traced and picked enough to hold" (*CP*, 156).

27.   Williams, "Preface," *Selected Essays*, xii: "It is not what you say that matters but the manner in which you say it; there lies the secret of the ages."

28.   Mannamatta is possibly Olson's pun joining "manner-matter" with Mannampatta, a village in Kerala, India.

29.   Olson refers to a performance of Ezra Pound's translation of Sophocles (Pound spells it Sophokles), *Women of Trachis*, at Black Mountain College.

30.   The reference to Pindar is unclear. It was not until 1957 that Duncan began composition on "A Poem Beginning with a Line by Pindar" (*The Opening of the Field*, 62–69; *Collected Later Poems and Plays*, 56–63). Pindar was a lyric poet from Thebes. Duncan's poem opens with Wade-Gery and Bowra's translation of "Pythian I" in *Pythian Odes*: "The light foot hears you and the brightness begins."

Letter 27 (June 1955)

31.   Four typed pages of Duncan's essay "Notes on Poetics Regarding Olson's 'Maximus'" accompanied this letter (*Essays*, 47–54).

32.   This is referring to Ezra Pound's "How to Read," in his *Literary Essays* (24): "There are three 'kinds of poetry.'" The three modes—melopoeia, phanopoeia, and logopoeia—are discussed in the essay.

33.   Baedeker guides are travel books that have been published since the 1830s.

Letter 28 (June 1955)

34.   The Museu Nacional d'Art de Catalunya in the Palau Nacional in Barcelona was constructed for the International Exposition of 1929 and became a museum in 1934. Both

Duncan and Jess were particularly inspired by Barcelona's Park Güell, constructed by Antoni Gaudí in the early twentieth century; to Duncan, it was "filled with wonders . . . with story-book fantasies of color and strange forms, grottoes, hanging terraces, arcades, dragon fountains, and little houses at the gate out of Grimm's world" (Duncan's letter dated June 26, 1955, to Ida Hodes, qtd. in Jarnot, *Robert Duncan*, 140).

35.   Frescos from two early twelfth-century churches, the Church at Pedret and St. Clement of Tahull, were on display in the Museu Nacional d'Art de Catalúnya.

36.   "Letters for Denise Levertov: For a Muse Meant," a poem first published in *Black Mountain Review* (1954) and then in Duncan's *Letters* as "For a Muse Meant: Letter I" (*CEPP*, 639–43). Levertov first wrote to Duncan in May or June 1953.

37.   See Olson's book on Melville, *Call Me Ishmael.*

38.   Lawrence, *Studies in Classic American Literature.*

39.   Jesus's response to Mary Magdalene is *noli me tangere*, "don't touch me" (John 20:17).

40.   Frieda was D. H. Lawrence's wife. No quotation in Lawrence's work has been found that matches what Duncan says here, but the discussion is close to Lawrence's passionate writing in *Look! We Have Come Through!*

41.   Ann is Robert Creeley's wife.

42.   A Cole Porter song from the musical *Wake Up and Dream* (1929).

Letter 29 (August 1955)

43.   Wallace Stevens died on August 2, 1955.

44.   Keres are malignant spirits, the bringers of all sorts of evil.

45.   San Roman de la Bons is a fresco in the apse of the church called Saint Clement of Tahull, dated circa 1123.

46.   In the fresco, *ego sum lux mundi* (I am the light of the world) appears in the pages of the book in Christ's left hand, while the symbols A and ω (alpha and omega) appear on either side of his head.

47.   Lluis Dalmau was a Spanish painter.

48.   This is from line 4 in the "Imaginary Instructions" section of "The Venice Poem," in Duncan, *Poems, 1948–49*, 29 (*CEPP*, 218).

49.   The final chorale of Stravinsky's *Symphonies of Wind Instruments* is the first time the composer's famous coda appears. Manuel de Falla, a Spanish composer, wrote a work for guitar *Homenaje pour "Le tombeau de Claude Debussy"* in 1920.

50.   This refers to Duncan's book of poems *Letters.*

Letter 30 (August 1955)

51.   Duccio di Buoninsegna combined the ancient Byzantine art traditions with the spirituality of the Gothic style to form the basis of the new Sienese school; Giotto di Bondone is regarded as the first great Italian art master, the man who broke the traditions of the Middle Ages; Giovanni di Paolo was an Italian painter.

52.   He means the famous luxury ship.

Letter 31 (August 1955)

53.   Olson quotes from Duncan's August 14 letter. Butterick observes the influence of this portion of the letter on Olson's poem "John Burke" (*MP*, 148), where he writes, "she holds a city in her hair" (Butterick, *Guide to the Maximus Poems*, 201).

54.   Olson again is quoting from Duncan's letter of August 14.

55.   See Whitehead, *Process and Reality*, 22–35.

56.   The letter to Creeley has not survived.

Letter 32 (August 1955)

57.   Patroclus and Achilles were companions at the battle of Troy. After Hector killed his friend, Achilles made human and animal sacrifices, and then sought vengeance on his enemies. Patroclus's soul went to Hades; he appeared as an eidolon, an image of himself. Homer, *Iliad*, 23.70ff.

58.   "Ubi, et qui" translates to "where, and who." In many ways, these are the central concerns expressed in *The Maximus Poems*. The assignment of value to place and the dramatic and daily actions that give meaning to specific locales are dominant in Olson's writing.

59.   On pankarpia and panspermia, see Harrison, *Themis*, 291–94.

60.   Ann is Robert Creeley's wife.

61.   Olson may be referring to his poem "The Morning News," where he quotes from an uncited source, probably Josef Strzygowski: "One of the less known names of that Omaha chief known to history as Handsome Slayer was, He-Who-Runs-Away-To-Play-Another-Day" (*CP*, 118). The poem was composed for Frances Boldereff in a March 7, 1950, letter (Maud and Thesen, *Charles Olson and Frances Boldereff*, 212–18) and published in *Origin* 10 (Summer 1953): 122–28. Olson assumed Duncan knew the poem.

Letter 33 (August 1955)

62.   Duncan heard the lectures that became *The Greeks and the Irrational* when he returned to the University of California at Berkeley in 1947.

63.   The reference is to Olson's "Letter 6": "There are no hierarchies, no infinite, no such many as mass, there are only / eyes in all heads, / to be looked out of" (*MP*, 33).

64.   A flyer attached to the *Pound Newsletter* 7 (July 1955) announced that the October issue would contain pieces in celebration of Pound's seventieth birthday. "Readers of the *Newsletter* who wish to add their voices to this collective celebration are cordially invited to send contributions, the forms of which may be of their own choosing" (n.p.).

Letter 34 (October 1955)

65.   E. R. Dodds cites Gilbert Murray's *Greek Studies* (66–67) as the source for the phrase "The Inherited Conglomerate" and then writes: "The geological metaphor is apt, for religious growth is geological: its principle is, on the whole and with exceptions, agglomeration, not substitution" (Dodds, *The Greeks and the Irrational*, 179). In discussing C. H. Douglas's concepts of social credit, Ezra Pound reached a summary in two definitions, the first involving teamwork or cooperation and the second focusing on the cultural heritage available to contemporary workers, which is close to Duncan's point in this letter:

> *Increment of association*: Advantage men get from working together instead of each his own, e.g., a crew can work a ship whereas the men separately couldn't sail ships each on his own.
> *Cultural heritage*: Increment of association with all past inventiveness, e.g., thus, crops from improved seed: American wheat after Carleton's researchers; a few men hoisting a locomotive with machinery. (Pound, *Social Credit*, 4)

66.   This is from Federico García Lorca, "Poetica," *Origin*, 1st ser., 16 (Spring–Summer 1955): 104. The translation is by Paul Blackburn.

67.   The references are to Duncan's poem "The Effort" (*CEPP*, 281–97), discussed above, and to Pound, *Confucius: Confucian Analects*. Kung is the fifth-century Chinese philosopher known in Western culture as Confucius. The "three joys" may be referring to study, friendship, and self-confidence or self-determination. See Pound, *Confucius*, 195.

68.   The reference is to the final line of Pound's "Canto XXVII," *The Cantos*, 132.

69.   The reference is to the story "Exit 3," in Rumaker, *Gringos*, 9–34.

70.   "Beautiful thing" is from Williams, *Paterson*, 99–112.

71.   Brancusi was a Romanian sculptor who generated radically new forms in modern sculpture.

Letter 36 (February 1956)

72.   Duncan quotes Graves's *The White Goddess* in the introduction to his *Book of Resemblances* and uses Graves's book to advance his own mythopoetics. See *CEPP*, 361–66.

Part Three

Letter 37 (September 1956)

1.   The letter was typed on the letterhead of San Francisco State College.

2.   Eberhart's review of Allen Ginsberg's *Howl*, "West Coast Rhythms," appeared in the *New York Times Book Review* on September 2, 1956.

3.   Marthe was Rexroth's wife.

4.   Field was an American painter and a former student at Black Mountain College.

5.   Alexander is an American painter. Duncan and Jess owned several watercolor paintings by him.

6.   Robert B. Heilman at this point was the chair of the Department of English at the University of Washington. A distinguished Shakespearean scholar, he wrote elegant and strenuous letters in support of Theodore Roethke, who was teaching in the English Department.

Letter 38 (December 1956)

7.   Caresse Crosby was the wife of Harry Crosby. The Black Sun Press, first operated by Harry and then by Caresse Crosby, printed Olson's *Y & X*.

8.   Charles Peter is Olson's son with Betty; their daughter's name was Katherine.

9.   The reference here is to Duncan's play *The Will*. The Mixons, Simone, and Weir were in the cast that read it at the Poetry Center in March 1957. *Medea at Kolchis* (in *Collected Early Poems and Plays* [hereafter *CEPP*], 591–631) was performed at Black Mountain College in August 1956. Huss played Garrow in the production.

10.   The Playhouse was a theater in San Francisco on the corner of Beach and Hyde Streets. Kermit Sheets was the artistic director of the Playhouse at the time Duncan's *Medea* was performed.

Letter 39 (December 1956)

11.   The letter was written on the letterhead of the Poetry Center, San Francisco State College.

Letter 40 (December 1956)

12.   The letter was typed on the letterhead of the *Black Mountain Review*.

13.   Bet and Pete are Olson's wife and son.

14.   Creeley was living in Albuquerque, New Mexico.

15.   Kramer, *Sumerian Mythology*; Güterbock, *Song of Ullikummi*. Olson also owned Gordon's *Ugaritic Literature*.

16.   This refers to Duncan's play *Medea at Kolchis: The Maidenhead* (*CEPP*, 593–631). Duncan wrote the play between 1951 and 1956. Olson may be confusing Duncan's working titles as separate productions.

17.   This poem was published as "Who slays the Spanish sun . . ." (Olson, *Collected Poems* [hereafter *CP*], 407–8).

18.   Thomas Oliver Larkin was the first American consul at Monterey, 1844–1848.

19.   John Sutter was a pioneer in California on whose land gold was discovered in 1848. Basques were among the immigrants who made up the labor pool during the gold rush.

20.   Joseph Facci was in exile from Mussolini's Italy. He worked in the Office of War Information in Washington, DC, with Olson.

Letter 42 (January 1957)

21.   Abraham Merritt was a prolific writer of fantasy stories and novels, including *The Moon Pool* and *The Ship of Ishtar*.

22.   Duncan's library contains a copy of Kirk and Raven, *Heraclitus: The Cosmic Fragments*; and Kirk and Raven, *The Presocratic Philosophers*. The memoir of the Pre-Raphaelites Duncan refers to is Hueffer, *Memoirs and Impressions*. The final reference in this sentence is to Moore, *Marianne Moore Reading Her Poems and Fables*.

23.   These were the final words of the British artist J. M. W. Turner.

Letter 43 (January 1957)

24.   This letter was written on the letterhead of Black Mountain College.

25.   Kenneth O. Hanson was an American poet who was teaching at Reed College in Portland, Oregon.

26.   Powell was a widely published and distinguished librarian at UCLA. Examples of his work include *The Alchemy of Books* and *The Prospect before Us*.

Letter 45 (April 1957)

27.   This is a carbon copy of a form letter. Olson has added the first line and the informal ending in his hand.

Letter 46 (April 1957)

28.   Duncan's narrative "From These Strands Becoming" consisted of four parts: "Introduction," "California Origins," "Teachers," and "The Drawing." Some of the material was later used in the beginning chapters of his *HDB*.

29.   James, "On a Certain Blindness," in his *Talks to Teachers*, 137.

30.   The typescript of Duncan's "Of Blasphemy" and a note to the poem accompanied this letter (*The Opening of the Field* [hereafter *OF*], 41; *Collected Later Poems and Plays* [hereafter *CLPP*], 36).

31.   Rumaker's story "The Desert" appeared in *Evergreen Review* in 1957.

32.   Hamilton and Mary Tyler were old friends of Duncan. See their article "In the Beginnning, or Recatching *The Years as Catches*," in Bertholf and Reid, *Robert Duncan: Scales of the Marvelous*, 1–13. Hamilton Tyler was an independent scholar who wrote books on the Pueblo peoples, for example *Pueblo Gods and Myths* and *Pueblo Animals and Myths*.

33.   Harrison, *Alpha and Omega*; Harrison and Mirrlees, *Book of the Bear*.

34.   Walt Whitman, "Song of Myself," in his *Complete Poetry and Selected Prose*, 43.

35.   Duncan paraphrases from the story of Ariadne and Theseus in book 8 of Ovid's *Metamorphoses*. Theseus defeated the Minotaur on the island of Crete and escaped the bull's labyrinth by following a thread supplied by Ariadne.

36.   Patchen, *Hurray for Anything*.

37.   Wolpe, *Instrumental Music*.

Letter 47 (April 1957)

38.   This is a form letter. Olson added the final greeting in his hand.

39.   See Duberman, *Black Mountain*, 409–13, for an account of the college's closing.

Letter 48 (April 1957)

40.   This letter was typed on the letterhead of San Francisco State College.

Letter 49 (May 1957)

41.   Bernhard De Boer of Nutley, New Jersey, was a distributor of both *Origin* and the *Black Mountain Review*.

Letter 50 (May 1957)

42.   Nicola Cernovich was at the time the manager at Orientalia, an occult bookstore in New York City on Twelfth Street.

Letter 52 (June 1957)

43.   This phrase refers to grey matter, or the brain.

44.   We have not been able to locate a source for what looks like a direct quote. Duncan is probably using the quotation marks for emphasis.

45.   Duncan combines two kinds of letters (the Greek would be ἰδιώτης) to indicate one's own private self rather than the more common usage of "idiots" designating ignorance or a lack of skill.

46.   Duncan owned and read Frankfurter and Jackson, *The Letters of Sacco and Vanzetti*. Voluntary actions in a community of people are recurring themes in the letters. He also owned Katherine Anne Porter's book *The Never Ending Wrong*.

Letter 53 (June 1957)

47.   The letter was typed on the letterhead of the Poetry Center, San Francisco State College.

48.   *Evergreen Review* (1957) contained three poems by William Carlos Williams, but no poems by Olson.

Letter 55 (August 1957)

49.   Olson's "(Variations, Done for Gerry Van De Wiele)."

50.   Also published in *Measure* (1957): Edward Marshall, "One" and "Two," 6–11; Edward Dorn, "The Rick of Green Wood," 15–16; Larry Eigner, "Millionem" and "Brink," 17–19.

51.   Duncan is referring to an unpublished essay titled "Three Poems in *Measure* One: An Open Letter."

52.   Douglas, "The Blanket," 32–33.

53.   The lines are from Jack Spicer's poem "Song for Bird and Myself."

54.   Moore, *Complete Poems*, 168.

55.   Opie, *Oxford Dictionary of Nursery Rhymes*.

56.   A typescript of "Of Despondencies" and "Poetry, a Natural Thing" followed. The latter poem's third from final line is "a little heavy, a little contrived." Duncan has inserted an asterisk and the following annotation: "John Crowe Ransom gave me this, writing in rejection of some poems: 'But I think you have an accurate poetic language; you get some difficult things said poetically. Some how it seems a little heavy, a little contrived, but you are a good prospect. If this doesn't seem impertinent.'" The letter of Ransom to Duncan is dated August 14, 1957.

Letter 56 (August 1957)

57.   This unfinished letter to Olson was not mailed.

58.   This refers to Marshall, "One" and "Two."

Letter 57 (September 1957)

59.   Pound, "Canto XLVI," *The Cantos*, 231.

60.   Rexroth, "San Francisco Letter."

61.   Mary Caroline Richards was a potter and teacher of English at Black Mountain College. She wrote an influential book, *Centering*.

62.   The text of "Sing Fair the Lady" accompanied this letter. "Sing fair the Lady and her knight" is the first line of Duncan's poem "A Song of the Old Order" (*OF*, 52–53; *CLPP*, 46–47).

Letter 58 (September 1957)

63.   Hell Gate is the name of a bridge over the East River connecting Queens and the Bronx in New York City.

64.   Duncan's poem in five parts is "(The Propositions)," which was later published in *OF*, 30–37; *CLPP*, 25–33.

Letter 59 (October 1957)

65.   Max Pulver, "Jesus' Round Dance and Crucifixion According to the Acts of St. John," in Campbell, *The Mysteries*, 179, 181–82. In an essay, Duncan wrote: "In the Gospel of John it is called the Round Dance, 'If thou wouldst understand that which is me,' the Christ says: 'know this: all that I have said, I have uttered playfully—and I was no means ashamed of it. I danced, but as for thee, consider the whole" ("From the Day Book," 43, in *HDB*, 558).

66.   This poem is Duncan's "Working Too Long at It" (*CEPP*, 376).

67.   "Upon Taking Hold" and "Light Song" were published in *Letters* as "letter iii" and "letter ix," and both are dedicated "(for Charles Olson)" (*CEPP*, 645–47, 654–55), while "(The Propositions)" (*OF*, 30–37; *CLPP*, 25–33) contains direct references to Olson.

68.   Duncan is referring to Oliveros, *Three Songs for Soprano and Piano*. A copy of the setting for Olson's poem accompanied this letter.

69.   Here, Duncan transcribed the musical notation from Oliveros's composition above Olson's "The Songs of Maximus: Song 6" (*MP*, 20): "you sing you who also wants."

70.   Duncan won this prize for five poems in *Poetry* (1957): "A Morning Letter," "The Temple of the Animals," "There's Too Much Sea on the Big Sur" (*CEPP*, 151–55), "Poem," and "A Ride to the Sea" (*CEPP*, 141–42).

71.   Duncan's essay "Three Poems in *Measure* One: An Open Letter" is unpublished.

Letter 60 (October 1957)

72.   The letter appears before and after a typescript of Duncan's poem "The Question" (*OF*, 54–55; *CLPP*, 48–49).

73.   Montague L. Rhodes James, "The Ash-Tree," in his *Collected Ghost Stories*, 62.

74.   Pound's assertion "DICHTEN=CONDENSARE," in *ABC of Reading* (77) might be behind this statement by Duncan.

75.   Moore read at the Poetry Center at San Francisco State University on October 11, 1957. Duncan wrote a short essay for the program titled "Notes on the Poetics of Marianne Moore" (Duncan, *Selected Prose*, 94–96).

Letter 61 (November 1957)

76.   Campion, "Observations in the Art of English Poesie."

77.   Coanda was a Romanian engineer who built the first jet-propelled plane.

Part Four

Letter 62 (January 1958)

1.   This is a reference to Isadora Duncan.

2.   "The Field" was the working title of the manuscript that was published as *The Opening of the Field* (hereafter *OF*). The reference is to the first line of "A Poem Beginning with a Line by Pindar": "The light foot hears and the brightness begins." The poem appears in *OF*, 62–69, and *Collected Later Poems and Plays* (hereafter *CLPP*), 56–63.

3.   The reference is to Olson's poem "Tyrian Business" (*Maximus Poems* [hereafter *MP*], 39).

4.   Olson's poem sequence *West* (*Collected Poems* [hereafter *CP*], 597) contains the following lines:

> World Travelers imagine Duncan in doe-skin
> with his fowling piece—between
> those romantic paintings and not Peter Rabbit Robert
> Duncan in fringed jacket against that bad sunset

5.   Typescripts of the following poems accompanied this letter: "The Performance We

Wait For" (*OF*, 55–57; *CLPP*, 49–51); "A Poem Beginning with a Line by Pindar" (*OF*, 62–69; *CLPP*, 56–63); "At Christmas" (*OF*, 58; *CLPP*, 52–53); "Proofs" (*OF*, 59; *CLPP*, 53); and "Yes, as a Look Springs from Its Face" (*OF*, 61; *CLPP*, 54–55).

Letter 63 (January 1958)

6.   In ancient Egyptian mythology, Thoth was depicted with the head of an ibis and a human body; Thoth invented writing and was the scribe of the underworld.

Letter 66 (March 1958)

7.   This refers to Whitman's "Darest Thou Now, O Soul," in his *Complete Poetry and Selected Prose*, 309.

8.   J. Edgar Hoover and "the Presidents" (Roosevelt, Truman, Eisenhower, and so on) appear in Duncan's "A Poem Beginning with a Line by Pindar" (*OF*, 64; *CLPP* 58).

9.   Levertov, *Five Poems*, contains drawings by Jess.

Letter 67 (Spring 1958)

10.   This message was sent to Olson on a postcard. In a letter to H.D. dated July 5, 1959, Duncan writes: "You will find in *Letters* an owl attendant (no. 27), and just before your 'Sagesse' appeared here in *Evergreen Review* with that beautiful visage of the Scops owl, I came across Bulletin 72 of the Smithsonian Institution, *The Owl Sacred Park of the Fox Indians*." H.D.'s poem "Sagesse" appeared in the *Evergreen Review* in the summer of 1958. Duncan's "letter xxvii" in *Letters* is "An Owl Is an Only Bird of Poetry" (*Collected Early Poems and Plays* [hereafter *CEPP*], 673–76).

Letter 68 (March 1958)

11.   The text and music of Oliveros's "Song No. Six (from Maximus)" accompanied this letter, as did the typescript for Duncan's "Structure of Rime VIII–XI" (*OF*, 70–73; *CLPP*, 64–66).

12.   Whitman, *Complete Poetry and Selected Prose*, 309, 372.

13.   See Lawrence, "The Ship of Death" (*Collected Poems*, 716).

Letter 69 (March 1958)

14.   These are all poems by Duncan in *Origin* 1.14 (Autumn 1954): 123–28. Of these, only "Love Poem" (republished as "Reflections," *CEPP*, 410–11) did not appear in *A Book of Resemblances* (hereafter *BR*): "Salvages. Lassitude" (*BR*, 83; *CEPP*, 411), "Friedl" (*BR*, 84–85; *CEPP*, 412), "A Conversion" (*BR*, 77; *CEPP*, 408–9), "Songs for the Jews from Their Book of Splendours" (*BR*, 86–87; *CEPP*, 413–14), "A Dream of the End of the World" (*BR*, 70–71; *CEPP*, 405–6). In "A Dream of the End of the World" is the line "We came down to Dar Ling Lake."

15.   Levertov, "Love Poem."

16.   Pound's "Canto 85" appeared as the first poem in *Section: Rock Drill*, 85–95.

17.   William Carlos Williams's "The Burden of Loveliness" was first collected in his *Make Light of It*, 245–50.

18.   Marshall, "Leave the Word Alone."

19.   Ginsberg, *Siesta in Xbalba and Return to the States*.

20.   Whalen, "Takeout," is collected in his *Like I Say*, 22–23.

21.   Olson's "Stiffening, in the Master Founders' Wills" (*MP*, 132) begins with the line "Descartes, age 34, Date Boston's"; the poem appeared in *Measure* 3 (Summer 1962): 30–35.

Letter 70 (May 1958)

22.   "Wright" is perhaps a reference to Nathalia Wright, *Melville's Use of the Bible*.

23.   Levin was a Harvard professor and the author of *James Joyce*, one of the first publications of New Directions.

24.   Adams was an American newspaper reporter, an editor, and the author of several books, including *The Shape of Books to Come* and *Literary Frontiers*.

25.   Purdy was an American novelist, short story writer, and playwright.

26.   Kazin was an American critic and poet, best known for *On Native Grounds*.

27.   Hoskins was an American poet. Her books include *A Penitential Primer* and *Villa Marcisse*.

28.   Booth was an American poet whose *Letter from a Distant Land* (1956) won the Lamont Poetry Prize for 1956.

29.   Bowers was an American poet and author.

30.   When Olson received Guggenheim Fellowships in 1939 and 1948, Moe was the secretary-general of the John Guggenheim Foundation.

Letter 71 (November 1958)

31.   In May 1956, James Broughton proposed a "Poets Theatre" to Ruth Witt-Diamant at the Poetry Center at San Francisco State University, but there was not enough money to fund the project. The backer for the new project of the Writers Theater was Humphrey Ireland.

32.   The letter from Turnbull to Duncan is dated October 30, 1958.

33.   "Prometheus Unbound," in Shelley, *Complete Works*, III.iv.77–83.

34.   The phonetic notation suggests that Duncan reads the indefinite article before "sky" as a mid front vowel, as in *pay*, not as a low-mid vowel sounded in words like *must*.

35.   "Prometheus Unbound," in Shelley, *Complete Works*, IV.i.192–93.

36.   Typescripts of Duncan's poems "The Natural Doctrine," "Structure of Rime XII," and "Structure of Rime XIII" follow the letter. These poems are collected in *OF*, 81–83; *CLPP*, 74–76.

Letter 72 (December 1958)

37.   The letter from Bobbie Creeley, Robert Creeley's wife, has not survived. Thomas Matthews Pearce, Cecil Vivian Wicker, and Morris Freedman were all members of the English Department at the University of New Mexico, where Robert Creeley was teaching.

38.   Duncan's poem "Masturbation: For the Innocence of the Act" appeared in *R*C* Lion* 3 (Spring 1957): 46–55. After revision, part of the original poem appeared as "Nor Is the Past Pure" (*OF*, 41–43; *CLPP*, 37–39).

39.   These were published as "Toward an African Elegy" (*CEPP*, 42–45); "King Haydn of Miami Beach" (*CEPP*, 48–50); "Medieval Scenes" (*CEPP*, 183–97); "The Temple of the Animals" (*CEPP*, 153–54); and "The Venice Poem" (*CEPP*, 211–40). "Homage to the Brothers Grimm" became "3 Poems in Homage to the Brothers Grimm": a poem not listed here, "The

Dinner Table of Harlequin" (*CEPP*, 243–44), was included with "The Robber Moon" (*CEPP*, 241–42) and "Strawberries under the Snow (*CEPP*, 242–43).

40.   Fredericks was a printer and the founder of Banyan Press. See the 2003 edition of *Letters* for Duncan's notes on the text, his memos, and the correspondence with Fredericks on the printing of the 1958 Jargon edition.

41.   Jeanne d'Orge was a British poet and painter who lived and worked in Carmel, California.

42.   Jess's show in January 1959 was at Gump's, a fashionable store for luxury goods at 135 Post Street just off Union Square in downtown San Francisco.

43.   *The Haywain Triptych* by Bosch is in the Prado Museum in Madrid.

Letter 74 (February 1959)

44.   This refers to Greville MacDonald, *George MacDonald and His Wife*.

45.   The reference here is to the first line of Dante's *Inferno*. Duncan later published a poem with the title "Nel Mezzo del Cammin di Nostra Vita," which quoted Olson and was collected in *Roots and Branches* (hereafter *RB*), 21–24; *CLPP*, 117–20.

46.   He is referring to Pound's "Canto XCIX": "Food is the root. / Feed the people" (*The Cantos*, 709).

47.   Valéry, *Art of Poetry*, 7:177. The full passage reads as follows: "Metaphor, for example, marks in its naive principle a grouping, a hesitation between several different expressions of one thought, an explosive incapacity that surpasses the *necessary* and *sufficient* capacity. Once one has gone over and made the thought rigorously precise, restricted it to a single object, then the metaphor will be effaced, and prose will appear."

48.   Duncan is referring to his poem "The Law I Love Is Major Mover," first published in 1956–1957 (*OF*, 10–11; *CLPP*, 6–7).

Letter 75 (April 1959)

49.   Duncan's review of Dahlberg's *The Sorrows of Priapus*, "Against Nature," appeared in *Poetry* (1959). Olson also refers to D. H. Lawrence's *Studies in Classic American Literature*. See Christensen, *In Love, in Sorrow: The Complete Correspondence of Charles Olson and Edward Dahlberg*.

50.   Dahlberg, *Flea of Sodom*.

51.   Olson's poem *O'Ryan 2 4 6 8 10* was published by White Rabbit Press in September 1958, with a cover illustration by Jess.

Letter 76 (May 1959)

52.   Duncan met Dahlberg in Palma, Majorca, in 1955.

53.   Duncan is referring to William Burroughs, with whom he had appeared in the final issue of the *Black Mountain Review* two years earlier. Burroughs's *The Naked Lunch* was published in Paris by Olympia Press two months after the date of Duncan's letter.

54.   The reference is to Olson's poem "In Cold Hell, in Thicket" (*CP*, 155–60).

55.   A "trimmer" is someone who changes their behavior to accommodate a particular situation. In a December 1959 letter to Denise Levertov, Duncan uses the term explicitly in reference to sexual hypocrites: "And there are wandering indefinite 'homosexuals' who belong with Dante's trimmers, whose sexual life is only an appearance: i.e{.} having no real

response psychicly or physically at all" (Bertholf and Gelpi, *The Letters of Robert Duncan and Denise Levertov*, 225). Trimmers has been used as a translation of *ignavi* in Dante's *Inferno*, 3:22–69.

56.   Boehme, *Six Theosophic Points*, is in Robert Duncan's library. The second volume of *The Works of Jacob Boehme* contains the essay "The Treatise of the Incarnation."

Letter 77 (May 1959)

57.   Olson quotes Everson (Brother Antoninus), "I'm pre-beat" from "The Beat Friar."

58.   The reference is to Olson's poem "May 20, 1959" (*CP*, 487–88).

Letter 78 (November 1959)

59.   This poem, quoted throughout the letter, is "The Distances" (*CP*, 491–92). Donald Allen, presumably, shared the poem with Duncan during the production of *The New American Poetry*, where "The Distances" also appears (37–39). A "thermofax" is a photocopy.

60.   Duncan's poem "Dream Data" appeared as the first poem in "A Sequence of Poems for H.D.'s Birthday" (*RB*, 10–16; *CLPP*, 107–13).

Letter 80 (December 1959)

61.   Olson gave lectures at Black Mountain College in the spring of 1956 and in San Francisco in February–March 1957 titled "The Special View of History." The lectures were published as *The Special View of History* and, like the essays "Projective Verse" and "Human Universe," articulate a "stance toward reality" (*Collected Prose* [hereafter *CPR*], 246), a way of negotiating the complex features of personal and environmental facts that emerge as occasions of energy and dynamic, interactive form.

Letter 81 (January 1960)

62.   The reference is: "We stick to the truth and we will undertake / our grievous sin rather than live / in peril of our souls" (Duncan, *Faust Foutu*, act 2, scene 12, 38; *CEPP*, act 2, scene 12, 559).

63.   He is referring to Creeley, "Three Prefaces."

64.   Duncan, "The Venice Poem" (*CEPP*, 234).

65.   The photograph by Patricia Merle Topalian appears on the rear cover of Duncan's *Roots and Branches*.

Letter 83 (February 1960)

66.   Duncan is quoting Olson's December 23, 1959, letter to him (letter 80).

67.   Duncan uses Roman script for the first three letters and moves to Greek for the final three letters of κόσμος ("cosmos" in English).

68.   The reference is to Duncan's poem "Apprehensions" (*RB*, 30–43; *CLPP*, 126–37).

69.   In Olson's hand in the right margin: "portentous, primordial, universal, transcendent."

70.   Nicholas of Cusa, a fifteenth-century cardinal, mathematician, scholar, experimental scientist, and philosopher, stressed the incomplete nature of man's knowledge of God and the universe. His principal work is *De Docta Ignorantia* (1440).

71.   The reference is to the following line: "We stick to the truth and we will undertake /

our grievous sin rather than live / in peril of our souls" (Duncan, *Faust Foutu*, act 2, scene 12, 38; *CEPP*, act 2, scene 12, 559). In Olson's hand at right: "confusion of novel with void a discord. seems backward overleap 'outward' star-worlds and is space-hung doesn't give time as function its 'novelty' no eternity! all infinity-pseudo flow." Olson also added: "Miscegenation! & notes—also space!—object."

72.   In Olson's hand at right: "Verdad 'Life which shows itself' Whitman."

73.   This refers to Olson, "Maximus, to Himself": "I stood estranged / from that which was most familiar" (*MP*, 56).

74.   In Olson's hand at right: "beautiful."

Letter 84 (February 1960)

75.   Above this sentence, Olson writes by hand: please make sure to let me see a carbon of *Apprehensions* when the rest is done, yes?

76.   Olson encountered Muhyi al-Din Ibn 'Arabi and the Islamic mystical tradition through the work of Henry Corbin, whose essay "Cyclical Time in Mazdaism and Ismailism" appeared in 1957. Cosmological imagery derived from Corbin appears in Olson's "Maximus at the Harbor" and other works. See Clark, *Charles Olson*, 282–83. Fritz Meier addresses Ibn 'Arabi's Islamic mysticism in "The Mystery of the Ka'ba." Additional texts on the Islamic philosopher in Olson's library include Nasr, *Three Muslim Sages: Avicenna-Suhrawardi-Ibn'Arabi*, and Husaini, *Ibn Al'Arabi, the Great Muslim Mystic Thinker*.

77.   Above this in Olson's hand: "una."

Letter 85 (February 1960)

78.   These two notes are written on a copy of Duncan's recommendation in support of Olson's application to the Guggenheim Foundation.

79.   The first act of the play *Faust Foutu* was read by Duncan at the Living Theater on May 2, 1960.

80.   This refers to Duncan's *The Opening of the Field* .

Letter 86 (February 1960)

81.   This letter is undated, and its conclusion has not survived.

Letter 87 (March 1960)

82.   Seaver was the managing editor at Grove Press.

83.   *Tricky Cad . . . Case VII: Whinemeals* (1959) is a newsprint *détournement* (a term used by the Situationists to describe co-opting works of capitalist production and reusing them for new artistic ends) comic strip collage by Jess. It is in the collection of the Los Angeles County Musem of Art and also available in *Jess: O! Tricky Cad and Other Jessoterica*. The typescript of the third movement of Duncan's poem "Apprehensions" accompanied this letter.

Letter 88 (May 1960)

84.   Richard Stone and Edward Klima had visited Duncan and Jess at Stinson Beach. Klima, a prominent linguist, purchased two paintings by Jess, *The Breakdown of the*

Haywain and *The Earth Is the Fire in the Head*. Stone and Klima lived in Boston and invited Duncan to stay with them when he came east.

Letter 90 (November 1960)

85.   *The Maximus Poems* was published in November 1960.

86.   Duncan's poem "Osiris and Set" appeared in *Set* 1.

87.   A typescript of the following poems by Duncan accompanied the letter: "Roots and Branches," "What Do I Know of the Old Lore," "Night Scenes I–III," "A Sequence of Poems for H.D.'s 73rd Birthday," "Dear Carpenter," "Nel Mezzo del Cammin di Nostra Vita," "A Dancing Concerning a Form of Women," "The Law," "Apprehensions," "Sonneries of the Rose Cross," "Variations on Two Dicta of William Blake," "Come, Let Me Free Myself," "Risk," "Four Songs the Night Nurse Sang," "Structure of Rime XV–XVIII," and "Osiris and Set." All are collected in *RB*, 3–46, 47–52, 67–69; *CLPP*, 101–40, 141–45, 147–61.

88.   The quote is from a note Gerrit Lansing sent to "a number of poets and poet-friends," including Duncan, in 1959 when he conceived of the small magazine *Set*. According to Lansing, the phrase "delighted Robert Duncan." See "Statement: How *SET* Was Conceived" (Lansing, *Heavenly Tree, Northern Earth*, 259).

Letter 91 (March 1961)

89.   This refers to Duncan's poem "The Ballad of the Enamord Mage" (*OF*, 23–24; *CLPP*, 18–20).

90.   "Bet" is Olson's wife. Olson gave a poetry reading at Brandeis University on March 9, 1961.

91.   The reference is to Carew's poem "An Elegy upon the Death of the Dean of Pauls, Dr. John Donne," which contains the following lines: "The Giant phansie, which had prov'd too stout / For their soft melting phrases" and "But thou art gone, and thy strict lawes will be / Too hard for Libertines in Poetrie" (388–90).

Letter 92 (March 1961)

92.   This was originally published as "From the Day Book (Excerpts from an Extended Study of H.D.'s Poetry)" in *Origin* (1963). The chapters were then collected and published as *The H.D. Book*.

93.   In Olson's hand in right margin: "I don't think so."

94.   H.D., *End to Torment*.

95.   Further information about this lecture is unavailable.

96.   "Some Good News" (*MP*, 124).

97.   In Olson's hand following: "Isn't that too much!"

98.   In Olson's hand following: "YA."

99.   The reference is to Olson's poem "Maximus, from Dogtown—I" (*MP*, 172–76).

100.   James Merry was a former sailor who fought and was killed by a bull in nine-teenth-century Dogtown. He figures prominently in "Maximus, from Dogtown—I" (*MP*, 172–76). See also Snow, "Bullfight on Cape Ann."

101.   The reference is to Olson's poem "To Gerhardt, There, among Europe's Things, of Which He Has Written Us in His 'Brief an Creeley und Olson,'" which was reprinted in *The Distances* and collected in *CP* (212–22).

102.   In Olson's hand at right: "thank you Robert Duncan."

103.   The following passages from H.D., *End to Torment*, appear on these pages in the published edition: 58, 37, and 44.

104.   Sheri Martinelli, a visual artist, poet, and literary publisher, was Pound's muse and mistress while he was at St. Elizabeths in Washington, DC.

105.   This quote is from Jung, *Memories, Dreams, Reflections*, 203.

Letter 93 (April 1961)

106.   The poem appeared in *Maximus Poems IV, V, VI* with the following dedication:

for Robt Duncan,
who understands
what's going on
—written because of him
March 17, 1961
(*MP*, 207–9)

107.   John Hays Hammond Jr. built a castle from stones taken from European ruins in Gloucester on Hesperus Avenue; it is now a public museum. Olson frequented Hammond's castle with other artists and gave a reading there in September 1960. See Butterick, *A Guide to the Maximus Poems*, 249–50; and Clark, *Charles Olson*, 285–87.

108.   Shayer had written to Olson as early as July 1959.

Letter 94 (May 1961)

109.   Duncan taught at the University of British Columbia in January 1961; the essay "Ideas of the Meaning of Form" was printed at that time for distribution to Warren Tallman's classes. This note is written at the beginning and at the end of the typescript. The essay was first published in *Kulchur* 4 (1961): 60–74, and collected in Duncan, *Essays*, 68–83.

110.   The reference is to Olson's "GRAMMAR—a book," which was later collected as part of the essay "Proprioception" (*CPR*, 191–95).

Letter 95 (August 1961)

111.   This refers to the Institute of Contemporary Arts in Washington, DC. Duncan read there with Denise Levertov on April 15, 1962.

112.   The YMHA for many years ran a distinguished poetry series in New York City. Elizabeth Kray worked for the YMHA and arranged readings for poets in New York and other cities. By 1969, she was the CEO at the Academy of American Poets.

Letter 97 (December 1961)

113.   This is referring to Olson's "Across Space and Time."

114.   Olson's birthday was December 27, Duncan's January 7, and Wieners's January 6.

115.   "Cultsure" is from Lansing, "Editorial: The Burden of *Set*, #1"; "economics" and "history of prehist." in the following paragraph are from the same article.

116.   Olson writes in "On History," collected in his *Mythologos*, 1:3: "And what Duncan did, it seemed to me, in that—was that a letter to me? He divided it into—it's a hell of a lot

further than any pun ever was—histology, or the study of cells, and story. 'Story' in the sense that the only thing that really counts, again is what's so exciting."

117.   The line is from Olson's "Across Space and Time" (*CP*, 509).

118.   From William Blake's "America a Prophecy," in his *Complete Poetry and Prose*, plate 14, lines 19–20.

119.   See Porcher, *Les grandes heures de Rohan*.

120.   An accompanying drawing by Duncan illustrates the scene described in the letter: a woman pours water from the sky; below, an older man warms by a fire. The following text is included under the image: "Let us drink of both springs that we may forget all other matters and yet remember what was reveald to us."

121.   Olson, "Across Space and Time" (*CP*, 508).

Letter 98 (December 1961)

122.   This refers to Olson's "On History," in *Mythologos*, 1:3, and Olson's poem "Letter 23": "I would be an historian as Herodotus was, looking / for evidence of / what is said" (*MP*, 104–5).

123.   The Christmas play is *Telepinas*, collected in Olson, *The Fiery Hunt*, 88–96. See the introduction by Butterick in that volume, xix–xx.

Part Five

Letter 99 (January 1963)

1.   The reference is to Olson's poem "The Gulf of Maine," which first appeared in *Maximus Poems IV, V, VI* and later in *The Maximus Poems* (hereafter *MP*), 278–80.

2.   Olson, *A Bibliography on America for Ed Dorn*. At this point, the booklet circulated in manuscript copies. Duncan quotes the essay below.

3.   Spicer, *The Heads of the Town*.

4.   McClure's "Revolt" appeared first in *Journal for the Protection of All Beings* (1961).

Letter 100 (January 1963)

5.   Anastas is a Gloucester resident and native speaker of Greek, who was a friend of Olson. His publications about Olson include (with Parson), *When Gloucester Was Gloucester* and *Maximus to Gloucester*.

6.   The Duke of Berry's "Zodiac" refers to the French Gothic manuscript illumination from the calendar of *Très Riches Heures*. Olson could be citing a 1956 *Time* magazine notice ("Art: Books of the Centuries") announcing the gift of two medieval *Books of Hours* to the Metropolitan Museum of Art. The Duke of Berry's *Books of Hours* have been reprinted several times. See, for example, Rorime, *The Belles Heures of Jean, Duke of Berry, Prince of France*.

Letter 101 (March 1963)

7.   Gertrude Stein was actually born on February 3, 1874.

8.   *The Waste Land* was published in 1922, not 1921.

9.   Duncan refers to H.D.'s *Trilogy*, written during the Second World War and published

in 1973 by New Directions. The three books of the trilogy are *The Walls Do Not Fall* (1944), *Tribute to the Angels* (1945), and *The Flowering of the Rod* (1946).

10.   New Directions actually published *The Pisan Cantos* in 1948.

Letter 102 (March 1963)

11.   Olson could be referring to statements made by Pope John XXIII, who met on March 7 with Nikita Khrushchev's son-in-law and wife—the first papal audience with high-ranking communist figures. The pope's encyclical "Pacem in Terris" was not delivered until a month later on April 11. In that address, he advocated for greater ties between nations of competing ideological views.

12.   Scapa Flow, an anchorage of about fifty square miles in the Orkney Islands, Scotland, is also a British naval base.

13.   Saône refers to a river and valley in Burgundy, France.

14.   Olson here could mean *ēthē* (ηθη), which is the plural of *ēthos*. In the *Ethics* Aristotle treats ethos as habit. Accordingly, habitual modes of character can contribute to multiple modes of ethical performance. Olson seems to be resisting automatic ways of responding to situations that call for moral judgment and action in favor of the actual conditions and circumstances of inhabited environments.

Letter 103 (March 1963)

15.   Olson refers here to "The Allegory of Wealth: A Poem from America Still" (*Collected Poems* [hereafter *CP*], 540), where he writes an American version of the Persephone myth: "I rushed to go across the space from one skyscraper office / to the other, to try to help, to see if there was anything / one might do, what the Milliardaire had done to the Maid." The poem was published in Tom Raworth's first issue of *Outburst*.

Letter 104 (April 1963)

16.   This refers to the publication of Schaff, "Some Statements on Projective Verse."

17.   The reference is possibly to Arthur Rimbaud's "Sun and Flesh" (Soleil et chair): "No more gods! No more gods! Man is King / Man is God!" (*Rimbaud Complete*, 13).

18.   "Pippa Passes" is a poem by Robert Browning.

19.   This quote is from Olson's poem "Maximus to Gloucester, Letter 27 [withheld]" (*MP*, 185).

20.   Wilson, "Continental Drift."

21.   Olson's wife and son.

22.   Warren and Ellen Tallman organized the Vancouver Poetry Conference, which took place July 29–August 16, 1963. Seventy-five poets attended, including Charles Olson, Robert Duncan, Robert Creeley, Denise Levertov, Allen Ginsberg, Margaret Avison, Michael Palmer, Clark Coolidge, George Bowering, and Robert Hogg. See Bergé, *The Vancouver Report*.

23.   Duncan wrote about the poem: "After Reading H.D.'s Hermetic Definitions." The actual title of H.D.'s poem is "Hermetic Definition."

24.   The reference is to Olson's poem "Maximus to Gloucester, Letter 27 [withheld]": "I have this sense, / that I am one / with my skin" (*MP*, 185–86).

25.   A typescript of Duncan's poem "The Continent" (*Roots and Branches*, 172–76; *Collected Later Poems and Plays* [hereafter *CLPP*], 251–56) accompanied this letter.

Letter 105 (May 1963)

26.   The references here are to "GRAMMAR—a book" and to "Proprioception" and "Logography," which appeared in *Kulchur* 1 under the editor's title of "Pieces of Time." These works were combined with "Theory of Society," "A Work," "Bridge-Work," "the hinges of civilization to be put back on the door," and "A Plausible 'Entry' for, like, Man" and published as *Proprioception*.

27.   Elias Wilintz was the proprietor of Corinth Books. The Jargon Society and Corinth Books jointly published Olson's *The Maximus Poems*.

28.   This is Latin for "it pleases."

Letter 108 (December 1963)

29.   For an account of Duncan's scene with his aunt Faye and his mother, see Hamilton Tyler and Mary Tyler, "In the Beginning, or Recatching *The Years as Catches*," in Bertholf and Reid, *Robert Duncan: Scales of the Marvelous*, 8–9; and Lubin, "'that lettrous mountain of friendship': The Selected Letters of Pauline Kael and Robert Duncan."

30.   See Duncan, "Beginnings: Chapter 1 of *The H.D. Book*, Part I" (*The H.D. Book* [hereafter *HDB*], 35–61).

31.   In Jewish wisdom writings, the Kelipah is the outer shell of reality, which conceals the light of God's creation.

32.   Duncan and Jess were in London in January 1956, not 1955.

Letter 110 (May 1964)

33.   This was published as an untitled statement in *Matter* 3 [December 1965]: [1–3].

34.   Duncan is referring to Havelock, *A Preface to Plato*.

35.   Typescripts of "Passages" 1, 2, 4, 5, 6, and 7 accompanied this letter, and the poems were collected in *Bending the Bow* (hereafter *BB*), 9–22; *CLPP*, 305–16.

36.   Jess's paintings were exhibited at the Odyssia Gallery in May–June 1971 and reproduced in the catalog *Translations*.

37.   Barbara Joseph, an old friend and patron of Duncan and Jess, advanced enough money so that they were able to buy a house at 3267 Twentieth Street in San Francisco.

Letter 111 (June 1964)

38.   The cover photograph of *Cardinal* (the undergraduate literary magazine of Wesleyan University) in the spring of 1964 was of Duncan.

39.   The cover of the first issue of *Niagara Frontier Review* (Summer 1964) included a photograph of Olson teaching in front of a chalkboard.

Letter 112 (June 1964)

40.   Olson lived in Wyoming, New York, about twenty miles southeast of Buffalo, when he taught in the English Department at the State University of New York at Buffalo in 1964.

41.   The typescripts for "Passages" 7, 8, and 9 accompanied this letter, and the poems were collected in *BB*, 22–28; *CLPP*, 316–21.

42.   Duncan's "Old Testament" and "New Testament" appeared in *Fuck You: A Magazine of the Arts* in 1964.

43.   Goodenough, "The Divine Fluid in Ancient Egypt," in his *Jewish Symbols*, 5:141–97.

Letter 113 (June 1964)

44.   Jung, *Memories, Dreams, Reflections*, 203.

45.   Ibid., 225.

46.   Ibid., 226.

47.   In Bertholf and Gelpi, *The Letters of Robert Duncan and Denise Levertov*, the June 20, 1964, letter of Levertov to Duncan (no. 320, 458–59) is incomplete; the passage cited here by Duncan completes that letter.

48.   See Pound, *Confucius: Confucian Analects, the Great Learning and the Doctrine of the Mean*, 137–38. Duncan is also referring to his poem "The Effort," in Peck, *The Green Tradition*, 263–80 (*Collected Early Poems and Plays* [hereafter *CEPP*], 281–97).

Letter 114 (July 1964)

49.   A typescript of "Passages" 12 and 13 accompanied this letter, and the poems are collected in *BB*, 34–35, 40–45; *CLPP*, 325–27, 330–35.

50.   The letter of Robert Creeley to Duncan is dated June 29, 1964. It is in the Robert Duncan Collection in the Poetry Collection of the University Libraries, University at Buffalo, State University of New York.

Letter 116 (January 1965)

51.   Olson's book *Human Universe and Other Essays* appeared in August 1965. His poem *Signature to Petition* was published as a broadside by Oyez Press of Berkeley in 1964.

52.   Duncan met Jackson Mac Low about 1945. The particular collage poems he mentions have not been identified.

Letter 117 (February 1965)

53.   The "Wahs" are Fred Wah and Pauline Butling.

54.   Raphael is the author of *Your Psychic Powers: The Key to Success*.

55.   This refers to Kelly and Leary, *A Controversy of Poets*.

56.   "Benefice" is the title of "Passages" 23.

Letter 119 (May 1966)

57.   Robert Creeley was living in Bellagio near Lake Como in Italy at this time.

Letter 121 (September 1966)

58.   Duncan cites Gobron, *Histoire et philosophie du caodaisme*, as a source for "Eye of God: Passages 29" (*BB*, 124–27; *CLPP*, 403–7).

59.   Duncan is referring to Thomas Vaughan's *Alchemical Works*.

60.   An advertisement for Duncan's book *The Years as Catches* contained a statement by Olson with the lines "Ancient, permanent wings of / Eros—& of Orphism."

61.   National Educational Television produced a thirty-minute film about Olson in Gloucester. The quotation is from the film.

Letter 122 (December 1966)

62.   This was written on Hotel Steinplatz letterhead.

63.   The reference is to Olson's poem *West*. A photograph of Red Cloud is the frontispiece.

64.   Barry Hall was the publisher of *West*.

65.   On October 28, 1966, Olson departed from Montreal on the *Empress of Canada* with the stylish New York City art patron Panna Grady and her young daughter. Together they briefly rented a London flat on Mount Street, near Hyde Park. A month later, Olson departed for Berlin, where he suffered chest pains. See Clark, *Charles Olson*, 330–34; and Maud, *Charles Olson at the Harbor*, 197–205, for conflicting views on Olson's relationship to Grady and her one-time paramour and former Black Mountain student John Wieners. See also Olson's poem "Hotel Steinplatz, Berlin, December 25 (1966)" (*MP*, 569).

66.   Renate Gerhardt is the widow of Rainer Maria Gerhardt.

67.   William Radoslovich married Jean, Betty Olson's sister. Lucy della Picola presumably was, as Olson says, his "guide near the Italian frontier."

68.   Linear A was an early form of Greek writing discovered at Knossos in Crete by Sir Arthur Evans. Olson owned copies of two books dealing with the ancient script: Gordon, *Before the Bible*; and Huxley, *Crete and the Luwians*.

69.   Hunkpatila is one of the two primary divisions of the Yanktonai Sioux, who live in South Dakota.

Letter 123 (January 1967)

70.   The reference is to Duncan's poem "The Scattering" (*CEPP*, 415), which appeared on the Christmas card in ink and various colors of crayon.

71.   German for "salvation, bliss."

72.   Bob Hawley was a student at Black Mountain College and then the publisher of Oyez Press, which produced Duncan's *The Years as Catches*.

Letter 124 (January 1968)

73.   Chilam Balam appears in "Passages 32" (*Ground Work*, 14–18; *CLPP*, 445–51).

74.   Olson read and commented on his work at the Berkeley Poetry Conference, July 23, 1965. See "Reading at Berkeley," in Olson, *Mythologos*, 137–40.

75.   Placer mining is a technique that allows the heavier gold to fall to the bottom of a container and the lighter materials to be washed away by water. This is the technique used by miners in a stream with a pan.

76.   This is a reference to Olson's poem "West 6" (*CP*, 599).

77.   Concerning the Modocs, see the discussion of Duncan's family line in his "A Poem Beginning with a Line by Pindar" (*Opening of the Field*, 62–69; *CLPP*, 56–63).

78.   In Olson's hand: "age 47 & age 49."

79.   In Olson's hand: "1954–1960, 1961–1968? Black Mountain—___?___?"

80.   The letter of Robert Creeley to Duncan is dated January 14, 1968. It is in the Robert Duncan Collection in the Poetry Collection of the University Libraries, University at Buffalo, State University of New York.

81.   Duncan is referencing the line "Let the human Mind loose!" from his "Passages 32" (*Ground Work*, 14; *CLPP*, 446).

Letter 125 (January 1968)

82.   Olson may be referring to the appearances of Isis and Venus in "Passages 32" (*Ground Work*, 18; *CLPP*, 450), which Duncan had sent with letter 124.

83.   See Duncan's essay "Rites of Participation" (*HDB*, 153–99).

84.   Cabeza de Vaca was a Spanish explorer who walked from about Galveston, Texas, to the Pacific Coast. See Long, *Interlinear to Cabeza de Vaca*; and Adorno and Pautz, *The Narrative of Cabeza de Vaca*. Olson was attracted to the historical figure of Cabeza de Vaca particularly for his survival in the American interior for nine years as a slave. He eventually became a shaman among indigenous tribes of the American Southwest and Mexico. The poem "As Cabeza de Vaca Was" appears in an undated manuscript. See Maud, *Charles Olson's Reading*, 197.

Letter 127 (March 1968)

85.   The preface was not published.

86.   This may refer to Creeley, *5 Numbers*.

Letter 128 (April 1968)

87.   Duncan, *Sweetness and Greatness of Dante's Divine Comedy*.

Letter 129 (December 1968)

88.   This is Duncan and Jess's Christmas greeting for 1968, which was written on the verso of a page from Jess's book *Gallowsongs* (1970).

Letter 130 (December 1969)

89.   This refers to the International Poetry Festival held at the University of Texas, Austin, November 17–22, 1969. Robert Creeley replaced Olson.

90.   Octavio Paz was a Mexican writer prolific in his publications and radical in his political views. He distinguished himself in poetry, prose, and political commentary. In 1990, he was awarded the Nobel Prize for Literature.

91.   The Tenth Muse was a bookstore in San Francisco operated by Julia Newman.

92.   The review mentioned is Zinnes, "Duncan's One Poem."

Glossary

Adam, Helen (1909–1993), was a Scottish poet, a writer of traditional and sometimes mystic ballads, whose reading of Blake's poetry in Robert Duncan's class at the Poetry Center in 1954 focused him on the Romantic and ballad traditions in poetry. This turn to the Romantic tradition countered the pull of Olson into a poetics based on myth, history, and geography. She and her mother and sister Pat were close friends of Duncan and Jess, even after the mother died and the sisters moved to New York City. Helen published several books, including the play *San Francisco's Burning* (1963, republished in 1985); *Ballads* (1964) with illustrations by Jess and a preface by Duncan; *Selected Poems and Ballads* (1974); and *Turn Again to Me and Other Poems* (1977). After Adam's death, Kristin Prevallet edited *A Helen Adam Reader* (2007).

Admiral, Virginia (1915–2000), met Robert Duncan at Berkeley in 1936 and was a friend and confidant about his political and literary views. She and Duncan published the little magazine, *Epitaph*, one issue, spring 1938. They moved to New York City separately and continued *Epitaph* as *Experimental Review* 2 (November 1940) with Sanders Russell also as an editor. *A Supplement* appeared in January 1941, and number 3, the final issue, appeared in September 1941. Both Admiral and Duncan were typists for Anaïs Nin in New York City. Admiral studied painting with Hans Hoffmann in Provincetown and had shows at Buecker and Harpsichords galleries. In 1942, she married the painter Robert De Niro and in 1943 gave birth to the actor Robert De Niro. Virginia Admiral's painting *The Red Table* (1944), hung in Duncan's writing office in his San Francisco home.

Allen, Donald Merriam (1912–2004), was an influential publisher, translator, and editor at Grove Press, who is best known for the publication of the seminal anthology *The New American Poetry* (1960), in which Olson's "Projective Verse" was republished along with notable work by Duncan, Philip Whalen, Frank O'Hara, LeRoi Jones, and other experimental writers working solidly within the Pound/Williams modernist tradition. In the 1960s in San Francisco Allen established Grey Fox Press and the Four Seasons Foundation, publishing work by both Duncan and Olson, as well as other writers associated with Black Mountain and the San Francisco Renaissance, including Robert Creeley, Edward Dorn, Joanne Kyger, Michael Rumaker, Jack Spicer, Gary Snyder, Philip Whalen, and others.

Angulo, Jaime de (1884–1950), was a widely published anthropologist, linguist, and ethno-musicologist of California indigenous tribes. During the second part of his life he lived on Big Sur, wrote fiction and poetry, and was a mentor to poets as well as adventurers of the free life. Duncan rented a room in his house in Berkeley from the summer of 1949 through October 1950, and typed manuscripts and looked after him when he was dying of cancer. See Callahan, "The World of Jaime de Angulo" (a conversation between Bob Callahan and Robert Duncan) (1979). William Carlos Williams praised his writing; Ezra Pound helped get de Angulo's work published during the 1940s. After his death Bob Callahan established the Turtle Island Foundation to print more of de Angulo's work, including *Coyote's Bones: Selected Poetry and Prose* (1974). Two later publications are *Indian Tales* (1953) and Guy de Angulo, *Jaime in Taos: The Taos Papers of Jaime de Angulo* (1985).

Antoninus, Brother. See **Everson, William**.

Artist's View. See **Mahl, Claire**.

Avison, Margaret (1918–2007), was a widely published and distinguished Canadian poet. Cid Corman featured her in *Origin*, 1st ser. (1957), and at the time of this correspondence she was the author of *Winter Sun* (1960) and *Sliverick* (1960), as well as a regular contributor to other literary magazines. She attended and participated in the Vancouver Poetry Conference in the summer of 1963. More recent publications include *Always Now: The Collected Poems* (2003), *I Am Here and Not Not-There: An Autobiography* (2009), and *The Essential Margaret Avison* (2010).

Baker, Richard (1936–), helped arrange poetry readings at the University of California Extension Center in San Francisco, and was the primary organizer of the Berkeley Poetry Conference (1965); he later became the spiritual leader of the Zen Center in San Francisco. He was close to many of the poets in San Francisco, including Philip Whalen, whom he ordained as a Buddhist priest in 1973.

Baraka, Amiri. See **Jones, LeRoi**.

Berkeley Miscellany was a magazine consisting of two issues edited by Duncan in 1948–1949, and it was printed by the Libertarian Press in New Jersey. Mary Fabilli, Jack Spicer, Gerald Ackerman, and Duncan appeared in the issues.

Big Table's editors Paul Carroll and Irving Rosenthal printed sections of William Burroughs's *Naked Lunch* and Jack Kerouac's *Old Angel Midnight*, which had been censored from the *Chicago Review* in the publication of this journal's first issue. Carroll went on to edit and publish four more runs from spring 1959 to fall 1960. Paul Blackburn, John Ashbery, Barbara Guest, Robert Creeley, Allen Ginsberg, and Denise Levertov all appeared in *Big Table*. Duncan published three poems in three issues, including "Apprehensions" (1960), which he had sent to Olson as a typescript previously.

Blackburn, Paul (1926–1971), was a New York poet, a translator, and a contributing editor to the *Black Mountain Review*. His translations of Provençal poetry were published by Robert Creeley as *Proensa* (1953). Other books include *The Dissolving Fabric* (1953), *Brooklyn-Manhattan Transit: A Bouquet for Flatbush* (1960), *The Journals* (1972), *Against the Silences* (1980), and *Collected Poems* (1985).

Black Mountain Review, edited by Robert Creeley, published seven issues from spring 1954 to autumn 1957. With *Origin*, the review was central to the emergence of the new American poetry, especially as inspired by the poetry and poetics of Charles Olson. Robert Duncan, Robert Creeley, Edward Dorn, Paul Blackburn, and Denise Lever- tov published in the review. Olson's essay on Duncan, "Against Wisdom as Such," appeared in the first issue, and Duncan's essay on Olson, "Notes on Poetics Regard- ing Olson's 'Maximus,'" appeared in the sixth issue, spring 1956.

Blaser, Robin (1925–2009), came from Idaho to Berkeley in 1944 and quickly became closely associated with Robert Duncan and Jack Spicer, and later connected to the San Francisco Renaissance in the sixties. In 1966, he moved to Vancouver, British Columbia, and became a Canadian citizen after starting a teaching career at Simon Fraser University. His early books include *The Moth Poem* (1964), *Les chimères* (translations from Nerval, 1965), *Cups* (1968), and *Syntax* (1982). *The Holy Forest* (1993) is his collected poems, with a foreword by Robert Creeley. His essays are in *The Fire: Collected Essays* (2006). Blaser also edited *The Collected Books of Jack Spicer* (1975).

Blok, Aleksandr A. (1880–1921), was a Russian symbolist poet of the Revolution whose most famous book was published in 1918, *The Twelve*. It was translated several times, but the one by Babette Deutsch and Avraham Yarmolinsky from 1931 could have been seen by Olson.

Borregaard, Ebbe (1933–), is a Bay Area poet and was part of the Jack Spicer circle. He also was one of Duncan's students at the Poetry Center at San Francisco State College. As editor of Oannes Press, he published two titles by Helen Adam and James Alex- ander. Borregaard has lived in Bolinas since 1969 and is the author of *The Wapitis* (1958), *Sketches for 13 Sonnets* (1969), and other works.

Brakhage, James Stanley (Stan) (1933–2003), considered one of the greatest experimental filmmakers of the twentieth century, developed a range of techniques that explored the formal and thematic potential of the visual medium. He is especially known for allowing chance events to enter his films's composition. As a young man new to San Francisco, he lived with Duncan and Jess for several months in 1952–1953 in exchange for domestic service. Duncan remained in contact with Brakhage over the years of this correspondence, and he and Jess stayed with Brakhage on several occasions during visits to New York City (see Jarnot, *Robert Duncan: The Ambassador from Venus*). Later Brakhage published essays with Zephyrus Image in San Francisco (the printer for Dorn's poem *Slinger*), while maintaining a place of operations in Colorado. Brakhage experimented with nonlinear plots in films, something like the serial forms of Duncan and Olson, employing such new techniques as painting, scratching, and other physical manipulations of film, as well as using collage work, multiple expo- sures, and in-camera editing. The "Dog Star Series," 1961–1964, resulted from these techniques, as did the "The Pittsburgh Trilogy," (1971), which included *The Act of Seeing with One's Own Eyes*. "The Dante Quartet," (1987), another series of films, is considered a great accomplishment in Breakage's later period.

Bronk, William (1918–1999), was an American poet, and an early follower of Wallace Ste- vens's poetry. He has the distinction of being one of two writers (Cid Corman is the other) to appear in all the series of *Origin*. Bronk's collected poems, *Life Supports: New and Collected Poems* (1981), was followed by a series of smaller books, including *Metaphor of Trees and Last Poems* (1999). He stands out as one of the leading poets of American literature in the late twentieth century.

Broughton, James (1913–1999), was a Californian poet and filmmaker, and long-time friend of Duncan. With Kermit Sheets, Broughton published Duncan's booklet *Medieval Scenes*. He was a member of the Maidens group, along with Madeline Gleason, Eve Triem, Duncan, and Jess, in San Francisco in 1957. *True and False Unicorns* (1957) was an example of his ecstatic and at times erotic poetry, which was followed by two collections: *A Long Undressing: Collected Poems, 1949–1959* (1971) and *Packing Up for Paradise: Selected Poems, 1946–1996* (1997). *Seeing the Light* (1977) is a filmography, and *The Androgyne Journal* (1977) is autobiographical prose.

Bryan, Ashley F. (1923–), is an American writer and painter who had a distinguished career as an artist and illustrator of children's books. He designed the cover for *Origin*, 1st ser., 5, and made the frontispiece for Robert Creeley's *Le Fou*.

Bunker, Constance (Connie) Wilcock (1919–1975), was Charles Olson's first common-law wife, beginning in 1941. They had a daughter, Kate Olson Bunker (1951–1998). The marriage ended while Olson was at Black Mountain College in 1956. Connie married George R. Bunker (1923–1991) in 1959.

Burroughs, William (1914–1997), was a Beat fiction writer who became a close friend of Allen Ginsberg and Jack Kerouac in New York. His works include *Junkie* (1953), *Naked Lunch* (1959), and *The Ticket That Exploded* (1962).

Butling, Pauline (1939–), was a Canadian student at the State University of New York at Buffalo when Charles Olson was teaching at the school; she also attended the 1963 Vancouver Poetry Conference. Butling wrote a master's thesis titled "Robert Duncan: The Poem as Process" (1966).

Butts, Mary (1892–1937), was a British novelist and poet. Duncan was familiar with her work as early as 1942, especially her novel *Armed with Madness* (1928). Her work informed and complicated his inherited Theosophical and spiritual knowledge from his adopted parents, and helped him articulate what he saw as the active dimensions of myth in daily life, what Jane Harrison referred to as *dromenon*, "the thing done," an exemplification of spiritual reality through enactments of everyday living. For Duncan, "the important revelation," put forward in Butts's writing, "was that intense personal experience suffered was more than psychodrama: it sought its realization as ritual and threshold of the sacred." See Duncan's contribution to *The Writings and the World of Mary Butts: A Conference* (1984), reprinted in *A Sacred Quest: The Life and Writings of Mary Butts* (1995).

Cernovich, Nicola (Nick) (1929–), was a Black Mountain College student and later a Broadway and off-Broadway lighting designer. At Black Mountain he printed Duncan's *Song of the Border-guard*, based on a design by Cy Twombly. He also performed dance pieces at Black Mountain, 1951; Olson admired Cernovich's choreographic interpretations and wrote "Apollonius of Tyana" for him that summer.

Church, Peggy Pond (1903–1986), was a poet from New Mexico who in the 1950s lived in San Francisco. Her poetry derives from the history, culture, and landscape of the Southwest: *Accidental Magic* (2004) and *Birds of Daybreak: Landscapes and Elegies* (1985). She was also a student of her region: *When Los Alamos Was a Ranch School* (with Fermor Church; 1974) and *Bones Incandescent: The Pajarito Journals of Peggy Pond Church* (2001); her account of Southwest writer Mary Hunter Austin was published as *Wind and Trail: The Early Life of Mary Austin* (1990). Pond's poetry is well represented in two collections: *New and Selected Poems* (1976) and *The Dancing Ground of Sky: The Selected Poetry of Peggy Pond Church* (1993). Sharon Snyder celebrates her life and accomplishment in *At Home on the Slopes of Mountains: The Story of Peggy Pond Church*.

Circle, a literary journal founded and edited by George Leite and Bern Porter, published ten issues from 1944–1948. (Leite also owned and operated Daliel's Bookstore and Gallery on Telegraph Avenue in Berkeley.) From the start the journal published images of art alongside poetry and other writing. The journal also encouraged political positions tending toward anarchist views and civil libertarianism, which explains why Kenneth Rexroth was an initial and sustaining supporter. *Circle* published poets of the Bay Area, including Robert Duncan, whose poems "The Years as Catches" appeared in nos. 7–8 (1946) and "Toward an African Elegy" in no. 10 (1948).

Clarke, John (1933–1992), was a devoted student of Olson's poetics and a charismatic teacher at the State University of New York at Buffalo. He wrote the booklet *Blake* (1974), which was part of the *Curriculum of the Soul* series. His later study *From Feathers to Iron* (1987) examined the significant influence of Olson's poetics.

Corman, Cid (1924–2004), was an American poet and editor of the magazine *Origin*. Corman was an intense and enthusiastic advocate for the new poetry and poetics growing out of Charles Olson and Robert Creeley's writing. The first of the five series of the magazine ran for twenty issues from spring 1951 to winter 1957. For Olson's instructions to Corman about the magazine, see Olson, *Letters for Origin*; see also Evans, *Charles Olson and Cid Corman: Complete Correspondence*. Seemingly going against the poetic direction of the magazine, Corman invited Samuel French Morse's essay "The Motive for Metaphor: Wallace Stevens: His Poetry and His Practice" to take up the whole issue of *Origin*, 1st ser., 5 (1952) (see Olson's letter to Duncan, November 25, 1951, above). Corman was also a dedicated poet who published more than a hundred small and regular volumes of poems, including the much-read and admired *Sun Rock Man* (1962) and *Livingdying* (1970). He published one selected volume, *Aegis: Selected Poems, 1970–1980* (1983), and then two volumes of the definitive selected poems in *OF* (1990), which was originally projected to run to five volumes. Some of his many notes and essays on poetry are collected in *Word for Word: Essays on the Arts of Language* (1977–1978).

Creeley, Robert (1926–2005), was a poet and fiction writer who became a close friend of Denise Levertov in 1949 and of Olson and Duncan in the 1950s. He established the Divers Press (1950–1954), taught at Black Mountain College (1954–1955), edited the *Black Mountain Review* (1954–1957), and taught at the State University of New

York at Buffalo and Brown University. He lived for a time with his first wife, Ann McKinnon, on Majorca, which is the setting for his novel *The Island* (1963). His many books include *Le Fou* (1952), *If You* (1956), *A Form of Women* (1959), *For Love: Poems, 1950–1960* (1962), *Words* (1967), *The Finger* (1968), *Pieces* (1969), *Collected Poems: 1945–1975* (1982), *Memory Gardens* (1986), *Collected Prose* (1988), *Collected Essays* (1989), *Life and Death* (1998), and *Collected Poems: 1975–2005* (2008).

Dahlberg, Edward (1900–1977), wrote autobiographical novels—*Bottom Dogs* (1930) and *From Flushing to Calvary* (1933)—that marked him as a proletarian author of the Depression era. His work includes *Do These Bones Live* (1941), *Because I Was Flesh: An Autobiography* (1964), *The Edward Dahlberg Reader* (1967), and *The Leafless American* (1967). Duncan reviewed his *Sorrows of Priapus* (1957).

Dorn, Edward (1929–1999), studied with Charles Olson at Black Mountain College. Fielding Dawson, Michael Rumaker, Jonathan Williams, and Dorn all became successful and recognized writers after Black Mountain's challenge to their creative thinking and analytic abilities. In a letter published later as *A Bibliography on America for Ed Dorn*, Olson defines a vision of the American experience based on the confrontation with the geography of the continent. That view showed up in Dorn's first book of poems, *The Newly Fallen* (1961), and continued into the books published while he was living in England, mainly *Geography* (1965) and *The North Atlantic Turbine* (1967). In the latter book, Dorn refined a condensed and precise style that matched the rapid articulation of his perceptions, and then which moved forward to the standing accomplishment of *Slinger* (1975), which collected the parts of *Gunslinger* published between 1968 and 1974. While Olson proposed a heroic vision of nineteenth-century America, compare the heroic quest of Ahab-Dorn, which turned that vision into a mock-heroic view that was still imbedded in a sense of geography, though now imbued with reference to the pervasive cultural issues of the 1960s and 1970s. It was a complex vision of cultural analysis and an eighteenth-century sense of satire as an intellectual corrective directed through a mode of social derision. *Collected Poems: 1956–1974* (1975) could be taken as a summary account of the early years, but it was *Slinger* and *Recollections of Gran Apacheria*, illustrated by Michael Myers (1974), which refocused Dorn's perception of the American West, as well as the sharp declarative lines and satirical accounts contained in the following books: *Hello, La Jolla* (1978), *Yellow Lola* (1981), and *Abhorrences* (1990). Dorn associated with poets and writers of many persuasions, but his own unique vision is firmly on view in recent collected editions of his work: *Way More West: New and Selected Poems* (2007), *Collected Poems* (2012), and *Derelict Air* (2015).

Duerden, Richard (1927–2000), was a part of the San Francisco Renaissance of poetry and participated in a group of poets that included Robert Duncan, Jack Spicer, Harold Dull, and Helen Adam. He published several books of poems, including *The Fork* (1965) and *The Left Hand and the Glory of Her* (1967). He edited the small magazine *Foot*, which ran for two issues in 1961 and 1962; issues three to seven ran between 1977 and 1979. Duncan's drawing of a foot appeared on the cover of the first issue, and then again on the cover of the third issue. In addition, two issues of Duerden's magazine *Rivoli Review* appeared in 1963 and 1964.

Dunn, Joe (1934–1996), was part of a circle of poets and artists in San Francisco that
included Robert Duncan, Jess Collins, Jack Spicer, Ebbe Borregaard, Helen Adam,
Harold Dull, and others. After Dunn and his wife, Carolyn, moved to San Francisco from Boston with Spicer, he learned how to operate an AM multilith offset
press and began printing books of poems under the imprint of White Rabbit Press,
including his own volume of poetry, *The Better Dream House* (1968). Jess illustrated
and made covers for books by Jack Spicer, Helen Adam, Denise Levertov, and
Charles Olson, while Duncan illustrated books by Ebbe Borregaard and George
Stanley. Later Paul Alexander, Knute Stiles, and Graham Mackintosh were associated with the press. The White Rabbit Press existed from 1957 until 1981. A fuller
story of the press appears in Johnston, *Bibliography of the White Rabbit Press*, while
Carolyn Dunn and Kevin Killian discuss White Rabbit and the writing of the period
in *Eyewitness: From Black Mountain to White Rabbit*.

Eigner, Larry (1927–1996), was a poet from Swampscott, Massachusetts, who published in
Origin and the *Black Mountain Review*. He lived with cerebral palsy, and his poems
are brief notations of immediate perceptions and observations, the phrases organized spatially on the page. He spent his last decades in Berkeley. His collections
include *From the Sustaining Air* (1953), *On My Eyes* (1960), *Selected Poems* (1972),
Waters, Places, a Time (1983), *Windows/Walls/Yard/Ways* (1994), and *The Collected
Poems of Larry Eigner* (2010).

Evergreen Review was edited by Donald Allen and Barney Rosset during its influential first
eight issues, beginning in 1957. Rosset remained the editor until the ninety-seventh
issue in 1973. The editors published emerging European writers such as Albert
Camus, Samuel Beckett, and Eugene Ionesco along with new American poets like
Ginsberg, Duncan, and Olson. Duncan appeared in a section of the second issue,
1957, on the "San Francisco Scene."

Everson, William (Brother Antoninus) (1912–1994), was a California poet and printer at
his Lime Kiln Press. He was an associate of Duncan's from the time he returned to
the Bay Area from a Conscientious Objectors camp in Oregon after World War II.
He was a serious contributor to the poetry of the Bay Area and Northern California,
which he celebrated in *The Veritable Years, 1949–1966* (1978). His early collections
became central texts in the San Francisco Renaissance: *Single Source: The Early
Poems of William Everson, 1934–1940* (1966), *The Crooked Lines of God* (1959), and
The Hazards of Holiness (1962). He was married to Mary Fabilli before converting
to the Catholic faith and taking the name Brother Antoninus when he joined the
Dominican Order in 1951. Two other volumes state Everson's loyalty to the poet
Robinson Jeffers and to the West: *Robinson Jeffers: Fragments of an Older Fury*
(1968) and *Archetype West: The Pacific Coast as a Literary Region* (1974). See also
"'Where as Giant Kings We Gatherd': Some Letters from Robert Duncan to William
Everson, 1940 and After" (1985).

Fabilli, Mary (1914–2011), and her sister Lillian became friends of Robert Duncan at
Berkeley in 1937–1938. Mary was a poet, short story writer, and artist, while Lil-
lian favored direct political action and labor organizing. Mary appeared in Robert
Duncan's *Berkeley Miscellany* publications, and early in her career was praised by

William Carlos Williams. She wrote under the name Aurora Bligh and was married to William Everson. Her early writing is collected in *Aurora Bligh and Early Poems* (1968); other books include *The Old Ones* (1966) and *The Animal Kingdom* (1975).

Ferlinghetti, Lawrence (1919–), is an American poet and painter well known as the co-founder of City Lights Bookstore in San Francisco, an institution that became the center of the Beat Movement and San Francisco Renaissance, and continues to be a gathering place for poets, readers, painters, and those who relish the atmosphere of Bay Area life in the 1950s and 1960s. He began the Pocket Poets series with his own first book, *Pictures of the Gone World* (1955), and the series soon included Allen Ginsberg's *Howl and Other Poems* (1956), Robert Duncan's *Selected Poems* (1959), Frank O'Hara's *Lunch Poems* (1964), Michael McClure's *Ghost Tantras* (1964), Charles Bukowski's *Notes of a Dirty Old Man*, and Gary Snyder's *Rip Rap* (1959). Jack Kerouac in his novel *Big Sur* (1962) depicted "Lorenzo Monsanto" as a Ferlinghetti figure. Ferlinghetti's later book *A Coney Island of the Mind* (1958) established him as a social critic with strong pacifist views, which turned to social satire in *Tyrannus Nix* (1969). His selected poems appeared in 1993 as *These Are My Rivers: New and Selected Poems*; he remains active as a poet, painter, and political activist.

Ferrini, Vincent (1913–2007), was an American poet who lived in Gloucester, Massachusetts. His early books include *No Smoke* (1941) and *The House of Time* (1954). He edited a poetry magazine titled *Four Winds* and published four issues between the summer of 1952 and the winter of 1953. In *The Maximus Poems*, "Letter 5," Olson writes to Ferrini as the "Editor of a Gloucester Quarterly":

> I do not know that Four Winds has a place
> or I a sight in it
> in a city where highliners breed
> if it is not as good as fish is.

And then in conclusion makes his final point:

> It's no use.
> There is no place we can meet.
> You have left Gloucester.
> You are not there, you are anywhere
> where there are little magazines
> will publish you.
> (*Maximus Poems*, 23 and 29)

Ferrini's collected poems are *Know Fish* (1979), *The Navigators: Know Fish* (1984), and *The Community of Self: Know Fish* (1986).

Floating Bear: A Newsletter began in New York City in 1961 with Diane di Prima and LeRoi Jones as editors; it came to an end in 1971 after thirty-eight issues. ***Floating Bear*** published a variety of poets from New York and San Francisco, including Duncan, Olson, Frank O'Hara, Denise Levertov, and Philip Whalen. Its distinguishing feature was that poems were published almost as soon as they were acccepted, so that it was possible to read the latest work very quickly.

Four Pages, a magazine edited by Dallam Simpson, appeared in nine issues, all literally four pages–or eight sides–in length, between January and September 1948. Simpson was also proprietor of the Cleaners Press, first of Galveston, Texas, and then of Washington, DC. Many well-known writers published pieces in *Four Pages*: William Carlos Williams, Marianne Moore, Stephen Spender, Frank Moore, W. S. Merwin, and Jackson Mac Low, among others; Duncan published three pieces. While being confined at St. Elizabeths, Pound was forbidden to publish his writing, but Dallam Simpson published selections of his prose and poetry in *Four Pages*. Under the name Dallam Flynn, he also published and prefaced Basil Bunting's *Poems 1950* (1950).

Fuck You: A Magazine of the Arts was an influential, mimeographed literary magazine produced from 1962 to 1965 in the home of poet, activist, and musician Ed Sanders in New York City. Thirteen issues were published along with numerous broadsides and manifestos.

Gerhardt, Rainer M. (1927–1954), was a German poet and the author of *Der tod des Hamlet* (1950); he edited a magazine titled *fragmente*; two issues appeared 1951–1952. Olson's poem "To Gerhardt, There among Europe's Things, of Which He Has Written Us in His 'Brief an Creeley und Olson,'" first appeared in *Origin* (Winter 1951–1952). See Michael Kellner, *Falk* (1984), which contains poems by Olson and Robert Creeley translated into German and other materials from *fragmente*.

Ginsberg, Allen (1926–1997), was a key figure in the Beat movement in New York and San Francisco. His poems combine anxiety, exaltation, radical politics, and a drive toward sexual and visionary ecstasy. He came to prominence following the Six Gallery reading in 1955 in San Francisco, where he performed with Philip Lamantia, Michael McClure, Gary Snyder, and Philip Whalen. In the 1960s, his political stances focused on resistance to the Vietnam War and to nuclear proliferation, and he vocalized and embodied many of the objectives of countercultural activism, especially gay rights. His books include *Howl* (1956), *Kaddish* (1961), *The Fall of America* (1972), *Collected Poems, 1947–1980* (1984), *White Shroud* (1985), *Death and Fame* (1999), *Deliberate Prose* (2000), and *Collected Poems, 1947–1997* (2007).

Gleason, Madeline (1903–1979), originally from North Dakota, arrived in San Francisco where she organized poetry readings and brought together a group of poets in the 1940s which grew into the founding of the Poetry Center by Ruth Witt-Diamant; that activity also built a foundation for the poetry renaissance of the 1950s. She was a painter of haunting cityscapes at night, a close friend and associate of Duncan and Jess, and also a poet of intense psychological and religious journeys. She wrote *The Metaphysical Needle* (1949) and *Concerto for Bell and Telephone* (1966), which led to *Here Comes Everybody: New and Selected Poems* (1975) and then to her final collection, *Collected Poems: 1919–1979* (1999).

Golden Goose was a little magazine coedited by Frederick Eckman and Richard Wirtz Emerson. The Golden Goose Press published books of poems, including Creeley, *Le Fou*.

Haeckel, Ernst Heinrich (1834–1919), was a German zoologist, naturalist, physician, and philosopher; he is the author of *The History of Creation*. He coined many commonly used words, such as biology, ecology, anthropology, and stem cell. He championed Charles Darwin's ideas of natural selection, but he is important for Duncan and Olson for propounding the theory that ontogeny recapitulated, or repeated, phylogeny. In other words, the growth of an individual organism (its ontology) repeats the evolutionary history of a species (its phylogeny). Olson cites Haeckel's theory in three letters: May 31–June 12, 1955; August 21, 1955; and August 24, 1955. In each instance he proposes the birth of form as a projective version of poetic forms.

Harrison, Jane Ellen (1850–1928), was a British classics scholar who helped found modern studies in Greek mythology. *The Prolegomena* (1903) and the second edition of her *Themis* (1927) were influential for both Duncan and Olson, though the latter especially embraced her descriptions of enactments of rituals in archaic Greece, with emphasis on the action and expressed terms, not just the individual feeling, of religious ceremony. Olson was particularly drawn to Harrison's description of *dromenon*, "the thing done."

Hawkins, Bobbie Louise (1930–), was born and raised in West Texas. She won a following as a short story writer, poet, and artist in various media. When she was attending art school in Albuquerque (University of New Mexico), she met Robert Creeley who was then teaching at Albuquerque Academy, a school for boys, and attempting to enter graduate school at the University. Hawkins and Creeley lived together in common law marriage until 1976; they had two children, Sarah and Katherine. The couple moved to Bolinas, California, in 1975, and it was there that Bobbie Louise Hawkins experimented with Xerox art and other forms of media and writing. Her first one-woman show of paintings and collages was at the Gotham Book Mart in New York City in 1974. Her early books include *Our Own Body* (1973), *Frenchy and Cuban Pete* (1977), and *Back to Texas* (1977). Her albums appearing in the early 1980s included *Live at the Great American Music Hall*, with Terry Garthwaite and Rosalie Sorrels. More poems and stories followed in *Almost Everything* (1982), *One Small Saga* (1984), and *My Own Alphabet: Stories, Essays and Memoir* (1989). She was on the faculty of the Jack Kerouac School of Disembodied Poetics in Boulder, Colorado, until 2010.

Hodes, Ida (1914–), a native of Chicago, was a figure in the San Francisco poetry scene from the early 1950s onward. She was assistant director of the Poetry Center at San Francisco State University after Robert Duncan. Olson was to deliver lectures and give a reading at the Poetry Center in February 1957 during her time there. She was a good friend of Duncan and Jess.

Horton, David T. See **Kasper, John**.

Huss, Wesley (1918–), taught drama and acting at Black Mountain College. When Duncan's play *Medea at Kolchis* was performed at Black Mountain on August 29 and 30, 1956, Huss played Garrow. A year earlier, as noted in his letter to Duncan June 12, 1955, Olson was not pleased with Huss's production of Sophocles's play *Women of Trachis* at the College. During the final period of Black Mountain College, Huss served as the bursar and therefore helped Olson settle the accounts of the college. He later moved to the Bay Area and remained active in the theater.

Inferno was a small literary magazine based in San Francisco, which was published by Leslie Woolf Hedley from 1950 to 1956.

Jacobus, Harry (1927–), is an American painter and longtime friend of Duncan and Jess Collins. Jess and Jacobus were students at California School of Fine Arts at the same time in the late 1940s. Jacobus traveled to Europe with Duncan and Jess in 1955, but when they went to Mallorca, he went to Greece and other cities in Europe. The three drove a car from San Francisco to New York, and because Jacobus was nervous about making the rental car drop-off on time, they had only a one-night stop at Black Mountain College to see Charles Olson. As a visual artist Jacobus began as a non-objective painter, which he remained during most of his career. He lived on the island of Hydra in Greece from 1966 to 1972, where he painted large, colorful abstract canvases, which excited both Duncan and Jess who bought a number of them from slides Jacobus sent them. For many years, Jacobus lived around the Bay Area, but now resides in Foley, Alabama. See Wagstaff's "An Interview with Harry Jacobus" and Duncan's "Statement on Jacobus for Borregaard's Museum," both reprinted in Duncan's *Collected Essays and Other Prose*.

Jargon Society was a run of publications initiated by Jonathan Williams in 1951. In the following years, he put out books by Olson, Creeley, Duncan, and others in the Williams-Olson line. Duncan's *Letters* was published by Jargon in 1958.

Jess [Collins] (1923–2004) was born Burgess Franklin Collins and grew up in Long Beach, California. He attended Long Beach State and, when drafted into the military, worked on the Manhattan Project as a chemist; in 1946 after leaving the army, he found employment with the Hanford Atomic Energy Project in Richmond, Washington. In 1949, he enrolled at what was then the California School of Fine Arts (now the San Francisco Art Institute). In January 1951, he began a domestic life with Robert Duncan that lasted until the latter's death in 1988. Many of the themes of his early works came from fairy tales, tales of fantasy, old legends, and romantic stories, as well as from scientific sources. Together with Duncan, in the 1950s, Jess worked on visual word collages that became a series of elaborate and complex images he called "paste-ups." Early showings of his work appeared at Gump's, 1959 (mentioned in the letters) and the Ubu Gallery, 1953. A large show of his *Paste-ups and Assemblies 1951–1983* appeared at the John and Mable Ringling Museum of Art, 1984. In 1959, Jess began a number of paintings called *Translations*, which grew into a series of complex visual works derived from public images. These compositions with an introduction by Duncan appeared in a catalog in 1971. Another series, *Salvages*, was begun that same year. For it, Jess used old paintings of his own and those he found in second-hand stores, revising them into his painterly vision. The culmination of art paste-up and translations appears in the completed *Narkissos* collage and graphite work, 1991, a visual accumulation requiring more than twenty years of careful attention. Jess and Duncan were strong and consistent supporters of artists and writers in San Francisco, even as the two produced their own books of drawings and holographic poems, the most handsome of which is *A Book of Resemblances*

(1966). Michael Auping assembled a retrospective of Jess's work called *Jess: A Grand Collage: 1951–1993* that began its national tour at Buffalo's Albright Knox Art Gallery, 1993.

Jones, LeRoi (Amiri Baraka) (1934–2014), was in 1963 an editor of *Kulchur*, where parts of Olson's essay "Proprioception" first appeared in 1960. As the coeditor (with Diane di Prima) of *Yugen* and *Floating Bear*, Jones oversaw the publication of other portions of the essay from 1960 to 1962. After the 1965 assassination of Malcolm X, Jones changed his name to Amiri Baraka and participated in the Black Arts movement, aiming a charged political critique at white supremacy in US society while also increasing awareness of African American culture, literature, and history. Throughout the many phases of his career as an author, music critic, activist, black nationalist, and Marxist, he remained devoted to Black Mountain poetics, especially as expressed by Olson, Edward Dorn, and others. Key works include *Blues People: The Negro Experience in White America* (1963), *The Autobiography of LeRoi Jones* (1997), *Amiri Baraka and Edward Dorn: The Collected Letters* (2013), and *S O S: Poems 1961–2013* (2015).

Kaiser, Augusta Elizabeth (Betty) (1925–1964), was Charles Olson's second common-law wife. She was killed in a car accident on March 28, 1964, in Wyoming, New York.

Kasper, John (1929–1998), and T. David Horton (1927–) were frequent visitors to Pound at St. Elizabeths Hospital in Washington, DC. Together they published the Square Dollar series of pamphlets, which included Ernest Fenollosa's *The Chinese Written Character as a Medium for Poetry* (1951), *Gists from Agassiz*, a selection of Louis Agassiz's writing edited by Kasper, and Alexander Del Mar's *Roman and Moslem Moneys*. See Seelye, *Charles Olson and Ezra Pound*, xxiv–xxv.

Katue, Kitasono (1902–1978), was a Japanese poet and the founder and editor of *Vou*, a magazine of experimental writing in Japan. Pound translated a selection of his writing for Ronald Duncan's magazine *Townsman* (1938). Katue translated Pound as well as William Carlos Williams. His volume *Black Rain* was published by the Divers Press in 1954.

Kelly, Robert (1935–), is a prolific American poet who helped establish the Hawk's Well Press in New York City; he was also the editor of the little magazines *Matter* and *Trobar*. With Paris Leary, he edited an anthology of poetry, *A Controversy of Poets* (1965). He teaches at Bard College, where he was a founding member of the Milton Avery Graduate School of the Arts. Some of his many books include *Armed Descent* (1961), *Cities* (1972), *Spiritual Exercises* (1981), *The Time of Voice: Poems, 1994–1996* (1998), *Opening the Seals* (2016), and *The Hexagon* (2016).

Lansing, Gerrit (1928–), is an American poet who was born in Albany, New York, grew up in northern Ohio, and was educated at Harvard and Columbia. He lived for a time in New York City working in a record store and was a participant in the poetic ambiance and friendships with poets around Frank O'Hara. For a time, he ran a bookstore in Annapolis, and then moved to Gloucester, MA. Like Duncan and Olson, Lansing has spent a lifetime reading and accumulating knowledge about literary, occult, and historical matters. His first collection, *The Heavenly Tree Grows*

Downward (1966), finds intellectual and spiritual resonance with the work of Robert Kelly, Chuck Stein, Kenneth Irby, and others. These poets have the wisdom of learning Olson confronted in Duncan, but all put their wisdom to the articulation of the imagination as a greater goal than wisdom itself. It is little wonder then when Lansing proposed a small magazine called *Set*, Duncan was enthusiastic. Lansing edited and published two issues of the journal in 1961 and 1963, and Duncan's poem "Osiris and Set" appeared in the first edition. Lansing has been a guiding figure behind Olson's legacy in Gloucester for generations of younger poets. His *Heavenly Tree, Northern Earth* (2009) includes the poems published in *Analytic Psychology* (1983), the twenty-third booklet in the *Curriculum of the Soul* series.

Levertov, Denise (1923–1997), met Duncan for the first time in New York City on his way to Europe in 1955. Levertov was a highly published and prolific poet whose work intersected with concerns proposed by Charles Olson, Robert Creeley, and Robert Duncan; Cid Corman published some of her earliest work in *Origin*. Her lyric range, however, remained consistently her own, based on a physicality and imagery derived early on from William Carlos Williams. She and Duncan maintained an intense and extensive correspondence that has been collected as Bertholf and Gelpi, *The Letters of Robert Duncan and Denise Levertov* (2004). Her strongly articulated political positions against the Vietnam War, a key focus of her correspondence with Duncan, appears most compellingly in *To Stay Alive* (1971). For Levertov's views on the correspondence, see "Some Duncan Letters: A Memoir and a Critical Tribute," in her *Light Up the Cave* (1981).

Loewinsohn, Ron (1937–2014), was a poet and novelist who was associated with the San Francisco Renaissance and taught at the University of California, Berkeley. Some of his publications are *Meat Air: Poems, 1959–1969* (1970), *Goat Dances* (1976), *Magnetic Field(s)* (1983), and *Where All the Ladders Start: A Novel* (1987).

MacDonald, George (1824–1905), was a Scottish preacher, poet, and novelist, best known for his romances, fairy tales, and fantasy fiction: *At the Back of the North Wind* (1871), *The Princess and the Goblin* (1872), *The Princess and Curdie* (1883), and *Lilith* (1895). He was a best seller in Victorian England, avidly admired by C. S. Lewis, W. H. Auden, and G. K. Chesterton, and in his American lecture tour of 1872–1873 he befriended Walt Whitman and Henry W. Longfellow; even Mark Twain was an admirer. Helen Adam, Jess, and Duncan read his work avidly. Some titles remain in the library of Robert Duncan.

Mac Low, Jackson (1922–2004), was an experimental poet, playwright, and composer who based his early writing and composing on chance operations in words and music. Since the 1970s, his work has been associated with Language Poetry. He met Robert Duncan in New York City in 1945. Some of his publication are *August Light Poems* (1967), *22 Light Poems* (1968), *Words nd Ends from Ez* (1989), and *Barnesbook: Four Poems Derived from Sentences by Djuna Barnes* (1996). John Cage and Kurt Schwitters provided models and influences for his work, some of which he honored in *42 Merzgedichte: In Memoriam, Kurt Schwitters* (1994). The range and vitality of his writing are everywhere obvious in the collection *Doings: Assorted Performance Pieces, 1955–2002* (2005).

Mahl, Claire (1917–1988), was a New York and California painter, editor, and friend of Duncan and Jess. She was the editor of the publication the *Artist's View*, which after an introductory issue in May 1951 published seven issues between July 1952 and March 1954. Jess, Duncan, Madeline Gleason, David Park, and Philip Roeber were some of the writers and artists featured. Each issue was two pages with four sides of writing and reproductions of paintings and drawings. Duncan's poem "An About Face," in his *Names of People*, is dedicated to her. His essay "Pages from a Notebook" first appeared in the *Artist's View* 5 and provoked Olson's response in "Against Wisdom as Such."

Marshall, Edward (1932–2005), was a poet associated with the Black Mountain and Beat groups; he published in the *Black Mountain Review*. His long poem "Leave the Word Alone" was included in Donald Allen's *The New American Poetry* (1960) and was a source for Allen Ginsberg's *Kaddish*. His books include *Hellan, Hellan* (1960) and *Transit Glory* (1967).

McClure, Michael (1932–), was born in Kansas and went to San Francisco to study painting, but after meeting Robert Duncan he began to focus on poetry instead. He was influenced by Charles Olson and Robert Creeley, a poet and playwright in the Beat Movement and the San Francisco Poetry Renaissance, and participated in the reading at Six Gallery with Ginsberg, Rexroth, Snyder, and others. His early books—*Hymns to St. Geryon and Other Poems* (1959), *The New Book/A Book of Torture* (1961), and *Ghost Tantras* (1964)—established his views on a Dionysian and erotic celebration of bodily and biological existence and natural process. Some of these works are collected in *Huge Dreams: San Francisco and Beat Poems* (1999), while his literary positions are confirmed in *Scratching the Beat Surface* (1982), talks given at SUNY at Buffalo as part of the Charles Olson Memorial Lectures. McClure's *Mysteriosos and Other Poems* (2010) continues his vision of poetry. The full range of his writing and thinking appears in *Lighting the Corners on Nature, Art, and the Visionary: Essays and Interviews* (1993) and *Of Indigo and Saffron: New and Selected Poems* (2011).

Measure, edited by John Wieners, published three issues between the summer of 1957 and the summer of 1962. The magazine was supported by Charles Olson and Robert Duncan, and published poets associated with Black Mountain College and the poetry world of San Francisco.

Merwin, William Stanley (1927–), is an American poet and translator whose early poetry in *A Mask for Janus* (1944) was selected by W. H. Auden for the Yale Younger Poets series. This early book attracted Olson's attention. His books include *Green with Beasts* (1956), *The Moving Target* (1963), *The Lice* (1967), *New Selected Poems* (1988), *The River Sound: Poems* (1999), and *Garden Time* (2016).

Migrant, edited by Gael Turnbull and Michael Shayer, published eight issues from July 1959 to September 1960. Ed Dorn, Robert Creeley, Denise Levertov, Robert Duncan, and Larry Eigner appeared along with Roy Fisher and Michael Shayer. The magazine helped introduce the new American poetry to British readers.

Miles, Josephine (1911–1985), was a poet and professor at the University of California,

Berkeley. Her professional publications include *The Vocabulary of Poetry: Three Studies* (1946), *Style and Proportion: The Language of Prose and Poetry* (1966), and *Poetry and Change: Donne, Milton, Wordsworth, and the Equilibrium of the Present* (1974). Her poems appeared in journals and magazines regularly, and she published them in a series of books, including *Prefabrications* (1955), *Fields of Learning* (1968), *Poems: 1930–1960* (1983), and *Collected Poems* (1983). She was impressed by Beat poetry and helped Allen Ginsberg publish *Howl* and was one of Jack Spicer's teachers. The English Department granted her tenure as full professor, the first woman at Berkeley to achieve that position.

Morse, Samuel French (1916–1985), was an American poet. Wallace Stevens published Morse's *Time of Year: A First Book of Poems* (1943) and wrote the introduction, and Morse's book about Stevens followed later: *Wallace Stevens: Poetry as Life* (1970). Morse's *Collected Poems* appeared ten years after his death (1995), and his essay "The Motive for Metaphor: Wallace Stevens: His Poetry and His Practice" comprised the whole of *Origin*, 1st ser., 5 (1952).

Niagara Frontier Review, edited by Charles Boer, Charles Olson, and then by Harvey Brown, published three issues from Buffalo, 1964–1966, where Charles Olson was teaching at the State University of New York at Buffalo. Harvey Brown established the Frontier Press, and so was the publisher of *Niagara Frontier Review*, as well as a series of books that includes Brooks Adams, *The New Empire* (1967), and Ed Dorn's novel *By the Sound* (1971). Charles Boer was also the coeditor, with George F. Butterick, of Charles Olson's book *The Maximus Poems*, volume 3, and Boer is the author of *Charles Olson in Connecticut*. *Niagara Frontier Review* published poets who were following Olson's poetry and poetics, including Robert Creeley and Robert Duncan as well as Ed Dorn, Robert Kelly, and John Wieners. The cover of the first issue (Summer 1964) reproduced a photograph of Olson teaching at a chalkboard.

Oliveros, Pauline (1932–2016), was a composer who lived in the Bay Area. Oliveros's compositions, performances, and conceptual approaches to postwar experimental music brought attention to ideas like "deep listening" and "sonic awareness." Her methods of improvisation and ritual, along with her interest in the processing of information in tonal patterns, correlate with Duncan's and Olson's proprioceptive understanding of poetry. *Three Songs for Soprano and Piano* (1980) contains settings of Duncan's "An Interlude of Rare Beauty" and Olson's "The Songs of Maximus: Song 6."

Origin, a journal edited by Cid Corman from the spring of 1951 to the fall of 1985, cultivated the poetry and poetics of Charles Olson and Robert Creeley, featured Robert Duncan, Denise Levertov, and others, and helped to shape reception of the new American poetry. The first series ran for twenty issues from the spring of 1951 to the winter of 1957; the second was fourteen issues, from the spring of 1961 to the summer of 1964; the third consisted of twenty issues, from the fall of 1965 to the winter of 1971; the fourth series ran for twenty issues, October 1977 to July 1982; and the short fifth series ran for four issues from the fall of 1983 to the fall of 1985. Corman was an active and involved editor even into the final series. For insight to the formation of the first series, see Olson's correspondence with Corman in Olson, *Letters for*

Origin; for context and discussion of *Origin*'s influence on shaping North American poetics, see Golding's "Little Magazines and Alternative Canons: The Example of *Origin*."

Oyez Press published authors connected to the Black Mountain school and the San Francisco Renaissance. Robert Hawley and Stevens van Strum offered books and broadsides by Duncan, Olson, Josephine Miles, Denise Levertov, and others beginning in 1964. Oyez published more than eighty books over a twenty-year period.

Paracelsus (1493–1541) was a Swiss doctor, astrologer, and alchemist who believed in diagnosing human illness instead of seeking explanations in the four elements. He wanted to cure diseases with chemical agents and so is known as the founder of modern medical chemistry. He proposed a system of symbolic correspondences between the macrocosm and the microcosm. The following books appear in Duncan's private library: Paracelsus, *Paracelsus: Selected Writings*; Jung, *Selected Writings: Alchemical Studies*; Jung, *The Spirit in Man, Art, and Literature*; Debus, *The English Paracelsians*; and Koyre, *Mystiques, spirituels, alchemistes*.

Parkinson, Thomas (1920–1991), was a poet and professor in the English Department, University of California at Berkeley. He and Duncan had been acquaintances and at times were friends from the period when Duncan returned to Healdsburg and Berkeley in 1946. He was a scholar of Yeats and a friend to many poets. His books of poetry include *Thanatos: Poems for the Earth* (1965), *Homage to Jack Spicer* (1970), and *Poems: New and Selected* (1988). Parkinson edited *Hart Crane and Yvor Winters: Their Literary Correspondence* (1978), and wrote several books of criticism, among them *W. B. Yeats: The Later Poetry* (1964).

Patchen, Kenneth (1911–1972), was an American poet, novelist, and artist. Duncan met him in New York City in the 1940s when he and Virginia Admiral were typists for Anaïs Nin. Patchen's volume *Fables and Other Little Tales* (1953) appeared as Jargon 6, and his book *Hurray for Anything: Poems and Drawings* (1957) was published as Jargon 21. In writing to Olson (April 15, 1957), Duncan said, "Jonathan sent—arrived in this morning's mail an absolutely lousy book by Patchen. O my dear God! It cast the fear of the lord in me for them, self-indulgences that so barely hide an insolence toward the orders of the art." Even though Duncan was not a fan of Patchen's writing, Patchen did publish a long list of books, including the popular *The Journal of Albion Moonlight* (1944), which appears in Robert Duncan's library. Patchen was both popular to and influential on the Beat poets, and his reputation continues with *Collected Poems* (1968) and *Awash with Roses: Collected Love Poems of Kenneth Patchen* (1991).

Perkoff, Stuart Z. (1930–1974), was an American poet. Two of his poems, "The Blind Girl" and "To Be Read on Festival Days," appeared in *Origin* (1951). Jonathan Williams published Perkoff's first book, *Suicide Room: Poems* (1956), as Jargon 17.

Porter, Bern (1911–2004), was an American publisher, poet, scientist, and, to some, a philosophical radical. He edited and published *Henry Miller Miscellanea* (1945) and *The Happy Rock: A Book about Henry Miller* (1945). From 1944 to 1948 he was a coeditor (with George Leite) of the literary magazine *Circle*, and as an editor he accepted poems by Robert Duncan. He later published Henry Miller's *Books Tangent to Circle*. He also had a career working on the Manhattan Project, though he became a pacifist. In his later years he turned to concrete and visual poems like those collected in his *Found Poems* (1972).

Raworth, Thomas Moore (1938–2017), was a British poet, and visual artist. As a young man be founded and edited the small magazine *Outburst* (1959–64) and co-founded, with Barry Hall, Goliard Press (1965–67), later Cape Goliard Press, publisher of Olson's *Archaeologist of Morning* (1970). Goliard Press published Raworth's early books, *Weapon Man* (1965), *Continuation* (1966), and *The Relation Ship* (1967). Though he is recognized as a leader in the British Poetry Revival, he developed close relationships with the Black Mountain poets, mainly Robert Creeley, Charles Olson, and Edward Dorn. In the 1970s he was associated with Holbrook Teeter's Zephyrus Image press in San Francisco and with the poetry of John Ashbery. Raworth has published books of poems steadily from the 1970s to the present; the volumes *Tottering State: New and Selected Poems, 1965–1983* (1984) and *Collected Poems* (2003) expanded his reputation on both sides of the Atlantic. His *Earn Your Milk: Collected Essays* was published in 2009.

Rexroth, Kenneth (1905–1982), was an American poet, man of letters, and political activist as well as a central figure in the San Francisco Renaissance. His program of news and review of poetry on KPFA shaped the literary taste of Bay Area listeners. His anarchist political views as well as his interest in Japanese literature and the fusion of Christianity and Buddhism, along with his focus on environmental issues, were highly influential. He published widely, but the volumes *Collected Shorter Poems* (1966), *Collected Longer Poems* (1968), and *World Outside the Window: Selected Essays* (1987), established the depth and vision of his achievement. A more recent publication, *The Complete Poems* (2003), was edited by Sam Hamill and Bradford Morrow. Duncan refers to Rexroth's *An Autobiographical Novel* (1966), 243–46, in the salutation "Dear Ole Olson" in an early letter (Berkeley 1949?).

Richardson, Lawrence (Larry) (1920–1991), was an American scholar and poet, the author of *Poetical Theory in Republican Rome* (1944). Richardson's "Avignon and Babylon" appeared in the *Yale Poetry Review* in 1945, and other poems appeared in three later issues of the *Yale Poetry Review*.

Roethke, Theodore (1908–1963), was a poet who drew on romantic and modernist impulses, whose poems alternated between traditional forms and free verse. He taught for many years at the University of Washington in Seattle. His books include *Open House* (1941), *The Far Field* (1961), *Collected Poems* (1966), *Selected Letters* (1968), and *On the Poet and His Craft: Selected Prose* (1965).

Rosset, Barney (1922–2012), founded the Grove Press and then became the publisher of the writers of the new and experimental prose and poetry of his time. Richard Seaver was the managing editor. He published the uncensored version of D. H. Lawrence's *Lady Chatterley's Lover* (1959), and with the publication of Henry Miller's novel *The Tropic of Cancer* (1961), he successfully won a victory for free speech. In 1957 the *Evergreen Review*, which enjoyed the editorial assistance of Donald Allen and

Fred Jordon, featured Jean-Paul Sartre and Samuel Beckett in the first issue and focused on the "San Francisco Scene" in the second. Contributions by Henry Miller, William Burroughs, Pablo Neruda, Harold Pinter, Tom Stoppard, Octavio Paz, and many other experimental and world-class writers appeared in the *Review* right through to the final 96th issue in 1973.

Roth, William M. (1916–2014), was an executive of a shipping company and a regent of the University of California, who served as US trade representative (1967–1969) and later taught at Princeton University. He was also a patron who supported Duncan's efforts at the Ubu Gallery in 1953. He and his wife, Joan Osborn, purchased several paintings by Jess, including a portrait of Joan.

Rukeyser, Muriel (1913–1980), was a poet, social and political activist, and translator. As a judge for the Bender Foundation, she read the manuscript of Duncan's first book, *Heavenly City, Earthly City*, and admired it. She reviewed the book after its publication in "Myth and Torment" (1948). Her *U.S. 1* (1938) is perhaps the most distinguished book of poems about the Depression. Her *Life of Poetry* (1949) is a passionate statement on the imperative for poetry to confront social and political issues; *Collected Poems* (1978) gives a summary of her career as a poet.

Rumaker, Michael (1932–), was a student of Duncan who graduated from Black Mountain College. In letters to Creeley and Olson, Duncan develops his rationale for endorsing his graduation from the college. Rumaker established his reputation as a short story writer in college, and then published a run of collections, including *Exit 3 and Other Stories* (1966), *Gringos and Other Stories* (1967), and *My First Satyrnalia* (1981). A history of his relationship with Duncan was described in Rumaker's narrative "Robert Duncan in San Francisco" (1978), which was reprinted in *Robert Duncan in San Francisco* (1996). His memoir *Black Mountain Days* (2003) reflects on his experiences as a writer.

Russell, Sanders (1909–1982?), was an American poet, whom Duncan met and admired as a writer when he was a student at Berkeley, 1937–1938. He was Duncan's first mentor in poetry. Duncan shared a cabin with Russell and Jack Johnson (a poet and artist) at Woodstock, New York, during the winter of 1940–1941. Russell published two volumes of poetry: *Poems* (1941) and *The Chemical Image* (1947).

Sauer, Carl Ortwin (1889–1975), was an American geographer whose work had an influence on Olson's, especially his "Environment and Culture during the Last Deglaciation" (1948) and "The Morphology of Landscape" (1925), both collected in Sauer, *Land and Life* (1963).

Set. See **Lansing, Gerrit.**

Shayer, Michael (1938–), is a British poet. His books include *Persephone* (1961) and *Poems from an Island* (1970).

Spicer, Jack (1925–1965), was a California poet associated with Robert Duncan and Robin Blaser in Berkeley in the late 1940s and with the San Francisco poetry scene of the 1950s and 1960s. His surreal and anti-poetic poems are self-conscious experiments testing the power and limits of language: *After Lorca* (1957), *Billy the Kid* (1959),

The Heads of the Town Up to the Aether (1962), *The Holy Grail* (1964), and *Language* (1965). *The Collected Books of Jack Spicer*, edited by Robin Blaser (1975), gathers these publications while Peter Gizzi and Kevin Killian have edited a more recent critical edition titled *my vocabulary did this to me: The Collected Poetry of Jack Spicer* (2008).

Tallman, Ellen (1927–2008) and **Warren** (1921–1994), held teaching positions at the University of British Columbia and were influential in introducing the projective poetics of Duncan, Olson, Creeley and others to western Canada. They invited Duncan to give a lecture on Charles Olson in 1961—the first lecture in this collection. In 1963 they helped organize and sponsor the Vancouver Poetry Festival, which brought together new American and Canadian poets. In the 1970s, Ellen Tallman shifted her interest to psychology and taught at Simon Fraser University and the Cold Mountain Institute. She invited Duncan to participate in several of the institute's seminars and retreats. Warren Tallman coedited (with Donald Allen) *Poetics of the New American Poetry* (1973) and a collection of literary criticism, *In the Midst* (1992). The Tallmans inspired the TISH movement, a group of UBC students who were influenced by the Black Mountain and New American traditions of poetry exemplified in the work of Duncan, Olson, and others.

Triem, Eve (1921–1999), was a poet who began her career as a translator of Greek poems with the book *Translations from the Greek Anthology* (1967). During this early period, she also knew E. E. Cummings and wrote a pamphlet about him, *E. E. Cummings* (1969), which established his place as a poet. She lived in San Francisco and Seattle and was the author of several books of poems, including *Parade of Doves* (1946) and *New as a Wave: A Retrospective, 1937–1983* (1984). In 1957, she was a member of the Maidens, a group of five poets led by Robert Duncan. After moving to Seattle in 1960, she was befriended by Denise Levertov, who was responsible for the publication of her final book, *Nobody Dies in the Summer: Selected Poems* (1993).

Trobar, edited by George Economou, Joan Kelly, and Robert Kelly, published five issues from New York City between 1960 and 1964. Robert Kelly's essay "Notes on the Poetry of Deep Image" appeared in the second issue. Robert Duncan published in each of the issues.

Tudor, David (1926–1996), was an American pianist who taught music at Black Mountain College. Later, in a company with John Cage, he became a leader in experimental and electronic music.

Turnbull, Gael (1928–2004), was a Scottish physician and poet. In his early life as a student and poet he moved back and forth between Scotland and North America. His first books were *Trio*, with Eli Mandel and Phyllis Webb (1954), and *The Knot in the Wood and Fifteen Other Poems* (1955). Cid Corman published his next book, *Bjarni Spike-Helgi's Son and Other Poems* (1956), and that publication brought him into the circle of the New American poets. While living in California, Turnbull edited, with Michael Shayer, eight issues of *Migrant* (July 1959–July 1960), which helped introduce the new American poets to British readers. He had close relationships with William Carlos Williams, Robert Duncan, Robert Creeley, Cid Corman, and Louis

Zukofsky, as well as with the British poets Charles Tomlinson, Edwin Morgan, and Ian Hamilton Finlay. The pamphlet was his favorite form of publication, and many of his were collected in *A Gathering of Poems, 1950–1980* (1983), while his prose journal appeared two years later as *A Year and a Day* (1985). After his death, his poems were gathered in *There Are Words: Collected Poems* (2006).

Twombly, Edwin Parker (Cy) (1928–2011), was an American artist and friend and colleague of Robert Rauschenberg who developed a calligraphic style of written figures on green, gray, or black bases. He enjoyed international acclaim as one of the artists (with Rauschenberg) who moved away from the directions established by abstract expressionism. As a student at Black Mountain College, he made the design for the cover wrapper of Duncan's *Song of the Border-guard* (1952), which is regarded as his first graphic work.

Wah, Fred (1939–), was a Canadian student at the State University of New York at Buffalo when Charles Olson was teaching at the school; Wah also attended the 1963 Vancouver Poetry Conference. He became the editor of a magazine titled *Sum*, which produced five issues, December 1963–April 1965, and he published Duncan's *Writing Writing*. Wah's book *Earth* (1974) appeared in the *Curriculum of the Soul* series.

Whalen, Philip (1923–2002), was a poet who was associated with Gary Snyder and Lew Welch. He became a figure in the San Francisco Renaissance and was also closely connected to Beat writers on the East Coast, including Jack Kerouac, who wrote about him in *The Dharma Bums*. Whalen was one of the readers at the Six Gallery in 1955. In 1973, he became a Zen Buddhist monk. His collections include *Memoirs of an Interglacial Age* (1960), *On Bear's Head* (1969), *Heavy Breathing: Poems, 1967–1980* (1983), *Canoeing Up Cabarga Creek: Buddhist Poems, 1955–1986* (1996), *Overtime: Selected Poems* (1999), and *The Collected Poems of Philip Whalen* (2007).

Whitehead, Alfred North (1861–1947), was a British mathematician and philosopher. His book *Process and Reality: An Essay in Cosmology* (1929) was central to Olson's poetics. He introduced the book to Duncan when he gave lectures in San Francisco during February–March 1957. Duncan also read and cited *The Aims of Education* (1929) and *Modes of Thought* (1938).

White Rabbit Press. See **Dunn, Joe**.

Wieners, John (1934–2002), was a poet who attended Black Mountain College from 1955 to 1956, studied under Charles Olson at the University at Buffalo, and was influenced by the Beats and by the Black Mountain group. He edited the journal *Measure*. His books include *The Hotel Wentley Poems* (1958), *Ace of Pentacles* (1964), *Asylum Poems* (1969), *Selected Poems: 1958–1984* (1986), and *Supplication: Selected Poems of John Wieners* (2015).

Williams, Jonathan (1929–2008), was an American poet, book designer, publisher, and photographer. He was a student at Black Mountain College and founder of the Jargon Society. His first book was *Garbage Litters the Iron Face of the Sun's Child* (1951), illustrated by David Ruff. Williams published Charles Olson's *The Maximus Poems 1–10* (1953) as Jargon 7, Robert Duncan's *Letters* (1958), and Robert Creeley's *A Form* *of Women: Poems* (1959). He planned to publish Kenneth Patchen's *Poemscapes*, and in a letter to Duncan dated July 19, 1954, wrote: "Anyway, an item I want by Xmas, along with the Patchen, is a Miscellanea of Olson: new verse, a bibliography, and notes & critiques by every capable man on the continent. Creeley thinks it cld be a good vehicle for raising funds for the rest of Maximus." The book was not published. Williams also had a career as a poet. *An Ear in Bartram's Tree: Poems, 1957–1967* (1969), with an introduction by Guy Davenport, was the first major collection, which was followed by *Blues and Roots, Rue and Bluets: A Garland for the Appalachians* (1971), with photos by Nicholas Dean, and *Elite/Elite: Poems, 1971–75* (1979), containing photos by Guy Mendes and an introduction by Guy Davenport. The eclectic collection *Blackbird Dust: Essays, Poems, and Photographs* (2000) was followed by the late selected poems, *Jubilant Thicket: New and Selected Poems* (2005). His essays appear in *The Magpie's Bagpipe: Selected Essays* (1982). Through the run of Jargon Society publications Williams stressed the relationship among photography, poetry, and book design. One of his final books of his own photographs specifies Williams's contributions as an artist, photographer, and publisher: *A Palpable Elysium: Portraits of Genius and Solitude* (2002), with an introduction by Guy Davenport.

Witt-Diamant, Ruth (1895–1987), was a professor at San Francisco State University, 1930–1962, where she founded and for many years (1954–61) directed the Poetry Center. As the director she was responsible for bringing many poets to read in San Francisco, including Robert Lowell, Dylan Thomas, W. H. Auden, Marianne Moore, Elizabeth Bishop, and Denise Levertov. She edited (with Rikutaro Fukuda) an anthology of poetry first published in Japan in 1968: *53 American Poets of Today* (1971). Duncan served as assistant director from September 1956 to June 1957. The Poetry Center continues the activity of inviting poets to read, and the recording of these readings has allowed the center to collect thousands of tapes, films, and discs (now digitally remastered for a research center in modern poetry).

Zukofsky, Louis (1904–1978), was a poet born in New York of Russian Jewish parents. Zukofsky was a friend of Ezra Pound and William Carlos Williams, and he was a central figure in the objectivist group of the 1930s, which included George Oppen and Charles Reznikoff. He edited *An "Objectivists" Anthology* (1932). His shorter experimental poems were collected in *All* (1966) and *Complete Short Poetry* (1992). His long poetic sequence *"A"* (1978) was influenced by Pound and Williams. His prose includes *Bottom: On Shakespeare* (1963); *Propositions: Collected Critical Essays* (1967); *Collected Fiction* (1990); and *Complete Short Poetry* (1992).

Bibliography

Robert Duncan's library, now housed in the Poetry Collection, State University of New York at Buffalo, contains some of the volumes listed below; their presence in his library can be checked with searches at http://p8991-bison.buffalo.edu.gate.lib.buffalo.edu.

Adam, Helen. *Ballads*. New York: Acadia, 1964.

———. *A Helen Adam Reader*. Edited by Kristin Prevallet. Orono, ME: National Poetry Foundation, 2007.

———. *San Francisco's Burning*. 1963. Brooklyn, NY: Hanging Loose, 1985.

———. *Selected Poems and Ballads*. New York: Helikon, 1974.

———. *Turn Again to Me and Other Poems*. New York: Kulchur Foundation, 1977.

Adams, Brooks. *The New Empire*. 1902. Introduction to the reprint by Charles Olson. Cleveland, OH: Frontier, 1967.

Adams, Charles Francis, ed. *The Works of John Adams, Second President of the United States with a Life of the Author, Notes, and Illus. by His Grandson, Charles Francis Adams*. 7 vols. Freeport, NY: Books for Libraries, 1969.

Adams, James Donald. *Literary Frontiers*. New York: Duel, Sloan and Pearce, 1951.

———. *The Shape of Books to Come*. New York: Viking, 1944.

Adorno, Rolena, and Patrick Charles Pautz, eds. *The Narrative of Cabeza de Vaca*. Lincoln: University of Nebraska Press, 2003.

Alcalay, Ammiel. *A Little History*. Edited by Fred Dewey. New York: re: public and UpSet, 2013.

Allen, Donald, ed. *The New American Poetry: 1945–1960*. New York: Grove, 1960.

Allen, Donald M., and Warren Tallman. *The Poetics of the New American Poetry*. New York: Grove, 1973.

Anastas, Peter. *Maximus to Gloucester: The Letters and Poems of Charles Olson to the Editor of the Gloucester Daily Times, 1962–1969*. Gloucester: Ten Pound Island, 1992.

Anastas, Peter, with Peter Parson. *When Gloucester Was Gloucester: Toward an Oral History of the City*. Photos by Mark Power. Gloucester: Gloucester 350th Anniversary Celebration, 1973.

Angulo, Guy de, ed. *Jaime in Taos: The Taos Papers of Jaime de Angulo*. San Francisco, CA: City Lights, 1985.

Angulo, Jaime de. *Coyote's Bones: Selected Poetry and Prose*. Edited by Bob Callahan. San Francisco, CA: Turtle Island Foundation, 1974.

———. *Indian Tales*. New York: Wyn, 1953.

Aristotle. *Nicomachean Ethics*. Translated by Robert C. Bartlett and Susan D. Collins. Chicago: University of Chicago Press, 2012.

"Art: Books of the Centuries." *Time* (December 10, 1956), http://content.time.com/time/subscriber/article/0,33009,808766,00.html.

Avison, Margaret. *Always Now: The Collected Poems*. Erin, ON: Porcupine's Quill, 2003.

———. *The Essential Margaret Avison*. Edited by Robyn Sarah. Erin, ON: Porcupine's Quill, 2010.

———. *I Am Here and Not Not-There: An Autobiography*. Erin, ON: Porcupine's Quill, 2009.

———. *Sliverick*. Toronto: Ganglia, 1960.

———. *Winter Sun*. London: Routledge and Kegan Paul, 1960.

Baraka, Amiri. *Amiri Baraka and Edward Dorn: The Collected Letters*. Albuquerque: University of New Mexico Press, 2013.

———. *The Autobiography of LeRoi Jones*. New York: Lawrence Hill, 1997.

———. *S O S: Poems 1961–2013*. New York: Grove, 2015.

Bartlett, Lee, ed. "'Where as Giant Kings We Gatherd': Some Letters from Robert Duncan to William Everson, 1940 and After." *Sagetrieb* 4.2–3 (Fall–Winter 1985): 137–70.

Baum, L. Frank. *The Emerald City of Oz*. Chicago: Reilly and Britton, 1910.

———. *The Road to Oz*. Chicago: Reilly and Britton, 1909.

———. *The Wonderful Wizard of Oz*. Chicago: Reilly and Britton, 1908.

Beach, Christopher. *ABC of Influence: Ezra Pound and the Remaking of American Poetic Tradition*. Berkeley: University of California Press, 1992.

Berdyaev, Nikolay Aleksandrovich. *Freedom and the Spirit*. Translated by Oliver Fielding Clarke. London: Bles, 1935.

Bergé, Carol. *The Vancouver Report*. New York: Fuck You Press, 1964.

Bernstein, Michael André. "Bringing It All Back Home: Derivations and Quotations in Robert Duncan and the Poundian Tradition." *Sagetrieb* 1.2 (1982): 176–89.

Bertholf, Robert J., and Albert Gelpi, eds. *The Letters of Robert Duncan and Denise Levertov*. Stanford, CA: Stanford University Press, 2004.

Bertholf, Robert J., and Ian Reid, eds. *Robert Duncan: Scales of the Marvelous*. New York: New Directions, 1979.

Bertholf, Robert J., and Dale M. Smith, eds. *Imagining Persons: Robert Duncan's Lectures on Charles Olson*. Albuquerque: University of New Mexico Press, 2017.

Blackburn, Paul. *Against the Silences*. New York: Permanent, 1980.

———. *Brooklyn-Manhattan Transit: A Bouquet for Flatbush*. New York: Totem, 1960.

———. *Collected Poems*. New York: Persea, 1985.

———. *The Dissolving Fabric*. Palma, Spain: Divers, 1953.

———. *The Journals*. Los Angeles, CA: Black Sparrow, 1972.

———. *Proensa*. Palma, Spain: Divers, 1953.

———. "The Search" and "The Assistance." *Black Mountain Review* 1 (Spring 1954): 20–21.

Blake, William. *The Complete Poetry and Prose*. Edited by David V. Erdman. Rev. ed. Berkeley: University of California Press, 1982.

Blaser, Robin. *Cups*. San Francisco, CA: Four Seasons Foundation, 1968.

———. *The Fire: Collected Essays*. Edited by Miriam Nichols. Berkeley: University of California Press, 2006.

———. *The Holy Forest*. Toronto: Coach House, 1993.

———. "Letters to Freud" and "Poem by the Charles River." *Measure* 1 (Summer 1957): 12–14.

———. *The Moth Poem*. San Francisco, CA: Open Space, 1964.

———. *Syntax*. Vancouver, BC: Talon, 1982.

Blaser, Robin, trans. *Les chimères*. San Francisco, CA: Open Space, 1965.

Blok, Aleksandr A. *The Twelve*. 1918. Translated by Babette Deutsch and Avraham Yarmolinsky. Illustrated by George Buddle. New York: W. E. Rudge, 1931.

Boehme, Jacob. *Six Theosophic Points and Other Writings*. Translated by John Roll. Ann Arbor: University of Michigan Press, 1958.

———. *The Works of Jacob Boehme the Teutonic Theosopher*. Translated by William Law. 4 vols. London: M. Richardson, 1764–1781.

Boer, Charles. *Charles Olson in Connecticut*. Chicago: Swallow, 1975.

Booth, Philip. *Letter from a Distant Land*. New York: Viking, 1956.

———. *Lifelines: Selected Poems, 1950–1999*. New York: Viking, 1999.

Borregaard, Ebbe. *Sketches for 13 Sonnets*. Berkeley, CA: Oyez, 1969.

———. *The Wapitis*. San Francisco, CA: White Rabbit, 1958.

Bowers, Edgar. *Collected Poems*. New York: Knopf, 1997.

———. *The Form of Loss*. Denver, CO: Allen Swallow, 1956.

Brenan, Gerald. *St. John of the Cross: His Life and Poetry*. Translated by Lynda Nicholson. Cambridge: Cambridge University Press, 1973.

Bronk, William. *Life Supports: New and Collected Poems*. San Francisco, CA: North Point, 1981.

———. *Metaphor of Trees and Last Poems*. Jersey City, NJ: Talisman, 1999.

———. "Round the Year Jazz." *Black Mountain Review* 1 (Spring 1954): 34.

Broughton, James. *A Long Undressing: Collected Poems, 1949–1959*. Highlands, NC: Jargon Society, 1971.

———. *The Androgyne Journal*. Oakland, CA: Scrimshaw, 1977.

———. *Packing Up for Paradise: Selected Poems, 1946–1996*. Santa Rosa, CA: Black Sparrow, 1997.

———. *Seeing the Light*. San Francisco, CA: City Lights, 1977.

———. *True and False Unicorns*. New York: Grove, 1957.

Browning, Robert. *Bells and Pomegranates*, vol. 1: *Pippa Passes*. London: Moxon, 1841.

Bukowski, Charles. *Notes of a Dirty Old Man*. San Francisco, CA: City Lights, 1969.

Bultmann, Rudolf. *The Theology of the New Testament*. Translated by Kendrick Grobel. New York: Scribner's, 1955.

Bunting, Basil. *Poems 1950*. Galveston, TX: Cleaners, 1950.

Burroughs, William. *Junkie*. New York: Ace, 1953.

———. *Naked Lunch*. Paris: Olympia, 1959.

———. *The Ticket That Exploded*. Paris: Olympia, 1962.

Bush, Ronald, ed. *The Correspondence of Ezra Pound and the Frobenius Institute, 1930–1959*. New York: Bloomsbury Academic, forthcoming.

Butling, Pauline. "Robert Duncan: The Poem as Process." Submitted in partial fulfillment for the degree of master of arts, University of British Columbia, 1966.

Butterick, George F. *A Guide to the Maximus Poems of Charles Olson*. Berkeley: University of California Press, 1978.

Butterick, George F., ed. *Charles Olson and Robert Creeley: The Complete Correspondence*. Vols. 6 and 10. Santa Barbara, CA: Black Sparrow, 1985, 1996.

Butts, Mary. *Armed with Madness*. London: Wishart, 1928.

———. *A Sacred Quest: The Life and Writings of Mary Butts*. Edited by Christopher Wagstaff. Kingston, NY: McPherson, 1995.

Callahan, Bob. "The World of Jaime de Angulo." *Nethualcoyotl News* 1 (Summer 1979): 1, 5, 14–16.

Campbell, Joseph, ed. *The Mysteries: Papers from the Eranos Yearbooks*. 1955. Princeton, NJ: Princeton University Press, 1990.

Campion, Thomas. "Observations in the Art of English Poesie." In *Campion's Works*, edited by Percival Vivian, 35–36. Oxford: Clarendon, 1909.

Carew, Thomas. "An Elegy upon the Death of the Dean of Pauls, Dr. John Donne." In *The Norton Anthology of Poetry*, 5th ed., edited by Margaret Ferguson, Mary Jo Salter, and Jon Stallworthy, 388–90. New York: Norton, 2005.

Cassirer, Ernst. *The Philosophy of Symbolic Forms*. 3 vols. Translated by Ralph Manheim. New Haven, CT: Yale University Press, 1953–1957.

Char, René. "Poems." Translated by Jackson Mathews. *Botteghe Oscure* 10 (1952): 128–62.

———. "To a Tensed Serenity," "Epilogue," and "To . . ." *Origin*, 1st ser., 16 (Spring–Summer 1955): 100–103.

Christensen, Paul, ed. *In Love, in Sorrow: The Complete Correspondence of Charles Olson and Edward Dahlberg*. New York: Paragon House, 1990.

Church, Fermor, and Peggy Pond Church. *When Los Alamos Was a Ranch School*. 1974. Edited by Barbara Storms. Los Alamos, NM: Los Alamos Historical Society, 1998.

Church, Peggy Pond. *Accidental Magic*. Albuquerque, NM: Wildflower, 2004.

———. *Birds of Daybreak: Landscapes and Elegies*. Santa Fe, NM: Gannon, 1985.

———. *Bones Incandescent: The Pajarito Journals of Peggy Pond Church*. Edited by Shelley Armitage. Lubbock: Texas Tech University Press, 2001.

———. *The Dancing Ground of Sky: The Selected Poetry of Peggy Pond Church*. Santa Fe, NM: Red Crane Literature Series, 1993.

———. *New and Selected Poems*. Boise, ID: Ahsahta, 1976.

———. *Wind and Trail: The Early Life of Mary Austin*. Albuquerque: Museum of New Mexico Press, 1990.

Clark, Tom. *Charles Olson: The Allegory of a Poet's Life*. New York: Norton, 1991.

———. *Edward Dorn: A World of Difference*. Berkeley, CA: North Atlantic, 2002.

———. *Robert Creeley and the Genius of the American Common Place*. New York: New Directions, 1993.

Clarke, John. *Blake*. Canton, NY: Institute of Further Studies, 1974.

———. *From Feathers to Iron: A Concourse of World Poetics*. Bolinas, CA: Tombouctou, 1987.

Corbin, Henry. "Cyclical Time in Mazdaism and Ismailism." In *Man and Time: Papers from the Eranos Yearbooks*, edited by Joseph Campbell, 115–72. Princeton, NJ: Princeton University Press, 1957.

Corman, Cid. *Aegis: Selected Poems, 1970–1980*. Barrytown, NY: Station Hill, 1983.

———. *Livingdying*. New York: New Directions, 1970.

———. *OF*. 2 vols. Venice, CA: Lapis, 1990.

———. Review. "*W. B. Yeats and Sturge Moore, Their Correspondence 1901–1937*, edited by Ursula Bridge." *Black Mountain Review* 1 (Spring 1954): 48–51.

———. *Sun Rock Man*. Kyoto, Japan: Origin, 1962.

———. *Word for Word: Essays on the Arts of Language*. 2 vols. Santa Barbara, CA: Black Sparrow, 1977–1978.

Creeley, Robert. *All That Is Lovely in Men*. Asheville, NC: Jonathan Williams, 1955.

———. *Autobiography*. 1990. Reprinted in Tom Clark, *Robert Creeley and the Genius of the American Common Place*, 122–44. New York: New Directions, 1993.

———. *Collected Essays*. Berkeley: University of California Press, 1989.

———. *Collected Poems: 1945–1975*. Berkeley: University of California Press, 1982.

———. *Collected Poems: 1975–2005*. Berkeley: University of California Press, 2008.

———. *Collected Prose*. Berkeley: University of California Press, 1988.

———. *The Finger*. Los Angeles, CA: Black Sparrow, 1968.

———. *5 Numbers*. New York: Poets Press, 1968.

———. *For Love: Poems, 1950–1960*. New York: Scribner's, 1962.

———. *A Form of Women*. New York: Corinth in association with Jargon, 1959.

———. *Le Fou*. Columbus, OH: Golden Goose, 1952.

———. *The Gold Diggers*. Palma, Spain: Divers, 1954.

———. *If You*. San Francisco, CA: Porpoise Bookshop, 1956.

———. *The Immoral Proposition*. Karlsruhe, West Germany: Jonathan Williams, 1953.

———. *The Island*. New York: Scribner's, 1963.

———. *Life and Death*. New York: New Directions, 1998.

———. *Memory Gardens*. New York: New Directions, 1986.

———. *Pieces*. New York: Scribner's, 1969.

———. "Three Prefaces." *Migrant* 3 (November 1959): 2–3.

———. *Windows*. New York: New Directions, 1987.

———. *Words*. New York: Scribner's, 1967.

Croce, Benedetto. *Aesthetic as Science of Expression and General Linguistic*. New York: Noonday, 1922.

Dahlberg, Edward. *Because I Was Flesh: An Autobiography*. Norfolk, CT: New Directions, 1964.

———. *Bottom Dogs*. New York: Simon and Schuster, 1930.

———. *Do These Bones Live*. New York: Harcourt, Brace, 1941.

———. *The Edward Dahlberg Reader*. New York: New Directions, 1967.

———. *Flea of Sodom*. Norfolk, CT: New Directions, 1940.

———. *From Flushing to Calvary*. London: Putnam's, 1933.

———. *The Leafless American*. Sausalito, CA: Beachman, 1967.

———. *The Sorrows of Priapus*. Norfolk, CT: New Directions, 1957.

Dante. *The Inferno of Dante Alighieri*. London: J. M. Dent, 1908.

Debus, Allen. *The English Paracelsians*. New York: Watts, 1966.

Del Mar, Alexander. *Roman and Moslem Moneys*. Washington, DC: Square Dollar, 1956.

Dodds, E. R. *The Greeks and the Irrational*. Berkeley: University of California Press, 1951.

Dorn, Edward. *Abhorrences*. Santa Rosa, CA: Black Sparrow, 1990.

———. *By the Sound*. Mount Vernon, WA: Frontier, 1971.

———. *Collected Poems*. Edited by Jennifer Dunbar Dorn. Manchester, England: Carcanet, 2012.

———. *Collected Poems: 1956–1974*. San Francisco, CA: Four Seasons Foundation, 1975.

———. *Derelict Air: From Collected Out*. Edited by Justin Katko and Kyle Waugh. London: Enitharmon, 2015.

———. *Geography*. London: Fulcrum, 1965.

———. *Hello, La Jolla*. San Francisco, CA: Wingbow, 1978.

———. *The Newly Fallen*. New York: Totem, 1961.

———. *The North Atlantic Turbine*. London: Fulcrum, 1967.

———. *Recollections of Gran Apacheria*. Illustrated by Michael Myers. Berkeley, CA: Turtle Island Foundation, 1974.

———. "The Rick of Green Wood." *Measure* 1 (Summer 1957): 15–16.

———. *Slinger*. Berkeley, CA: Wingbow, 1975.

———. *Way More West: New and Selected Poems*. Edited by Jerome Rothenberg. New York: Penguin, 2007.

———. *Yellow Lola*. Santa Barbara, CA: Cadmus, 1981.

Douglas, Clifford Hugh. *Economic Democracy*. London: C. Palmer, 1920.

———. *Social Credit*. London: Eyre and Spottiswood, 1933.

Douglas, Gavin. "The Blanket." *Measure* 1 (Summer 1957): 32–33.

Duberman, Martin. *Black Mountain: An Exploration in Community*. New York: Dutton, 1972.

Duerden, Richard. *The Fork*. San Francisco, CA: Open Space, 1965.

———. *The Left Hand and the Glory of Her*. San Francisco, CA: Cranium, 1967.

Dunbar, William. "Lament for the Makaris." In *The Norton Anthology of Poetry*, 5th ed., edited by Margaret Ferguson, Mary Jo Salter, and Jon Stallworthy, 86–89. New York: Norton, 2005.

Duncan, Robert. "After Reading H.D.'s Hermetic Definitions." *Trobor* 4 (1962): 1–3.

———. *As Testimony: The Poem and the Scene*. San Francisco, CA: White Rabbit, 1964.

———. "Beginnings: Chapter 1 of *The H.D. Book*, Part I." *Coyote's Journal* 5–6 (1966): 8–15.

———. *Bending the Bow*. New York: New Directions, 1968.

———. *A Book of Resemblances: Poems, 1950–1953*. New Haven, CT: Henry Wenning, 1966.

———. *The Collected Early Poems and Plays*. Edited by Peter Quartermain. Berkeley: University of California Press, 2012.

———. *Collected Essays and Other Prose*. Edited by James Maynard. Berkeley: University of California Press, 2014.

———. *The Collected Later Poems and Plays*. Edited by Peter Quartermain. Berkeley: University of California Press, 2014.

———. "A Conversion." *Origin*, 1st ser., 14 (Autumn 1954): 125.

———. "A Dream of the End of the World." *Origin*, 1st ser., 14 (Autumn 1954): 127–28.

———. "Early History: The First Day," "The Cities of the Plain," "The Golden Age," "The Second Night in the Week," "Processionals of the Dead," "Africa Revisited," and "The Horns of Artemis." *Origin*, 1st ser., 6 (Summer 1952): 76–88.

———. *Faust Foutu*. 1953. Barrytown, NY: Station Hill, 1985.

———. "Friedl." *Origin*, 1st ser., 14 (Autumn 1954): 124–25.

———. "From the Day Book." *Origin*, 2nd ser., 10 (July 1963): 1–47.

———. *Ground Work: Before the War*. New York: New Directions, 1984.

———. *The H.D. Book*. Edited by Michael Boughn and Victor Coleman. Berkeley: University of California Press, 2011.

———. *Heavenly City, Earthly City*. Berkeley, CA: Bern Porter, 1947.

———. "The Law I Love Is Major Mover." *Ark II/Moby I* (1956–1957): 12.

———. "Letters for Denise Levertov: For a Muse Meant." *Black Mountain Review* 3 (Fall 1954): 19–22.

———. *Letters: Poems, 1953–1956*. 1958. Edited by Robert J. Bertholf. Chicago: Flood Editions, 2003.

———. "A Little Freedom for Poets, Please." *Artist's View* 0 (May 1952): [3].

———. "Love Poem." *Origin*, 1st ser., 14 (Autumn 1954): 123.

———. *Medieval Scenes*. San Francisco, CA: Centaur, 1950.

———. "A Morning Letter," "The Temple of the Animals," "There's Too Much Sea on the Big Sur," "Poem," and "A Ride to the Sea." *Poetry* 90.6 (September 1967): 350–55.

———. *Names of People*. Los Angeles, CA: Black Sparrow, 1968.

———. "near-far Mister Olson." *Origin*, 1st ser., 12 (Spring 1954): 210–11.

———. "Notes on Poetics Regarding Olson's 'Maximus.'" *Black Mountain Review* 6 (1956): 201–11.

———. "Old Testament" and "New Testament." *Fuck You: A Magazine of the Arts* 7 (September 1964): [18–20].

———. *The Opening of the Field*. New York: Grove, 1960.

———. "Osiris and Set." *Set* 1 (Winter 1961–1962): 2–3.

———. "Pages from a Notebook." *Artist's View* 5 (July 1953): [2–4].

———. *Poems, 1948–49*. Berkeley, CA: Berkeley Miscellany Editions, 1949.

———. *A Poet's Mind: Collected Interviews with Robert Duncan, 1960–1985*. Edited by Christopher Wagstaff. Berkeley, CA: North Atlantic, 2012.

———. "(The Propositions)." *Measure* 1 (1957): 40–48.

———. Review. "Against Nature." *Poetry* 94 (April 1959): 54–59.

———. "Rites of Participation." Part 1. *Caterpillar* 1 (October 1967): 6–29.

———. *Roots and Branches*. New York: New Directions, 1964.

———. "Salvages. Lassitude." *Origin*, 1st ser., 14 (Autumn 1954): 123–24.

———. *Selected Poems*. San Francisco, CA: City Lights, 1959.

———. *Selected Poems. 1993*. Edited by Robert J. Bertholf. New York: New Directions, 1997.

———. *A Selected Prose*. Edited by Robert J. Bertholf. New York: New Directions, 1995.

———. *The Song of the Border-guard*. Broadside No. 2. Black Mountain, NC: Black Mountain College, 1952.

———. "Songs for the Jews from Their Book of Splendours." *Origin*, 1st ser., 14 (Autumn 1954): 126–27.

———. "Statement on Jacobus for Borregaard's Museum." *Northern Lights* 2 (1985–1986): 119, 121.

———. *The Sweetness and Greatness of Dante's Divine Comedy*. San Francisco, CA: Open Space, 1965.

———. "Toward an African Elegy." *Circle* 10 (Summer 1948): 94–96.

———. *The Truth and Life of Myth: An Essay in Essential Autobiography*. New York: House of Books, 1968.

———. Untitled statement. *Matter* 3 [December 1965]: [1–3].

———. "Variations upon Phrases from Milton's the Reason of Church Government." *Contour Quarterly* 1.1 (April 1947): 3–6.

———. *Writing Writing*. Albuquerque, NM: Sumbooks, 1964.

———. "The Years as Catches." *Circle* 7–8 (Fall 1946): 1–4.

———. *The Years as Catches: First Poems (1939–1946)*. Berkeley, CA: Oyez, 1966.

Dunn, Carolyn, and Kevin Killian. *Eyewitness: From Black Mountain to White Rabbit*. New York: Granary, 2015.

Dunn, Joseph. *The Better Dream House*. San Francisco, CA: White Rabbit, 1968.

Eberhart, Richard. Review of *Howl*. "West Coast Rhythms." *New York Times Book Review* (September 2, 1965): 7, 18.

Edwards, John Hamilton, and William W. Vasse. *Annotated Index to the Cantos of Ezra Pound*. Berkeley: University of California Press, 1957.

Eigner, Larry. *The Collected Poems of Larry Eigner*. 4 vols. Palo Alto, CA: Stanford University Press, 2010.

———. "A Fete." *Black Mountain Review* 1 (Spring 1954): 33.

———. *From the Sustaining Air*. Palma, Spain: Divers, 1953.

———. "Millionem" and "Brink." *Measure* 1 (Summer 1957): 17–19.

———. *On My Eyes*. Highlands, NC: Jonathan Williams, 1960.

———. *Selected Poems*. Berkeley, CA: Oyez, 1972.

———. *Waters, Places, a Time*. Santa Barbara, CA: Black Sparrow, 1983.

———. *Windows/Walls/Yard/Ways*. Santa Rosa, CA: Black Sparrow, 1994.

Emerson, Richard Wirtz. *The Greengrocer's Son*. Denver, CO: Allan Swallow, 1950.

———. *Poems from the River Lo*. Columbus, OH: Golden Goose, 1949.

Evans, George, ed. *Charles Olson and Cid Corman: Complete Correspondence, 1950–1964*. 2 vols. Orono, ME: National Poetry Foundation, 1987.

Everson, William [Brother Antoninus]. *Archetype West: The Pacific Coast as a Literary Region*. Berkeley, CA: Oyez, 1974.

———. *The Crooked Lines of God*. Detroit: University of Detroit Press, 1959.

———. *The Hazards of Holiness*. Garden City, NY: Doubleday, 1962.

———. "I'm pre-beat" from "The Beat Friar." *Time* 73 (May 25, 1959): 58.

———. *Robinson Jeffers: Fragments of an Older Fury*. Berkeley, CA: Oyez, 1968.

———. *Single Source: The Early Poems of William Everson, 1934–1940*. Berkeley, CA: Oyez, 1966.

———. *The Veritable Years, 1949–1966*. Santa Barbara, CA: Black Sparrow, 1978.

Fabilli, Mary [Aurora Bligh]. *The Animal Kingdom: Poems and Drawings, 1964–1967*. Berkeley, CA: Oyez, 1975.

———. *Aurora Bligh and Early Poems*. Berkeley, CA: Oyez, 1968.

———. "The Garden." *Berkeley Miscellany* (1949): 12–24.

———. *The Old Ones*. Berkeley, CA: Oyez, 1966.

Facci, Joseph. *A Plan for a Democratic Public Opinion*. 1947. Patzcuaro, Mexico: Published by the author, 1967–1968.

Fenollosa, Ernest. *The Chinese Written Character as a Medium of Poetry*. Washington, DC: Square Dollar, 1951.

Ferlinghetti, Lawrence. *A Coney Island of the Mind*. New York: New Directions, 1958.

———. *Pictures of the Gone World*. San Francisco, CA: City Lights, 1955.

———. *These Are My Rivers: New and Selected Poems*. New York: New Directions, 1993.

———. *Tyrannus Nix*. New York: New Directions, 1969.

Ferrini, Vincent. *The Community of Self: Know Fish*. Books 4 and 5. Storrs: University of Connecticut Library, 1986.

———. *The House of Time*. London: Fortune, 1954.

———. *Know Fish*. Books 1 and 2. Storrs: University of Connecticut Library, 1979.

———. *The Navigators: Know Fish*. Book 3. Storrs: University of Connecticut Library, 1984.

———. *No Smoke*. Portland, ME: Falmouth Publishing House, 1941.

Frankfurter, Marion Denman, and Garden Jackson, eds. *The Letters of Sacco and Vanzetti*. New York: Vanguard, 1930.

Frazer, James George. *The Golden Bough: A Study in Magic and Religion*. 12 vols. London: Macmillan, 1915.

Frobenius, Leo, and Douglas C. Fox, eds. *African Genesis*. New York: Stockpole, 1937.

Gerhardt, Rainer M. *Der tod des Hamlet*. Freiberg: Gruppe der Fragmente, 1950.

Ginsberg, Allen. *Collected Poems, 1947–1980*. New York: Harper and Row, 1984.

———. *Collected Poems, 1947–1997*. New York: Harper Perennial, 2007.

———. *Death and Fame*. New York: Harper Flamingo, 1999.

———. *Deliberate Prose: Selected Essays 1956–1995*. New York: HarperCollins, 2000.

———. *The Fall of America*. San Francisco, CA: City Lights Books, 1972.

———. *Howl and Other Poems*. San Francisco, CA: City Lights, 1956.

———. *Kaddish*. San Francisco, CA: City Lights, 1961.

———. *Siesta in Xbalba and Return to the States*. Near Icy Cape, Alaska: Privately published, 1956.

———. *White Shroud*. New York: Harper and Row, 1985.

Gleason, Madeline. *Collected Poems: 1919–1979*. Edited by Christopher Wagstaff. Jersey City, NJ: Talisman House, 1999.

———. *Concerto for Bell and Telephone*. San Francisco, CA: Unicorn, 1966.

———. *Here Comes Everybody: New and Selected Poems*. San Francisco, CA: Panjandrum, 1975.

———. *The Metaphysical Needle*. San Francisco, CA: Centaur, 1949.

Gobron, Gabriel. *Histoire et philosophie du caodaisme*. Paris: Bervy, 1949.

Golding, Alan. "Little Magazines and Alternative Canons: The Example of *Origin*." *American Literary History* 2.4 (Winter 1990): 691–725.

Goodenough, Robert Edwin R. *Jewish Symbols in the Greco-Roman Period*. 13 vols. New York: Bollingen Foundation and Pantheon Books, 1956.

Gordon, Cyrus H. *Before the Bible*. New York: Harper, 1963.

———. *Ugaritic Literature: A Comprehensive Translation of the Poetic and Prose Texts*. Roma: Ponticium Institutum Biblicum, 1949.

Graves, Robert. *The White Goddess: An Historical Grammar of Poetic Myth*. London: Faber and Faber, 1948.

Güterbock, Hans Gustov. *The Song of Ullikummi: Revised Text of the Hittite Version of a Hurrian Myth*. New Haven, CT: American Schools of Oriental Research, 1952.

Haeckel, Ernst. *The History of Creation; or, The Development of the Earth and Its Inhabitants and Its Actions by Natural Causes*. 2 vols. New York: Appleton, 1880.

Hanson, Kenneth O. *Poems*. Portland, OR: Portland Art Museum, 1959.

Harmon, James. "For Dance," "For Henry Miller," "On Leaving for Prison," "Love," "Barb," and "An Ineluctable Modality." *Inferno* 6–7 (July 1952): 34–37.

Harrison, Jane. *Alpha and Omega*. London: Sidgwick and Jackson, 1915.

———. *The Prolegomena to the Study of Greek Religion*. 1903. Cambridge: Cambridge University Press, 1908.

———. *Themis: A Study of the Social Origins of Greek Religion*. 2nd ed. Cambridge: Cambridge University Press, 1927.

Harrison, Jane, and Hope Mirrlees. *The Book of the Bear: Being Twenty-One Tales Newly Translated from the Russian*. London: Nonesuch, 1926.

Harvey, William. *Exercitatio anatomica de motu cordis et sanguinis in animalibus* [*On the Motion of the Heart and Blood*]. 1628. London: Bell and Sons, 1889.

Havelock, Eric. *A Preface to Plato*. Cambridge, MA: Belknap, 1963.

Hawkins, Bobbie Louise. *Almost Everything*. Toronto: Coach House Press, 1982.

———. *Back to Texas*. Berkeley, CA: Bear Hug Books, 1977.

———. *Frenchy and Cuban Pete*. Bolinas, CA: Tombouctou, 1977.

———. *Live at the Great American Music Hall: Terry Garthwaite, Bobbie Louise Hawkins, Rosalie Sorrels*. Chicago: Flying Fish Records, 1981.

———. *My Own Alphabet: Stories, Essays and Memoir*. Minneapolis, MN: Coffee House, 1989.

———. *One Small Saga*. Minneapolis, MN: Coffee House Press, 1984.

———. *Our Own Body*. Los Angeles, CA: Black Sparrow, 1973.

H.D. [Hilda Doolittle]. *End to Torment: A Memoir of Ezra Pound*. Edited by Norman Holmes Pearson and Michael King. New York: New Directions, 1979.

———. "Sagesse." *Evergreen Review* 2.5 (Summer 1958): 27–36.

Hedley, Leslie Woolf. *Death of a World*. San Francisco, CA: Inferno, 1951.

———. *Selected Poems, 1946–1953*. Sausalito, CA: Golden Goose, 1953.

Hellman, Robert. "The Quay." *Black Mountain Review* 1 (Spring 1954): 8–17.

Henderson, Linda Dalrymple. "Mysticism as the 'Tie That Binds': The Case of Edward Carpenter and Modernism." *Art Journal* 46.1 (Spring 1987): 29–33.

Hoskins, Katherine. *A Penitential Primer*. Cummington, MA: Cummington, 1945.

———. *Villa Marcisse: The Garden, the Statues, and the Pool*. New York: Noonday, 1956.

Hueffer, Ford Madox. *Memoirs and Impressions: A Study in Atmosphere*. New York: Harper and Brothers, 1911.

Humphries, Rolfe, ed. *New Poems by American Poets*. New York: Ballantine, 1953.

Husaini, Abdul Qadir. *Ibn Al'Arabi, the Great Muslim Mystic Thinker*. Lahore, Pakistan: Muhammad Ashraf, 1963.

Huxley, George. *Crete and the Luwians*. Oxford: Privately published, 1961.

James, Montague L. Rhodes. *The Collected Ghost Stories*. London: Edward Arnold, 1931.

James, William. *Talks to Teachers on Psychology and to Students on Some of Life's Ideals*. 1899. Cambridge, MA: Harvard University Press, 1983.

Jarnot, Lisa. *Robert Duncan: The Ambassador from Venus*. Berkeley: University of California Press, 2012.

Jess. *Gallowsongs*. Los Angeles, CA: Black Sparrow, 1970.

———. *Jess: O! Tricky Cad and Other Jessoterica*. Edited by Michael Duncan. Los Angeles, CA: Siglio, 2012.

———. *Translations*. Introduction by Robert Duncan. Los Angeles, CA: Black Sparrow, 1971.

Johnson, Samuel. *The Lives of the Most Eminent English Poets: A Selection*. Edited by John Mullan and Rodger Lonsdale. 1779. Oxford: Oxford University Press, 2009.

Johnston, Alastair. *A Bibliography of the White Rabbit Press*. Berkeley, CA: Poltrooon Press and Anacapa Press, 1985.

Jones, LeRoi. *Blues People: The Negro Experience in White America*. 1963. New York: Harper Perennial, 1999.

Jung, C. G. *The Archetypes and the Collective Unconscious*. Translated by R. F. C. Hull. New York: Pantheon, 1959.

———. *Memories, Dreams, Reflections*. Edited by Aniela Jaffe. Translated by Clara Winston Richard. New York: Pantheon, 1963.

———. *The Secret of the Golden Flower: A Chinese Book of Life*. Translated by Richard Wilhelm. London: Kegan Paul, Trench, Trubner, 1945.

——. *Selected Writings: Alchemical Studies*. Translated by R. F. C. Hull. Princeton, NJ: Princeton University Press, 1967.

——. *The Spirit in Man, Art, and Literature*. New York: Pantheon, 1966.

——. *Synchronicity: An Acausal Connecting Principle*. Princeton, NJ: Princeton University Press, 1973.

Kasper, John, ed. *Gists from Agassiz; or, Passages on the Intelligence Working in Nature*. Washington, DC: Square Dollar, 1953.

Katue, Kitasono. *Black Rain*. Palma, Spain: Divers, 1954.

Kazin, Alfred. *On Native Grounds: An Interpretation of Modern American Prose Literature*. New York: Reynal and Hitchcock, 1942.

Kelly, Robert. *Armed Descent*. New York: Hawk's Well, 1961.

——. *Cities*. West Newbury, MA: Frontier, 1972.

——. *The Hexagon*. Boston: Black Widow, 2016.

——. *Opening the Seals*. New York: Autonomedia, 2016.

——. *Spiritual Exercises*. Santa Barbara, CA: Black Sparrow, 1981.

——. *The Time of Voice: Poems, 1994–1996*. Santa Rosa, CA: Black Sparrow, 1998.

Kelly, Robert, and Paris Leary, eds. *A Controversy of Poets: An Anthology of Contemporary American Poetry*. Garden City, NY: Doubleday, 1965.

Kenner, Hugh. *The Poetry of Ezra Pound*. Norfolk, CT: New Directions, 1950.

——. *The Pound Era*. Berkeley: University of California Press, 1971.

Kerouac, Jack. *Big Sur*. New York: Farrar, Straus and Cudahy, 1962.

——. *The Dharma Bums*. New York: Viking, 1958.

——. *Old Angel Midnight*. N.p.: Booklegger/Albion, 1973.

Kirk, G. S., and J. E. Raven. *Heraclitus: The Cosmic Fragments*. 1954. Cambridge: Cambridge University Press, 1962.

——. *The Presocratic Philosophers: A Critical History with a Selection of Texts*. Cambridge: Cambridge University Press, 1957.

Koyre, Alexandra. *Mystiques, spirituels, alchemistes du XVIe siècle allemand*. Paris: Gallimard, 1971.

Kramer, Samuel Noah. *Sumerian Mythology: A Study of Spiritual and Literary Achievement in the Third Millennium*. Philadelphia: American Philosophical Society, 1947.

Krishnamurti, Jiddu. *Education and the Significance of Life*. New York: Harper and Row, 1953.

Lanier, Sidney. *The Centennial Edition of the Works of Sidney Lanier*. Baltimore: Johns Hopkins Press, 1945.

——. *The Science of English Verse*. New York: Scribner's, 1880.

Lansing, Gerrit. *Analytic Psychology*. Canton, NY: Glover, 1983.

——. "Editorial: The Burden of *Set*, #1." *Set* 1 (Winter 1961–1962): 8–12.

——. *The Heavenly City Grows Downward*. Annandale-on-Hudson: Matter, 1966.

——. *Heavenly Tree, Northern Earth*. Berkeley, CA: North Atlantic, 2009.

Laubiès, René. "Eight Reproductions." *Black Mountain Review* 1 (Spring 1954): 25–32.

Laughlin, James, ed. *New Directions in Prose and Poetry 14*. New York: New Directions, 1953.

Lawrence, D. H. *The Complete Poems of D. H. Lawrence*. Edited by Vivian de Sola Pinto and Warren Roberts. New York: Penguin, 1994.

——. *Lady Chatterley's Lover*. New York: Grove, 1959.

——. *Look! We Have Come Through!* London: Chatto and Windus, 1917.

——. *The Plumed Serpent*. London: Martin Secker, 1926.

——. *Studies in Classic American Literature*. New York: T. Seltzer, 1923.

Layton, Irving. "Lacquered Westmount Doll." *Black Mountain Review* 1 (Spring 1954): 19.

Leed, Jacob. "Robert Creeley and the *Lititz Review*: A Recollection with Letters." *Journal of Modern Literature* 5 (April 1976): 243–59.

Levertov, Denise. *Five Poems*. San Francisco, CA: White Rabbit, 1958.

——. *Light Up the Cave*. New York: New Directions, 1981.

——. "Love Poem." *Origin*, 1st ser., 14 (Autumn 1954): 86.

——. *Relearning the Alphabet*. New York: New Directions, 1970.

——. *To Stay Alive*. New York: New Directions, 1971.

Levin, Harry. *James Joyce: A Critical Introduction*. Norfolk, CT: New Directions, 1941.

Lewis, Wyndham. "Editorial." *Enemy* 1 (January 1927): ix–xv.

——. *Time and Western Man*. London: Chatto and Windus, 1927.

Loewinsohn, Ron. *Goat Dances*. Santa Barbara, CA: Black Sparrow, 1976.

——. *Magnetic Field(s)*. New York: Knopf, 1983.

——. *Meat Air: Poems, 1957–1969*. New York: Harcourt, Brace and World, 1970.

——. *Where All the Ladders Start: A Novel*. New York: Atlantic Monthly Press, 1987.

——. *The World of the Lie*. San Francisco, CA: Chance, 1963.

Long, Haniel. *Interlinear to Cabeza de Vaca: His Relation of the Journey from Florida to the Pacific, 1528–1536*. New York: Frontier, 1969.

Lubin, Bradley, ed. "'that lettrous mountain of friendship': The Selected Letters of Pauline Kael and Robert Duncan, 1945–1946." *Lost and Found: CUNY Poetics Documents*, ser. 4, 4.1 (Fall 2013): 31–35.

MacDonald, George. *At the Back of the North Wind*. 1871. London: Blackie, 1911.

——. *Fairy Tales*. Edited by Greville MacDonald. London: Allen, 1924.

——. *The Light Princess and Other Fairy Tales*. New York: Putnam's, 1893.

——. *Lilith: A Romance*. London: Chatto and Windus, 1895.

——. *The Princess and Curdie*. Illustrated by Marie L. Kirk. 1883. Philadelphia: Lippincott 1908.

——. *The Princess and the Goblin*. 1872. Philadelphia: Lippincott, 1907.

MacDonald, Greville. *George MacDonald and His Wife*. New York: Dial, 1924.

Macleod, Norman. *Horizons of Death*. New York: Parnassus, 1934.

——. *Pure as Nowhere*. Columbus, OH: Golden Goose, 1952.

——. *Selected Poems*. Boise, ID: Ahshata, 1975.

Mac Low, Jackson. *August Light Poems*. New York: Caterpillar, 1967.

——. *Barnesbook: Four Poems Derived from Sentences by Djuna Barnes*. Los Angeles, CA: Sun and Moon, 1996.

——. *Doings: Assorted Performance Pieces, 1955–2002*. New York: Granary, 2005.

——. *42 Merzgedichte: In Memoriam, Kurt Schwitters*. Barrytown, NY: Station Hill, 1994.

——. *22 Light Poems*. Los Angeles, CA: Black Sparrow, 1968.

——. *Words nd Ends from Ez*. Bolinas, CA: Avenue B, 1989.

Marshall, Edward. *Hellan, Hellan*. San Francisco, CA: Auerhahn, 1960.

——. "Leave the Word Alone." *Black Mountain Review* 7 (Autumn 1957): 38–51.

——. "One" and "Two." *Measure* 1 (Summer 1957): 6–11.

——. *Transit Glory*. New York: Carp and Whitefish, 1967.

Martinelli, Sheri. *La Martinelli*. Milan: Vanni Scheiwiller, 1956.

Maud, Ralph. *Charles Olson at the Harbor*. Vancouver: Talonbooks, 2008.

——. *Charles Olson's Reading: A Biography*. Carbondale: Southern Illinois University Press, 1996.

Maud, Ralph, and Sharon Thesen, eds. *Charles Olson and Frances Boldereff: A Modern Correspondence*. Hanover, NH: Wesleyan University Press, 1999.

McClure, Michael. *Dark Brown*. San Francisco, CA: Auerhahn Society, 1961.

——. *Ghost Tantras*. San Francisco, CA: City Lights, 1964.

——. *Huge Dreams: San Francisco and Beat Poems*. New York: Penguin, 1999.

——. *Hymns to St. Geryon and Other Poems*. San Francisco, CA: Auerhahn, 1959.

——. *Lighting the Corners on Nature, Art, and the Visionary: Essays and Interviews*. Albuquerque: University of New Mexico, College of Arts and Sciences, 1993.

——. *Mysteriosos and Other Poems*. New York: New Directions, 2010.

——. *The New Book/A Book of Torture*. New York: Grove, 1961.

——. *Of Indigo and Saffron: New and Selected Poems*. Edited by Leslie Scalapino. Berkeley: University of California Press, 2011.

——. "Revolt." *Journal for the Protection of All Beings* 1 (1961): 38–52.

——. *Scratching the Beat Surface*. San Francisco, CA: North Point, 1982.

Mead, G. R. S. *Thrice-Greatest Hermes*. 3 vols. London: John M. Watkins, 1949.

Meier, Fritz. "The Mystery of the Ka'ba: Symbol and Reality in Islamic Mysticism." 1944. In *The Mysteries: Papers from the Eranos Yearbooks*, edited by Joseph Campbell. Princeton, NJ: Princeton University Press, 1955.

Merritt, Abraham. *The Moon Pool*. New York: Avon, 1944.

——. *The Ship of Ishtar*. New York: Avon, 1945.

Merwin, William Stanley. *Garden Time*. Port Townsend, WA: Copper Canyon, 2016.

——. *Green with Beasts*. London: Hart-Davis, 1956.

——. *The Lice*. New York: Atheneum, 1967.

——. *A Mask for Janus*. New Haven, CT: Yale University Press, 1944.

——. *The Moving Target*. New York: Atheneum, 1963.

——. *New Selected Poems*. Port Townsend, WA: Copper Canyon, 1988.

——. *The River Sound: Poems*. New York: Knopf, 1999.

——. "The Sapphire." *Poetry* 84 (August 1954): 255.

Miles, Josephine. *Collected Poems*. Urbana: University of Illinois Press, 1983.

——. *Fields of Learning*. Berkeley, CA: Oyez, 1968.

——. *Poems: 1930–1960*. Urbana: University of Illinois Press, 1983.

——. *Poetry and Change: Donne, Milton, Wordsworth, and the Equilibrium of the Present*. Berkeley: University of California Press, 1974.

——. *Prefabrications*. Bloomington: Indiana University Press, 1955.

——. *Style and Proportion: The Language of Prose and Poetry*. Boston: Little, Brown, 1966.

——. *The Vocabulary of Poetry: Three Studies*. Berkeley: University of California Press, 1946.

Miller, Henry. *Books Tangent to Circle*. Belfast ME: Bern Porter, 1971.

——. *The Tropic of Cancer*. New York: Grove, 1961.

Miller, J. Hillis. *The Linguistic Moment: From Wordsworth to Stevens*. Princeton, NJ: Princeton University Press, 1985.

Moore, Marianne. *The Complete Poems*. New York: Viking, 1981.

——. *Marianne Moore Reading Her Poems and Fables*. New York: Caedmon, 1955.

Morse, Samuel French. *Collected Poems*. Orono, ME: National Poetry Foundation, 1995.

———. "The Motive for Metaphor: Wallace Stevens: His Poetry and His Practice." *Origin*, 1st ser., 5 (Spring 1952): 3–65.

———. *Time of Year: A First Book of Poems*. Cummington, MA: Cummington, 1943.

———. *Wallace Stevens: Poetry as Life*. New York: Pegasus, 1970.

Murray, Gilbert. *Greek Studies*. Oxford: Clarendon, 1947.

Nasr, Sayyed Hossein. *Three Muslim Sages: Avicenna-Suhrawardi-Ibn 'Arabi*. Cambridge: Harvard University Press, 1964.

O'Hara, Frank. *Lunch Poems*. San Francisco, CA: City Lights, 1964.

O'Leary, Peter. "Previews and Supplements: Peter O'Leary on Robert Duncan's *The Origins of Old Son*." *Kenning Editions* (April 3, 2010), http://www.kenningeditions.com/kenning-editions/previews-supplements-peter-oleary-on-robert-duncans-the-origins-of-old-son.

Oliveros, Pauline. *Three Songs for Soprano and Piano*. Baltimore, MD: Smith, 1980.

Olson, Charles. "Across Space and Time." *Set* 1 (Winter 1961–1962): 4–5.

———. "Against Wisdom as Such." *Black Mountain Review* 1 (Spring 1954): 35–39.

———. "The Allegory of Wealth: A Poem from America Still." *Outburst* 1 (1961): n.p.

———. *Anecdotes of the Late War*. Highlands, NC: Jonathan Williams, 1955.

———. "Apollonius of Tyana." *Origin*, 1st ser., 6 (Summer 1952): 90–110.

———. *Archaeologist of Morning*. London: Cape Goliard, 1970.

———. *A Bibliography on America for Ed Dorn*. San Francisco, CA: Four Seasons Foundation, 1964.

———. *Call Me Ishmael*. New York: Reynal and Hitchcock, 1947.

———. "The Carpenter Poem 1 (Letter 33)." *Olson: The Journal of the Charles Olson Archives* 6 (Fall 1976): 52–54.

———. *The Collected Poems of Charles Olson Excluding the Maximus Poems*. Edited by George F. Butterick. Berkeley: University of California Press, 1987.

———. *Collected Prose*. Edited by Donald Allen and Benjamin Friedlander. Berkeley: University of California Press, 1997.

———. *The Distances*. New York: Grove, 1960.

———. *The Fiery Hunt and Other Plays*. Edited by George F. Butterick. Bolinas, CA: Four Seasons Foundation, 1977.

———. "GRAMMAR—a book." *Floating Bear* 7 (1961): [8–12].

———. *Human Universe and Other Essays*. Edited by Donald Allen. San Francisco, CA: Auerhahn Society, 1965.

———. *In Cold Hell, in Thicket*. Published as *Origin*, 1st ser., 8 (1953).

———. "Letter #29" [from *The Maximus Poems*]. *Beloit Poetry Journal* 5.1 (1954): 27–32. Reprinted in *Olson: The Journal of the Charles Olson Archives* 6 (Fall 1976): 19–20.

———. *Letters for Origin: 1950–1956*. Edited by Albert Glover. London: Cape Goliard, 1969.

———. *The Maximus Poems*. 1960. Edited by George F. Butterick. Berkeley: University of California Press, 1983.

———. *The Maximus Poems*. Vol. 3. Edited by Charles Boer and George F. Butterick. New York: Grossman, 1975.

———. *Maximus Poems IV, V, VI*. London: Cape Goliard Press and Grossman Publishers, 1968.

———. *The Maximus Poems 1–10*. Stuttgart, Germany: Jonathan Williams, 1953.

———. *The Maximus Poems 11–22*. Stuttgart, Germany: Jonathan Williams, 1956.

———. *Mayan Letters*. Palma, Spain: Divers, 1953.

———. *Muthologos: Lectures and Interviews*. Edited by Ralph Maud. Vancouver, BC: Talonbooks, 2010.

———. *Mythologos: The Collected Lectures and Interview*. Edited by George Butterick. Bolinas, CA: Four Seasons Foundation, 1978.

———. "On First Looking Out of La Cosa's Eyes." *Black Mountain Review* 1 (Spring 1954): 3–7.

———. *O'Ryan 2 4 6 8 10*. San Francisco, CA: White Rabbit, 1958.

———. "Pacific Lament." *Atlantic Monthly* 177 (March 1946): 103.

———. "Projective Verse." *Poetry New York* 3 (1950): 13–22.

———. "Proprioception" and "Logography." *Kulchur* 1 (Spring 1960): 19–22.

———. *Proprioception*. San Francisco, CA: Four Seasons Foundation, 1968.

———. Review. "*Captain John Smith, His Life and Legend* by Bradford Smith." *Black Mountain Review* 1 (Spring 1954): 54–57.

———. *Selected Writings*. Edited by Robert Creeley. New York: New Directions, 1966.

———. *Signature to Petition*. Berkeley, CA: Oyez, 1964.

———. *The Special View of History*. Berkeley, CA: Oyez, 1970.

———. "Theory of Society." *Yugen* 7 (1961): 53–54.

———. *This*. Broadside no. 1. Black Mountain, NC: Black Mountain College, 1952.

———. "To Gerhardt, There, among Europe's Things, of Which He Has Written Us in His 'Brief an Creeley und Olson.'" *Origin*, 1st ser., 4 (Winter 1951–1952): 241–48.

———. "(Variations, Done for Gerry Van De Wiele)." *Measure* 1 (1957): 2–5.

———. *West*. London: Goliard, 1966.

———. "A Work." *Floating Bear* 21 (1962): [4–6].

———. *Y & X*. Washington, DC: Black Sun, 1948.

Opie, Iona Archibald. *The Oxford Dictionary of Nursery Rhymes*. Oxford: Clarendon, 1951.

Ortega y Gasset, Jose. *The Dehumanization of Art*. Translated by Helen Wey. New York: P. Smith, 1951.

Ovid. *Metamorphoses*. Translated by Charles Martin. New York: Norton, 2004.

Paracelsus. *Paracelsus: Selected Writings*. Edited by Lebendiges Erbe. New York: Pantheon, 1951.

Parkinson, Thomas. *Homage to Jack Spicer*. Berkeley, CA: Ark, 1970.

———. *Poems: New and Selected*. Orono, ME: National Poetry Foundation, 1988.

———. *Thanatos: Poems for the Earth*. Berkeley, CA: Oyez, 1965.

———. *W. B. Yeats: The Later Poetry*. Berkeley: University of California Press, 1964.

Parkinson, Thomas, ed. *Hart Crane and Yvor Winters: Their Literary Correspondence*. Berkeley: University of California Press, 1978.

Patchen, Kenneth. *Awash with Roses: Collected Love Poems of Kenneth Patchen*. Edited by Larry Smith and Laura Smith. Huron, OH: Bottom Dog, 1991.

———. *Collected Poems*. New York: New Directions, 1968.

———. *Fables and Other Little Tales*. Karlsruhe, West Germany: Jonathan Williams, 1953.

———. *Hurray for Anything: Poems and Drawings*. Highlands, NC: Jonathan Williams, 1957.

———. *The Journal of Albion Moonlight*. New York: United Book Guild, 1944.

Peck, Daniel H., ed. *The Green Tradition: Essays and Poems for Sherman Paul*. Baton Rouge: Louisiana State University Press, 1989.

Perkoff, Stuart Z. "The Blind Girl" and "To Be Read on Festival Days." *Origin*, 1st ser., 2 (Summer 1951): 109–11.

———. *Suicide Room: Poems*. Highland, NC: Jargon Society, 1956.

Perle, George, and Paul Lansky. "Twelve-Tone Composition." In *The New Grove Dictionary of Music and Musicians*, 19:286–96. Oxford: Oxford University Press, 1980.

Peyre, Henri. *History of Modern Culture: Addresses at the First Meeting of the French History Society*. New York: French History Society, 1950.

———. *Writers and Their Critics: A Study of Understanding*. Ithaca, NY: Cornell University Press, 1944.

Pindar. *Pythian Odes*. Translated by H. T. Wade-Gery and C. M. Bowra. London: Nonesuch, 1928.

Porcher, Jean. *Les grandes heures de Rohan*. Geneva: Skira, 1953.

Porter, Bern. *Found Poems*. Millerton, NY: Something Else, 1972.

———, ed. *The Happy Rock: A Book about Henry Miller*. Berkeley, CA: Bern Porter, 1945.

———, ed. *Henry Miller Miscellanea*. Berkeley, CA: Bern Porter, 1945.

Porter, Katherine Anne. *The Never Ending Wrong*. Boston: Little Brown, 1977.

Pound, Ezra. *ABC of Reading*. New York: New Directions, 1934.

———. "Canto 85." *Hudson Review* 8 (Winter [1954]–1955): 487–501.

———. *The Cantos*. 11th ed. New York: New Directions, 1989.

———. *Confucius: Confucian Analects, the Great Learning and the Doctrine of the Mean*. 1893. Translated by James Legge. New York: Dover, 1971.

———, trans. *Confucius: The Great Digest*. New York: New Directions, 1951.

———, trans. *Confucius: The Unwobbling Pivot and the Great Digest, with Ciu-Hsi's "Preface" to the Chung yung and Tseng Commentary on the Testament*. Washington, DC: Square Dollar, 1951.

———. *Guide to Kulchur*. London: Faber and Faber, 1938.

———. *Literary Essays of Ezra Pound*. Edited by T. S. Eliot. New York: New Directions, 1968.

———. Review. *Economic Democracy* [by Major C. H. Douglas]. *Little Review* 6.11 (April 1920): 39–42.

———. *Section: Rock Drill*. New York: New Directions, 1956.

———. *Social Credit: An Impact*. London: Stanley Nott, 1935.

———. "Some Notes by a Very Ignorant Man." In Ernest Fenollosa, *The Chinese Written Character: An Ars Poetica*. London: Stanley Nott, 1936.

Powell, Lawrence Clark. *The Alchemy of Books and Other Essays and Addresses on Books and Writers*. Los Angeles, CA: W. Ritchie, 1954.

———. *The Prospect before Us*. San Francisco, CA: Grabhorn, 1963.

Purdy, James. *Don't Call Me My Right Name and Other Stories and a Novella*. New York: New Directions, 1957.

Raphael, Maryanne. *Your Psychic Powers: The Key to Success*. Cobalt, ON: Highway Book Shop, 1974.

Raworth, Thomas Moore. *Collected Poems*. Manchester, England: Carcanet, 2003.

———. *Continuation*. London: Goliard, 1966.

———. *Earn Your Milk: Collected Essays*. Cambridge, England: Salt, 2009.

———. *The Relation Ship*. London: Goliard, 1967.

———. *Tottering State: New and Selected Poems, 1965–1983*. Great Barrington. MA: Figures, 1984.

———. *Weapon Man*. London: Goliard, 1965.

Rexroth, Kenneth. *An Autobiographical Novel*. Garden City, NY: Doubleday, 1966.

——. *Collected Longer Poems*. New York: New Directions, 1968.

——. *Collected Shorter Poems*. New York: New Directions, 1966.

——. *The Complete Poems*. Edited by Sam Hamill and Bradford Morrow. Port Townsend, WA: Copper Canyon, 2003.

——. "Lament for Dylan Thomas." *Yale Literary Magazine* 122 (November 1954): 26–27.

——. "San Francisco Letter." *Evergreen Review* 1 (1957): [5]–14.

——. *Thou Shalt Not Kill: A Memorial for Dylan Thomas*. Mill Valley, CA: Goad, 1955.

——. *World Outside the Window: Selected Essays*. New York: New Directions, 1987.

Rhine, Joseph Banks. *Extra-Sensory Perception*. Boston: Bruce Humphries, 1935.

Richards, Mary Caroline. *Centering in Pottery, Poetry, and the Person*. Middletown, CT: Wesleyan University Press, 1964.

Richardson, Lawrence. "Avignon and Babylon." *Yale Poetry Review* [2] (Autumn 1945): 25–29.

——. *Poetical Theory in Republican Rome*. New Haven, CT: Yale University Press, 1944.

Rilke, Rainer Maria. *Duino Elegies*. Translated by Robert Hunter and Gary Miranda. New York: Norton, 1939.

——. *Neue Gedichte*. Translated as *New Poems* by J. B. Leishman. London: Hogarth, 1964.

Rimbaud, Arthur. *Rimbaud Complete*, vol. 1: *Poetry and Prose*. Translated by Wyatt Mason. New York: Modern Library, 2003.

Roethke, Theodore. *Collected Poems*. Garden City, NY: Doubleday, 1966.

——. *The Far Field*. Garden City, NY: Doubleday, 1961.

——. *On the Poet and His Craft: Selected Prose*. Seattle: University of Washington Press, 1965.

——. *Open House*. New York: Knopf, 1941.

——. *Selected Letters*. Seattle: University of Washington Press, 1968.

——. *The Waking: Poems, 1933–1953*. Garden City, NY: Doubleday, 1953.

Rorime, James J., trans. *The Belles Heures of Jean, Duke of Berry, Prince of France*. New York: Metropolitan Museum of Art, 1958.

Rukeyser, Muriel. *Collected Poems*. New York: McGraw-Hill, 1978.

——. *The Life of Poetry*. New York: Curnut, 1949.

——. "Myth and Torment." *Poetry* 72 (April 1948): 48–51.

——. *U.S. 1*. New York: Covici, Friede, 1938.

Rumaker, Michael. *Black Mountain Days*. Asheville, NC: Black Mountain, 2003.

——. "The Desert." *Evergreen Review* 1 (1957): 65–105.

——. *Exit 3 and Other Stories*. Harmondsworth, England: Penguin, 1966.

——. *Gringos and Other Stories*. New York: Grove, 1967.

——. *My First Satyrnalia*. San Francisco, CA: Grey Fox, 1981.

——. "Robert Duncan in San Francisco." *Credences* 2.3–4 (March 1978): 12–55.

——. *Robert Duncan in San Francisco*. San Francisco, CA: Grey Fox, 1996.

Russell, Sanders. *The Chemical Image*. San Francisco, CA: Ark, 1947.

——. *Poems*. Woodstock, NY: Capricorn, 1941.

Sadie, Stanley, ed. *New Grove Dictionary of Music and Musicians*. 20 vols. London: Macmillan, 1980.

Sauer, Carl Ortwin. *Land and Life: Selections from the Writings of Carl Ortwin Sauer*. Edited by John Leighly. Berkeley: University of California Press, 1963.

Schaff, David. "Some Statements on Projective Verse." *Yale Literary Magazine* 131.3–4 (April 1963): 5–14.

Seelye, Catherine, ed. *Charles Olson and Ezra Pound: An Encounter at St. Elizabeths*. New York: Grossman, 1975.

Seymour-Smith, Martin. "Where Is Mr. Roethke." *Black Mountain Review* 1 (Spring 1954): 40–47.

Shayer, Michael. *Persephone*. Ventura, CA: Migrant, 1961.

———. *Poems from an Island*. London: Fulcrum, 1970.

Shelley, Percy Bysshe. *The Complete Works of Percy Bysshe Shelley*. 10 vols. Edited by Roger Ingpen and Walter E. Peck. London: Ernest Been, 1927.

Snow, Edward Rowe. "Bullfight on Cape Ann." In his *Mysteries and Adventures along the Atlantic Coast*, 146–56. New York: Dodd, Mead, 1948.

Snyder, Gary. *Rip Rap*. San Francisco, CA: City Lights, 1959.

Snyder, Sharon. *At Home on the Slopes of Mountains: The Story of Peggy Pond Church*. Los Alamos, NM: Los Alamos Historical Society, 2011.

Sophokles. *Women of Trachis: A Version by Ezra Pound*. New York: New Directions, 1981.

Spicer, Jack. *After Lorca*. San Francisco, CA: White Rabbit, 1957.

———. *Billy the Kid*. Stinson Beach, CA: Enkidu Surrogate, 1959.

———. *The Collected Books of Jack Spicer*. Edited by Robin Blaser. Los Angeles, CA: Black Sparrow, 1975.

———. *The Heads of the Town Up to the Aether*. Lithographs by Fran Herndon. San Francisco, CA: Auerhahn, 1962.

———. *The Holy Grail*. San Francisco, CA: White Rabbit, 1964.

———. *Language*. San Francisco, CA: White Rabbit, 1965.

———. *my vocabulary did this to me: The Collected Poetry of Jack Spicer*. Edited by Peter Gizzi and Kevin Killian. Middletown, CT: Wesleyan University Press, 2008.

———. "Song for Bird and Myself." *Measure* 1 (1957): 34–37.

Stein, Gertrude. "Capitals, Capitals." *This Quarter* 1 (Summer 1925): 13–23. Reprinted in *New Music* 20 (April 1947): 3–34, with music by Virgil Thomson.

———. *The Making of Americans: The Hersland Family*. Paris: Contact Editions and Three Mountains Press, 1925.

———. "Reflections on the Atomic Bomb." *Yale Poetry Review* 7 (December 1947): 3–4.

Tallman, Warren. *In the Midst*. Vancouver, BC: Talonbooks, 1992.

Triem, Eve. *E. E. Cummings*. Minneapolis: University of Minnesota Press, 1969.

———. *New as a Wave: A Retrospective, 1937–1983*. Seattle, WA: Dragon Gate, 1984.

———. *Nobody Dies in the Summer: Selected Poems, 1934–1989*. Edited by Bernard G. Dack. Seattle, WA: Broken Moon, 1993.

———. *Parade of Doves*. New York: Dutton, 1946.

———. *Translations from the Greek Anthology*. Homestead, FL: Olivant, 1967.

Turnbull, Gael. *Bjarni Spike-Helgi's Son and Other Poems*. Ashland, MA: Origin, 1956.

———. *A Gathering of Poems, 1950–1980*. London: Anvil, 1983.

———. *The Knot in the Wood and Fifteen Other Poems*. London: Revision, 1955.

———. *There Are Words: Collected Poems*. Edinburgh: Shearsman, 2006.

———. *A Year and a Day*. Glasgow: Mariscat, 1985.

Turnbull, Gael, with Eli Mandel and Phyllis Webb. *Trio*. Toronto: Contact, 1954.

Turner, Frederick. *The Frontier in American History*. New York: Henry Holt, 1920.

Tyler, Hamilton. *Pueblo Animals and Myths*. Norman: University of Oklahoma Press, 1975.

———. *Pueblo Gods and Myths*. Norman: University of Oklahoma Press, 1964.

Valéry, Paul. *The Art of Poetry*. Translated by Denise Folliot. Princeton, NJ: Princeton University Press, 1958.

Vaughan, Thomas. *The Works of Thomas Vaughan*. Edited by Arthur Edward Waite. London: Theosophical Publishing, 1919.

Wagstaff, Christopher. "An Interview with Harry Jacobus." *Northern Lights* 2 (1985–1986): 81–118.

Wah, Fred. *Earth*. Canton, NY: Institute of Further Studies, 1974.

Waldman, Anne, and Andrew Schelling. *Disembodied Poetics: Annals of the Jack Kerouac School*. Albuquerque: University of New Mexico Press, 1994.

Webb, Walter Prescott. *The Great Frontier*. Boston: Houghton Mifflin, 1952.

West, Nathanael. *Miss Lonelyhearts*. New York: Liveright, 1933.

Whalen, Philip. *Canoeing Up Cabarga Creek: Buddhist Poems, 1955–1986*. Berkeley: Parallax, 1996.

———. *The Collected Poems of Philip Whalen*. Middletown, CT: Wesleyan University Press, 2007.

———. *Heavy Breathing: Poems, 1967–1980*. San Francisco, CA: Four Seasons Foundation, 1983.

———. *Like I Say: Poems*. New York: Totem/Jargon Books, 1960.

———. *Memoirs of an Interglacial Age*. San Francisco, CA: Auerhahn, 1960.

———. *On Bear's Head*. New York: Harcourt, Brace and World, 1969.

———. *Overtime: Selected Poems*. New York: Penguin, 1999.

Whitehead, Alfred North. *The Aims of Education*. 1929. New York: Free Press, 1967.

———. *Modes of Thought*. 1938. New York: Free Press, 1968.

———. *Process and Reality: An Essay in Cosmology*. New York: Macmillan, 1957.

Whiteman, Bruce. "A Search in Obedience: On the Collected Works of Robert Duncan." *Los Angeles Review of Books*, December 28, 2013, https://lareviewofbooks.org/article/search-obedience-collected-works-robert-duncan.

Whitman, Walt. *Complete Poetry and Selected Prose*. Edited by James E. Miller Jr. Boston: Houghton Mifflin, 1959.

Wieners, John. *Ace of Pentacles*. New York: Carr and Wilson, 1964.

———. *Asylum Poems*. New York: Angel Hair, 1969.

———. *The Hotel Wentley Poems*. San Francisco, CA: Auerhahn, 1958.

———. *Selected Poems: 1958–1984*. Santa Barbara, CA: Black Sparrow, 1986.

———. *Supplication: Selected Poems of John Wieners*. New York: Wave, 2015.

Williams, Jonathan. *Blackbird Dust: Essays, Poems, and Photographs*. Brooklyn, NY: Turtle Point, 2000.

———. *Blues and Roots, Rue and Bluets: A Garland for the Appalachians*. Photos by Nicholas Dean. New York: Grossman, 1971.

———. *An Ear in Bartram's Tree: Poems, 1957–1967*. Chapel Hill: University of North Carolina Press, 1969.

———. *Elite/Elite: Poems, 1971–75*. Photos by Guy Mendes. [Highlands, NC]: Jargon Society, 1979.

———. *Garbage Litters the Iron Face of the Sun's Child*. Illustrated by David Ruff. San Francisco, CA: Jonathan Williams, 1951.

———. *Jubilant Thicket: New and Selected Poems*. Port Townsend, WA: Copper Canyon, 2005.

———. *The Magpie's Bagpipe: Selected Essays*. Edited by Thomas Meyer. San Francisco, CA: North Point, 1982.

———. *A Palpable Elysium: Portraits of Genius and Solitude*. Boston: David Godine, 2002.

Williams, William Carlos. *The Collected Poems of William Carlos Williams*, vol. 1: *1909–1939*. Edited by A. Walton Litz and Christopher MacGowan. New York: New Directions, 1986.

———. *The Collected Poems of William Carlos Williams*, vol. 2: *1939–1962*. Edited by Christopher MacGowan. New York: New Directions, 1988.

———. "The Desert Music." *Origin*, 1st ser., 6 (Summer 1952): 65–75.

———. "The High Bridge above the Tagus River at Toledo," "Sappho," and "View of a Woman at Her Bath." *Evergreen Review* 3 (1957): 56–58.

———. *Make Light of It: Collected Stories*. New York: Random House, 1950.

———. "Of Asphodel: Coda." *Poetry* 84 (August 1954): 249–54.

———. *Paterson*. Edited by Christopher MacGowan. New York: New Directions, 1992.

———. *Selected Essays*. 1954. New York: New Directions, 1969.

Wilson, Edmund. *Axel's Castle: A Study in Imaginative Literature*. New York: Scribner's, 1931.

———. *Patriotic Gore: Studies in the Literature of the American Civil War*. New York: Oxford University Press, 1962.

Wilson, J. Tuzo. "Continental Drift." *Scientific American* 208 (April 1963): 86–100.

Witt-Diamant, Ruth, and Rikutaro Fukuda, eds. *53 American Poets of Today*. Folcraft, PA: Folcraft Library Editions, 1971.

Wolpe, Stefan. *Instrumental Music: Selections*. Hollywood, CA: Counterpoint/Esoteric, 1954.

Wright, Nathalia. *Melville's Use of the Bible*. Durham, NC: Duke University Press, 1949.

Zinnes, Harriet. "Duncan's One Poem." *Prairie Schooner* 43 (Fall 1969): 317–20.

Zukofsky, Louis. *"A."* Berkeley: University of California Press, 1978.

———. *All*. New York: Norton, 1966.

———, ed. *An "Objectivists" Anthology*. New York: TO Publishers, 1932.

———. "Bottom: Essay on Shakespeare." In *New Directions in Prose and Poetry 14*, edited by James Laughlin, 288–307. New York: New Directions, 1953.

———. *Bottom: On Shakespeare*. 2 vols. Austin: University of Texas Press, 1963.

———. *Collected Fiction*. Elmwood Park, IL: Dalkey Archive, 1990.

———. *Complete Short Poetry*. Baltimore, MD: Johns Hopkins University Press, 1992.

———. *Propositions: Collected Critical Essays*. London: Rapp and Carroll, 1967.

Index